Storytelling in Daily Life

Performing Narrative

Storytelling in Daily Life

Performing Narrative

Kristin M. Langellier
and Eric E. Peterson

TEMPLE UNIVERSITY PRESS

PHILADELPHIA

For our families,

and especially for Raymond Langellier (1919–1996),

family storyteller *par excellence*

Temple University Press, Philadelphia 19122
Copyright © 2004 by Temple University
All rights reserved
Published 2004
Printed in the United States of America

♾ The paper used in this publication meets the requirements of the
American National Standard for Information Sciences—Permanence of
Paper for Printed Library Materials, ANSI Z39.48-1984

Library of Congress Cataloging-in-Publication Data

Langellier, Kristin, 1951–
    Storytelling in daily life : performing narrative / Kristin M. Langellier and
Eric E. Peterson.
        p.   cm.
    Includes bibliographical references and index.
    ISBN 1-59213-212-X (cloth : alk. paper) — ISBN 1-59213-213-8 (pbk. : alk. paper)
        1. Storytelling. 2. Folklore—Performance. I. Peterson, Eric E., 1954– . II. Title.
GR72.3.L35 2004
808.5′43—dc21

2003050791

2 4 6 8 9 7 5 3 1

Contents

Acknowledgments

Storytelling happens—but only through the participation of many people. Before we begin our narrative, we take a moment to recognize the people whose participation and support made it possible for us to write this book.

Storytelling matters—it involves effort and risk for storytellers and audiences. We first gratefully acknowledge the participants in our research who shared their stories with us. For reasons of confidentiality in research, we have not named the individuals who invited Kristin to join them around kitchen tables to talk and laugh and eat, but we hope that the attention we bring to Franco-Americans in Maine will help to express our appreciation and regard for the vibrancy of their lives and stories. We thank them for their gifts of storytelling. We also thank two storytellers highlighted in the case studies: Jane, for her curiosity about our work and for volunteering to contribute her stories to our study; and Craig Gingrich-Philbrook, for his many stimulating conversations on performing narrative and his willingness to share a videotape of his performance.

Storytelling changes things—but by the time we realize it we are already enmeshed in a world of stories. We recognize the importance of our families, to whom we dedicate this book, in nurturing and shaping our intrigue with and understanding of storytelling. We especially recognize the role of our son, Keir, whose birth crystalized for us the significance of family storytelling and whose enjoyment of wide-ranging narrative performances spurs us on.

Storytelling endures—as students of narrative and performance, we continue as audiences to our first mentors. We are deeply indebted to our generous and inspiring teachers: to Richard Lanigan and Tom Pace for guiding us in phenomenology and philosophy of communication; to Marion Kleinau, William Haushalter, and Elbert Bowen for initiating us in performance studies. Our colleagues in performance studies, too numerous to list and some—but not all—of whom are cited in the following pages, have also informed, enlivened, and enriched our understanding of narrative through their performances, scholarship, and conversations. Our students, too, keep us learning.

We owe a particular debt of gratitude to Cathy Riessman for her friendship and support, for late night and early morning discussions about all things narrative, and for introducing us to Elliot Mishler and the narrative study group of Cambridge, Massachusetts. This local group of narrative scholars, who monthly gather under Elliot's guidance in his and Vicky Steinitz's home, responded to many of the ideas and examples we explore in this book. In addition to Cathy and Elliot, we acknowledge Susan Bell, Michael Bamberg, Jane Attanucci, Sara Dickey, Mark Freeman, Arlene Katz, Brinton Lykes, Angeliki Nicolopoulou, John Rich, Michael Rich, Ellen Rintell, Jill Taylor, Lucie White, and Krista Van Vleet. We thank our dear friend Deborah Pearlman, who finds room for us in her home on our trips to attend narrative study group meetings.

We recognize the University of Maine for providing a grant to support Kristin's fieldwork and then simultaneous sabbaticals that gave us much needed time to devote to our writing. Susan Pinette (Franco-American Studies), Lisa Michaud (Franco-American Center), and Amy Morin (Canadian American Center) helped Kristin find participants for the fieldwork. Our colleagues in the Department of Communication and Journalism, with the constant support of Dean Rebecca Eilers, covered our responsibilities while we were away. Although finding time to write was difficult, finding the space was easy thanks to Celeste Langellier and Karen McMillin, who helped us make a sabbatical home near theirs and near our families in the Midwest.

We thank Peter Wissoker of Temple University Press, who expressed interest in this project early on and then patiently waited several years until we found time to write. We thank Della Pollock for introducing us to Peter and for her reading and suggestions to improve the manuscript.

Finally, portions of Chapter 7 written by Eric were originally published in *Narrative Inquiry* as "Narrative Identity in a Solo Performance: Craig Gingrich-Philbrook's 'The First Time'" (vol. 10, 2000, pp. 229–251) and "One More First Time: A Response to Katz and Shotter" (vol. 10, 2000, pp. 475–481). Copyright © 2000, John Benjamins B. V., Amsterdam.

Part I

A Communication
Approach to Storytelling

Here, I would like to recount a little story
so beautiful I fear it may well be true.
—Michel Foucault (1976, p. 225)

"Let me tell you about something that happened to me," one friend tells another as they walk through the park. "So, how did your school day go?" asks a family member at the dinner table. "Did you see last night's episode on television? Let me tell you what happened," a worker says to a colleague during their coffee break. "Once upon a time," intones a pre-school teacher to a group of children. "I would like to tell you my version of what is going on," a petitioner states at a town meeting. "You'll never guess what happened today," begins the latest entry in an online Internet journal. "Here is how I experienced it," a patient confides to a doctor. These simple speech acts announce, request, declare, promise, and invoke stories. They perform narrative. Such storytelling matters: it is an integral and consequential part of daily life.

As audiences gather around storytellers, narrative becomes a significant site of communication and study. Embedded in the daily lives of ordinary and extraordinary people, storytelling flourishes. People make sense of their experiences, claim identities, interact with each other, and participate in cultural conversations through storytelling. Narrative is performed everywhere. Writers pen autobiographies and fiction; scholars recount the dramas of history and science. Storytelling permeates newspapers and magazines, radio, television, and film. Advertisers tell stories to sell their stock, and politicians package their lives in stories during campaigns. On stage, in the workplace, and at home, storytelling thrives. In the postmodern idiom, we "get a life" by telling and consuming stories (Smith & Watson, 1996). The study of narrative surged in the United States after World War II, fueled by at least five contemporaneous phenomena: the narrative turn in the human sciences; the memoir boom in writing; the new identity movements based in race and ethnicity, gender and sexuality, age and ability; the therapeutic cultures of self-help and talk shows reciting illness, trauma, and victimization; and the self-performance practices of performance art, popular culture, and electronic media, including the Internet.

Narrative studies have emerged to address the storytelling performances all around us. As part of that effort, this book sifts through the wide spread and far reach of contemporary narrative performance to concentrate on storytelling practices rooted in people's daily lives, families, and communities. As storytelling is embedded in daily life, so, too, our narrative interests are located in our personal and intellectual lives, kindled by our biographies as spouses, parents, colleagues, and researchers. We listen to stories about siblings, for example: "Remember when Larry and Dennis went fishing, and Dennis ate the bait," or "the time we forgot Kevin at home when we went to Grandma's house," or "how Maria broke her arm and no one believed her," or "when Tom nearly burned down the house." We also tell stories when we talk with colleagues, friends, and family. Now that our son Keir is away at college, we narrate in e-mail: a tale of how our cat, Hobbes, got caught in the neighbor's live trap two nights running, or an update on the health of a close family friend who has cancer, or a chronicle of the new metal roof as it weathers its first Maine winter, or an anecdote from one of the classes we teach. If, as Jack Zipes (1997, p. 132) writes, storytelling is "an experiential moment in which one learns something about oneself and the world," this study is our effort to share some of what we have learned about storytelling and about performing narrative in daily life.[1]

We present a critical interpretation of narrative in daily life, an interpretation rooted in our academic disciplines of communication and performance studies. This intervention shifts analytic focus from story text to storytelling performance as embodied, situated, and embedded in fields of discourse. The mundane experience of performing narrative—listening to and telling stories—suggests that storytelling is first and foremost a human communication practice. The simple act of saying "let me tell you a story" establishes a communication relationship that constitutes the speaker as a storyteller and the listeners as audience. The utterance "let me tell you a story" is, in other words, *performative* in that it does what it says it is doing. It performs the storytelling that it announces. "Let me tell you a story" also establishes a story, the "something that happened" that the storyteller reenacts, recites, or represents. The telling of the story is a *performance.* As a human communication practice, performing narrative combines the performative "doing" of storytelling with what is "done" in the performance of a story.

The term *performing narrative* incorporates both performance and performativity. Narrative performance materializes performativity in that "experiential moment" of learning something about oneself and the world: a risky and dangerous negotiation between a doing (telling and listening to stories) and a thing done (the story of experience) where participants reiterate norms of storytelling and where discursive conventions frame interpretations of stories. Performing narrative is risky and dangerous because, as Elin Diamond (1996) asserts, "as soon as performativity comes to rest on a performance, questions of embodiment, of social relations, of ideological interpellations, of emotional and political effects, all become discussable" (p. 4). The emphasis on storytelling performance conceptualizes narrative as act, event, and discourse—a site for understanding and intervening in the ways culture produces, maintains, and transforms relations of identity and difference (Strine, 1998). Performing narrative refers to any act of doing storytelling, not just to a heightened act of communication, aesthetically marked, framed in a special way, and put on display for an audience (Bauman, 1986). Performing narrative constitutes the event and conditions of communication, not as a singular or intentional act but as the reiterative practice by which discourse produces the effects it names (Butler, 1990a). Performing narrative focuses on doing things with words and asking what difference(s) it makes to do it.[2]

The combination of the performative and performance in storytelling is illustrated by the often-quoted words of Walter Benjamin (1969): "The storyteller takes what he tells from experience—his own or that reported by others. And he in turn makes it the experience of those who are listening to his tale" (p. 87). Benjamin's description emphasizes the sense of storytelling as performance. At a minimum, performance involves a two-step process of "taking" and then "making" experience for someone: first, as an embodied listener at work in the world, the storyteller takes her or his consciousness of experience and "in turn" makes it an experience of consciousness for the audience. Storytelling, Benjamin states, comes from "the realm of living speech" and goes back into it. Benjamin's insistence that experience can include one's "own experience or that reported by others" suggests that this process is not a linear conveying of experience to an audience but a reversible and reflexive process. Storytelling is reversible in that an audience can "take" her or his consciousness of the storyteller's experience and "in turn" become a storyteller and make it an experience for another audience. Audiences can become storytellers and vice versa. Telling one's story invites listeners to respond and often to reciprocate with their own stories (Geissner, 1995). Storytelling is reflexive in that, as Benjamin's description suggests, storytellers begin as audiences to themselves and others before becoming storytellers. It is the reflexivity of the storyteller that makes it possible for her or him to shift from audience to storyteller and storyteller to audience, to shift consciousness to experience and experience to consciousness.

The discovery of reflexivity in performance underscores the sense of storytelling as performative. That is, the constitution of a person as a storyteller or an audience is a contextual feature of a particular material, social, and cultural situation. Storytelling is performative in that possibilities for our participation are marked out in advance, so to speak, by the discourse and by our material conditions. Stories also live after as well as live before performance. When we participate in storytelling, whether as storytellers or audiences, we reenact storytelling as a conventionalized form of communication as well as collaborate in the production of a unique story or performance. This storytelling event recites, recalls, reiterates previous storytelling events in general and in particular. In brief, storytelling is socially and culturally reflexive. Storytelling is not a natural form of communication but a habitual and habituating practice. However, because it is reflexive, any particular storytelling event has the potential to disrupt material constraints and discourse conventions and to give rise to new possibilities for other storytelling events and for how we participate in performing narrative. Our approach to performing narrative theorizes both the transgressivity and the normativity of storytelling (McKenzie, 1998): storytelling's productive potential for creativity and resistance, and storytelling's reproductive capacity to reinscribe conventional meanings and relations.

Our study develops a theory of performing narrative and illustrates it with a variety of examples in order to understand the storytelling that surrounds us in daily life, and, further, to participate critically in conversations about what stories, what meanings, and what bodies matter. We present performances and analyses of family storytelling, storytelling on the Internet, breast cancer storytelling, and personal narrative of gay identity performed on stage. We selected these examples to illuminate the diversity of narrative performances and, in several instances, to examine new sites of storytelling. The book thus integrates a sustained theoretical argument for approaching storytelling as a communication practice with empirical analyses and case studies of performing narrative in daily life.

We organize our study into three parts, with each part introduced by a brief orientation that situates the succeeding chapters within narrative theory and methodology. Part I: A Communication Approach to Storytelling encompasses this introduction and a chapter on storytelling in daily life. In this chapter we examine a story told among a group of women on a weekend trip to Quebec City as an instance of narrative performance in social interaction. We use this story, "We'll See You Next Year," to accomplish two simultaneous tasks: to develop our approach to performing narrative as a communication practice that is embodied, material, discursive, and political; and to illustrate the significance of a communication approach through the description, analysis, and interpretation of a particular narrative performance.

Part II: Family Storytelling: A Strategy of Small Group Culture turns to a somewhat more traditional site for storytelling, the family as experience and institution. We take family storytelling—a communication practice in which families remember, transmit, and innovate stories through generations—as a research model for the study of performing narrative. We devote three chapters to thematically analyze empirical data on family storytelling from fieldwork conducted among Franco-American families in Maine.

Whereas Part II features an in-depth analysis of one way to perform narrative, Part III: Storytelling Practices: Three Case Studies emphasizes the diversity in narrative performance. We offer three case studies to call into question the very familiarity of storytelling and to suggest boundary conditions for performing narrative. We selected these particular cases—storytelling in weblogs, breast cancer storytelling, and a staged performance of autobiographical storytelling—in order to question or problematize the taken-for-granted habits and institutions of performing narrative. In particular, we question the assumption of orality and face-to-face interaction, the assumption of coherence in crafting a recognizable story, and the assumption of representational conventions that privilege visibility in developing narrative identity and agency. Now let us "recount a little story" about performing narrative, about what matters in storytelling, and how and why storytelling matters.

CHAPTER I

Performing Narrative in Daily Life

A group of eight women, gathered in a hotel room in Quebec City, share stories after a day of sightseeing and touring the city. They listen as Marie (a pseudonym) begins another story:

Marie: when I was in the hospital having Lisa
         when he [Paul] was eleven months old
         the <u>morn</u>ing that Richard took me to have Lisa
         <u>while</u> I was delivering Lisa he took his first step

These few phrases open Marie's story, which we title "We'll See You Next Year," and illustrate the daily experience of listening to and telling stories. Whatever its significance for the participants, as a communication event it is unremarkable, a common occurrence. How shall we understand what is happening here? In this chapter, we explore *performing narrative* as a communication practice. To do so, we bring together two research traditions: a speech act or semiotic tradition of studying symbolic activity, or what is communication; and a phenomenological tradition of studying conscious experience, or what is human. The combination of these traditions as an approach to the study of human communication has been called semiotic phenomenology by Richard L. Lanigan (1988, 1992).[1] We use semiotic phenomenology as a way to understand and describe what happens in the experience of storytelling. The story that Marie tells serves as an exemplar to illustrate this analysis throughout the chapter.

In developing semiotic phenomenology as an approach to human communication, Lanigan draws primarily upon the work of Maurice Merleau-Ponty and Michel Foucault. As we suggest through the following analysis, we find the confluence of these thinkers particularly productive for understanding storytelling matters—especially their emphasis on communication as embodied in a social world and as a locus of material action and power. As Nick Crossley (1996) argues, Merleau-Ponty's and Foucault's attention to the lived body and the inscribed body, to the existential and the institutional, can "be brought into a mutually informing and enriching dialogue" (p. 99). We develop four aspects of this dialogue in separate chapter sections to argue that performing narrative is (1) embodied, (2) situated and material, (3) discursive, and (4) open to legitimation and critique.

The first section looks at how storytelling is *embodied* by participants in a system of relations among audiences, storytellers, narrators, and characters. Any access to performing narrative is made possible by bodily participation, including the researcher's body. The second section examines how storytelling is *situated* in particular material conditions by looking at the constraints of language, history, and culture among storytellers and audiences. Situational resources and material conditions suggest how the communication context gives rise to particular stories, to particular performances of stories, and to particular performance practices. The third section asks "why is this story performed in this way and not that way?" by exploring the *discursive regularities* that constitute rules of exclusion and inclusion for stories and storytelling, and rules for who listens to and who tells stories. Performing narrative as a communication practice makes conflict over experience and identity concrete, accessible, and therefore discussable and open to change. The fourth section considers how performing narrative is open to *legitimation and critique*. That is, what does particular storytelling "do": how does it normalize experience and identities, and how does it transgress social and cultural norms and institutions? Questions about the consequences of performing narrative cannot be answered by a focus on any one system component—story text, storyteller, audience—but only within a multilevel model of strategies and tactics that examines relations of power. At the end of each section of this progressive argument, we offer a set of questions which guide the analysis of storytelling in daily life as *a communication practice* and which reflect our emphasis on performing narrative as performance and performativity. Finally, the chapter concludes with a discussion of the significance of this emphasis on communication in a theory and model of performing narrative.

The Embodied Context of Performing Narrative

We begin with a most mundane and obvious description: some *body* performs narrative. Performing narrative requires bodily participation: hearing and voicing, gesturing, seeing and being seen, feeling and being touched by the storytelling. The challenge comes in describing this bodily participation in ways that do not reduce the body to a collector or information processor of stories outside of any body. Performing narrative is not a discrete event—somehow external to the body—of processing and recounting prior events. The body of the storyteller does not function as a kind of organic video camera or tape recorder. Rather, the storyteller takes up some part of bodily activity (such as the perception of an event) and moves it to another activity of the body (such as the performance of a story): as Benjamin writes, "The storyteller takes what he tells from experience—his own or that reported by others. And he in turn makes it the experience of those who are listening to his tale" (p. 87). Nor can the body be reduced to thought and consciousness. Performing narrative is not a cognitive or reflective process for which the body is a container. The body of the storyteller is not a film or video screen upon which or through which stories may be projected. Before performing narrative is conceived or represented, it is lived through the body as meaningful. Our task is to explicate the context of relations in which the body is both part and participant.

Benjamin's description of storytelling suggests that the storyteller is embodied before an audience simultaneously as both a narrator and a character, both a speaking subject and a subject of discourse. The speech act "let me tell you about something that happened to me" situates the storyteller as a narrator in a relationship with a listener in a particular setting ("let *me* tell *you*"), with a larger audience which includes the storyteller and listener (the "us" implied by "let me tell you"), and with potential listeners beyond the immediate context (a more general or public "you"). At the same time, it situates or positions the storyteller as a narrator in a relationship with herself as a character ("something that happened to *me*") and in relationship as a character with other characters within the story (Maclean, 1988; Bamberg, 1997b). In phenomenological language, these multiple and ambiguous relations are lived through as bodily conduct, and they constitute a "system of four terms" (Merleau-Ponty, 1964a, p. 115; Lanigan, 2000). In storytelling, this embodiment constitutes a system of relations among storyteller, narrator, character, audience. That is, these embodied relations are extensions of an incarnate subject capable of moving reciprocally between perception and expression. The storyteller lives as both narrator and character in performing narrative for an audience. Narrator and character are not things the storyteller can withdraw from or hide behind. The storyteller does not change bodies to become a narrator or a character or a listener. Nor is the storyteller a composite of narrator and characters. Both narrator and character are sensible to the extent that they are dimensions of the storyteller's bodily conduct; they are ways of grasping the world, of moving voice and body to tell stories.[2]

Narrator and character are sensible for the storyteller—they are seen and heard and felt—because they are postures of a body that can see itself seeing, hear itself speaking, and touch itself touching. This description of storytelling as a bodily capability follows the phenomenological tradition of emphasizing the lived body, or what Merleau-Ponty calls *le corps propre* ("the body proper"). Merleau-Ponty (1964a) focuses on the undividedness of the lived body when he writes: "The enigma is that my body simultaneously sees and is seen. That which looks at all things can also look at itself and recognize, in what it sees, the 'other side' of its power of looking. It sees itself seeing; it touches itself touching; it is visible and sensitive for itself" (p. 162). In performing narrative, the storyteller is an audience for herself or himself. Furthermore, because the bodily comprehension of narrator and character are forms of conduct sketched out in the world, such embodiment is always already accessible to others. The body that can touch itself can also touch and be touched by others, can gesture and feel emotion. Narrator and character form part of an intersubjective system that is lived through by storyteller and audience. Let us turn now to the story "We'll See You Next Year" in order to illustrate these aspects of embodiment in performing narrative.

"We'll See You Next Year"—Introduction

The story "We'll See You Next Year" is told during an evening of conversation and storytelling among eight women in a hotel room in Quebec City. The women, who range in age from forties to sixties, have joined together for an "immersion weekend" organized in connection with the Franco-American Center at the University of Maine. The women live in the local communities that surround the university and share a connection, direct or indirect, with the university or someone at the university. Five of the women are or were part of university administrative staff (two are now retired), one is a friend of one of the other women, one is a teacher in a local high school who heard about the trip, and one—Kristin—is university faculty. Prior to making the trip, Kristin contacted the participants to obtain permission to audio tape-record storytelling that might happen during the trip. The primary storyteller in what we call the "We'll See You Next Year" story, Marie (a pseudonym, as are all the participants named in this book), is one of the trip co-organizers for this first-time event. She takes up the role of tour guide during the five-hour van ride to Quebec City, occasionally talking to the group as a whole about landmarks, architecture, and other points of interest. For most of the drive the women talk in pairs with their seat-mates. All the women are white, but not all are Franco-American. Some are interested in practicing French language skills; others are more interested in the trip to Quebec City. Some are old friends; others are new acquaintances.

During the weekend, Marie drives the group to Laval University, L'Ile d'Orleans, St. Anne de Beaupre cathedral, and to shopping centers, museums and markets, the cinema, and restaurants. At the end of the first day, the group gathers in Marie and Louise's room to talk about the day, about things they did, French language interaction, Canadian currency and culture, and shopping. Over evening dinner on the second day of the trip, the women begin to tell some personal experience stories. At this moment, Kristin asks if the group would "save" the stories until they return to their hotel after dinner so they could be audio taped. So, after returning to the hotel, the women change into pajamas and robes, open some wine, and gather again in Marie and Louise's room. Marie and Louise sit on the inside edges of their adjacent beds with a woman on the outside edge of each bed. Three women sit on chairs around the beds; one woman sits on the floor. They talk and tell stories: sometimes overlapping each other and talking simultaneously while moving between conversation and storytelling, sometimes withholding interruptions to encourage one person to become the sole storyteller.

After the tape recorder is turned on, Marie begins by telling about coming home from the hospital after the birth of Paul, her first child, to much laughter and audience participation. She concludes by saying, "Okay, that's my story. Somebody else." One of the group encourages Blanche, sitting next to Marie on the other side of the bed, to tell her story about directions and getting lost on the way to a lake. After Blanche finishes, Marie asks if Rebecca, sitting on a chair next to Blanche, has a story. Rebecca links to one of the stories that Marie told before this session and tells about how her young son and nephew turned into "little devils" in a store. After she concludes, Marie begins what will turn into a series of related stories in which she interweaves descriptions of her experiences with some childhood tales about her son, Paul. In the first of these, a description of how she "cried for five months" upon finding out she was pregnant with her second child, is woven around another often-repeated tale of her threat to put a sign up on the lawn listing Paul, her firstborn, as "for sale" if he kept misbehaving. Louise comments that "Oh, Paul used to do some awful things." Then Marie begins the "We'll See You Next Year" story. She tells the story with much animation, moving around and bouncing on the bed, waving her arms to suggest action, gesturing and taking in all of her listeners. The entire story lasts about three minutes and begins nine minutes after the tape recorder is turned on.

A description of embodiment does not merely specify who speaks and who listens, or even what is said and not said. To describe storytelling we focus on what is said and what is not said within a horizon of speaking, listening, and feeling—a lived unity of bodily participation. Storytelling occurs within a field of bodily practices. The story Marie tells is not outside her body or the bodies of the women in the hotel room with her. They do not hear, feel, or look at the story as they would a disembodied thing; rather, they participate and join in storytelling as bodily practices that are of the world in which they are embedded. Storytelling, we might say, is the focus of their activity. At the same time, this focus is possible because the field has been cleared of other activities. They have put aside other possibilities, such as reading, watching television, sleeping, and individual conversation, in order to give a hearing to, *to audience*, storytelling. If we were to locate a beginning point to this or any storytelling episode, then, it would be found not in the action of an individual storyteller but in the joint project of storyteller and audience. Certainly it is appropriate to say that Marie *tells* the story, but she does so only because the women (including Marie) participate to create a space and time within which the story can be heard, seen, and felt.

Thus, the description of "We'll See You Next Year" begins with the question of what relationships exist so that this story, told in this way, by this person, for this audience, can come into being. A description of these relationships explicates the lived meanings that come to constitute the group and their practice of storytelling. We emphasize these relationships as human communication practices in order to focus on bodily conduct and embodied discourse rather than to create an inventory of information about individuals and their behavior. Marie's conduct as the first person to tell a story once the tape recorder is turned on and her subsequent emergence as the primary story-teller for the evening's session is not arbitrary but distinctive. There is a continuity or "carryover" of group relations and interaction patterns established throughout the weekend trip. Marie continues to act for and with the encouragement of the group by working to help manage their mutual contact—in other words, Marie continues to act as a kind of tour guide in this storytelling session. She initiates the storytelling round, invites others to tell stories, manages turn-taking by directing dialogue, and then "takes on" or accepts an opportunity to be the primary storyteller. All of the women participate in this contact; they collaborate in laughter and exclamations, they contribute stories, they coax others to tell stories, they coach and coerce speakers by asking questions and filling in details. And while all of the women participate, this participation varies; that is, some speak more than others, some laugh and respond more than others, some listen better or are more engaged than others, and so on.

The relationships that make it possible to perform narrative go beyond the intersubjective relations of the immediate group. The audience for Marie's story includes past listeners in the sense that aspects of her past tellings of this story—such as selection of details, dialogue, intonation patterns—persist and shape her bodily conduct on this particular evening. A few of the present audience members have heard one or more of her stories before. Louise, a life-long friend, has heard these stories on many occasions. And Marie has written versions of some of these stories to share with her adult children, some of whom have children of their own. Beyond those present in the hotel room, the audience includes persons who have the potential to listen to the tape or read a transcribed version of her story. The presence of the tape recorder, too, contributes to and shapes the conduct of the audience and storyteller in performing narrative. Beyond this potential audience, Marie uses her story to "talk back" to the institution of the Roman Catholic Church, as discussed in the analysis below. It is unlikely that such institutions will ever actually "hear" this story. Instead, they function as a virtual addressee for Marie's story. Thus, performing narrative binds relationships across time and space in that it brings together actual, potential, and virtual audiences in a shared world.

Performing narrative is the site of interpersonal contact; storytelling brings together audiences in such a way that a story emerges. At the same time, performing narrative is a site of *intra*personal contact. The storyteller, Marie, tells about something that happened to her when her daughter, Lisa, was born; she brings to consciousness a past experience. That is, she embodies her experience—she is the narrator of herself as a character. As Merleau-Ponty (1964b) writes, "this subject which experiences itself as constituted at the moment it functions as constituting is my body" (p. 94). It is important to emphasize that it is the conduct of embodiment—the body that touches itself touching—that makes possible the representation of experience in narrative. Bodily conduct in performing narrative gives rise to representation and not vice versa. As Katherine Young (2000), in an essay on emotion in narrative, clarifies: "narratives do not excavate emotions out of the past or the unconscious but rather construct them in the present in the body" (p. 81). Marie is not merely representing or displaying what happened to her on some past occasion but living her experience by occasioning it for this particular audience in the present situation.[3]

The embodied context of performing narrative forms a system of relations among storytellers, audiences, narrators, and characters. Participation in this system depends upon bodily capabilities to see and be seen, to touch and be touched, to speak and to hear. The mundane observation with which we began, some *body* performs narrative, contains an important ambiguity: that is, this body may be a person (my body, or intrapersonal communication), a few persons (a body of women, or interpersonal and small group communication), many people (the body politic, or public communication), and many groups of peoples (cultural bodies, or intercultural communication). To look at the embodied context of performing narrative is to ask questions about the conduct of bodies in storytelling: What body/bodies participate in performing narrative? To what extent do bodies participate that are not present in the immediate storytelling situation? How do these bodies participate as audiences and storytellers, narrators and characters? Whose body or bodies speak, see, narrate, watch, feel, listen? How is the body the performative boundary—a horizon of speaking, listening, and feeling—for storytelling? How do bodies perform narrative in gestures of voice and hand? How do these performative boundaries accumulate around and accrete sexuality, gender, race, and age? What patterns of behavior (bodily conducts) are shared, coaxed, coached, coerced, and collaborated on among participants? What bodily conducts does storytelling occasion? What systems of social relations—intrapersonal, interpersonal, public, and cultural—emerge in storytelling?

Situational and Material Constraints in Performing Narrative

The embodied context gives Marie and her audiences the possibility to perform narrative; however, only *some* of these possibilities are materialized in the performance situation. Some body performs narrative; and this body, capable of touching others and of touching itself touching, recaptures its corporeal existence and uses it to perform narrative. Merleau-Ponty (1964a) writes that "as an active body capable of gestures, of expression, and finally of language, it turns back on the world to signify it" (p. 7). Performing narrative, like the other examples Merleau-Ponty gives for symbolic uses of the body, "is not yet a conception, since it does not cut us off from our corporeal situation; on the contrary, it assumes all its meaning" (p. 7). What is this corporeal situation?

As the previous discussion of audience suggests, the human context includes all the actual, real, and virtual relations of daily life. Despite traditions of individualism which would suggest otherwise, we argue that the person is embedded in and "assumes all the meaning" of its environment. The body is dependent upon its corporeal situation and is not independent of or in opposition to it (as suggested by such formulations as nature vs. culture or text vs. context). A simple test of this argument can be performed under what phenomenologists call "imaginative variation": vary—in imagination—an aspect of the situation and examine the result. For example, would a person survive the removal of oxygen from the environment? Or, to use the case suggested by our previous discussion, would a storyteller begin to tell a story without an audience? Through such variations of what is possible, we come to discover the meanings of our corporeal situation.

The body that performs narrative is constrained by the material conditions of its corporeal situation. The body is constrained: it depends upon but is not caused or determined by its environment. We use the term *constraint* here in the semiotic and phenomenological sense of a boundary that defines the conditions of what is possible.[4] A constraint is not merely a restriction or obstruction. Constraints define what is possible in the sense that an organism which breathes oxygen is both "restricted" in that it cannot live in an oxygen-depleted environment, and "facilitated" in that the ability to take in and make use of oxygen from its environment makes possible a range of activities. An audience constrains the storyteller in a similar way: storytelling is restricted in that it takes an audience to make it happen, and storytelling is facilitated in that the storyteller can draw upon the shared language, history, and culture of the audience in order to tell a story. The audience constrains the constitution of what can be a story, of how a story can be told, and of the meanings that emerge from storytelling. Thus, constraints both facilitate and restrict possibilities for expression and perception.

The body that performs narrative is oriented toward its project in a particular corporeal situation. Performing narrative depends upon, but is not determined by, the material conditions of its particular corporeal situation. There are no transparent situations or neutral material conditions for storytelling. Instead, we ask what situational resources exist and how are they mobilized and ordered? How do material conditions constrain storytelling? These situational resources are most often taken for granted in both descriptions of and the actual doing of storytelling. For example, in "We'll See You Next Year," Marie tells her story in English, although she also speaks French. She does not explain what she is doing when she begins storytelling. Nor do audience members negotiate with each other as to how they will listen or how much they will contribute. There is an economy to the project of storytelling that facilitates participation in habitual forms of interaction—Marie and her audience can focus on storytelling and do not have to invest a lot of effort in making explicit what they are doing or how they do it so long as they continue to employ habitual forms. Consider the first part of her story:[5]

"We'll See You Next Year"—Part I

Marie: when I was in the hospital having Lisa
     when he [Paul] was eleven months old
     the <u>morn</u>ing that Richard took me to have Lisa
     <u>while</u> I was delivering Lisa he took his first step

Louise: aww

Marie: and he walked

Louise: [laughter]

Marie: I will tell you that

Louise: right on his tip toes

Marie: right on his tip toes
     like a little I-don't-know-what

Louise: about ninety miles an hour

Marie: I know it oh geez
     he—and he never stopped
     he'd get up at six o'clock in the morning
     and he wouldn't stop
     'til he went for his nap
     of course Lisa woke up about the time for his nap
       she was ready to eat
     by the time I got her done
       he'd be up
     and then she <u>screamed</u> all night
     she screamed <u>all</u> night from . . eleven o'clock
     she'd have her ten o'clock feeding she'd scream 'til four o'clock in the morning

[?]: yeah that's just like [unintelligible]

Marie: of course you know Richard god love him
      he slept upstairs in his bed
      he had to work

Louise: oh yeah [laughter]

Marie: so Marie was downstairs running walking the floor
     <u>crying</u>
     Lisa's screaming
      I'm crying

           wa::lking the floor
              fi::ve hours
           finally she'd go to sleep
  Louise: ohhh::
  Marie: Paul would get up at six o'clock
  Louise: yep yep
  Marie: so here we go
           I got an hour's sleep
           Paul would get up and away he'd go
  Louise: [laughter]
  Marie: there's Paul

Louise serves as an instigator and interlocutor for the first part of the story. She draws upon her shared history with Marie—life-long friends—to interject observations about how Paul walked. In so doing, she extends her comment that "Oh Paul used to do some awful things" made moments before during the end of Marie's previous story (which interwove her threat of putting Paul up for sale with her tale of crying for five months when she found out she was pregnant again). Louise's efforts here work to amplify one aspect of Marie's previous story, thereby encouraging her to tell similar stories. Louise invokes "stories about the awful things Paul would do" as a series of stories that could be told at this time. Even for women in the group who are not as familiar with Marie, this story falls easily within the more widespread "infant tales of child-hood antics" genre of family storytelling (discussed in the next chapter as the ordering of content). In both cases, the familiarity of the story as *a kind of story to tell*, whether as an instance of "Paul stories" or "tales of childhood antics," constrains participation.

Marie incorporates Louise's comments; in fact, her easy collaboration with Louise on how Paul walks ("up on his tip toes") and how fast ("about ninety miles an hour") suggests their shared history as conversational partners. Marie confirms Louise's comments but, as will become evident as the story pro-gresses, she uses Paul's behavior to help develop a different kind of story than another "Paul story." Instead, the continuity of Marie's crying in the previous story (when she finds out she is pregnant) and her crying in "We'll See You Next Year" is used to elaborate the daily routine she lives after Lisa's birth. Rather than provide a focal point for the story, Marie situates Paul's behavior as part of a larger pattern: Paul running, newborn Lisa screaming, husband Richard sleeping, and Marie crying. This pattern occurs on a regular schedule each day ("so here we go"). She uses temporal details to make her routine con-crete: clock time (six o'clock, ten o'clock, eleven o'clock, four o'clock in the morning, six o'clock in the morning), duration (an hour, five hours, all night), speed (ninety miles an hour), calendar dates (eleven months), and life markers ("<u>while</u> I was delivering Lisa he took his first step").

Marie employs temporal details to construct her daily life for this audience. But the meaning of these details depends upon a shared understanding for the larger context of what might be called a political economy of mothering. Marie situates herself as being at the mercy of a schedule she does not control—a common feature of the social relations of production and reproduction in the middle and latter parts of the twentieth century in the United States. Some elements of her story suggest this larger context of social relations: the medicalization of childbirth ("when I was in the hospital having Lisa"), the mother as sole childcare provider in a private home isolated from other support ("I got an hour's sleep"), a wage-earning husband employed outside the home ("he had to work"), the replacement of breast feeding with bottle feeding according to a schedule rather than demand ("her ten o'clock feeding"), and, as we will see in the next part of the story, compulsory heterosexuality and the control—both secular and religious—of sexual relations (the "timing" of children). This larger context of social relations is not uniform or continuous, however. It varies—it is punctuated differently—by race, class, ethnicity, and, as we will see in the next section, religious practices. In fact, Marie's efforts to incorporate a variety of details suggest that the political economy of her life-world is a juxtaposition of discontinuous but regular elements that have been, could be, or might become something different.

The temporal details and markers of "We'll See You Next Year" point to the material conditions of mothering which constrain what can be told in the story, how the story is told, and the meanings that emerge. The story supposes that the participants are already installed in a political economy of mothering. They participate both in what Young (1985) calls the immediate "surround" as eight women who are all mothers and in the larger social and cultural context of production and reproduction. Thus the particular case of mothering that Marie constitutes in performing this narrative comes to symbolize other possible situations. The meaning of mothering in "We'll See You Next Year" is not to be found in the series of clauses and temporal details that compose the narrative but in following them where they go, where they project or point. As Merleau-Ponty (1964b) concludes, "it is at the heart of my present that I find the meaning of those presents which preceded it, and that I find the means of understanding others' presence at the same world; and it is in the actual practice of speaking that I learn to understand" (p. 97). The women in the immediate surround, as well as the potential audience represented by the tape recorder, depend upon—are constrained by—the material conditions of a particular corporeal situation. It is in performing narrative that they are able to realize a common project and understand the meanings of that particular corporeal situation.

Performing narrative occurs under particular *situational and material constraints*. Storytelling mobilizes the resources of language, history, culture, and material conditions to perform narrative. To ask about situational and material constraints is to ask how these resources give rise to particular stories, to particular performances of stories, and to particular performance practices. We ask: What resources in the situation make storytelling possible? What material conditions, what economic and cultural resources, does storytelling draw upon and mobilize? In what places and spaces is narrative performed? How is it embedded in surrounding discourse? What kind and how much time is given to perform? How do the situation and material conditions constrain—both restrict and enable—participation? How much and what kind of effort does it take to perform? How does storytelling point to or assume social conditions of its production? Are there economies of performance made possible by habitual forms of bodily conduct? How do particular historical and cultural formations—such as race, sexuality, gender, age, and class—serve as resources? How does the distribution of resources constrain what stories and meanings can emerge, who can tell them, how they are told, and to what audiences?

Discursive Regularities in Performing Narrative

Through their bodily capabilities and within their situated context, a group of women performs the story "We'll See You Next Year." What are they doing in telling this particular story and in telling it this way? Performing narrative, embodied and constrained by material conditions, is known through the discursive practices in which it participates. To our earlier observation that some body performs narrative, we add an equally mundane and obvious corollary: to perform narrative is to do something in and with discourse. The focus on "doing something in and with discourse" emphasizes performing narrative as an event. Discourse as event, Foucault (1976) reminds us, "must not be confused with the expressive operation by which an individual formulates an idea, a desire, an image; nor with the rational activity that may operate in a system of inference; nor with the 'competence' of a speaking subject when he constructs grammatical sentences" (p. 117). Foucault questions these traditional themes—the creativity of a founding subject, the originality of experience, the operation of a universal mediation—by exploring the "ordering" of discourse. As suggested by the title of his lecture, *L'Ordre du Discours*, Foucault asks how discourse is ordered. In particular, he asks how is it that this discourse event appears rather than others, how is it distributed in this series, according to what specific regularities, and in what possible conditions of existence? Let us explore each of these regulatory principles that order discourse: event, series, regularity, and the possible conditions of existence.

As a first step in analyzing the ordering of discourse, Foucault explores the formation of discourse as *event* through systems of exclusion, what he calls external rules governing power and knowledge. These external rules work to delimit discourse, to specify the boundaries that locate "just what discourse is," through a web of prohibitions, divisions and rejections, and the opposition between true and false. As mentioned earlier, a storyteller is not free to narrate just anything, in just any way at any place or time, to any audience. A story-teller utilizes and enacts prohibitions, in other words, when she or he performs narrative. A different system of exclusion operates in the ways that discourse divides and rejects what is meaningful from what is meaningless, what belongs to the narrative and what does not, what contributes to understanding and what does not. These divisions and rejections make possible the opposition of true and false as a third system of exclusion. The division between discourse as an act of enunciation and discourse as what is enunciated makes possible a judgment as to which is true and which is false. In storytelling, this system of exclusion is an effort to fix or locate the "truth" of storytelling either in what the narrative says or in what the performance does. Indeed, this opposition makes possible the common dismissal of storytelling as mere entertainment or fiction, and its reverse valorization as an aesthetic or artistic performance—in both cases, storytelling is excluded from an exercise of power; it says and does nothing in the social world.

A second regulatory principle governs the internal formation of discourse through classification, ordering, and distribution. Discourse exercises control over itself through internal rules that locate regularities in a *series*. This regulatory principle makes it possible to classify types of discourse by locating gradations of repetition and sameness—that is, to locate a series. These repetitions allow us to identify what Foucault (1976) calls a society's "major narratives, told, retold and varied; formulae, texts, ritualised texts to be spoken in well-defined circumstances; things said once, and conserved because people suspect some hidden secret or wealth lies buried within" (p. 220). Another type of series is the ordering of discourse according to an individuality or "I." In storytelling, we identify utterances as belonging to speakers; we identify point of view, narrators, and characters as types of coherence of action in discourse. But a series may also be distributed in discourse which takes neither the form of repetition nor the action of an individual. Foucault names this type of series "disciplines" to indicate that it is an anonymous system of rules for generating new discourse. An example of a distributed discipline in story-telling can be seen in the operation of "the voice of medicine" which can be spoken by anyone—not just doctors or medical personnel—to anyone in stories of health and illness (see Mishler, 1984).

The third regulatory principle controls discourse by governing the conditions under which it is employed by speaking subjects. As Lanigan (1992) summarizes, the conjunction of knowledge and power produces subjects, that is, "persons who are 'subject to' knowledge and yet the 'subject of' power" (p. 23). These *regularities* in discourse, in the conjunction of knowledge and power, reveal rules for who is qualified to speak on a specific subject, rules for how speaking and listening roles are appropriated and the extent of their interchangeability, rules for the diffusion of discourse through the doctrinal adherence of subjects, and rules for differences in the ability to appropriate discourse. In storytelling, we ask what qualifies someone to tell a story, for example, to speak for herself or himself from the "authority of experience," or to speak for others as an expert. Discourse rules also govern who can or who has to listen and to what extent audiences can contribute, interrupt, or challenge what is told. Storytelling has rituals to determine which subjects are eligible to speak and listen and which subjects are enforced speakers or audiences. When Marie speaks to her experience as a mother in "We'll See You Next Year," she enacts a prior adherence to the subject of mothering and childcare that links all of the women as mothers. Their reciprocal, though variable, allegiance to a discourse on mothering regulates the storytelling.

The final regulatory principle is a critical effort to discuss the conditions of discourse that frame what can be said, what can be understood, and what can be done in storytelling. This effort does not look to find a hidden core of truth or universal meaning in discourse but reverses this tendency to find and fix meaning and, instead, looks to its *possible conditions of existence* for that which gives rise to and limits discourse. The analysis of discourse as event, series, and regularity is a critical effort in that it explicates the rules and regularities that frame discourse: it "brings to light the action of imposed rarity" (p. 234). The focus of analysis is to explicate the struggles over meaning rather than to explain their causes or motivations in the storyteller, audience, or text. That is, analysis elucidates regularities by exploring variations in relations of knowledge and power as the possible conditions of storytelling: this story could be told differently. Analysis does not explain storytelling as the exercise of creativity, as an originary experience, or as a movement of universal signifying system. Let us look at the second part of "We'll See You Next Year" in order to illustrate the four regulatory principles in discourse.

"We'll See You Next Year"—Part II

Marie: so
Lisa I think was two and half months old when we had her baptized
so we . had her baptized
[to Blanche] and you know [names parish member]
I think she was having her fifth

Blanche: yes

Marie: something like that
she was having that one baptized at the same time

okay
so <u>after</u> he baptizes
no:w this <u>priest</u> has baptized two kids in eleven months honey

[general]:   [laughter]

Marie: and the priest says to me
we'll see you next year

[?]:   ohhhh

[?]:   oooo

Marie: and I says you won't if I can help it

[general]:   [laughter]

Marie: and <u>wa::s he:: mad</u>
<u>oh::</u> mother
he went up one side of me and down the other

Cora: oh Marie

Marie: I had to do my: duty darlin'
and well I said
I said Father
that I didn't say I wouldn't have any more children
I <u>want</u> more children
but <u>you're</u> not going to see me next year if I can help it
and I picked up my little Lisa and I walked out the door
so Richard [husband] says
You shouldn't have said that
I said
YOU:: SHUT UP

[general]:   [laughter]

Marie: I said let me tell you one thing
if I hear one more word out of <u>you</u>
and one more word out of that <u>priest</u>
I'm taking these <u>two kids</u>
they're going on <u>his</u> doorstep for <u>three days</u>
and I'll tell you he'll change his tune

[?]:   [unclear] my god

Marie: and I never heard anything from either one of them you can imagine

[general]:   [laughter]

Marie: ay:: *maudit*

What external rules of power and knowledge regulate this storytelling? The question of what is prohibited, the operation of a system of exclusion, is an explicit point of contention in this segment of the story. Marie "talks back" to the priest in multiple ways. Her response to his prescriptive comment "we'll see you next year" suggests three types of prohibition: (1) she voluntarily ("if I can help it") will not follow the teachings of the Roman Catholic Church to "do her duty" to bear children, which would constitute a sin, a prohibited object; (2) she breaks with expected behavior—silence or simple acceptance—that characterizes baptism as a ritual; and (3) she is disrespectful in that her response challenges the priest's exclusive right to speak on a subject. Her husband Richard's comment, "you shouldn't have said that," marks out a similar ambiguity: you should not say such things (prohibited object), you should not talk that way during a baptism (ritual), and you should not talk that way to a priest (right to speak). The variation in the extent of these prohibitions is demonstrated by the difference between Marie's direct response to Richard ("YOU:: SHUT UP") and her indirect challenge to the priest. The priest's response to Marie's statement suggests the operation of the second system of exclusion, that of a division and a rejection. The priest takes her statement as an unreasonable abdication of her "duty" as a wife, mother, and, in institutional terms, a daughter of the Church. His rejection of her folly is clear ("he went up one side of me and down the other"). Marie repunctuates even while accepting the validity of this division; that is, she does not reject the distinction between reason and folly, but she resituates her response as reasonable by putting it in the context of mothering ("he'll change his tune" if he has to take care of her two infants). She does not reject her duty ("I want more children"), but she redefines the priest's expectation that she return next year with another child as the unreasonable one ("and wa::s he:: mad").

This part of the story also illustrates the function of repetition and the exercise of internal rules, Foucault's second regulatory principle. The repetition of temporal details in this part of the story ("two kids in eleven months," "two kids . . . on his doorstep for three days") combine with the temporal details from the first part of the story to form a series. This series regulates how we classify what kind of story Marie tells: given the series of temporal details, the question about the timing of children becomes a story about doing one's best under difficult conditions rather than a story of rebellion against the Father/priest and father/husband. These internal regularities also work to position Marie as a character in relation to other characters, as a narrator in relation to herself as a character, and as a storyteller in relation to actual and virtual audiences (Bamberg, 1997b). She performs as a character interacting with other characters by occasioning participant speech coming from the character as quoted or direct discourse. For example, in her interchange with the priest, she moves from narrating the action in present tense ("and the priest says to me") to speaking his discourse ("we'll see you next year"). She maintains the same form for herself as character by narrating her response in the present ("and I says") and her speech ("you won't if I can help it"). As she speaks this line, she straightens up on the bed in her seated position as if standing up as tall as possible—living the action as character for the audience in the hotel room.

Contrast this gesture of speech and posture with the following report of the priest's response which she narrates from an "observer" position. The past tense speech, "he went up one side of me and down the other," accompanies a sweep of Marie's hand held out in front of her moving upwards to a peak about head-high during the first part of the phrase and downwards in the second half. Her hand gesture literalizes, as it were, the figure of speech she uses to describe how the priest chastises Marie. She does not place the action in or on her own body, but displaces and projects Marie-as-character in front of Marie-as-narrator for her audience.

The positioning of Marie in relation to the audience is emphasized in her report of the priest's speech "I had to do my: duty darlin'," which simultaneously functions as indirect discourse set in the past (a reference to what the priest said) as well as direct address to the audience in the present that evaluates and positions this action (as seen by the use of "had to do" rather than "have to do" and the addition of "darlin'," which the priest is unlikely to have used). The "matter of fact" tone of voice used to correct the priest's interpretation of her behavior ("I didn't say I wouldn't have any more children / I want more children"), suggests that Marie can speak Church doctrine as well as the priest. It is the careful ambiguity of her statement of desire ("I want more children") coupled with her knowing modification ("but you're not going to see me next year if I can help it") that challenges the disciplinary rebuke of the priest and places Marie within the limits of the Church's "truth."

The differentiation of speaking subjects, the third regulatory principle, is evident in the contrast between the reported interaction with the priest and the reported interaction with her husband. Marie responds calmly to the emotionally charged criticism by the priest, whereas Richard's indirect and brief correction ("you shouldn't have said that") triggers the vociferous "YOU:: SHUT UP" and subsequent scolding ("If I hear one more word out of you"). This reversal in emotions suggests that the priest's and Richard's speech are not interchangeable. At the same time, however, the ritualistic aspect of this scolding works to align Richard's speech with the speech of the priest: it is not accidental that the parallel phrases, "if I hear one more word out of you and one more word out of that priest," suggest a mother disciplining children. This ritualistic speech defines the qualifications of who can speak; that is, only someone who can take care of "these two kids [. . .] for three days" can speak on this subject ("and I'll tell you he'll change his tune"). While all three speaking subjects share doctrinal adherence to the pronatalism of the Church, the discourse constructs motherhood as a privileged (non-interchangeable) access to speech, thereby excluding both priest and husband from its appropriation ("and I never heard anything from either one of them").

What possible responses are made or can be made to this disciplinary action? What becomes discussable as a consequence of this particular story-telling? Within the narrative, a space for response is marked out but not performed by the storyteller. Marie says, "and I never heard anything from either one of them you can imagine." She does not say that they never said anything, nor does she say that they were silent; she describes an absence in her hearing, not the presence or absence of their speech. In a similar way, this phrase marks a possible closure or ending to the story for the audience of the narrative. That is, the phrase "and I never heard anything from either one of them" functions as resolution (a variation on "and they all lived happily ever after") that marks out the possibility for, but does not perform, audience response. In both cases, the meaning of response—whether that of the subjects in the narrative ("*I* never heard anything from either one of *them*") or the audience subject to the narrative ("*you* can imagine")—is not a question of a hidden truth, a universal meaning, or a system of signification located in storyteller, audience, or story. Rather, the meaning of response is a question of the possible conditions of existence of discourse performed by the ordering of event, series, and regularities of speaking subjects. The conditions of existence make some stories, some ways of telling stories, and events of storytelling more easily performed. If the storytelling was performed in this way, it can be performed in another, different way.

To perform narrative is to do something in and with discourse. The *regularities of discourse* lead us to ask questions about why storytelling is performed in a particular way and not in other ways. We ask: What regularities order storytelling as an event? What web of prohibitions, divisions and rejections, and oppositions make possible this particular event rather than others? What rules regulate what gets to be told and retold? How does the way narratives are performed help us to locate repetitions in discourse? Upon what major narratives does this particular event rely? What types of coherence does discourse create around narrators, characters, and action? How do internal regularities work to position narrators and characters, storytellers and audiences? How does discourse frame what can be said? What institutions and rituals operate in the discourse event? How does the narrative work to empower some subjects and disempower others? What qualifies someone to tell a story? Who can and who has to listen? How are possibilities for speaking and listening appropriated and distributed? To what extent are speaking and listening interchangeable? How does discourse discipline the bodies of participants?

Legitimation and Critique in Performing Narrative

An analysis of discourse gives us the rules and regularities that frame the storytelling event of "We'll See You Next Year." These conditions of possibility emerge within the specific material situation of storytelling and its embodied context. What are the consequences of performing this narrative, of performing narrative? Foucault poses a question toward the beginning of his lecture on *L'Ordre du Discours* that we would do well to ask about storytelling. He asks, "What is so perilous, then, in the fact that people speak, and that their speech proliferates? Where is the danger in that?" (p. 216). Or, as we would phrase it: what is so perilous in performing narrative? Where is the danger in that? The danger of performing narrative is that by doing something in and with a discourse that is neither uniform nor stable, we risk changing the bodily practices and material conditions in which they are embedded: what is done can be undone. As discourse, performing narrative "transmits and produces power; it reinforces it, but also undermines and exposes it, renders it fragile and makes it possible to thwart it" (Foucault, 1980, p. 101). When Marie speaks in the voice of the Church ("I want more children"), she reinforces and legitimates it. At the same time, however, her participation in this discourse makes it possible for her to render it fragile and thwart it at least temporarily ("but you're not going to see me next year if I can help it"). Storytelling, therefore, can work both to legitimate and to critique relations of power. For this reason, we ask about the tactical productivity or efficacy of storytelling rather than divide it into discourses of power on the one hand, and counterdiscourses on the other.

In order to ask about the efficacy of storytelling, we examine how these tactics carry out an overall strategy. We employ a strategic model here because, as Anthony Wilden (1987b) argues, "strategy and tactics are characteristic of all goal-seeking, adaptive, open systems" (p. 232). In the case of storytelling, an open system of communication involves a lived-body capable of perception and expression, constrained by situational and material conditions, and organized by the ordering of discourse. Wendy Patterson (2002) emphasizes narrative as strategic in order to illuminate the operation of power and "the complexity of the processes involved in narration as action and interaction" (p. 2). Strategy concerns the goals around which a system is organized; while tactics concern how a system goes about accomplishing these goals. Tactics concern the precise and sometimes tenuous ways strategy is put into practice. Under ordinary circumstances, a strategy envelops or constrains the tactics within it: tactics are dependent upon strategy. However, as Foucault (1980) points out, "one must conceive of the double conditioning of a strategy by the specificity of possible tactics, and of tactics by the strategic envelope that makes them work" (p. 100). Tactical changes can lead to alterations in strategy. For this reason, Wilden describes the hierarchy of strategy over tactics as semi-dependent. That is, tactical innovations may rupture or restructure the constraints of strategy. Once strategy is restructured, however, the hierarchy of strategy enveloping tactics returns.

The question of strategy and tactics in "We'll See You Next Year" is not one of who possesses power but of how power is distributed even as it is transformed in discourse. Indeed, Marie's story challenges simplistic notions of power that would allocate power to individuals or to institutions. The priest does not rule over the family, nor does the father rule over the mother within the family. Both Church and family, however, link their survival to shared strategies of reproduction. The Church utilizes familial reproduction—among other strategies—to ensure its survival over generations. The family, in turn, utilizes this reproductive strategy to support and facilitate its own survival. Childcare responsibilities are tactical issues in familial and religious reproduction. Marie's storytelling maintains the strategic emphasis on reproduction but she uses the variability of tactics—there are many ways to achieve the same goal—to suggest a different distribution of relations. As she suggests, childcare could be performed within the family by the father or outside the family by the priest. Marie's "threat" of this possibility suggests that such a tactical innovation would require strategic restructuring of the sexual division of labor in current arrangements of reproduction in both Church and family. By contrast, the proposed modification in the timing of reproduction is less disruptive because it can be "contained" as a transformation in tactics rather than in strategy.

The danger that storytelling poses is this potential to critique or reinscribe ongoing strategic arrangements. Performing narrative can rupture or reaffirm the sedimentation of discourse in lived experience. Let us look at the final part of "We'll See You Next Year" to see how family storytelling functions as strategic, as a "local center" of power and knowledge.

"We'll See You Next Year"—Part III

Cora:	how many years between Lisa and
Marie:	Roger
Cora:	Roger?
Marie:	two and a half
Anna:	Marie what did you just say?
	I *mau*
Marie:	<u>eh maudit</u>
	oh son of a gun
Anna:	*eh maudit, eh maudit?* [other participants repeat line; overlapping speech]
Marie:	a l<u>it</u>eral translation is word said
	which makes no sense
	but it's a sort of a it's a . semi-curse [laughs]
[general]:	[laughter]
Marie:	it's not a swear not really a swear but a
	yeah it's sort of like that
Blanche:	but you know how she feels

[?]: yeah

Marie: that was enough of that story
         we've had enough of those . those beans for awhile

After the general laughter that greets Marie's proffered resolution and coda, "and I never heard anything from either one of them you can imagine," Cora asks an indirect question about the timing of children. Cora does not comment directly on the behavior of the priest or Richard, nor does she directly evaluate Marie's resolution or her work as storyteller. However, the phrasing of her question regarding "how many years between" Lisa and Roger suggests that Cora already knows that Marie has a third child and that the interval between children is longer than one year. Why, then, does she ask this question in this way? We ask about the appearance and phrasing of this question not to establish a motive or explanation for it, but to ask how it functions, to interrogate its tactical efficacy in the discourse. Cora's question can function in several ways: to affirm Marie's claim to "<u>want</u> more children" but not within the year, to testify to Marie's veracity as a storyteller, to confirm Cora's ongoing knowledge of and relationship with Marie, to share in the work of storytelling by providing additional information, to corroborate the "kinwork" of keeping track of familial relations and names (di Leonardo, 1984; Baldwin, 1985), and to attest to Cora's participation in the storytelling situation as a good audience.

Cora's question suggests a larger strategic one: would the story have been told in this way or told at all if there was not a delay of more than a year between children? The choice of the narrative form itself, with its construction of a life "and all lives as something that can in every sense of the word be told as a 'story'" (Merleau-Ponty, 1964b, p. 75), provides stability—however temporary—for Marie's efforts to loosen the grip of prevailing interpretations for the timing of reproduction. Marie's intervention within ongoing secular and religious discourses on reproduction is effective because the tolerance it demands trades off on its acceptance of the interwoven discourses of pronatalism and mothering. Telling this story *as a story* works strategically to maintain Marie's identity as a good mother and wife (established by her childcare efforts in Part I of "We'll See You Next Year") and as a good daughter of the Church (established by the baptism and her statement "I <u>want</u> more children" in Part II of the story). At the same time, telling the story as a story works tactically to demonstrate her agency: her ability to manage a difficult schedule of mothering and childcare (the labor of reproduction) supports her claim to manage the "schedule" of reproduction ("but <u>you're</u> not going to see me next year if I can help it"). Tactically, she can "out-mother" both the priest and Richard—she is better at the actual work of childcare, and she is better at managing behavior as she illustrates by "talking back" and silencing them.

But why tell this story at this time and place to this audience? Or, rather, what strategic functions does this storytelling perform decades after the events it narrates? We can interrogate the strategic function of performing narrative by comparing the distribution of communication relations in the story with the distribution of communication relations in the telling of it. Within the story, Marie participates in normative discourses on reproduction in order to redistribute control over timing of reproduction. Beyond relations embedded in the story, however, the telling of it does something more than report on a successful discourse tactic used decades ago. How then, in the telling of this story, are the normative discourses of storytelling distributed and redistributed? Clearly, knowledge of the story events is not equally shared among all of the audience. However, the asymmetrical relation of knowledge, and the differential work of memory and recall that this entails, is situated within a larger collaborative context of equity wherein everyone has the potential to tell a story and to participate in its telling. Even during sections of the story where Marie serves as the primary speaker or solo narrator (Part II in particular), she does so with the encouragement of the audience, who recognizes her descriptions ("yep yep"), who empathizes with her situation ("ohhh::," "ooooo"), who shares her shock at the priest's comment ("Oh Marie"), and who joins her in laughter. By contrast, the communication relationships within the story are posed as a symmetrical challenge (Marie can manage the timing of reproduction as well as the priest or her husband) within a larger context of inequity in the labor of reproduction (Marie has little say regarding the construction of what constitutes a "good" mother, wife, and daughter of the Church).

The contrast in these communication relationships is illustrated in the final section of "We'll See You Next Year" by Marie's exclamation "*eh maudit*" and her subsequent response to Anna's question, "Marie what did you just say?" Anna's question functions as a request for clarification in knowledge rather than a challenge to knowledge such as that posed by the priest and then by Richard. Marie responds in the context of the "immersion" weekend where questions about French language and expression are part of the ongoing shared dialogue. Their collaborative "talk about talk" unsettles the sedimentation of discourse habits. Marie addresses the force of this habitual expression by providing an alternate English expression, "oh son of a gun," that might substitute for the French "*eh maudit.*" Then she offers a word-for-word translation but for the homophone ("*mot dit*") that, while providing a literal substitute for her expression, "makes no sense." Finally, she suggests its pragmatic function by describing it as "not really" but "sort of like" a swear word or "semi-curse." Interestingly, she avoids the more literal translation, "damnation," which would invoke religious meanings and would cast a different interpretation on her actions. Meaning, in short, is not to be found in semantics, syntactics, or pragmatics—the bits of verbal material sedimented in speech—but in the embodied and strategic function of the discourse. As Blanche volunteers, "but you know how she feels." For it is precisely this unnamed "feeling" that is performed by the narrative. The discussion of *"eh maudit"* unearths the sedimented "words said" and moves indirectly to "say what it means." So, too, "We'll See You Next Year" moves indirectly to unsettle how we feel about "that story."[6]

When Marie restates her phrase, "that was enough of that story," she recaptures it strategically within the discourse of family storytelling. When she casts about for a way to say what "we've had enough of," she turns to the expression "those . those beans," perhaps reinscribing her storytelling efforts as if they were a meal that she has prepared and served to guests. And, just as she takes on the timing of reproduction within the story, she replicates this tactic in taking on the timing of storytelling: "we've had enough of those . those beans for awhile." In this case, however, the use of the same tactic works to further a different strategic goal. The expression functions both to postpone direct discussion or more critique of reproduction and, at the same time, turns the floor over to other possible speakers and other possible topics. In both cases, her tactical efforts to claim agency are performed by strategically acceding to normative forms that she performs: Marie can only perform her desire for more children by having them, and she can only perform "that story" by temporarily deferring it. Thus the timing of interaction in storytelling is part of a collaborative effort that works to avoid forcing the story or particular meanings on the audience. Performing narrative does not resolve or conclude these strategic efforts; it risks the danger of audience response and continued storytelling. Marie invites, but cannot guarantee, audience response or that the audience will return to and take up "that story" after "for awhile" has passed.

As a communication practice, performing narrative makes conflict over experience, speaking, and identity concrete and accessible. The danger of performing narrative, then, is that it is political, it is open to *legitimation and critique*. We ask about this danger when we ask about the consequences of performing: How does storytelling regularize—transmit, reproduce, and legitimate—existing power relations? How does it work to thwart, critique, and render such power relations fragile? Rather than ask about individual motivation or social pressures, we ask what strategic functions storytelling performs. Why tell this particular story in this way to this audience? How might it be performed differently? Who has access to storytelling? Who benefits? How do particular patterns of discourse—such as turn-taking, intonation, pauses, hand movement, posture, gaze, spatial arrangement—work to open up or close off possibilities in storytelling? What subjects and voices are heard more readily than others? What does narrative construct as normal? What strategies and tactics does storytelling employ to reproduce itself within what is considered normal? How do strategies constrain the availability of tactics that may be employed? How does the use of particular tactics alter the definition of strategies? In what contexts are performances circulated and distributed, produced and commodified?

Performing Narrative: A Theory and Model

We began this chapter with what we take to be a common phenomenon: the mundane experience of listening to and telling stories, of performing narrative. This phenomenon emerges whenever we perform one of the multitudinous ways of saying "here, I would like to recount a little story" or "let me tell you about something that happened to me." We discover in this communication practice the human capacity for storytelling. We take *performing narrative* as our object of study in order to emphasize the communication functions of storytelling as a performative doing and as what is done in a performance of narrative. Narrative performance is not a disembodied invention waiting to be found by any knowledgeable observer and analyzed within a neutral or stable context. Rather, it is through our participation in performing narrative, as researchers in this case, that we come to understand the context within which we locate relations which constitute a doing and a thing done. The doing of storytelling and the thing done by storytelling are contextual facts of a particular situation wherein performativity comes to rest on a performance. Performing narrative is radically contextualized: in the bodies and voices of participants; in its situated and material conditions; in the discursive regularities that shape language, experience, and identity; and in the consequences storytelling poses for legitimation and critique of personal, social, and cultural norms and institutions.

The theoretical approach we take—semiotic phenomenology—contributes both a new perspective and a sustained analysis of performing narrative. As a critical interpretation of the theory and practice of narrative, this approach moves from story text to storytelling performance. Simultaneously, it argues for a series of related analytic shifts: from the traditional concerns of literature and linguistic stylistics to the pragmatics of communication; from the disembodied theories and models of structuralism to the embodied participation of audiences and storytellers, near and remote; from decontextualized strategies of textual coherence to multivoiced and multileveled contexts of performance; from essentialized notions of experience to post-structuralist conceptualizations of identity as a performative accomplishment; and from the evaluative function of narrative as a textual feature—the "so what?" of a story—to the larger and more crucial issues of power and the political consequences of specific narrative performances and practices. Our theoretical approach focuses on understanding *performing narrative,* the phenomenon of storytelling in daily life, and participating critically in conversations about what stories, what bodies, and what meanings matter.

Family storytelling matters in "We'll See You Next Year," in part because one of the participants in this body of women, Kristin, has asked to hear family stories. Kristin's participation—and, by extension, the participation of those reading a transcript or hearing a tape recording of the performance long after that evening in Quebec City—is a contextual fact of the situation. The request for family stories is not an unusual one, even though the group engaged in other types of storytelling. For example, the women told stories about living in Maine, about working outside the home, about Franco-American culture, and about world events. The choice of family storytelling is motivated or strategic, as we have argued, for both the women in the hotel room and for us as researchers analyzing the communication practice of storytelling. The choice of "We'll See You Next Year" as an illustration of storytelling in daily life functions as a research exemplar.[7] That is, as researchers we move from our experience participating in storytelling to discover an example of the phenomenon for analysis. In analyzing the phenomenon of storytelling in daily life, we reverse this process: we move from the description of the phenomenon to discover its typicality by specifying the logic of similarities and differences in our experiences of it. Thus, the choice of a research exemplar is a judgment regarding the quality of the example, "We'll See You Next Year," to define the phenomenon *performing narrative*.

In Part II, we turn to family storytelling in order to illustrate the strategic distribution of knowledge and power in performing narrative. If "We'll See You Next Year" serves as a research exemplar for a theory of performing narrative, then family storytelling serves in parallel fashion as a research model for performing narrative. Family storytelling, in other words, is one way to perform narrative. The accuracy or research value of this model for performing narrative can be established by locating empirical variations in family storytelling and using those variations to define the typicality of the strategic operations it puts into play. Therefore, we analyze family storytelling as a multilevel hierarchy of strategy and tactics, recognizing as we do that not all forms of storytelling mobilize strategies and tactics in the same way. What the many varieties of storytelling share, however, is the strategic ordering of stories, storytelling tasks, and group and personal identities.

Part II

Family Storytelling: A Strategy of Small Group Culture

The study of family storytelling is particularly salient at the beginning of the twenty-first century, when the family is the subject of moral panic: in decline, under duress, and everywhere debated in terms of "family values." Discussions usually begin with the divorce rate (holding steady at about 50%) and continue with a host of political, legal, economic, and ethical controversies: no-fault divorce, custody rights, family leave, welfare and workfare, assisted reproduction, childcare quality and options, the rights of biological parents and adopted children, domestic violence, the care of aging parents, globalization and immigrant families, and many others. To take one specific controversy, the campaign to secure civil rights for gays and lesbians was met with the proposed federal Defense of Marriage Act in 1996. Poor, working-class, ethnic, and "alternative" families are especially vulnerable in these debates, but even the "traditional" nuclear family is targeted by the self-help and psychotherapeutic literature on the dysfunctional family. Among the responses to this panic over family is a new mainstream magazine for families, *Becoming Family: Helping to Build Stronger Families*. In the throes of all this attention, the family has been described as a fatal abstraction because the pervasive and persistent appeals to "family values" are increasingly detached from the social and material production of the family (Armstrong, 1994).

Family is a human communication practice—as much a way of "doing things with words" as it is a set of ties and sentiments. The increasingly public and ritualistic ways we display, document, photograph, video, put on the Internet, stage, and in all ways narrate family characterizes modern Western family life (Pleck, 2000). Social historian John Gillis (1996) argues that the contemporary family is asked to create and preserve its own myths, rituals, and images, mapping the *family we live by* onto the *family we live with*. Creator and custodian of "a world of its own making," the family performs itself with special urgency, "representing ourselves to ourselves as we like to think we are" (p. xv). The spectacle of "the family"—its discursive power as a word, image, fiction, and figure of speech—masks the particularities of how particular families are performed in daily practices such as storytelling.

Family storytelling is a way of doing things with words. In Part II we flesh out the "fatal abstraction" of family and its performance by investigating the embodied, situated, discursive, and political practice of family storytelling. Our approach mediates between the scenario of decline and the spectacle of display to examine how some families today tell their stories. We examine family storytelling as one of many possible strategies for doing family and producing family culture. Our aim is to illuminate how families perform narrative in daily life to constitute and reconstitute themselves and, in so doing, reproduce themselves in changing social and material conditions. This study is reliant upon our earlier conceptual work on family storytelling and its critical trajectory (Langellier & Peterson, 1993, 1995); it is distinguished from this earlier work by its empirical focus. However, we intend this three-chapter section to be an extended discussion of family storytelling as a human communication practice rather than a report of empirical findings pertaining to it.

Family storytelling is performed in the speech act, "let me tell you a story about my family." Within this performative perspective, a family is both the human communication medium of expression and the ordering of information and meanings inscribed in that medium: families tell stories, and families are narrative formations. Performing narrative emphasizes the dual sense in which family storytelling is both performance, something a family does, and performative, the doing of storytelling that constitutes and forms the family. As performance, family storytelling ritually and routinely enacts a family and enhances its stories of experience. As performative, family storytelling constitutes the social and historical relations of family as well as the practices of storytelling. Performing family storytelling emphasizes bodily relations in a reflexive sense: it encompasses the cultural formation of telling relations (families that matter) and relations of telling (storytelling matters).

The approach we develop, as outlined in the previous chapter, embeds family storytelling in bodies, material situations, and discursive relations that are open to legitimation and critique. We try to avoid an individualistic or isolated group approach that limits its focus to relationships within the family, effectively ignoring how family is a social product mutually interpenetrated by historical, political, and economic forces. We have called this constant focus on the "insides" of a family as a container of communication a form of overpersonalization that diverts attention from family storytelling as a discursive and social production (Langellier & Peterson, 1995). Yet our approach to family storytelling tries to resist the overgeneralizing moves of master narratives whose totalizing explanations forego or forget embodied and material differences among families. To understand storytelling as a communication phenomenon, we approach the family as a small group culture, following the work of Thomas McFeat (1974), and as a discursive formation, following the work of Foucault (1976).

Families are our first culture, and family stories are the cornerstones of family culture: "The family is always jerry-rigged and has to be imagined and re-imagined every generation" (Stone, 1988, p. 40). In acts of imagination and reimagination, families perform themselves to themselves. Performing family stories creates an imagined community to celebrate identity and values (Anderson, 1991; Myerhoff, 1992). As the production of small group culture, family storytelling is more the work of invention than of blood, language, and land (Appadurai, 1996). Exposing the "myth of blood," Elizabeth Stone asserts that narrative provides what blood cannot, dramatizing blood connection (1988, pp. 39–40). Approaching family storytelling as small group culture resists the idealization or romanticization of a "natural" family to examine how communication practices produce family. To paraphrase McFeat's (1974) observation, families are what culture uses to produce more culture (p. 39). Family storytelling is survival strategy of small groups in which they articulate who they are to themselves, for themselves and for the next generations, engaging memory and anticipation as embodied and material practices of human communication.

To approach family as a communication practice is to ask how its storytelling orders and transmits information and meanings within and through generations. In storytelling, families order content, tasks, and identities. Chapter 2 examines content-ordering: how the meanings and sensibilities constituted and lived by families are created, stored, retrieved, and transmitted over generations. Meaningful stories may include family "classics" that are told and retold, such as ancestor stories, infant tales, childhood memories, and family character sketches; genres of family markers, such as courtships, marriages, births, and deaths; and stories about family time and homeplaces. Task-ordering, developed in Chapter 3, focuses on the labor of family storytelling as a situated performance event: how lived meanings are transmitted in a particular material situation, by whom, to whom, and for whom. Task-ordering examines interactional dynamics of participation in family storytelling, for example, roles and rights allocated between genders and generations. In group-ordering, the subject of Chapter 4, we examine how families negotiate the meanings of stories to adapt and innovate identities under changing social and historical conditions. In each chapter we consider how family storytelling legitimates and critiques particular content to produce "good family stories," particular tasks to produce "good tellings" of family, and particular family definitions to produce "good families." In sum, we conceptualize family story-telling as multileveled strategies, carried out in diverse situations by multiple participants within and among generations, which generate and legitimate certain meanings and relations of power and resistance (Langellier & Peterson, 1993). Family storytelling both produces a family as an embodied small group culture, and it reproduces The Family as a discursive formation.

We can understand more fully the discursive constraints of cultural pro-duction when we substitute "family" for "sex" in the following quotation from Judith Butler (1993):

> The category of "[family]" is, from the start, normative; it is what Foucault has called a "regulatory ideal." In this sense, then, "[family]" not only functions as a norm, but is part of a regulatory practice that produces the bodies it governs, that is, whose regulatory force is made clear as a kind of productive power, the power to produce—demarcate, circulate, differentiate—the bodies it controls. (p. 1)

Family storytelling, in other words, produces that which it purports to repre-sent. To focus on performativity in family storytelling is to take on the task of locating the power of this regulatory practice in producing "good stories," "good tellings," and "good families." Again to paraphrase Butler, family story-telling is a socially embodied performance, a "stylized repetition of acts" that makes bodies visible and audible, for example, family bodies, mother's and father's bodies, children's bodies.

Family storytelling promises a performance and constitutes storytellers and audience, narrators and characters. Elinor Ochs and Lisa Capps (2001) argue that "active narrative involvement defines what it means to participate in mainstream American family" (p. 8). Performing narrative, as discussed in the previous chapter, establishes a particular system of relations among partici-pants—including researchers—which is context-dependent: family storytell-ing is a situated practice constrained by "ground rules" that frame interpreta-tions of experience and identity.[1] These three chapters draw on a corpus of interviews with families across Maine who identify themselves as Franco-American.[2] Throughout the following three chapters we present and analyze materials that Kristin gathered in interviews, at family gatherings, and in ca-sual interaction with families. We selected Franco-American families because they present an opportunity to investigate small group cultures informed by ethnicity, language, class, religion, and region. The corpus includes approxi-mately thirty hours of talk in sessions with individuals, with same-generation partners (e.g., husband and wife, cousins, sisters), and with multigenerational sets (e.g., grandmother-mother-daughter, father-son).

No communication situation is neutral or disembodied. Shoshana Blum-Kulka (1997) reminds that because of research ethics we cannot record people without their consent, and therefore "the choice is among different modes of intrusion into the lives of the people studied, through the presence of researchers, and/or use of tape recorders and video camera" (p. 18). As Kenneth J. Gergen writes: "if I approach the family as a group of persons engaged in creating meaning together, meanings that will create their future, then I realize that I am a participant in the process. I cannot remove myself and remain aloof without having an effect on those meanings" (in Rosenblatt, 1994, p. v). With Esther Schely-Newman (1999), we describe Kristin's position as that of a ratified audience as she went to family homes, gatherings, and meals, and we make her presence visible in transcriptions. As Blum-Kulka (1997) writes, "the presence of a semi-official guest for dinner certainly affected the proceedings; no doubt there is a stronger element of family self-representation in the talk than would have emerged otherwise" (p. 280). For some members, elderly storytellers in particular, Kristin provided an audience not otherwise available as she listened to and valued their family experiences and ethnicity (Myerhoff, 1992).

CHAPTER 2

Ordering Content and Making Family Stories

What is a family story and what stories do families tell about themselves? Stone (1988) provides a useful starting point with her definition of a family story: "almost any bit of lore about a family member, living or dead, qualifies as a family story—as long as it's significant, as long as it's worked its way into the family canon to be told and retold" (p. 5). Stories may be oral genealogies, life histories, or fully developed Labovian narratives, but would as characteristically include kernels, fragments, and remnants as well as coded family myths and shrouded family secrets.[1] In the daily life of families, stories may be told in more extended narrative events, such as occur at anniversaries, reunions, or wakes; or in briefer narrative acts around daily interactions and chores. All families tell stories and members bear them "under their skin" as weightless pleasures or painful tattoos (Stone, 1988, pp. 6–7).

However, from our human communication approach, we prefer the term *family storytelling* over family stories and other options such as family history, genealogy, and biography, for a number of reasons. First, family storytelling highlights the evaluative function of telling—the "so what?" and "what matters?" in the narrative performance event that makes sense of family and constructs the sensibilities of family. *Storytelling* as a term focuses on the making of meaningful stories to tell and retell rather than assuming significance. Second, families do not routinely perform their genealogies, histories, and biographies in family events and interactions. The bits and pieces of family storytelling emerge within mundane activities of *doing family*—fragmentarily, circumstantially, promiscuously, fleetingly, messily—often invisible to themselves as well as to others. Third, family storytelling calls attention to the strategic communication practice that forms and performs family. If narrative is not to become just an artifact or text transmitting information about a culture, then it must be looked at as a strategic performance within specific and multileveled contexts that order embodiment, situation, and discourse. Family storytelling is an evolving expression of small group culture rather than a collection of stories.

The study of content-ordering gives us access to how lived meanings and information work their way into a family canon. Content is not arbitrary but rather the ordering of information by and for a particular group which transforms information to communication. Families order information in particular performances as sites of struggles over meanings for particular acts, events, and identities. Content is the *effectivity* of this ordering, the constitution of significance particular to a small group culture (Grossberg, 1993). Families create meaning about their past in present interactions that anticipate a future. Any act or event can always be narrated in multiple and sometimes conflicting ways; there are always other ways to tell what happened. Folklorist Nancy Thym-Hochrein (1981) contrasts how the U.S. and German branches of her family told the story of her great-grandfather's exodus from Germany. The U.S. version portrayed an adventurous and respectable person who left home to found a town and family in the New World because he felt limited in the Old World. The German version highlighted the scandalous details of the great-grandfather's hasty departure and the painful mistake of leaving the family of origin behind. The "same" information about the "same" event is ordered as content in each version but differently, under different conditions, and with different significance and effectivity.

The emphasis on storytelling over story, on the evaluative over referential function, on performance over text, places issues of meaning and sensibility at the heart of family narrative. To some extent, what will become meaningful content is not predictable outside particular performance conditions and consequences. For example, at one breakfast that included grapefruit, the husband spontaneously remembered an act of his father's. He recounted to his wife, daughter, and Kristin, miming the gestures as he narrated, how his father had carefully cleaned off his pocketknife at the kitchen table and then lovingly, crisply, meticulously sectioned grapefruit halves for the children's breakfast. Nor can one foretell which family activities and events will survive to be retold once put into words. During a taping by Kristin and a colleague with a husband and wife in their home, for example, an adult son dropped by. His mother had recently cared for the adult son's toddler, Ashley, and the mother interrupted her narrative to us to relate an episode about Ashley to her son. Ashley had been tracking autumn leaves into the house as she went in and out to play. Asked on yet another entry into the house, "Are you coming in for good this time?" "No, Nana," the child replied, "I'm coming in for bad." Whether these stories work their way into the family canon or not depends on a family's strategies and tactics of ordering content. Will one or more of the grandparents, parents, children, or grandchildren remember it and pass it on?

Will it be retold with some frequency and over time? Benjamin (1969) observes that "storytelling is always the art of repeating stories, and this art is lost when the stories are no longer retained" (p. 91). In the sections that follow, we analyze how families remember and make stories by ordering content.

"It usually takes a lot of people to bring those memories back": Generality and Group Memory

We begin our consideration of content-ordering through an extended and embedded example from a session with two male cousins in their seventies, Gerald and Alain, who are related through their mothers. The session takes place in Gerald's kitchen with Madeline, his wife, in the background but not at the kitchen table with the cousins and Kristin. The window framing the table overlooks a river, and the cousins often point out houses, fishing spots, or town landmarks as they narrate. About ten minutes into the session, Gerald introduces what we call the story of "The Sewing Sandwiches." To examine content-ordering as a communication process involving generality and group memory, we will look at the seven-minute section in its entirety but segment it into units for discussion.

> *Gerald:* the my <u>grand</u>mother's <u>daughters</u>
> had a sewing circle
> and and my wife belonged to it too also
> and the <u>wives</u> of the the men in the family were always invited to join the sewing circle
> and they would meet every::
>
> *Alain:* Monday
>
> *Gerald:* Monday night and . ah
> they would talk a lot of French
>
> *Kristin:* okay
>
> *Gerald:* and my wife ah didn't know half of what they were saying when they did talk French
>
> *Madeline:* just from the French that I knew just a little bit in school
> like I could recognize some of the words but their grammar was
>
> *Kristin:* that's that's fascinating
> I've never heard
> was it a <u>family</u> sewing circle or a <u>community</u> sewing circle?
>
> *Gerald:* a family just a family

As storyteller, Gerald initiates the narrative sequence, but he is not the only narrator of this memory as Alain and Madeline participate in ordering information about the sewing circles, shifting relations between storyteller and audience. A few minutes before this segment Alain had commented that "it usually takes a lot of people to bring those memories back." At first it seems that Gerald is a storyteller of someone else's experience—the wives'—but all three family members have some kind of participant knowledge of the sewing circles: each will also perform as a character. Such generality of performance relations makes this content more likely to be remembered and transmitted. The participants have a common focus on the sewing sandwiches but from different angles of experience. Content-ordering requires that the sewing circles be remembered, but it does not require group consensus on their details and meanings. To Gerald's opening, Alain contributes the detail of Monday, the night the circle met, and Gerald readily incorporates this into his telling. At this point Madeline comes over to the table to explain her relationship to "the French" announced by him. She married into the family; she is not French although she understands some French words. Their content ordering suggests that the French language is a significant aspect of family definition, a performative boundary that differentiates the family body and bodies within the family.

Information about ritualistic family gatherings, French language use, and food are material resources ordered in this segment to create meanings for this family. The sewing circles are habitual activities, repeated through at least two generations, rather than discrete events. They have a special night, Monday, but also illustrate a repeated and mundane way of *doing family* and spending family time. They are organized by gender (a women's activity) and, as we will see, by generation (adults downstairs, children upstairs). "Because stories recount events that depart from the ordinary, they also serve to articulate and sustain common understandings of what the culture deems ordinary" (Ochs, 1997, p. 193). Like personal narratives, family stories must be about something that happened or happens or could have happened. Narrative studies usually discuss content in terms of tellability: what is interesting to the family? How is it interesting? In family storytelling, tellability is related not only to remarkable events with high tellability but also to mundane meanings for participants, a particular family—Stone's "so long as it's significant" criteria. In content-ordering, families sort through and negotiate tellability, discovering and evaluating what happened and its significance to family culture now and for the future. Tellability emerges within and from a family's ordering of content rather than from the decontextualized remarkableness of an event.

Because Kristin is familiar with the historical traditions of sewing circles and contemporary quiltmaking groups based in communities rather than families, she asks her question. Gerald gives the answer "a family just a family," but Alain offers additional information on Mrs. Lillie Bouchard, which Gerald then supplements:

Alain: well

there was a French family across the stree— across the river there

the <u>Bouchards</u>

weren't the same <u>Bouchard</u> as my mother

my mother was a Bouchard too and his mother was a Bouchard

Kristin: and my neighbor was a Bouchard by the way

Alain: yeah

they weren't the same <u>clans</u> but they moved in here

and she was kind of accepted in the family old Mrs. Lillie . Lillie Bouchard

she: belonged to the ah sewing circle

but it was all family it was ah . .

Gerald: yeah and

to get back to Lil for she used to no matter

she'd come to <u>all</u> the sewing this ah times

but she'd <u>row</u> across the river in the summertime

and <u>leave</u> about nine or ten o'clock at night <u>ro:w</u> back

in the wintertime she'd <u>cross</u> the ice she'd <u>cross</u> the ice to go to church

and . . <u>everybody</u> in the wintertime on French Island used to cross the ice

and then had to cross the <u>railroad tracks</u> to go to church when it was frozen over

Alain and Gerald answer Kristin's question, but they do much more. This section may seem a digression unless we focus on how participants are ordering content. Through the Bouchard name, the cousins explain their relationship to each other through their mothers as well as how a non-family member was admitted within a family activity. Kristin even inserts a brief link here, making a lighthearted effort to connect her Midwest French background to theirs in Maine through the Bouchard name. This citing and sorting exemplifies how participants create and maintain boundaries for family, working out its parameters and meanings. Boundaries mark space and belonging: who is in the family, who is in the sewing circle, who is in the community. Interestingly, the case of Mrs. Lillie Bouchard suggests that family in this instance is not strictly limited by biology or marriage but by place, in this case excluding Kristin. Gerald's ensuing content-ordering on crossing the ice may seem puzzling unless one considers how the narrating creates place: the island, the river, the railroad tracks, the church. Like beaten paths between homes, the specificity of geographic detail and sedimented patterns of movement anchor characters in place. Not only Lillie but "<u>everybody</u> in the wintertime used to cross the ice." Collective knowledge of place evokes collective memory that creates a sense of belonging in a group (Johnstone, 1990). Gerald's ordering of content constructs meaning here less as an individual life or family history and more as a bygone life, a form of heritage and nostalgia.

If information about sewing circles is to survive to future generations, their content-ordering must provide a sense of place and community for this particular family. And if the family is to survive in this particular place, then such content must find a place within it. Gerald's information also seems to be designed for an audience beyond the present listeners and outside the family, providing a context for family, through the situated details of community and place. Acknowledging the detour through place and audiences not present, Gerald takes us back to the sewing circle:

Gerald:	but to get back to the sewing circle
	like I said that— they each had a <u>turn</u>
	each week they had a turn
	and they would put on a . . a little lunch
Madeline:	oh a full <u>meal</u>
	you always had ham <u>sandwiches</u> or a <u>casserole</u> or something
Alain:	now see I don't remember that
Madeline:	yeah when <u>I</u> was in it there was cause I made chop suey one time
Alain:	I remember sewing circle before the before the grandchildren started getting into it
	I I remember just the aunts just the aunts and Mrs. Lillie Bouchard
	and it was just sandwiches
	they used to have they used to always make what we called <u>sewing sandwiches</u>
	and it was all it was was chopped
Alain &	
Gerald:	bologna and eggs
Madeline:	and onions
Alain:	and of course all the kids we couldn't wait until everybody left
	cause we got the <u>leftovers</u>
	and sewing sandwiches
	and in <u>my</u> family my immediate family my <u>kids</u>
	I started making those at home
	and my kids started calling them <u>daddy</u> sandwiches
Madeline:	ooh ooh
Alain:	but they were the <u>sewing</u> the sewing circle's sandwiches

The participation of multiple tellers may appear to change direction, delay, derail, backtrack, or bring in irrelevant information, but this narrating is not an instance of *a story* but of *stories* being ordered. When Gerald steers the conversation back to the sewing circle, his "little lunch" is corrected by his wife based on her generational and gendered participation, sewing with and cooking for the group, distinct from the men's childhood memories. Alain also distinguishes generational memories, specific to the time of the aunts and the sandwiches. Amusingly, Gerald and Alain name the ingredients of the sandwiches simultaneously—they concur on this information—to which Made-line adds "and onions," perhaps because she prepared as well as ate the "lunches." The ordering of content next moves to Alain's depiction of the living generations and how he made sewing sandwiches for his children, now called "<u>daddy</u> sandwiches." Madeline responds with two audible "oohs" that suggest this is new and interesting information for her, now ordered as content within the sewing circle memories.

In this segment, the information about sewing sandwiches is retained but reordered as content. Sewing sandwiches have moved from the grandparents' generation as a site of women's activity and an extended family gathering to a father and his nuclear family two generations later. The sewing sandwiches serve as an example of cultural transformation and transmission of this information. This example of how family storytelling orders content by gender and over generations would appear to end the story of the sewing sandwiches. However, without a pause the discussion continues:

Madeline: <u>his</u> [Gerald's] mother used to make lilies

Gerald: lilies

Madeline: for dessert
          it was some kind of a . really . almost like a sponge
          but it was . even more delicate than that
          she'd bake these on saucers and
               while they were still hot she'd curl the sides in
               they were rou:nd so they were just like . just like a lily
          and she'd when they were cool before the sewing came
          she'd fill them with whipped cream
               and then she'd put a little strip of ah you know those big orange jellies
               ah gumdrops
          she'd cut little pistles out of those and put them on
          [exhales] oh: go:d those were heaven

Alain: now isn't that funny how <u>you</u> remember that too
          but see I don't I don't remember the years of
               because my wife never she never belo:nged to it
               but like you and Ida and Amy and them they were they were mostly
               ah . not
          well <u>you</u> were an in-law though
               I was thinking like Ida and Amy and . ah . all the girls

Madeline: <u>Cathy</u> never was in it

Gerald: no

Madeline: and Jeanne had one of her own
               well she had a different one it was . <u>her</u> generation
          Claude's wife used to belong to that and maybe Ida did

> I don't know
>
> *Alain:*   no I don't think Ida ever belonged

If the earlier passage on Mrs. Lillie Bouchard seemed a digression, this segment is even more tangential. Admittedly, our first inclination was to spare the reader: to delete it, use ellipses, or provide a brief summary. But what is going on here? One thing that is going on is gendered content-ordering reminiscent of Karen Baldwin's (1985) work with men's and women's roles in family storytelling.[2] Madeline's description of how to make lilies is enhanced by iconic hand gestures that mime the work for the listeners (McNeill, 1992). Her "detour" details how delicate and delicious the lilies were and the time and skill required to make them for the sewing circle lunches. This is her lengthiest contribution to the session, and after it she returns to work in other parts of the house and ends her participation in the storytelling. The content-ordering about the lilies also recalls Michela di Leonardo's findings (1984) on gendered patterns of memory where daughters recall mothers' labor whereas sons remember their nurturing. Content-ordering involves both retrieving (Alain and Gerald) and correcting memory (Madeline) within a generation of participants. When Alain attempts to discern a logic for who is in the groups, we see not only remembering and monitoring but also sense-making geared to family cultural boundaries. If some of Gerald's detail on local geography was designed for an audience outside the family, this collaborative section on sewing circle members bears the marks of intrafamilial address. Even though Kristin does not know Ida, Amy, Cathy, Jeanne, or Claude, no one makes an attempt to explain to her their identities and family relations.

Narratives of Nostalgia and Loss

To summarize so far, as effort to create and transmit family culture through remembering, the ordering and reordering of information on sewing circles transforms sewing sandwiches to daddy sandwiches. Sewing circles no longer meet but sewing sandwiches survive as family practice and as story, both subject to changes in meanings but with enduring significance. The content about sewing sandwiches is collectively remembered but not fixed into a received narrative configuration as participants work over its meanings. In fact, there is not one story being worked out here but (at least) three open-ended narrative threads of content: the sewing circles, the lunches, and French language. These threads converge to emphasize the significance of family gatherings to cultural survival, capturing the sense in which they are both habitual and special resources in family formation. Gerald returns to the French language thread as the discussion continues:

> *Gerald:*   well us— we— ah our— my brothers and sisters never . talked . French
>   they could understand very little of it

and we'd <u>listen</u> to the women talk downstairs
   it was always *chèrrrrre!* [exaggerates the rolling of his "r"]
   we used to go *chèrrrrre* and we'd laugh upstairs
but as soon as it got quiet down the stairs
we'd come to have a some sewing sandwiches or
   ah get the rest of and
they always made more so that the kids would have some you know

Gerald clarifies that the children were listening upstairs and mimicking the French of adults downstairs before coming down for the sewing sandwiches. He and his siblings did not grow up speaking French, although Alain's family did. The French language is ordered here as narrative content, but neither the participants nor their children and grandchildren currently speak French. Family storytelling occasions talk about French, and occasionally talk in French, but Gerald and Alain's families tell these stories in English. It is also significant to note that although Kristin has some competency in French, she is more comfortable in English. Participants undoubtably adapt to this performance situation. We cannot capture nor calculate what is no longer present, but this content-ordering suggests a loss of information and sensibilities in family storytelling when the French language as a medium of expression yielded to English. The loss of French language suggests that what cannot be expressed has not survived in subsequent generations.[3] Language retention and loss is a complex and variable process of generation and geography, still in active contention and differentially performed across the corpus. Even through the marks of embodied difference fade, they may be remembered, as Gerald's playfully performed *"chèrrrrre"* suggests. The strategy to perform and repeat this word brings past pleasures to the fore, as Gerald performs as character what he tells as narrator. In these moments, participants enjoy a nostalgia for childhood imbued with pleasure and a spirit of worth and meaning.

Transmission of culture is facilitated by the generality of knowledge that diffuses content among multiple participants, those who take their own experience or that of others to create significant stories for family. Generality of knowledge provides some safeguard against both loss and distortion. "It takes a lot of people to bring those memories back" suggests the collective but dispersed memory that supports the ordering of content. We take a communication approach to memory that is embodied, interactional, and social rather than cognitive, individual, and psychological. Group memory is enabled by participation in family storytelling and supplemented by alternative storage, such as the photographs, books (e.g., a mother's book, a journal), videos, and genealogies which some participants offered to us. Group memory is constrained by embodied differences among participants, by changing social history, and by rules for excluded talk, as we next see.

"It wasn't talked about":
Family Secrets, Scandals, and Skeletons

Gerald continues his speaking turn and associates the sewing circle, sandwiches, and memories of French with what families do not talk about: gossip, "dark horses," and scandals. These exclusions are corroborated by Alain and explained in terms of local family models:

Gerald: but ah they used to meet and ah
    very little gossip about the family
        you know I mean ah if somebody did something wrong
    it wasn't talked about

Alain: yeah yeah it's true what he says and ah
    you find that most every family any la:rge families
        like we're considered large families and they were twelve fourteen

Gerald: twelve

Alain: twelve
        and most most of them my mother had nine kids his mother had seven
        seven or eight
        they were all large families
        so when you had a family reunion it constitutes a lot of people
    and ah . you know . us growing older
    like when we get in our fifties we always wonder about
        about the dark horses in the family
        or the scandals in the family
    there's some
    but try to ask . like we had a couple of scandals
        and we'd ask one of the aunts well what about this how come this is this
        you couldn't get anything out of them
    nothing

Gerald: not a word [chuckles]

Alain: like my mother she was one of the oldest and ah
    you'd ask her . no nothing
        you wouldn't get any
    and eventually as they die off and everything
        some of it comes out a little bit what really happened and everything
    but they used to conceal things they used to protect each other

Gerald: oh you wouldn't believe it

Alain: you know and I'm not saying that derogatively
    I think that's that's good to keep things in the closet
    but eventually they do come out what it is and
        and it's not . it's not that bad

it's a lot of things that's— are . almost accepted today
but <u>then</u> it was real scandals

Gerald and Alain bring up stories not told, marking their absence with a lengthy discussion. These memories enact a nostalgia that is more reflexive than the talk on the sewing circles, that does more than sentimentalize the past and censure, even if only implicitly, the present. The past was not all innocent and good. "He or she summons to thought and feeling certain empirically oriented questions concerning the truth, accuracy, completeness, or representativeness of the nostalgic claim" (Davis, 1979, p. 21)—and, as Alain notes, "<u>some</u> of it comes out a little bit what really happened." The specific scandals and secrets are less our analytic focus than the family rules around content-ordering. The ordering of content is constrained not only by memory and language, as developed above, but also by embodied participants, by the situation with other family members and the researcher, and by the normalizing discourse of powerful institutions, such as the law, religion, and the family itself. The family's first concern is itself and its own survival. With a stake in perpetuating itself it "must relentlessly push the institutions that preserve it" —heterosexual love, marriage, and childbearing especially (Stone, 1988, p. 50; Langellier & Peterson, 1993, 1995)—and ward off other threats to family image and practices ("doing something wrong," as Gerald puts it). Excluded content in Franco-American family storytelling includes alcoholism, domestic violence, abortion, sex, incest, child abuse, homosexuality, divorce, leaving the Church, anger, and disparaging the deceased. However, excluded discourse may still be named and narrated despite regulatory rules, as we discuss below.

The idea of family is normative, a regulatory ideal that reproduces the bodies it controls. Narrative participates in social control (Mumby, 1993). One cannot hear Alain's "It's good to keep things in the closet," things that when they come out "are almost accepted today," without thinking of homosexuality and its exclusion from family storytelling. Kath Weston (1991) problematizes "gay" and "family" as mutually exclusive terms that render homosexuals as "exiles from kinship" based on a paradigmatically heterosexual and procreative notion of family: "straight" is to "gay" as "family" is to "no family" (pp. 22–29). Controlling narratives, such as the pervasive heterosexual narrative of family storytelling, marginalize lesbians, gay men, the "homosexual choice" (O'Connell, 2001), and "intentional families" of lesbians and gay men. However muted, these choices and voices still emerge, particularly as the changing social and historical circumstances create opportunities for telling sexual stories (Plummer, 1995). In the Franco-American corpus studied here, one family member asks, "where are they [lesbians and gay men]? I know they're there." Franco-American writers such as Alain Bérubé (1997) and Paul Brouillette (April, et al., 1999) document gay identities as variations in ordering content in family narrative.

Narrative analysts have identified a general rule around moral stance, the "looking good" principle of narrators. "Narrators of personal experience evaluate protagonists as moral agents, whose actions, thoughts, and feelings are interpreted in light of local notions of goodness" (Ochs & Capps, 2001, p. 47). Gerald and Alain suggest two local notions developed by Franco-American families to promote survival: first, large families; and second, protecting each other. The history of the French in North America has been characterized by pronatal social policies and the Roman Catholic Church's highest priority on childbearing: in the 1600s and 1700s to populate New France in Canada; and after French defeat by British in 1763 as the only hope for the future because immigration from France was cut off. The mystique of *la survivance*, the passionate and valiant effort to maintain French identity in North America, included "the revenge of the cradles," a program of heroic fecundity that doubled the population every two decades from the eighteenth to the twentieth century. Large families are obviously important for biological reproduction, but they also are significant for cultural reproduction. The more people who know and remember the content of a small group culture, the more likely the group is to survive. Size itself is no guarantee of survival, but in larger families information and memories may be distributed among more individuals. Based upon his studies of natural and experimental small groups, McFeat (1974, pp. 150–152) argues that the greatest risk of information loss and distortion occurs in two-member groups where individual preferences for outcomes fall under less scrutiny than they do in groups larger than three, where information exchange undergoes routine monitoring.

Alain suggests that someone in the family knows what happened, even if they are not telling. "They conceal things to protect each other" implies that some things *are* secrets and justifiably protect family members and the younger generations. A family survives by not talking as well as talking, so that is why it is "good to keep things in the closet." Family members can count on themselves and on their caring group. Moreover, they can protect each other as family groups in a society that is unsupportive and even hostile to their survival. The French in North America traditionally "hid out" from the English in the face of powerful forces of assimilation and discrimination that threatened cultural survival, turning inward for help and security. Thus group-based secrets both maintain a boundary between a family and its environment and help a family survive in a challenging environment. Family secrets were sacred, and family problems were confided only to each other or to the parish priest, when necessary (Langelier, 1996).

But family secrets are not an all-or-nothing proposition, as the session here demonstrates when Gerald and Alain refer to, but decline to narrate, family scandals. One grandmother in the sample declares that she "didn't know things were supposed to be secrets," told them throughout her life, and faced family reproaches. At a three-generation family dinner, topics of alcoholism and a father's drinking were narrated and deliberated. Taboo topics were narrated by other participants, summarily or partially. In an individual interview, one daughter briefly disclosed instances of alcoholism and domestic violence in an earlier generation and an instance of sexual abuse in the extended family—none hinted at in the preceding interview with her mother, father, and herself present. Other taboo topics were coded more discreetly; for example, one daughter referred to her mother's going into therapy for "some childhood recollections" that are not specified or elaborated. Some events were narrated more fully to Kristin—of domestic violence, an abortion attempt, a divorce in progress—but the participants requested that we not disclose specific transcriptions. Criminal activities exhibited a more humorous tone and valence—for example, stories of illegal beer or whiskey cleverly concealed behind false walls in a basement during Prohibition, of a grandmother's smuggling butter across the border to sell for higher U.S. dollars, of distant relatives in the "Canadian Mafia" and cousins in jail.

Our point here is not to force family disclosure, lament its absence, nor speculate about details but rather to understand how families order content, through privileged and excluded discourse, in their storytelling as a function of transmitting family culture. Silence and secrets may contribute to family survival as surely as telling family stories. The repressed also transmits family culture. One grandmother stated that "I put things out of my mind," and a mother of eleven living in a rural region challenged, "don't ask me how I did it. I don't remember." Nor do we wish to deny the possibility of memories too painful or impossible to recall, as in instances of childhood amnesia or trauma (Ochs & Capps, 2001). Family therapists have explained how "black sheep" can be used to contain "deviance" in a family system, and that families may sacrifice an individual for the sake of family survival. "It wasn't talked about" can refer to what is known and narrated in selective ways (family secrets widely known and conditionally disclosed); to what is known and not narrated (family secrets not told); or to what is not known and not narrated (family secrets inaccessible for social-historical or psychological reasons).

"We tell that story a lot": Performing Family Classics

Storytelling about sewing sandwiches shows family at the communication work of content-ordering. This story may become a "family classic," depending on the frequency and duration of its telling. Family classics are the result of content-ordering over time and generations. In distinction from "it's not talked about," family classics are told and retold. They are the sedimentation of remembered information and negotiated meaning as a family narrates itself. Family classics assume the cultural work of ordering content and its transmission most often within but also outside family. Classics enter the family canon and bear the marks of repeated telling, fixing, and polishing. For example, in the precision of the line "February 27, 1954, I got my accident," we can hear a ritualized opening, keying a familiar story. Family classics may be nothing more than a scrap of language, a line of dialogue, or a vibrant image. For example, the grandchildren have transformed the French dish *ragoût de boulettes* (meatball stew) to "bullet soup"; a man, now in his eighties, quotes his father: "I never had a tractor until I had a boy big enough to run it"; and a mother recalls the image of her mother with doughnuts stacked all the way up her arm, ready to fry. Or family classics can be as lengthy as the lineage of fathers begetting sons, the details of a life-threatening accident, the intricate history of a family business.

Classics are widely known in a family and may be requested by other family members or offered in response to an interview question. A story about a Sunday drive during which the daughter blows ice cream through the bottom of the cone into her brother's mouth and out his nose, ends with, "We tell that story a lot." A story about how, during a girl's first visit to the family, she eats three helpings of the baked beans—unknowingly finishing the last of the beans before the mother has anything to eat—concludes with, "all the kids know that story." In the family it is called the "city girl story," a kernel familiar to the whole family. Because family classics carry information about family history, they often take the form of a kernel story that may be or may not be developed into a full story, depending on conversational context (Kalčik, 1975; Langellier & Peterson, 1992).

For example, in one session with Kristin, Yvonne narrates an infant tale, that is, a story about a child or children repeated in the family. She describes the Friday night meetings which her family convened when their father returned from work in Massachusetts. During his weekday absences, her mother kept a notebook in order to report to the father on the children's behavior. These reports are narrated like a Roman Catholic confession as Yvonne quotes her mother: "'everyone was pretty good but [son] sassed me thirteen times.'" Yvonne continues, "Well, one day when my dad was gone my mother got a phone call." The call is from a neighbor with the message that the two older children (Yvonne's siblings) are smoking cigarettes. Her mother grabs Yvonne and drags her to where the other children are. The mother hides in the bushes and catches the older children in the act of smoking, and then marches all three kids back home. The story concludes:

Yvonne: my <u>brother</u> got a licking for smoking
             my <u>sister</u> got a licking for smoking
             <u>I</u> got a licking I still don't know to this day why
             She [mother] says because I'm probably going to do something bad next week
             but everybody still laughs about that
             they say "why did Yvonne get a licking? She was home with you"

The coda "everybody still laughs at that" suggests this story is told both with some frequency and has endured over several years. The structural and linguistic repetitions in the closing lines emphasize the poetic features of the story (see Gee, 1986, 1989, 1991). The story encodes family values of discipline and is told within a description of how the children were brought up. Other examples of family classics anchor character (e.g., how the narrator did the best job milking the new family cow and got the job for the rest of the cow's life), teach a family lesson (e.g., how a daughter steals milk money and gets caught), or capture a family monument (e.g., the grandmother's one-hundredth birthday party in Canada). Family classics may be self-narratives, rich with the details of narrated events and delights of evaluation by the protagonist. But family classics are also told about other family characters and ancestors, and told by parents about children and by children about parents. In fact, their status as a family classic suggests that they may be told by more than one family member as settings and generations change. For example, the story of a middle-aged father getting his GED (General Education Diploma) is told by the daughter in one interview setting and by the mother at a family dinner—neither time by the protagonist.

Because family classics solidify content into a more stable text through retellings, they can become sites to display performance skills more than a social forum for ordering content. Here we emphasize performance in its definition as a special mode of communication that is aesthetically marked (Bauman, 1986). Consider the following classic told at a family meal with three generations: grandmother Pauline and grandfather, their daughter and her second husband, and the twelve-year-old granddaughter, plus a family friend, and Kristin. Dinner talk may occasion narrative performance (Blum-Kulka, 1997), and Monday night suppers are a weekly ritual for this family. The daughter's family is always there, sometimes alone but often with a changing cast of family friends. Pauline and her husband have been co-narrating bits about Pauline's parents, both deceased. The talk turns to how nervous Pauline's mother was about riding in a car. The story exhibits the Labovian structure of a fully developed narrative, which we code in brackets (on the right) and with numbered lines (on the left) to reference the performance analysis that follows. The story is clearly a family favorite, and the granddaughter requests it and then giggles after the abstract, signaling her familiarity and anticipation. There is much laughter throughout the telling, by Pauline and the audience.

1 I can tell about the time . my mother was older and she wasn't so well   [abstract]
2 and she needed a pair of shoes
3 so I took her down to Standard Shoe   [orientation]
4 and out behind you could go in the back door there you could park out behind there
5 [Kristin]: downtown Bangor
6 uh huh so we went in and we got the shoes and everything
7 we come ba:ck and so I opened up the door   [complicating action]

8   and she <u>sa:::t</u> I thou::ght on the <u>se:at</u>

9   I went around to the driver's seat and I looked across and my <u>god</u> she's not <u>there</u>

10 [Laughs to self] my <u>god</u> where is she? [granddaughter and others laughing over line]

11 and I run around the car and she had <u>slipped</u>

12 she was <u>laying</u> underneath the car
    [everyone laughing, laughter continues through rest of story]

13 and when I get nervous I giggle [she giggles]

14 and she says "leave me alone . I'll get up"

15 "just leave me alone . I'll get mad enough in a minute and I'll get up"

16 well sure enough she did . she got up

17 and after I'm trying not to laugh because—and I'm going "my god mother"

18 she never broke anything ever when she fell . we've got good strong bones
    apparent—   [resolution]

19 but my god I was dying when I go to get back in the car   [evaluation]

20 and I said "my god Mama I'm so sorry"

21 And so <u>I tell you now</u> when I'm going to help somebody in the car   [coda]

22 I don't <u>leave</u> until they've got <u>both cheeks</u> on the seat and I can shut the door

23 because it was aw:ful poor thing

"I can tell about the time" keys a performance that can be organized on a continuum of theatrical devices and poetic features (Wolfson, 1978; Georgakopoulou, 1998; Langellier, 2001) that enhance the experience. Theatrical features include the use of narrative present (e.g., the switch in line 14 from past tense to "and she says," and the alteration of narrative present with past tense); characters' speech (e.g., "leave me alone . I'll get up" in line 14); the teller's inner speech/thought (e.g., lines 9 and 10, "my <u>god</u> she's not <u>there</u> / my god where is she?" and line 17 "and after I'm trying not to <u>laugh</u> because"). Poetic features include rhythm (e.g., the stanza of lines 7–11 that alternate between "I" and "she," and the structural pair of line 14 with line 16); repetition (e.g., of words, "my god" in lines 9, 10, 17, and 20 and three uses of "get up" in lines 14, 15, and 16); and expressive phonology and intonational variations (e.g., emphasis and elongation to set a phrase apart from others in line 8, "and she <u>sa:::t</u> I thou::ght on the <u>se:at</u>"). These theatrical devices and poetic features render the text self-focusing and display the teller's competence as she assumes responsibility to the audience for performance (Bauman, 1986). The effect of performance is to enhance experience and crystallize family culture. The experiential immediacy and dramatization of performed narration works to increase audience involvement and sweep them into a community of rapport that deters critical responses and deflects discussion (Georgakopoulou, 1998). The focus on performance in the family classic subordinates the negotiations of content-ordering to the bonding of the family group, here especially through shared laughter. Audience participation is active but less substantive in terms of contributing narrative content.

The shaping and structuring of content in family classics suggests how they can survive both multiple tellings and multiple tellers. Further, they can travel, decontextualized from a family setting and recontextualized into other settings. The story about driving her mother inaugurates a performance series by Pauline, a trilogy of humorous stories on the same topic. About fifteen minutes later, another couple from the neighborhood drops by and is invited to join the table. The newcomers are told that we have been telling stories, including the one "about her mother laying under the car." This kernel is not developed and retold at this point, but the new arrival tells another driving story, about a time when she was with Pauline and her mother. This example suggests how classics may be told to outsiders and outside the family. The recontextualized story by the family friend focuses less on the mother-daughter characters and more on the narrator's long-standing relationship with Pauline.

Family classics may be shared more widely, too, in settings outside the home. Although the text of a classic becomes relatively fixed through the polishing of theatrical and poetic features, narrators strategically differentiate audiences. Another story, this one about an invention, suggests how a story is told differently within and outside the family. The narrating father in this story has been ordered by a doctor to stop working in construction because of a very serious injury to his leg at age twenty that has never healed. The story is about an invention, the idea for which comes to the father in a dream. His telling with his wife, daughter, and Kristin involves aspects of faith: "So I said one night, I was saying my prayers eh and I said 'you [Lord] gotta find me a job that I can do.'" The detailed story of designing the invention, patenting, and marketing it, concludes:

Father: so . hey . it's got to be <u>great</u> where it comes from
            it comes from the Lord to me

Mother: so . usually he never tells that at all

Father: no . I don't tell that to nobody
            they laugh at me

Mother: [laughs]

Father: especially some people that don't believe in nothing . so
            you know . you gotta . you gotta restrain yourself sometimes in places
            but that's the <u>fruit</u> . so
            everybody knows it in town

This example suggests that family classics can travel ("everybody knows it in town") and how the text changes in this context. This narrator strategically adapts to audiences and, in this telling, situates Kristin as one who does not laugh. The people in town cannot be assumed to share the family's belief in the divine origin of the invention. Occasionally a family story even enters the media, as when a father is featured in a Portland news story about the 9-foot

2-inch tomato plant he grew. The media experience is incorporated into the family story (he quotes the reporter as saying "a man in Lewiston is bragging about his tomato plant"), as is information about the reporter measuring the vine and counting the tomatoes. Classics do not prescribe a singular or transparent relationship among storyteller, narrator, and character, nor even between the classic and the family. A story introduced as "cute" in another narrator's repertoire had only a tangential link to her family. However, it seemed to be told and retold because of the gendered humor focusing around an incident in which a woman who disturbs the peace is put in jail for the night. When the jailor appears with breakfast the morning after, the woman says "'Mr. Charette, I'd like to have a Kotex.'" He responds, "'you eat these cornflakes just like the others.'" The rationale offered by the narration following the story, that perhaps her aunt still used "rags" for her menstrual period, weakly linked the story to family meanings being developed. Hence, performance value may outweigh family significance. In fact, in rereading this paragraph, we realized we unreflectively wrote it in the narrative present, enhancing its performativity. Textually solid and competently performed, family classics are the family stories most likely to be passed on and circulated in other settings.

Because of their sedimented content, family classics are more geared to teller performance and audience identification than they are to social questioning. The self-focusing text can anchor a family's definition and bolster cultural survival. They are often, though not always, entertaining or dramatic. The performance display can distinguish the talents or authority of a family storyteller. Like literary classics, family classics tend to endure through time as texts and to adapt to numerous contexts, within and outside family. Simultaneously, however, they may mute participation and critique as the sorting and making sense of content is subordinated to sedimented content and social affirmation. Family classics recall the ritual storytelling that Barbara Myerhoff (1992) observed among elderly American Jews: "It seemed, in fact, that their purpose was to allow things to stay the same, to permit people to discover and rediscover sameness in the midst of furor, antagonism, and the threats of splitting" (p. 263). Family classics may enchant experience, personalize family meanings, and close family boundaries to social exchange. In their (relative) stabilizing of content and meanings, they may naturalize family identity as more singular, solid, consensual, and "clean" than the messiness of family life.

That said, however, we should not assume that the process of content sedimentation fixes meaning. Family classics can be reworked and reinterpreted. For example, one story from the father's side and generation was about a young son who was "kicked all the way home" for some transgression. The phrase was memorable and kept intact and repeated three times by the daughter in a session with her husband and Kristin. The story had been told nu-

merous times in the family by the father in a matter-of-fact manner as an unremarkable event that tended to normalize its meanings and naturalize the
history of his childhood. However, the adult daughter is now retelling and
reinterpreting the episode as a story of abuse. She initiates the topic of child
abuse with Kristin, asking for her thoughts on the subject. The exchange among
the daughter, her husband, and Kristin is collaborative, probing, and provisional. It occurs near the end of a lengthy evening, following a family dinner
and getting three young children ready for bed. The family is in the process of
critiquing some family values and reordering the content of a family classic
to tell a different story within their own generation and for their children.

"When we get in our fifties" or "eventually as they die off": Timing and Tellability

Family classics stabilize content, although stability is always provisional. By
virtue of their textualizing, classics acquire high tellability for the family and
are less sensitive to context and timing. In this section, we consider how timing informs and constrains content-ordering. That is, we examine how a
muted or marginal story might be told for a period of time, at a particular point
in time, or within a special relationship or specific setting. Alain's comment
in the sewing circle segment suggests the variable tellability of story when he
says "when we get in our fifties" and want to know more family stories, or
"eventually as they [older family members] die off" some new stories come
out. What formerly was not narrated may be told later, may be told just once
or twice, or may be limited to a particular audience or occasion. Again, a focus on performing narrative argues that tellability is not inherent in the event
itself but in its embodiment, the situation, and material context. Content-
ordering is responsive to timing, place, and relationship as resources and constraints on family storytelling.

For example, a specific historical event, such as the September 11, 2001, terrorist attacks in the United States, may precipitate family storytelling. In one
instance, maternal grandparents were visiting a family with two boys in grade
school. The grandparents used the opportunity to talk about their memories
of Pearl Harbor when they were dating. It was funny and soothing for the boys
to hear about grandparents in their teens, before marriage and family, and to
imagine their grandparents, always old, as young. Moreover, it was the first
time the adult daughter and her husband of more than twenty years had heard
the story. In this instance, the events of September 11, 2001, create a shared
space, where similarities in the timing of events emerge and are ordered as
story content, and have now entered the family canon, at least for a time.

Or something as mundane as a family meal may evoke a new ordering of
content. In a session with a father and mother in their nineties, their recently

retired daughter, and Kristin, the daughter recounts a family story that emerged when she was nine years old. Her parents were in the same hospital at the same time as young children, "and no one ever realized it until all these years later 'cause it came up at the dinner table and I was about nine years old and ah somehow or other dad said something about the children's hospital in Portland and they got to talking about it . . . ." The newly discovered story of the father and mother meeting as young children becomes a staple of their family canon and reworked as a cornerstone of their marriage, now narratively constructed as predestined.

Ritual occasions designed for remembering, such as holidays, anniversaries and birthdays, family reunions, funerals and memorial services, often evoke family storytelling. Charlotte Linde (1997) distinguishes between occasions designed for narrative remembering, for example, an anniversary, and those which allow remembering as part of another activity but do not require narration, for example, visiting a homeplace. Narrative remembering may be most heightened around family deaths (Taylor, 1993) when storytelling functions in public and informal spaces to mark the transition for the deceased and survivors. Family storytelling constructs not only remembrance of deceased family members but the marking of significant transitions in family history. Timing may inform content-ordering to embrace the experience of death by survivors outside occasions designed for narrative remembering of the deceased. Many of the sessions and family gatherings that were part of our research became opportunities for participants to narrate deaths in ways not encouraged in other spaces and at other times.

Storytelling about the death of family members details the circumstances of the death, the shock and grieving. These stories were told from a personal stance with embodied emotion for events that had happened long ago. Young (2000) argues that emotions are occasioned, not represented, in narrative: "emotion is constructed by the way narrative assimilates memory to meaning on the occasion of telling, not by making the past present to the narrator imaginatively, but by making the narrator present to the past corporeally" (p. 102). One speaker, for example, recalled his brother who was missing in action during the Korean War when the narrator was a young boy, using the event as an emotional touchstone to weave his own memories, his mother's hope and sorrow, and current family dynamics around this long-ago event. In another instance Kristin was briefed by her local contact that the narrator in her next session had lost her husband and two sons in a small plane crash several years before, a tragedy that she might or might not recount. This content was not a question of a family secret, as everyone in the area (except Kristin, of course) knew the story, but an issue of timing and relationship. The woman did narrate the event, very near the end of the session. Another interviewee made the loss of her mother the emotional epicenter of the storytelling, transporting her bodily as a character into the realm of story. We came to recognize that interviews or family gatherings to meet with a researcher can become an opportunity to tell what is deflected or excluded in other settings. In at least one session, the great grandmother's sadness over her husband's and son's deaths several years before was listened to but not encouraged or developed by other family members present. Timing and situation inform and constrain content-ordering; an event's tellability is variable and changeable.

By contrast to deaths and their aftermaths, pregnancy and births were rarely narrated and even more rarely embodied emotionally in this corpus. Births were reported summarily, often at a distance, by women and men. A narrating father concludes, "So here we are four kids later," with no information on these family milestones.[4] This brevity prevailed, despite very large families of previous generations and considerable birthing experience within the current generation. The narrators, between mid-twenties to late eighties in age, had between two and five children; two were childless and one had eleven children. Peterson (1987) argues that stories of pregnancy are sensitive to both timing and relationship. This content is usually narrated *after* a pregnancy is announced, insuring appropriateness, salience, and orderly transmission of information. Or pregnancy and birth stories may be situated in mother-daughter relations or other women's settings that invite them. For instance, the storytelling session described in Chapter 1 also contained stories about breast milk and the exigencies of early motherhood as part of the women's weekend trip. Della Pollock (1999) historicizes the performance of birth stories, focusing on mothers who gave birth between the mid 1980s and mid 1990s. She notes that some of their stories skipped back a generation to their grandmothers' stories when home births were still routine and family women assisted the birthing mother. Their mothers' generation, giving birth in the 1950s and 1960s, however, either could not tell birth stories because medicalization of the process made common the use of general anesthesia and left few memories to tell, or would not tell birth stories because of the taboo on sexual talk in families.

Our corpus contained two brief birth stories from the grandmothers' generation, told by men, about family women assisting poor women: one woman dies in childbirth, as do her newborn twins, a memorable tragedy; the second woman is so poor "she didn't even have a nightgown or anything." A story from the middle generation was co-narrated by a husband and wife and focused on the medical setting for the birth of a baby who was "born jackknife," the medical problems the mother faced, and the doctor's role. Similar to Pollock's narrators, one of the younger mothers in the corpus narrated the births in the 1990s of each of her three children, with her husband co-narrating and Kristin as audience, while the children played cards in the next room.

The timing of birth stories is informed by changing social history as well as the specific situation. However, the local norms of storytelling in Franco-American families may further constrain if and how content about pregnancy and birth is ordered. Constraints on telling birth stories must be understood within historical discourses on pregnancy and sexual behavior and within the prohibition of birth control by the Roman Catholic Church. In these large French Catholic families, pregnancy and childbirth were not discussed with children. A man now in his sixties with ten siblings declared, "I never knew my mother pregnant." The mother of eleven who gave birth in the 1960s and 1970s insisted that her children "would never know I carried a baby. We never told them." In a separate interview with Kristin, her daughter tells a story about her and her sister asking their mother about where babies came from. When her mother replies "they come from God," the daughter says, "It was obvious to me in her manner and her actions and the way she said it that it wasn't true, and that was for me an indication that I was not allowed to ask her any more questions." Questions about sex and reproduction were not to be asked. One of the narrators, now a great grandmother, says, "it [pregnancy or birth] was never talked about." Nonetheless, she goes on to narrate a poignant story of a pregnancy seven years after her previous child and after she had returned to work in a shoe shop. In keeping with social conventions of the day, she had to inform her boss of her pregnancy, although she had not yet told anyone in the family. The family found out when she brought baby shower gifts home from the shoe shop and her young son asked, "What are those for?"

Thus, stories of pregnancy and birth may emerge for individual narrators later in life, after the announcement of someone else's pregnancy, and within changing social history that invites birth stories. Timing brings content-ordering and issues of tellability into changing circumstances of lived time and lived space as well as changing social history. Timing enables new stories and new interpretations. It embeds family storytelling in other family activities, such as dinner talk, birthdays, weddings, and funerals. On the one hand, the intimacy and familiarity of family suggest that storytelling does not require a special time or place. On the other hand, particular occasions offer spaces for specific stories or for unanticipated connections to be made between stories. From a communication perspective, performing family narrative is a situated practice, responsive to embodied emotions and interpersonal dynamics that emerge in particular relationships and are shaped by both local norms and larger discursive forces that prohibit or welcome certain content. The researcher is part and participant in the system of relations in which muted stories customarily not deemed either appropriate to the family or worthy of telling to outsiders may be told.

The consideration of timing suggests another facet of family storytelling as a communication practice in addition to the exclusions of "we don't talk about that" and the high tellability of family classics. To the processes of social memory and excluded or privileged talk, the consideration of timing contributes to the changing tellability of family stories. Temporal relations internal and external to the family shape the communication conditions under which content is created, remembered, and performed.

"Did you tell her how we met?": Genres and Genealogies

Content must be ordered into some format, according to discursive regularities that organize experience and events. In this section we consider narrative resources and genres that enable some family experiences to be more readily and easily narrated, and others that are less easily transmitted. For example, birth stories considered in the previous section privilege biological parenting and marginalize adoption, technologically assisted childbirth, and childlessness—content more difficult to encode and transmit. In narrative terms, we consider here issues of intelligibility, visibility, and audibility that inform and constrain how families order content about their experiences and history.

Attention to narrative format helps us understand an initial, formulaic response by some families and individuals that "we don't have any family stories." Beyond a display of modesty, this response may mean that family storytelling is invisible even to family members because it is quotidian and embedded in other talk and activity. But family experiences may also not fit generic forms. "The shape of a [family] life is as much a function of the conventions of the genre and style in which it is couched as it is, so to speak, of what 'happened' in the course of that life" (Bruner & Weisser, 1991, p. 129). Narrative resources for family storytelling pervade the larger culture where story forms are articulated in television and radio, newspapers and books, folklore and film. Culturally available resources and ready-made narrative templates organize experiences and history. Like a bricoleur, a family takes up bits and pieces of narrative forms and identities to assemble them into stories told at a particular place and time (Smith &Watson, 1996). Discursive regularities reveal how some content is easier to remember, articulate, and perform than is other content.

Scholars have recognized genres of family storytelling—for example, how we arrived and succeeded (Rubin, 1994), family fortune and misfortune (Brandes, 1975), infant tales of childhood antics (Baldwin, 1985), and courtship stories of how couples met and married (Silberstein, 1988) and how they divorced (Riessman, 1990). Genres provide a template to organize a text and a frame of understanding for responding to information (Briggs, 1993). To illustrate how genre facilitates content-ordering, we consider courtship stories as a form of the romance plot embodied in movies and books as well as family stories. Marriage founds family lines, but it simultaneously poses a threat to the family because it requires the acceptance of a stranger. A good courtship story lays a family's narrative groundwork and cements its foundation. A staple of family storytelling, courtship stories narrate origins, a family's genesis, how grandparents, parents, and stepparents met. Linde (1997) asserts that if an institution, including a family, has only one story that everyone knows, it will be an origin story.

Courtship stories were readily offered in response to researcher questions or they were initiated by family members, as when a husband joins his wife, already a half-hour into a session, with "have you told her [Kristin] about how we met?" Some courtship stories, particularly by male narrators, were woven into larger narrative frames, for example, service in World War II, a life-threatening accident, and a work history (for other examples, see Silberstein, 1988). By contrast, in one of our research sessions, three sisters and their mother devoted extensive and exclusive time to a courtship storytelling round. First one sister, then another, and then the third tells her courtship story. They then request their mother's story, contributing their own bits of remembered narrative to the mother's telling. During the third sister's story, her oldest daughter Nicole drops by with her young son, and she is coaxed by her aunt into the round to contribute a third generation story. Family members tell their own courtship stories, but they may also tell others' stories. One mother enthusiastically narrated her son's recent and unfolding courtship. An adult son narrated his widowed father's courtship of his second wife.

As a genre, courtship stories are characterized by predictable motifs (Stone, 1988) and by the romance plot (Modleski, 1982; Radway, 1984). The cluster of narratives by the three sisters (Monica, Susan, and Annette) and their mother draws on predictable motifs of courtship. For example, consider the "love at first sight" figure in the mother's story about seeing her future husband for the first time when he was a young boy getting a cat out of a tree: "I had this feeling I was going to marry him." Content reflects traditional sex roles, for example, powerful sexual attraction on the men's part: "that was _it_ when he saw me," declared one sister, Monica, about her husband-to-be; "I was a summer fling," begins a second sister, Susan, a story opening that is greeted with laughter from her sisters. Male sexual attraction is complemented by initial resistance on the female's part. Pursued by her future husband's persistent attentions, Monica says, "Well, anyway I gave up" and dated him until they married. We cannot know the relationship between the event as it happened and how it has come to be remembered and narrated, and "Whatever happened after the original glance or encounter—the developing relationship, the marriage—was made to cast its shadow back to the first encounter, as if it had been there to begin with" (Stone, 1988, p. 67). The hindsight of making great destiny out of an ordinary act is an example of the retrospective teleology that tells stories from the end to the beginning (Brockmeier, 2001), but as significantly it casts stories within powerful romantic conventions for narrating love and marriage in the United States.

Let's look at the granddaughter's story more closely to examine this family's content-ordering as a romance plot. Granddaughter Nicole responds to her aunts' requests for her courtship story:

Nicole: we met in high school
he just— you know teasing me
until one of my friends said "do you like him?"
and I said "yeah I guess so"

I was desperate for a <u>date</u> [lots of laughter]
 I wanted to go on a date so bad
 I hadn't been on one and I was finally 16 and I wanted to go on a date
I wasn't allowed to date until I was 16 that was the house rules

so . we . we went to the movies
 and uh then he just kept coming <u>back</u> so
we dated all through— it was the end of my junior year
 we dated all through my senior year
[slowly] he broke my heart at the end of my senior year
and uh . [softly] left me for another woman [she laughs self-consciously]

Annette: a three-month hiatus [said with a laugh]

Nicole: a three-month hiatus
[quickly] but he came back crawling on his hands and knees
so:: I took him back [group laughter starts in background and continues]
and he's been a really good husband ever since

The story follows the basic outline of the romance plot: an inexperienced young woman becomes involved with a man who breaks her heart and then returns to reveal his love and good character. The content-ordering reflects the courting conventions of male initiation and female response against the backdrop of family rules. The language, such as "he broke my heart," "left me for another woman," and "he came crawling back on his hands and knees," draws on conventional tropes. On the whole, the story appears to satisfy the staples of the courtship genre. However, it does not satisfy the storyteller's audience of family women. They prompt her to more detail and contribute narrative material of their own which fleshes out the "three-month hiatus" and information gap between "he broke my heart" and "I took him back." The granddaughter complies with her aunt Annette's request to "tell about the prom," first with the dismal but humorous story of the prom after he "dumped" her, and then with the following year's triumphant prom after they were reunited. But the family women are still not satisfied. Next begins a group ordering of content about the three-month hiatus during which the granddaughter "cried for those months" and was comforted by these three women. Monica, her mother, recalls the wet shoulder Nicole soaked repeatedly with her tears. Her aunt Annette narrates how she heard Nicole sobbing in the shower and consoled her. Aunt Susan tells about Nicole's trip to stay with her in northern Maine, where she holds and rocks Nicole on the living room floor as Nicole weeps and weeps. Nicole offers little content during this segment, saying at one point that she does not remember all that and at another point, "I knew he [husband] was a good one," justifying the heartache she went through. The courtship round concludes with Annette's declaration that if Nicole ever complains, she hears, "remember: you wanted him, you got him."[5]

This example of content-ordering is interesting for the ways it draws upon and deviates from the discursive regularities of the romance plot. In distinction from the classic courtship of Romeo and Juliet, the modern courtship plot notably excludes the family as content and context of story, or the family is positioned as an obstacle to be overcome in the plot. The content-ordering illustrates the participants' knowledge of the genre and their call to flesh out the experiential details that "make it their own" family story by becoming co-narrators and characters in the storytelling. In mediating between what happened, what was recalled, and what was told, they bring the genre to particular embodied and material details. The information originally omitted from the granddaughter's story adds to its drama and emphasizes her misery. Their backtracking delays the pay-off of "he's been a good husband ever since" and the elision of boyfriend to husband. Especially it makes an individual story into a family experience: the mother concludes, "it was an awful time" and "we would never want to go through that again." The storytelling becomes a site to bring family into courtship and to display their values of loyalty and support. The courtship experience is organized by generic conventions, but it is enriched, complicated, and critiqued by the ongoing content-ordering of family. Becoming a family through courtship is not just about a conjugal relationship between man and woman but a small group culture of family participants. The group production of content establishes meanings of courtship to *this family*, or at least to the five family women and three generations gathered together with Kristin.

Other courtship narratives in the corpus were less dramatic and developed, downplaying romance and heightening the familiarity of shared background. "We've been together all our lives," one mother narrates, beginning with kindergarten and grade school, through high school, and then marriage. Another's "I knew him most of my life" codes marriage within their ethnic group and religion. One narrator declined to narrate a courtship story, stating, "I am about to become a statistic," referring to a pending divorce. As the "other side" of courtship, few divorces were narrated, or they were sparingly developed. At this time and in these settings, the divorce narrative is not a genre of Franco-American family storytelling like the courtship story, although it is clearly tellable and conventionalized in other situations (see Riessman, 1990). Again, local norms animate our corpus. French Roman Catholicism has traditionally opposed intermarriage and divorce, although Franco-Americans after the 1940s began marrying outside their ethnic group, and divorce statistics for Franco-Americans now parallel the national rate (Langelier, 1996, p. 485). Generic resources suggest why some information is more difficult to encode in family storytelling than other information, for example, the narrative challenge undertaken by one family to tell the story of a son who is a single parent.

The complex interactions among genre and embodied, situated telling also apply to family history as it is constructed in family storytelling. "Family exists only because somebody has a story, and knowing the story connects us to a history" (Ng, 1994, p. 36). The temporal ordering of the courtship genre has an analog in the chronological ordering of the life history and family genealogy. Both genre and genealogy have their roots in linearity that brings coherence to events. The interview setting often keyed content-ordering by chronology, particularly in interviews with an individual or a married couple. One participant was distressed that her stories kept "jumping around" in time, despite Kristin's efforts to reassure her that family storytelling is associative and fragmentary. The presence of multiple active co-tellers in several of the other storytelling sessions thwarted chronology for the contingencies of content-ordering that derails linearity.

Genealogy offers a ready-made template for family history. "Tracing one's ancestors is a hedge against mortality in an increasingly mobile, global world" (Watson, 1996, p. 297). It is a highly codified practice that orders the particulars of family history into a coherent, demonstrable chart. Julia Watson (1996) argues that genealogy participates in discursive micropractices of power, including sexism, racism, and classism. For example, who begat whom, where, and in what line secures a patriarchal mooring that renders women, as well as orphans and the adopted, invisible. Silent or ambivalent on the historically dispossessed, such as Native Americans and African Americans, genealogy functions as an exclusionary practice because it was formed around the normative WASP subjects who first invaded and ordered the Americas. "Through establishing their genealogy, family members are assured that their everyday lives have transpersonal significance and are embedded in a historical chain" (p. 298).

Two sessions began by recalling family origins through tracing genealogy and articulating lineage. Of these, one participant had conducted extensive research on the family history, using archives, written records, and CD sets. The other participant traced his family name through four generations of fathers, from the great-grandfather in 1838 to himself. A third family inserted genealogy near the end of the session, based on research the daughter had done and about which she was instructing her parents, whose own stories did not go back beyond their grandparents. Let us consider a narrative sequence of content-ordering from a session with a mother and daughter that incorporates genealogy they learned from a male cousin in Quebec City. The segment occurs about an hour into the session, introduced by the mother:

Mother:	as a matter of fact uh doing genealogy
	we found out that we were <u>related</u> to King Louis the 15th
	the reason being is that his <u>mistress</u> was related to us
Daughter:	one of <u>one</u> of his mistresses
Mother:	and she bore him three sons
	who are related to <u>him</u> and related to <u>us</u>
	that's my story I wanted to tell you about
Kristin:	well there you go
Mother:	so we have royalty [laughs]
	we're so impressed [said with self-mocking and another laugh]
Daughter:	one of the three [sons] was the one who came over .
Mother:	escaped the Rev— the French Revolution
	landed in Quebec
	was so <u>sca:red</u>
	took off for the north country
	uh *Côte du Nord* is what they call it
	and uh <u>hid</u> there for many many years
	<u>ma:rried an Inuit</u>
	and <u>that's</u> where she [daughter] gets her hair
	look at that <u>dark . coarse</u> hair
	and that's a story that my mother will <u>not</u> accept
	not at all
	so we don't bring it up often
	she <u>refuses</u> to believe that that happened

We see here the weaving of genealogy and content-ordering that provides royal heritage and simultaneously links the daughter five generations later to an Inuit ancestor. The mother's first segment on their connection to royalty is quite brief and self-contained: "that's my story I wanted to tell you about." But the daughter also knows this history and prompts the story of the son who came to North America from France, which the mother continues to tell. Mother and daughter appear to attach more significance to the Inuit link than to the king of France. Such genealogy shares in the powerful narrative resource of the myth of blood (Stone, 1988), which emphasizes physical attributes passed on through generations, despite very remote genetic probabilities of their being transmitted. These meanings that the mother and daughter embrace, the grandmother rejects; this appears to be an ongoing issue because the mother asks Kristin not to bring it up when they move to the grandmother's upstairs flat to continue the storytelling in French. This example illustrates the potential conflict over who is qualified to speak on family history. Class and race hierarchies situate the grandmother's denial of the Inuit ancestry; conversely, the mother and daughter may be indulging in the contemporary trend to "exoticize" their ancestry.

What is interesting for our discussion of content-ordering is the template genealogy offers to found family lineage, here reportedly a mixture of French royalty and Native American heritage. Although history in France and North America supports the possibility of this lineage, the facts are less important to family culture than is the communication process of ordering content. Genealogy functions simultaneously to bring transpersonal significance to family history and to locate a point of contention in this family's storytelling, conflict over both facts and meanings. Indeed, genealogy resists family storytelling, and family storytelling ruptures genealogy's ordering. In subordinating personal story to the history of family, genealogy sees memory and imagination as dangerous to facts. This example suggests how genealogy both bolsters and threatens family sensibilities. Mother and daughter appear to be aware of the narrative possibilities of genealogy to ply the boundaries of fiction and fact:

Daughter: it would make for a fascinating novel

Mother: it would

Daughter: a historical epic

The genres of novel and historical epic belie the factual basis of genealogy at the same time that they suggest the imagination of history in a family's hands as they order content and make meaning of their lives. Genealogy is a strategy for writing the family into larger history, but putting together family history is polyvocal and contested. Content-ordering reveals an ongoing tension between information and communication and between personal and collective family history. Genre and genealogy are resources that inform content-ordering but certainly do not contain it.

In ordering content, families alter genres to fit their lives and rework genealogy in their own interests. Genres and genealogy enable families to more easily order content, but these narrative structures do not successfully discipline family storytelling. Family facts do not always stay in place; family bodies do not always stay in line. Against the forces of coherence and closure, family storytelling remains open to the contingencies and messiness of ongoing lives. Families live narrative. Content-ordering in our oral narrative corpus has a written counterpart in Vivian Lee Dills's (1998) lifestory-in-process. Her notion of performing narrative embraces the doing of family as well as telling stories, incorporating those ancestors and deceased family members who have not written and those living who will not write autobiographies—or balk even at telling family stories. Performing narrative honors family as medium (a doing) and as cultural formation (a thing done). Family storytelling creates living narratives that strategically respond to forces within and outside themselves as they survive and transmit culture to succeeding generations.

The Politics of "Good" Family Stories
as a Strategy of Cultural Survival

Family stories are not found but made in the ordering of content by small group cultures as they perform themselves to themselves. Like Benjamin's storyteller, families take what they tell from experience—their own or that reported by others—and, in turn, make it the experience of those who are listening to the tale. Small group cultures survive to the extent that they keep information moving through generations by ordering content in the lived time and lived space of doing family. The moral panic over the decline of the family is challenged by the complex human communication practice of family storytelling in daily life. The postmodern pronouncement for families to create a world of their own making is concretized in the mundane practice of performing narrative.

Narrative is perhaps the most ancient and widespread form in which people remember information as it is stored, retrieved, and transmitted in storytelling practices. In performing narrative, families order what happened to them, what is happening, and what could happen as memory and anticipation meet in daily life. In family storytelling, families remember, monitor, and manage information. They create content, make sense of events, and make meanings for the experiences of their family lives. They drop content from their repertoire; they recite from the family canon. They innovate new content, relocate or reinstate information that has lapsed or been muted or marginalized, and they reinterpret content in new ways. The ordering of content generates family stories in their differing forms and local occasions. This chapter specifically examines content-ordering of Franco-Americans as the transmission of information within and through generations in family storytelling. Throughout we consider how content-ordering is embodied by participants in interactions, situated within particular material conditions, and informed by discursive practices of institutions (e.g., English language, the Roman Catholic Church, popular culture) and changing forces of social history that order context and knowledge. Family storytelling simultaneously enables and constrains the transmission of particular content as families make their stories.

Family storytelling is a site of struggle and discussion over what stories are told and what are "good" family stories to tell. Families work on and work over information about what happened and what is meaningful to them. Transmission within and through generations is facilitated by the generality of information that diffuses content among multiple participants in the communication practice of collective remembering. The frequency and duration of telling sediments content, stabilizes family meanings, and canonizes family classics. Timing and occasions link and contextualize emotional content, emergent stories, and new interpretations of content. Families enlist and resist formats of genre and genealogy that make content intelligible, visible, and more easily ordered and transmitted. Against the coherence and closure that both enable and constrain content, families remain open to contingencies that reflect the messiness of daily family life, the sometimes conflicting involvements of multiple tellers, the complexities of family history, the changing conditions of tellability, and the provisionality of outcomes.

In communication terms, the inflow of information becomes distinctive in small group cultures and its outcome assumes a particular form. In a word, content-ordering is not arbitrary. Family storytelling legitimates certain meanings, sensibilities, and relations of power over other possibilities. The adoption of particular strategies of family storytelling makes available a limited variety of narrative meanings and structures. For example, family storytelling is constrained by strategies that put collective interests over individual interests; show the family in a favorable light; preserve family boundaries and protect family privacy; foster family institutions of heterosexual love, marriage, and procreation and downplay alternative choices and arrangements; reproduce traditional gender roles; regenerate generic formats for turning points in family life; naturalize family events and family history as a coherent and linear sequence; and participate in race and class hierarchies.

This list is not exhaustive but it clearly displays how content-ordering tends to reproduce The Family as a discursive construct with wide-ranging power to constitute and regulate normative family stories. "Good" family stories align families with the environmental interests of large social and cultural forces, for example, the patriarchal family (Nelson, 1997; Thorne & Yalom, 1981), the heterosexual family (O'Connell, 2001; Weston, 1991), the privatized, neobourgeois family (Rubin, 1994; Poster, 1978), and the monolithic family (Coontz, 1992, 1997; Langellier & Peterson, 1993), that project the nuclear, biological family as the singular, natural, and unchanging norm. Stated in terms of cultural transmission, these "good" family stories support survival of small group cultures, at least in the short run; at the same time, they exert social control that restricts alternative content offering other possible meanings and arrangements for families. Our methodology cannot predict which particular content and families will survive, but it can illuminate the politics of "good" stories in the content-ordering of the families in our corpus.

Family storytelling also engages in critique of and resistance to normative regularities. Family storytelling by particular embodied families may rupture master narratives of The Family. Our analysis also locates gaps and leaks where individual voices belie family consensus and contradict content; where family borders are opened to include others; where family flaws are divulged and family taboos on talk are criticized; where generic forms are complicated and reworked; and where the coherence and closure of linearity are thwarted and refused. Unquestionably, such gestures are small and local, but they open up and develop possibilities for variation to the mythic and monolithic family. In the case of Franco-Americans, perhaps the greatest resistance is exerted to an assimilated "American" identity that subordinates the embodied differences of ethnic family. The muted though continued audibility of the French language, the visibility of faith, the anchor of place, the significance of family gatherings, and the coded injuries of class and ethnicity all signal ethnic difference in performing narrative. The next two chapters will further flesh out these differences and the difference they make in small group culture. Our intent is not to tell the Franco-American story hinted at here, nor all the particulars of its contents, but to suggest the cultural survival of difference among American families despite the myth of the monolithic family. The multileveled model of family storytelling offers general access to content-ordering as a strategy of family survival, but this access must consider embodied, material, and discursive differences that both ground and disrupt local norms and local family models. Other families and family groups would differ from our corpus in terms of the specific content and stories ordered, but all families must order content and make stories in order to survive as small group cultures.

Family storytelling as a human communication practice focuses on one way of doing family. It suggests the power and effectivity of this communication practice in daily life, but there are other ways of doing family and alternate means of storing family culture. Participants offered photographs, a mother's book, a journal, genealogical charts, a map, a website, and family videos as well as family foods as aspects of content and their family narrative. By whatever means, a family must order content in some way for its culture to be reimagined and survive: someone must do the labor of remembering, sorting, telling, listening, and saving. In the next chapter we turn to the labor of task-ordering as communication practices that support the content-ordering of family cultures.

CHAPTER 3

Family Storytelling

Ordering Tasks in Small Group Cultures

We have situated family storytelling in relation to the moral panic in the new millennium over the changing family and the fear of losing "family values." Today's families have witnessed change more profound than at any other time in history. Twentieth-century family elders lived through technological innovations propelling them from horse and buggy to automobiles and airplanes and into space and cyberspace. The global and local contexts in which families now live have been rapidly reshaped as political, cultural, and social transformations extend notions of individual worth and human rights to democratize the family and alter relations among the young and old, women and men, and children and parents. Economic pressures refashion nuclear and extended families as they search for security. A worldwide feminist movement reconfigures and expands women's knowledge of their opportunities.

Throughout an era of transformation rupturing traditional forms of stability and continuity, family storytelling persists. In her recent book *Celebrating the Family*, Elizabeth H. Pleck argues that the United States has perhaps witnessed an increase rather than a decline in family rituals since the 1970s. But these are not simply sentimental rituals, with roots in Victorian culture (Gillis, 1996), whose main purpose is "to pay homage to an ideal of the privatized, affectionate family, with a mother nurturing her children at the center" (Pleck, 2000, p. 1). Pleck argues that we have now entered a postsentimental celebration of family, a shift in attitude and performance that both critiques the excesses of sentimentalism and recognizes ethnic and racial diversity among families. These postsentimental rituals acknowledge the more fluid and flexible forms of the postmodern family rather than a single dominant form. Judith Stacey (1990) argues that the postmodern family emerged from a host of changes: in attitudes toward sex, contraception, and abortion; intermarriage across religious, ethnic, and racial lines; divorce; women's roles; race relations; and homosexuality. To these considerations, Pleck adds consumer culture and popular entertainment as forces remaking family rituals. In the processes of both continuity and change, modernism and sentimental rituals have not disappeared; they exist side by side with the postmodern family and its postsentimental celebrations, intertwined in debates about and practices of family.

In the previous chapter we examined how, as small group cultures, families order content in telling stories about themselves. In storytelling, families order information using strategies of generality, timing, sedimentation, and genre to make and perform stories. We turn now from the problem of generating "good" family stories to the work of telling stories, from tales to "good" storytellings. This chapter examines task-ordering in performing narrative: what work does a family do in order to transmit its culture through storytelling? How is information about family-as-lived processed? How does the allocation of the work of storytelling, and the definition of those tasks, form different small group cultures? For example, how does the ordering of tasks reflect gender and ethnicity, such as Franco-American patterns of family storytelling? Task-ordering accounts for different communication processes than does content-ordering. By shifting our focus to the tasks of storytelling—to listening and telling, narrating and co-narrating—we take into account the communication work done in a small group ecology.

Family storytelling is one form of cultural work by which a small group intervenes to survive its environment. Task-ordering attends to particular kinds of environments and particular kinds of technologies of storytelling. Family storytelling responds to transformative changes in social, economic, and political structures as well as to the changing media of retrieval and transmission. In the liminal space of storytelling, families define tasks to order the inflow, outflow, and distribution of information from internal and external environments. What tasks are necessary for storytelling to take place and for family culture to be transmitted? Someone must do the work of remembering, composing, and telling stories in such a way that they are memorable and told again. Someone must listen and be able to understand and act on what she or he hears. Stories must not only be remembered but also be acted upon— that is, innovated and interpreted if they are to remain salient, adapt to changing conditions, and survive for future generations.

We can look at the sewing sandwiches story of the previous chapter to illustrate the analytic shift from content-ordering to task-ordering. In the memory work engaged in by Gerald, Alain, and Madeline they *retrieve basic information* about the rituals of the family sewing circles. When they work to figure out who in the family and community belonged to the sewing circles and to link the sewing sandwiches of the women's circles to the daddy sandwiches of Alain's family, they *innovate information* to fill in gaps, flesh out traces, connect actions, and make associations. A third order of work calls for the making of meaning. *Interpreting information* is the task they engage when they identify themes and rules for what was not talked about in their families: the meanings of absence and explanations for what is not narrated. The emergence and invention of new meanings show the heuristic function of storytelling to exceed memory of the past, participate in problem-solving in the present, and anticipate a future. According to McFeat (1974), the tasks of ordering basic, interpreted, and innovated information are required to reproduce small group culture over time. Unless someone does the work of ordering basic information, no cultural memory succeeds in the next generation. Unless someone does the work of innovating and interpreting information, a culture becomes stagnant, closed, and dead.

The analysis of task-ordering in family storytelling examines what work has to be done and who does it, who speaks and who listens under what conditions and with what consequences for the survival of family culture. We look first at how the tasks of retrieving, innovating, and interpreting information are distributed among generations, including several varieties of co-narrating and listening among subsets of family. Next we turn to the allocation of storytelling work by gender, considering patterns of difference and dominance, the interactional work family women do to nurture conversation and storytelling, and strategic goals women and men share. We then examine tactics that maximize family participation in storytelling and strategically promote cultural survival. We also explore conditions for storytelling, the mundane and ritual occasions that make it possible, focusing on the intersection of gender, ethnicity, and class. The chapter concludes with a discussion of how particular patterns of participation generate internal rules—to use Foucault's term—for family storytelling. Performing family stories involves interaction among participants and social action: that is, a performance with political consequences. Task-ordering generates internal rules that constitute and designate "good tellings" to promote and ensure the survival of family culture.

Between Generations: Multitasking in the Middle

McFeat (1974) states that "the positive feature stressed in small group culture is the creation of generations" (p. 114). In family, generations are specially related: preceding generations are not merely precursors but ancestors, and following generations are not merely successors but children. The continuity of generations so profoundly defines family that childless couples are sometimes said to have no family. How do the tasks of family storytelling define generations? In an ideal situation, each generation has work to do and participates in storytelling tasks. McFeat (1974) identifies one possible structure among

three generations: the second generation narrates content to the third generation and is corrected by the first generation; in family terms, parents tell stories to children as grandparents monitor the legitimacy of the information.

In a session with a mother (in her sixties), her only daughter (in her thirties),
and Kristin, the mother narrated how her mother, who lives in an upstairs flat,
came to the United States from Canada at age nineteen to join her sister who
was working in a Maine textile mill. Later, when the storytelling session moved
upstairs to include the grandmother, the grandmother says she came at age
sixteen. The mother responds to the grandmother that she herself had the age
wrong; turning to Kristin and her daughter she revises, "she came at sixteen
years old. I thought it was nineteen." Basic information in family storytelling
tends to generate consensus, even though generations or individuals may disagree about content. Notably, this is the same mother-daughter pair described
in Chapter 2 who have accepted a genealogical version of family history which
the grandmother patently rejects. Recall that they shared this genealogy with
the researcher but asked her not to bring it up in the grandmother's presence.

Different task definitions form different small group cultures. In the Franco-
American sample, we became acutely aware of the narrative respect accorded
the senior generation. When locating families to interview, we were repeatedly referred to the oldest family members for storytelling, often with appreciation for the project and even some urgency to document their narration.
"Oh, you'll want to talk to Agnes or to Odile," in their eighties or nineties, because "they know the stories." Family storytelling seemed to be equated with
family history, ancestors, and an orientation to a past "always on the brink of
disappearing" (Lanza, 1994). We attribute some of this orientation around the
senior generation to the desire to preserve Franco-American culture, a motivation for some, though not all, of our participants who self-identify as French.[1]
Assigning the task of family storytelling to the senior generation responds in
part to a historical shift from "melting pot" to multicultural America. The
philosophy of assimilation once imposed a uniformity that discouraged newcomers from speaking their own languages and maintaining ties with their
homelands. However, the landmark Immigration Act of 1965, coupled with
the civil rights movement of the 1960s and ethnic revivals of the 1970s, have
diminished the pressure to conform to a single, national ideal. In Maine, the
Northeast, and Cajun Louisiana, as well as the ongoing identity movement of
the Québécois, the North American French are a site for examining how ethnicity takes local form (Appadurai, 1996).

Honoring the senior generation may also embody the specifics of ethnic culture. The generational position of grandparents provides a starting place for
understanding how task-ordering emerges from and differentiates families
embedded in particular environments. Celebrations of family can be used as
a special time to assert a waning ethnic identity (Pleck, 2000). Women in particular guarantee ethnicity as they produce cultural foods, religious rituals in

the home, holiday traditions, and family storytelling. The working-class ethnic mother is a "cumbered self," the "most folk of the folk," who embodies the gender and class stereotypes of family ethnicity (di Leonardo, 1984), for example, the Jewish mother, the Black granny, the Native American grandmother, the German Oma, and the Italian Mama. The Franco-American *mémère* (grandmother) is the most French of the French, a privileged icon and a locus of performative power in the family. She is at the center of the defining ritual of Franco-American identity, the extended family's Sunday-after-Mass visit to *mémère*'s, with its storytelling, music, and meal (Dufresne, 1996). As keeper of folk and family memory, she is both a narrator of and a character in family stories (Langellier, 2002; Edelman, 1999). Our storytelling data, however, will show a more particularized and complicated picture than "*mémère* at the center" as cultural ideals are enacted in family settings.

If a theory of diffusion on the spread of the English language, for example, could account for task-ordering, then families everywhere would assume similar forms. All families would tell stories in English, and the master narrative of assimilation would triumph. However, task-ordering responds to specific environmental pressures and technologies, thereby differentiating families. The generational work of task-ordering finds graphic illustration when we consider the French language as a technology of telling. The straight-line theory of language loss assumes a three-generational structure in which the senior generation speaks exclusively or primarily French, the middle generation is bilingual French and English, and the third generation speaks only English (Gordon, 1964). The storytelling session cited above, when mother, daughter, and Kristin join the *mémère* upstairs in the house which the grandfather built and in which the mother was born and then raised her own children, both illustrates and challenges this three-generational pattern. While we talk, the mother sets *Mémère*'s hair in plastic curlers, a ritual the mother has performed every Saturday morning since before she married forty years before. On the way up the stairs, the mother cues Kristin that "this may be in French," and in French, she tells *Mémère* that she can speak French even though Kristin is present and *Mémère* also speaks English. In Anglophone North America, the use of the French language not only was lower prestige but also was punished in public schools and prohibited in some work settings by language laws (Doty, 1995). Bilingual Franco-Americans habitually adapt to even one English speaker in their audience. One family, for example, spoke French exclusively at home until they changed to English when a local teacher, who stayed with them for thirty-seven years, moved in. Another family, whose *pépère* forbade English in his home, changed to English when the first grandson married "one English-speaking Protestant" who thereafter "took over" the family language.

The session in *Mémère*'s apartment features her as the primary narrator while the mother engages in interactional work that facilitates storytelling.

The mother assumes the role of asking questions in French about *Mémère*'s youth in Canada, her coming to the United States, and her life here, spanning topics of home, work, and community. The mother monitors Kristin's understanding, switching to English to clarify where necessary. The granddaughter listens to and understands both the French and the English, but with one exception contributes her comments in English. In the following excerpt, *Mémère* (MM) has just finished describing to the mother (M) and Kristin (K) how she worked in textile mills when she first arrived in the United States. We provide translations of French in brackets.

> MM: *après [?] j'ai travaillé dans une maison privée* [after [?] I worked in a private home]
>   M: *qu'est-ce que c'est le nom de famille?* [what's the family's name]
>   [to Kristin] you're gonna love this
>   [to *Mémère*] *que vous avez travaillé?* [that you worked for?]
> MM: Provost
>   K: Provost! aaah! *ça c'est ma mémère* [that's my grandmother]
>   *ma mere s'appelle Provost!* [my mother's name is Provost!]
> MM: *ah oui?* [oh yes?]

Right after this interchange, the mother explains to Kristin that "when you said that [Provost is a family name] last night I didn't say a word." She adds, to her daughter, "my mother will tell her." So long as *Mémère* can (she is in her nineties), this is the grandmother's information to tell—her story—but the mother knows and elicits the information as the daughter and Kristin listen. It is *Mémère*'s work to retrieve the basic information that tells the story of her past youth in Canada and life in the United States, and participants request her stories and give her the floor to tell them (in fact, the mother coaches her at one point not to answer "*oui*" but to tell the story). The bulk of the session, particularly *Mémère*'s more extensive segments, are in French. Other segments are less monologistic, however, when the grandmother, mother, daughter, and Kristin discuss different card games played in their families, gardening, family pets, and family parties, as all participants switch primarily, though not exclusively, to English. This segment displays the three-generational pattern of language assimilation at the same time that it shows each generation to be, with different competencies, bilingual.

The mother's work, as the middle generation, is especially varied, demanding, and complex. In addition to the bilingual demands of eliciting talk from *Mémère* and periodically translating to Kristin, the mother provides additional background information for the grandmother's stories, she inserts how her own experiences and opinions intersect with *Mémère*'s ("I had to work in the garden and I hated it"), and she contributes stories about her own children. She operates as an interface of languages and generations. In a generational deviation, she also gently corrects her mother about the mileage of a family trip.

Whereas *Mémère* is the featured speaker, the mother's labor to coordinate and interlock generational tasks makes it all happen.

Nor does the mother's daughter simply listen. She facilitates the grandmother's storytelling after a pause to ask, "[working at a local site] was later?" She connects *Mémère*'s stories to her own generation (the local site now houses "where I work," and the grandmother's knitting produces "my winter wardrobe"). She initiates a story about the grandmother with "oh, I have to show the picture of her modeling career" in which *Mémère* is photographed with friends in a Dunkin Donuts brochure. Although the daughter characteristically speaks in English, when the talk turned to family pets, she asked *"les lapins qui ont été volé?"* to cue the grandmother, and then she co-narrates in English with her the story of the stolen rabbits. During segments in French when the grandmother describes scenes from her childhood, the daughter offers Kristin translations of unfamiliar vocabulary ("barrel staves," "spigot").

The generational labor in this storytelling reveals the interdependence of mutual determination and support that defines different tasks for each generation. But generations may also engage in the same storytelling tasks. For example, the mother also retrieves and corrects basic information like the senior generation, the daughter performs the facilitative work of the middle generation, and the grandmother listens to the mother's stories. The French language as a communication technology clearly distinguishes generations, but it is the intricate coordination and code-switching that produces this family storytelling. To accomplish the tasks of storytelling, generations complement one another as speakers and listeners. The code-switching between the English and French languages marks task distinctions between generations and creates a shared identity as family. The work of code-switching, particularly by the middle generation, functions as a strategy to both alter and maintain ethnic differences in a relatively unyielding environment that prefers the English language.

A different three-generational session suggests a variation in family structure based on task-ordering. This family exhibits the complementary pattern of generational labor described above, but it also enacts more symmetrical relations among generations. In talk near the end of a family dinner about the family rule to "marry Catholic," the grandmother (MM) has just told a story for Kristin (K) and a family friend (FF) about a time she and her husband-to-be attended a Protestant wedding against the wishes of their parents. Her daughter, the mother (M), follows with the observation that she has never been to non-Catholic religious services, while the twelve-year-old granddaughter (GD) interjects, "I have":

> *M:* The only thing I've been to is um
>
> *GD:* Yeah but I think Jewish people
>
> *M:* to a funeral and a service

MM: [to M] you went to a Baptist funeral or something for your for Mary's husband

GD: and and

MM: at the funeral parlor there was a service

  M: that was just a minister coming and saying a couple of nice things

MM: well I <u>know</u> but that's what they did
       that was the <u>service</u>

GD: I've been to two
       I've been to one bar mitzvah and one bat mitzvah

  K: mhmm

  M: I've been to two bat mitzvahs we
       [to GD] with your dad to something a few years ago

GD: oh I don't know but we only went to the parties

  M: okay

MM: you didn't go to church

GD: oh but I've been to <u>Hannah's</u> whole thing three times two times

FF: you live in a different world than your mother and father

  M: oh yes

MM: amen
       and your mother lived in a different world than we did as far as that was concerned
       oh yeah

For a time, generational status is suspended as grandmother, mother, and granddaughter contribute their experiences. The storytelling task is not so much to retrieve information as it is to understand what it means to "live in a different world." The task of interpreting change is distributed among generations, including the twelve-year-old granddaughter, although her contributions are at first muted in the overlapping interaction. The more distributed participation that characterizes the task of interpreting information blurs boundaries between narrative and conversation, sometimes making them nearly seamless. Symmetrical relations among generations characterize the conversational narrative described by Ochs and Capps (2001). Participation in the interpretation does not depend on retrieving basic information about the past but rather on "working through who we are and how we should be acting, thinking, and feeling as we live our lives" (p. 17). Ochs and Capps argue that conversational narrative promotes exploration, possibilities, and diverse thoughts, requirements of the tasks of innovating and interpreting information. Whereas this family differs from the preceding one in speaking only English, it is the task definitions—here innovating and interpreting information —that produce their more symmetrical generational structure. Following this excerpt, members of all three generations, including the mother's second husband and a family friend, discuss other issues around religion and family, including divorce, conversion, annulments, and tangled "step" relations.

The task-ordering of family storytelling creates generations with internal rules for participation. Members of the senior generation are regarded as "special people" (McFeat, 1974), and they are responsible for the memory work of monitoring basic information and for telling stories when called upon (by family members or researchers), although they may also participate in innovating and interpreting information. The task of the younger generation is to listen, but they, too, may innovate and interpret information. The middle generation has both the greatest latitude in storytelling labor and the greatest demands. Their labor might be described as multitasking and multidirectional in that it both elicits information from seniors and transmits it to the younger generation. Changing environments and technologies require that they innovate and interpret as well as alter the media of telling, in some instances here between two languages. Within this generational labor, the middle generation incurs the greatest responsibility for cultural transmission and greatest risks of loss. If that generation fails to retrieve information, a family loses its sense of heritage, and the three-generational structure is collapsed to two generations who can only innovate family culture. The future of family culture depends on their abilities to both preserve from memory and create from living narrative their family stories, to both remember the past and anticipate the future.

Yet generations are precisely relative, that is to say, they are positional, contextual, and shifting rather than stable and fixed. Our communication emphasis on task-ordering focuses on the labor of storytelling rather than on identity characteristics to render an account of differences among families. In fact, for survival over time, older generations listen to new stories and younger generations will assume the tasks of ordering basic information more characteristic of the senior generation. Our examples have so far featured settings in which three generations were present; however, even in an interview with an individual family member, generational structures emerge in the narrative labor. For example, in an interview with a middle-aged man, the participant recalled his grandparents' and parents' lives in a French community in New Hampshire (task of retrieving), generated stories from his own experience about his children (innovating), and defined a family identity (interpreting the difference between living his childhood as Franco-American and his present "intellectualized" experience of being Franco-American). In performing these storytelling tasks, he shifted among narrator and character relations, positioning himself within narrated events as a grandchild to his grandparents, as a child to his parents, and as a father to his children. In relation to Kristin, the researcher in the narrative event, he played out the multiple tasks of the middle generation in the absence of an older generation to legitimate information and of a younger generation to listen. Kristin thus "sits in" for the younger generation but remains non-family. Telling family stories to a researcher depends on intergenerational information but it gives only indirect access to generational task-ordering *in situ* as the tasks of retrieving, innovating, and interpreting information are collapsed into one narrator.

The significance of listening as narrative labor also merits further comment. In intergenerational settings, our corpus tends to show the youngest generation as listeners whose access to telling is more limited. By contrast, Blum-Kulka's (1997) study of dinner talk emphasizes the conversational involvement of children in Israeli and Jewish American families, co-narration between parents and children, and respect for children's storytelling rights. She argues that this feature emerges from contemporary parenting ideologies: "The families manifest the hallmarks of child-centeredness that characterize White, middle-class mainstream American families" (Blum-Kulka, 1997, p. 265). Child-centeredness requires adult accommodation and the adaptation of the situation to children's needs. Blum-Kulka locates the discourse correlate of child-centeredness "to parents' allusion to being *more involved* and *listening more* to their children than to their own parents in their tendency to grant center stage to children's topics at dinner and in the modes of facilitation through which adults help children participate and gain the skills needed for full and equal participation" (p. 266, emphasis in original). In our corpus, the presence of a researcher may have defined storytelling as a speech event for first and second generations. The youngest generation may well narrate in other family activities, during the day or at special events unavailable to researchers. The difference in our corpus may also be linked to a cultural rule in traditional Franco-American families that, although cherished, children are not placed at the center of family interaction (Langelier, 1996; French 1981).

Differences in the ratio of speaking and listening among generations alerts us to variations in task-ordering that differentiate generational structures in families by race, ethnicity, class, and so forth (e.g., Scollon & Scollon, 1981). For example, Terry Tafoya (1989) identifies a generational structure among Native Americans based upon family organized in concentric circles of relations. Siblings, including cousins, form the innermost circle; grandparents form the next circle (which may include great-aunts and great-uncles); biological parents and their siblings form the outermost circle. The resulting task-ordering differs from the three-generational structure where the middle generation transmits basic information, subject to correction by the senior generation, to the junior generation. In the case of Native Americans, the senior generation ("grandparents") are responsible for storytelling, training, and discipline of the junior generation ("all siblings"). These elders do not "transmit" information by direct teaching but rather "guide by creating a situation where a youth comes to 're-cognize' what they [the elders] already know" (Tafoya, 1989, p. 40). This task-ordering also contrasts with the group production and interpretation of stories which Shirley Brice Heath (1983) identifies in African American families. These stories are told cooperatively "with the help of the audience and with two or more participants in an event sharing the recounting" (Heath, 1983, p. 183). Both Tafoya and Heath suggest that individuals outside these cultures may not understand such events as family storytelling or even recognize that a story has been told.

To the extent that families assume generational forms from variations in task-ordering, families may exist in environments where others are unlike them. One family in our corpus was particularly remarkable for how it continued to speak French into the 1980s and 1990s even though isolated from a larger French community. Family narrative attributed this difference to the commanding presence of *Pépère*, the father of the mother who was interviewed with her husband and daughter, who forbade any English in his home among his children and grandchildren. Interviews and observations suggest to us that narrative tasks are ordered nonverbally as powerfully as they are in French or in the English now spoken in this family home. Both parents and the adult daughter concurred on the primacy of actions over words in family culture. The mother quotes that "children should be children," "children are to be seen and not to be heard," and they do not belong in adult conversation. The father asserts that love is shown rather than said, and then he mockingly performs a verse from a Hallmark card for grandparents and calls it "moosh, moosh, moosh" whose "words don't mean anything." This father participates in a long tradition of criticism of consumer culture, but more so he critiques the sentimental excess of the modern family. The daughter observes about her upbringing that "you were just supposed to do what you saw in the house" and "pass it on." In this family, narrative is performed more than told. In the words of French writer Annie Ernaux (1990), who describes her mother's rural Catholic upbringing, "in our lives nothing is thought, everything is done" (p. 50). Basic information is located in the context of daily actions and relationships rather than in messages; task-ordering is lodged in work done, with and without words.

This family structure is not organized around centering children in language by inviting their topics and listening to them. This example also highlights the significance of technologies of telling. Participation in this family's narrative depends on knowing context, and information located in context is not easily transmitted outside of that context. Participation invokes an interpretive strategy based on a stock of knowledge that must be filled in without being explicitly communicated. Successful survival to the next generation relies upon face-to-face interaction, proximity, and time together, particularly if the storage of family culture is not augmented by other technologies, such as writing, photographs, video, or electronic media. The persistence of French language and culture in this family suggests the remarkable power of small group culture to endure in unsupportive environments at the same time that it reveals its fragility.

Working Together and Apart:
Co-narrating Between Couples and Sides

The creation of generations is necessary for cultural survival. Tasks ordered by generations position the family as a unit engaged in retrieving and transmitting information over time. Tasks also are ordered by subsets within the family, formations of alliances between, for example, husbands and wives, father-son and mother-daughter dyads, and family sides. Task-ordering allocated to subsets raises the possibility of tension and struggle over who gets to do and who has to do which tasks. The capacity for families to subdivide suggests that the work of storytelling can create and maintain subgroups as various alliances work together to tell stories. Recall the assertion that "active narrative involvement defines what it means to participate in a mainstream American family" (Ochs & Capps, 2000, p. 8). Family storytelling involves the work of multiple participants. In this section we examine some varieties of co-narrating and co-listening.

In one interview with Louis and Bernice, Louis concludes the session by saying "we're old but we take care of each other. We have problems but we can live with it." Louis and Bernice are both eighty years old, with birthdays two days apart. They have been married for fifty-eight years. At the outset of the interview, Bernice declares that "Louis will be the one to be the commentator," but not long into the session, she joins him in narrating their stories. Together they tell of his World War II service and how they got married before he shipped out to the Pacific. In some segments they tell unshared events of their own experiences, but in other segments they narrate each other's experience, unshared and shared. For example, Louis describes how Bernice got picked up in a command car and driven to the church for their wedding. Bernice quotes Louis to tell how the wedding was planned: "He says, 'what do you say we go visit the priest?' He says, 'we signed—I signed the payroll for the checks, you know, so that means we're going to be here another month.' And he says, 'we could get married.' Because we always intended to get married when he was on furlough." Bernice's correction from "we signed" to "I signed" suggests the close alignment of their perspectives. Her quotation of his speech forges their interactional alliance, diffuses agency between them, and widens the base of support for her narrative contributions.

Louis (L) and Bernice (B) team up not just on narrated events but also on the evaluation and emotional meanings of these events: pleasure over a special *soirée* [party] they hosted; pride in their children's ability to speak French; and resentment over having repeatedly to house and feed extended family in their home. They also co-narrate their children's births:

> L: it took <u>eight years</u> for our first one
>
> B: eight . nine years

L: eight years . and then <u>Renee</u> came . thirteen months later
    when <u>Rick</u> came he came <u>jack</u>knife

B: [chuckling] breech

L: it took two doctors and two surgeons to go and get him
    and Dr. [checks name with B] he was a <u>family</u> doctor
        but he was also a <u>surg</u>eon
    so in order to get Rick— he weighed eight pounds ten ounces
    so while he was there he explor:ed
  and when she came to the next day or two days later
    he told her . he said "Bernice . if you want some more children
    you better go because it's not going to <u>last</u> long"
  and sure en<u>ough</u> she had <u>Renee</u>

B: because I had had <u>surg</u>ery
    so all the time I carried at three months I almost lost it

Bernice continues to narrate how she went to the doctor for a six-week checkup after the breech birth, received hormone injections, soon became pregnant, and gave birth to their second child thirteen months after their first, "so I had two babies there." She and Louis then talk animatedly and simultaneously, overlapping similar information in their desire and delight to recall their infant son's appetite, growth, and diet, bringing out a baby picture they had published in the local paper for his fiftieth birthday.

Together Louis and Bernice retrieve basic information. They are both narrators of and characters in each other's story. By distributing both these tasks between them, they work together to tell a single story and to create a family history that modifies their individual biographical standpoints. But how they join in storytelling tasks suggests not just that they know information about each other and share experiences together as a couple (Mandelbaum, 1987). The symmetry of their telling also has a sense of reciprocity in perspective and mutuality in affect. Their standpoints are not interchangeable (he describes the birth from his own and the doctor's views; whereas she describes the treatments she underwent to have a second pregnancy), but they are actively constructed around a common standpoint of family relationship. In this way, "more or less symmetrical biographical differences are actively and progressively modified and even eliminated by a process of biographical reconstruction" that Raymond McLain and Andrew Weigert (1979, pp. 176–177) call "biographical fusion." Tasks of retrieving information about family events are distributed quite reciprocally and equally between the two participants, and a consensus on content and emotion is achieved in their narrative reconstructions. Fusion, of course, can never be total or fixed, but the common labor and perspectives can ground both the unique creativity and potential destructiveness of marriage to individuals.

Fusion suggests a merging of narrative perspectives. A variation performed by another married couple explores and even preserves biographical differ-

ences at the same time it fuses modes of talking. This variation is distinguished from the previous one by its focus on the task of interpreting rather
than retrieving content. After a family dinner during which stories from each
family side were told, a pattern of story-explication-exploration emerged
among the husband, wife, and Kristin. The participants were telling stories
about the general topic of what being a Franco-American might mean. These
stories were not so much evidence documenting a family history as they were
texts to think with and think through (Sarris, 1990). For example, stories about
family foods were followed by alternative definitions of Franco-American
foods in relation to other ethnic foods and then by more abstracted possibilities for the relations of food and cultural identity. Each participant performed
tasks of narrating, explicating meanings, and raising additional questions,
working together through a range of topics from education, work ethics, class
issues, gender relations, and child-rearing practices. The exploration of possibilities for meanings and unresolved issues blurred distinctions between
narrating and listening and between participant and researcher. Kristin did
not know these participants prior to the session, and she was older than the
couple, rather than younger, as in the case of Louis and Bernice. Their fusion
around the task of interpreting content retained biographical differences between the couple rather than reconstructing one story.

We call another variation in task allocation between husband-wife pairs
"parallel lives." In one example, the father's work biography frames almost
the entire family storytelling session. His physical and economic survival organizes the family narrative as his wife and daughter request stories, fill in,
and expand on his stories. At the end of the interview, the daughter gives
Kristin a do-it-yourself autobiography of a mother's life, which her mother
composed for her oldest daughter.[2] Entitled *Reflections from a Mother's Heart:
Your Own Life Story in Your Own Words*, the book is organized in a twelve-
month format with space to write personal answers to questions that "explore
family history, childhood memories, lighthearted incidents, cherished traditions, and the dreams and spiritual adventures encountered in a lifetime of living." Its promise is "to open a richer, fuller understanding of who you are as
a family." The mother has answered every question, filled in every page. A
comparison of the narratives reveals virtually no overlap between the events
written by the mother in the book and the oral storytelling session ordered
around the father's telling, even though a common standpoint of family, religion, and local culture is called upon and achieved. This allocation of narrative labor created more a sense of parallel lives than of biographical fusion.
This variety of co-narration relied on respect and support for individual telling
rights and self-accomplishments, albeit in the context of family and traditional gender roles.

Families may also subdivide by sides. One husband and wife develop parallel stories rooted in childhood place, hers in the more urban Franco-American

community of southern Maine, his in the rural farms of northern Maine. Another variation in husband-wife labor is situated in a multigenerational family activity. Four generations gathered at a family dinner. The dinner took place during the summer in the daughter and her husband's home, to which the granddaughter's parents and grandmother have driven from approximately two hours away. Dinner is underway. Adults are seated at one table and the three young children (ages seven, four, and two) at another. Food is being passed around and talked about as the father begins this story (F is Father, M is Mother, D is Daughter, and K is Kristin):

> F: one thing when we used to be at the house
>   when I first got married OK
>
> D: [chuckle/laugh]
>
> M: I know what's coming
>
> K: you do?
>
> F: she's a wonderful cook OK?
>   but there was a lot of things I wouldn't eat
>   because we weren't eating <u>that</u> way at home
>   at home it was <u>plain</u>
>   I mean . like spaghetti sauce you throw in some tomatoes
>   and mash them all up and that was your sauce . that's it
>   and the sauce she used to make there was no way I would touch it
>   You got a bunch of <u>onions</u> in there
>   and gee I used to come home at night
>   and the first thing I'd do if she'd cooked something
>   I'd open up the pot
>   and if there was an onion in there
>   I'd go eat at the corner store
>   and that's the God honest truth

This story is quickly followed and elaborated by his wife:

> M: well we should start from the beginning
>   knowing how <u>fussy</u> he was
>   I'd cook my meals and I'd leave my onions <u>whole</u>
>   and I'd take them out
>   and he'd eat with gusto
>   and so one day he came home early
>   [unintelligible because of others' voices; we infer in the story that
>   F opened the pot and discovered M's secret]
>   and so I told him I always cooked with onions
>   and before he got home I always took them out
>
> F: and to be truthful you gotta cook with onions

This story narrates family sides that appear to converge in the perspective on cooking with onions and on an evenhandedness in telling between husband and wife as she matches his onion story with her own, as well as meeting his "fussiness" in eating with her own cooking stratagem. Like the retrospective teleology of courtship stories that make fate of everyday encounters, these matched stories about a marriage's beginnings are told from the end of forty years together. The resolution ("you gotta cook with onions") applies both to the conflict over onions and to the implied conflict over storytelling roles and rights ("well, we should start from the beginning"). The husband initiates the topic and closes the frame by pronouncing the evaluation in the last line. The wife backtracks in time, fills in behind the scenes, and thereby responds to his narrative challenge. The matched telling simultaneously exposes and submerges conflict. It embodies a habitual pattern of allocating the tasks of telling between husband and wife, as suggested when the wife says, "I know what's coming" as the daughter laughs. We return to this interaction in the next section on gendered telling.

Our attention to task-ordering between husband and wife can also be turned to the larger and longer intergenerational family event in which it is embedded. The maternal grandmother is occasionally called upon to tell stories, but her narratives are subordinated to the father (her recently retired son-in-law) who is spotlighted throughout the day, both through his own initiations and the supportive work especially of his daughter, but also of his wife and son-in-law. Nor can the grandmother provide correctional labor in retrieving content of the senior generation because the stories are from the other side of her daughter's family. The granddaughter's labor centers the father as family storyteller and forges an alliance between them. For example, she invites his story about holiday celebrations, toys he made for her children, and an injury to his hand. This father-daughter alliance also emerged in another session with multiple participants when a father cries and the daughter helps him recover his composure and then continue his narration. With the exception of this family's son-in-law, who addressed questions to his mother-in-law, our corpus did not have examples of sons facilitating mothers' tellings, perhaps because our sessions were not varied enough or because this pattern is more rare. Research on the Franco-American family identifies father-daughter and mother-son pairs as characteristic of patriarchal arrangements (French, 1981; Langelier, 1996). This possibility raises issues already intimated in previous discussions, that is, on the significance of gender as it informs and constrains task-ordering in family storytelling.

Gendered Lines

Our discussion of content-ordering and task-ordering has anticipated some gendered dynamics of family storytelling. Here we make gender thematic in examining the labor of performing narrative, and we continue to trace the echoes of gender throughout the analysis. The storytelling sessions were permeated with everyday references to gender: in the language of "the girls" and "the boys"; in gendered references in stories that placed the women inside and the men outside (e.g., the women going home after Mass to fix dinner while the men visited in the parking lot); and in interpretive links between generations by a father ("I'm not my father's son" and "my son is like me"). If we wanted to hear the funny and crazy stories, we were advised to go to the men in the family. A *mémère* who was the second of eight daughters and one son identified herself as "the boy in the family" because of the farmwork she did outside with her father. The family is a privileged—some argue the original—site of the sexual division of labor. Feminist scholars of the family have developed analyses of how culture maps distinct ideological constructs of gender roles and family onto biological raw material of sex, procreation, and nurturing. These mappings create, among other consequences, the sexual division of labor in the family, including the reproduction of mothering (Chodorow, 1978), the organization of housework (Hartmann, 1981), the "double shift" of women (Hochschild, 1989), and the standpoint of black women (Collins, 1991). Feminist analyses of the sexual division of labor in the family target oppression and differences in power.

As some feminists expose the patriarchal family, others focus on women's relationships with each other as expressions of "women's culture." These latter views focus on women's differences from men, citing characteristics of moral superiority to men, female nurturance and cooperativeness, selfless maternity, and benevolent sexuality (di Leonardo, 1998). Some tout matriarchal traditions and goddess tropes in, for example, ancient, black, or Native American families that imbue women, particularly older women, with performative power within the family. Matriarchs are most often cited in families at opposite ends of the race/class system: wealthy white women or working-class ethnic women. Hope Edelman (1999) captures the irony of the matriarch when she writes: "the more patriarchal the culture, the more likely you are to wind up with families that have older women of power" (p. 137). Patricia Boscia-Mulé (1999) notes that matriarchal power is contingent on its conformity to patriarchal interests and performance as a traditional wife and mother. Most forceful is di Leonardo's (1998) critique of the feminist essentialism in "women's culture" conflated with "white ethnic community." She argues that acclaiming the moral superiority of ethnic women makes false claims that lop off and deny the negative poles of women's and ethnic cultures. Moreover, when women's culture has also annexed the oppressed and heroic woman of color, the resulting traditional ethnic woman is transmuted as easily to antifeminist as to feminist causes.

Feminist scholars of narrative underwent a somewhat similar process of theorizing and documenting gender patterns (Sawin, 1999; Cameron, 1998). Work in the 1970s and 1980s responded to the question "Do men and women tell stories about their lives differently?" In mixed-sex settings, scholars empirically located both difference (Tannen, 1984, 1990; Maltz & Borker, 1982; Johnstone, 1990) and male dominance (e.g., Fishman, 1983; Henley & Kramarae, 1991; Kramarae & Jenkins, 1987; Spender, 1980). In parallel fashion to matriarchs of family, "women's ways of telling" were extolled as models of collaboration (Kalčik, 1975), corroboration (Baldwin, 1985; Yocum, 1985), and collective description (Hall & Langellier, 1988). These studies were followed by critiques of essentialism, especially by poststructuralist feminists who argued that naturalized categories of sex/gender were social, historical, and culturally variable constructions rather than biological givens. Moreover, the normalizing of women's talk and storytelling privileged white, heterosexual, middle-class practices. In the place of pan-gender models, we argue for a strategic and contextualized performance of gender, based in our approach to performing narrative as embodied, situated, and discursive.[3]

With the constructs of difference and dominance, we can now revisit one of our earlier examples of storytelling in mixed-sex settings to examine task-ordering. To take the example of the stories of cooking with onions, the habitual gendered patterns of telling can be analyzed as differences or, alternatively, as dominance. An analysis of gender differences focuses on what meanings the husband and wife contribute to a story and how they are expressed (Johnstone, 1990). The husband tells a self-oriented story in which he acts alone and builds his personal image as one who eats at the corner store rather than eating the food his wife prepares with onions. The story is focused around the dramatized action of looking in the pot. Its linear plot builds to the punch line, is told without interruption, and could stand on its own. The wife's story is linked to her husband's, dependent on it, and backtracks in time to offer the context of his autonomous action in their marriage. She tells an other-oriented story set in an interdependent social world in which harmony is crucial and conflict submerged. Her story is also linear, but its point is more indirect, left for the audience to supply and corroborate. In Baldwin's terms (1985), the gender differences form a "team telling" that makes a more complete family story.

From an analysis of gender dominance, the analysis would highlight a culture of power that underlies gender differences, differences that are structural, rather than individual, inequalities. This explanation would interpret the husband's story in terms of the prerogative of greater social power, whether understood in terms of how men's conversational dominance parallels their social and political dominance (e.g., West & Zimmerman, 1983) or the unconscious consequence of gender role training that serves to obscure the issue of power (e.g., Fishman, 1983). In this light, the husband's story is a performance of verbal aggressiveness and the power to define conversational topic and control a situation. He both sets the topic and has the last word. The wife, in this view, links her story to his previous story, jointly producing a story on his topic and within his definition of the situation. Although she is not acquiescent and his final comment accepts her narrative and relational move, the evidence of differential social power remains. She adjusts not only to his definition of topic and situation but also to his food preferences. That he eats sauce with onions requires nothing additional on his part. Furthermore, their interaction can be situated in the family context and lengthier narrative event in which these tasks are ordered. There the patterns of work allocation in which wives support husbands, and daughters support fathers, intimated above, become clearer. Scholars call this the conversational work that women do to support and serve men. The father is centered as storyteller through a combination of his own initiation and family women's interactional labor. This interactional work is a task distinct from but necessary to the transmission tasks of retrieving, interpreting, and innovating information.

When the father and son-in-law go into the yard to play with the young children, the grandmother, mother, daughter, and Kristin continue to talk around the kitchen table as the tape recorder runs. A large proportion of this now same-sex narrating is devoted to stories about the father which both the wife/mother and daughter tell. They engage in the narrative labor of interpreting content in an effort to understand, empathize with, and explain him. At an earlier occasion, the daughter and her husband had told brief versions of the father getting his GED, which the daughter calls "a really big deal for the whole family," a source of pride for him. They tell the father's stories but not vice versa. The story is repeated and expanded by the mother and daughter, and the mother remarks that "I'm surprised he didn't tell you" this story. His version would have been interesting for comparative purposes; however, our interest at this point is with the layering of narrative labor performed by women in family storytelling. They perform interactional work to support the father's storytelling in a mixed-sex setting, they tell and interpret his stories in their same-sex setting, and they provide the labor for the family gatherings which occasion narrative events. The result is the contradictory mixture of women's deference and performative power that fuels some scholars to make matriarchal arguments about patriarchal arrangements, such as Stone's (1988) conclusions about family stories:

> Family stories—telling them and listening to them—belong more to the women's sphere. When I interviewed married couples, it was not unusual for the woman to know more of her husband's family stories than he did, usually because she'd heard them through her mother-in-law. In this way, despite the convention of patrilineality, the family is essentially a female institution: the lore of family and family culture itself—stories, rituals, traditions, icons, sayings—are preserved and promulgated primarily by women. (p. 19)

Our concern is not that Stone's conclusion is false and groundless but rather that it is partial and decontextualized from storytelling as task-ordering. The gendered division of labor requires situated and material analysis of the power relations that produce families and reproduce unequal burdens for interactional work between women and men.

Motherlines

In distinction from a fatherline grounded in patrilineality and scaffolded by patriarchal arrangements, family storytelling affords occasions for bonding among family women and feminist resistance. In the same-sex setting just described, mother, daughter, and grandmother turn to their own stories after the labor of telling the father's story of education is completed. The mother distinguishes her educational opportunities from her mother's and her husband's: she went to high school. She tells the story of going to nursing school at age thirty-seven, a decision not supported by her husband, which the daughter expands as not supported by her husband's family. Mother and daughter collaborate to interpret the family's resistance, citing several gender dynamics. The daughter then tells a story of how she received her mother's approval when she went back to work and had to put her young children in childcare. Their co-narrating combines mutual support and critique of gender relations. In this way, the labor of storytelling differentiated by gender may combine to create maternal, or paternal, alliances.

One way to read task-ordering among family women is in terms of what Kathleen Woodward (1999) calls the motherline. She argues against reading the family from a logic of two generations in the Freudian mother-father-child triangle and the mother-daughter plot of identification and conflict. She advocates the invention of three-generational models where the expressly missing older woman—the grandmother, or *mémère* in our case—is included and where historical time intersects with biological, developmental time. In the motherline, three generations of women establish a heritage based not on struggle for domination but on the pleasurable interactions of play and performance (Cook-Gumperz, 1995). For example, Pauline talks about conflict with her mother over keeping family secrets, which her daughter echoes about her own daughter. Taken as discreet mother-daughter interactions, these play out the struggle and conflict between the two generations. However, put in the context of the motherline and situated as it is with laughter and light-heartedness, the interactions among three generations are playful and pleasurable. The talk about telling family secrets leads to a brief round of humorous stories in which the *mémère* tells about how her wearing head scarves thoroughly embarrasses her daughter, which the granddaughter then picks up to tell about "when you [grandmother] made me wear a kerchief." Edelman (1999), watching her daughter play, captures the sense of continuity through differentiation in the motherline: "she is a child and I am her mother; she is me and I am my mother; she is my mother and I am my grandmother" (p. 254).

Task-ordering in storytelling among women has produced several empirical descriptions of "women's narrative" as distinct from men's. Segments of the group performance of the courtship story among a grandmother, her three daughters, and a granddaughter (analyzed in Chapter 2) reveal the collaborative strategies of Susan Kalčik's (1975) women's rap groups that developed one point together, the corroborative tactics of Baldwin (1985) in which family women reinforce each other's points, the spinstorying of Langellier and Peterson (1992) that produces horizontal relations and a shared reality among women, and the overlays and spiraling of Gillian Bennett's (1986) female narrators of events that require exposition. However, we also wish to emphasize that the range of strategies that women (and men) can do depends upon the demands, resources, and constraints of particular performance situations (Hall & Langellier, 1988). Family women across our sample did not produce identical labor in family storytelling, nor did individual women across settings. For example, one cross-generational triad engaged for a time in telling competing stories that challenged each other's points and realities and structured hierarchical relations among them. By essentialist standards, another mother performed "like a man" in a mother-daughter session and "like a woman" in a three-generational setting. Another *mémère* regally presided over a session, displaying a range of tasks that included initiating stories, directing interaction, narrating, and listening. From the communication perspective taken here, it is the definition of task in a situation, not identity characteristics, that informs the use of particular strategies.

Common Task, Different Tactics

When men define a task as facilitating narrative, they, too, can perform the interactional work of storytelling. We conclude the section on gendered lines by looking at same-sex family interactional alliances, first between a father and son and then between a mother and daughter. These pairs come from families with comparable histories and class backgrounds from the same French community in northern Maine. The father-son session was conducted in the father's home, with our local contact person (a man) present as well as Kristin and a colleague (a woman) in Franco-American studies.

The father begins his storytelling with a genealogy, describing his great-grandparents, grandparents, and parents, how he lived in [name of town] "all my life," his houses, and children, after which he says to Kristin, "so what else do you want to know?" Before Kristin can respond, the son replies, "I want to interview him about the family business, which I am the third generation of the family business." He, in fact, does this, and more, by assuming the interviewer role, prompting his father to numerous stories, the first invited by "You had some stories about—I don't know how personal you want to get—

but I remember a story about you guys milking a cow on the side of the hill here." Other stories he elicits include the biography of a priest in the family, and his father's leading role in developing the local hospital, ski area, and the family insurance business. The father narrates these stories in lengthy turns, filled with the details of times, places, quantities, and events. He is clearly comfortable in his narrative role, accustomed to having the floor and in command of information.

The son serves as a host who announces and showcases his father's stories. He occasionally supplements factual information or provides evaluations of the content; for example, the missionary priest "was very active and very well liked," the hospital is a unique contribution to the community and "has just hired eight new doctors," his father is "one of the first ten who signed the note" for the ski area, and the family business is very successful, now located in three states and "you [father] were on the Board of Directors for fifty years." The son's labor corroborates the facts of his father's stories and reinforces his father's experiences and meanings. His interactional work constructs a moral stance for his father, and, by extension, himself. It is a performance of pride in their accomplishments, which situates the family within their work history, town history, and regional history. The sense of performance was perhaps augmented by the presence of several listeners. The co-narrating is characterized most strongly by complementary roles, where father retrieves information and the son upholds and advances his stories. Notably, the son's interactional labor centers and supports his father.

The interview with the mother-daughter pair took place in the mother's home with the daughter, the same female colleague, and Kristin as listeners. The contact person was not present. Like the father above, the mother begins with a life summary. Hers, however, starts not with genealogy but with her own marriage at age eighteen, her five children, and the small family farm on which she worked. After her opening statements, her daughter prompts:

> D: <u>before</u> you got married Mom?
>
> M: oh I was a [?] my mother and dad my dad was a sick man
>   but they brought us eight girls and a boy
>   so:: we worked with them all the time
>   picked the rocks and then
>
> D: you had <u>hors</u>es back then too huh
>
> M: oh yeah we had horses
>
> D: <u>tractors</u> were not a common thing
>
> M: no there wasn't much of a tractor
>   we had horses . on a farm
>
> D: you'd spend days picking strawberries and mulberries
>
> M: [laughs] yes

The mother next launches a brief, humorous story about a daughter who hates to pick strawberries. The contrast between the father-son tactics and mother-daughter tactics for accomplishing narrative tasks is striking. The mother takes brief turns and the daughter patiently prompts and coaches her to narrative. The mother is responsive but declines long turns and waits for the daughter or Kristin to pose questions. Together mother and daughter establish a pattern of co-narrating that holds throughout the interview: question-narration-explanation. The daughter or Kristin asks a question ("before you got married Mom?"), the mother tells about the farm work, and the daughter expands ("you had horses back then too huh") or explains ("tractors were not a common thing") with the mother. In this way, stories by the mother about a wake, a willful horse, and living with her in-laws the first year of marriage are further developed by the daughter: why there were no funeral parlors, how horses were shod, and that newly married couples stayed with their parents because they did not have enough money to have their own place, and so on. By mid-interview, the pattern has evolved such that Kristin asks a question to which mother and daughter co-narrate responses from their respective generations, usually the mother speaking first followed by daughter. Throughout the session, turns are brief and the floor is shared, a pattern identified by Carole Edelsky (1981). The shared floor structure seems most comfortable for the mother in this session.

Each same-sex pair achieved the family goal of transmission of content—however differently—through tactics that facilitated retrieval. The performance of gender is strategic and multiply contextualized. The father-son pattern was augmented by the larger audience (six, and, briefly, seven when a guest dropped by), the mixed-sex setting, and the father's acknowledged profile within the town's history. The contact person occasionally participated in the telling, too, by filling in or confirming statements about the hospital and university. The father was raised in a French-speaking household with an English mother who spoke French. We speculate that he had ongoing opportunities to speak English, especially in more public settings. The mother-daughter pattern emerged in a same-sex setting with fewer participants. Near the end of the session, the mother says, "I wanted [daughter] to come over because I knew she could explain it better." When in their mother's home, they speak French with each other, although they spoke English during the session. Each pattern is a strategic, situational negotiation of the constraints and resources rather than a general gender model. Each pair draws on resources—language, interaction, and situation—that are informed and constrained by gender, as well as class.[4] We present these paired variations on the interactional labor that either men or women may perform when the narrative task is defined as facilitating storytelling.

Rather than focus on sex differences in storytelling, we consider how task-ordering constructs gender in family culture formation. While we vigorously critique an essentialism that directs or explains task allocation according to biology or social history, we cannot ignore gendered patterns in our corpus. Nor can we ignore the unequal burden of narrative work borne by family women. The Franco-American family, particularly as it intersects with Roman Catholicism, is moored in patriarchy. Despite these moorings, these families enact a variety of gender formations, and they continue to undergo and respond to ongoing changes in women's roles. Other families and groups of families would yield additional variations of task-ordering by gender. Finally we note that women's storytelling labor is not necessarily burdensome nor unwelcome—joy and satisfaction emerge as emotions throughout our sessions. But still, the layers of narrative labor are disproportionately assumed by women in the family. This labor is critical to the storytelling enterprise and under increasing stress as transformative changes of social history continue to press on all families.

Storytelling Tasks and Tactics

Family members work together and apart to retrieve and transmit their culture. We have considered how families allocate and routinize tasks between generations, supplemented by interdependent subsets of spouses and other pairs who work together to co-narrate. We also considered how tasks are distributed by gender, often asymmetrically in terms of women's responsibilities for family interaction. Family storytelling is a joint enterprise that produces family culture through multiple actors who take on a range of tasks in a variety of ways. Generational and gendered patterns of telling that become habitual can contribute to the maintenance of family culture over time. Families, however, are always in flux, always undergoing internal change through births and deaths, marriages and divorces, new and waning relationships. Put another way, families are always incorporating new members as children are born or adopted and raised, and as new members enter by way of marriage and conjugal relations. Conversely, families are always losing members as children grow up and leave home, as well as through deaths and divorce.

Changes internal to a family are often linked to environmental forces that also press families to adapt. Among these are changes in women's roles, ethnic group consciousness and racial tensions, work patterns, life expectancy, family residential arrangements, and the pervasiveness of popular culture and consumerism. Economic decline places working-class families precariously on the faultline (Rubin, 1994). How can families withstand the waves of change, internal and external, to continue their culture? Transmission addresses the relations among tasks of retrieving, interpreting, and innovating. McFeat (1974) argues that the importance of generations and genders to family cultural survival does not derive from the differences of age, sex, or authority but "rather it has to do with the possibility of communication among members in which *some* remain predominantly senders while *others* remain predominantly receivers, and each has or will experience the other's role" (p. 114). In this section we explore some additional tactics families use to order the tasks of storytelling in ways that promote cultural survival so that "each has or will experience the other's role."

One tactic of cultural survival is to build redundancy into the narrative process. We have already seen evidence of this in the story of the father's attaining his GED, "a big story for the whole family" that was told, with differing development and contextualizing, four times by four different tellers across two storytelling sessions. As a kernel story which depends upon its conversational context for development, the GED story is a narrative possibility for communal sharing and transmission (Langellier & Peterson, 1992, p. 164). Its first telling, by the daughter, was couched in conversation about how working hard was more important than education in many Franco-American families, and how "educated people were put up above us." The story of her father's GED ends with her performance of his speech that shuts down many of their conversations: "Well, you're right, I'm wrong; you're smart, I'm dumb; you went to school, I didn't." The story surfaces later in the same session, this time by the son-in-law, within a discussion of how the parent generation broke the cycle of abuse they inherited. The kernel story here is used as evidence that the father's accomplishments were a greater stride than the son-in-law's law degree.

At a second family gathering, the father himself refers to the story, again in kernel form, this time contextualized within a description of childhood work on the farm that precluded his going to high school or participating in after-school sports. The story is in this conversation to reinforce a point about his upbringing, but it is not developed in its own right. The story is told in its most fully developed form by the mother and daughter, later the same day with the *mémère* and Kristin present. It emerges after *Mémère's* story of having to quit school to help care for younger siblings. The mother explains that family took care of family, linking this sensibility to her husband's family in which only the youngest three of eleven children received a high school education. Her version carries more emotional information ("he gets very very bitter" about this) than the telling by her daughter and son-in-law. She repeats the same speech with the same intonations as did her daughter: "You're right, I'm wrong; you're smart, I'm dumb; you went to school, I didn't." Together mother and daughter flesh out the event's emotional meanings, the wound of the father's lack of education. The mother adds the event before the GED of her husband's losing a lifelong job and, when interviewing for a new one, the insult he suffered at the hands of a female personnel officer who "was way out of line but she did him a favor" because it spurred him to enroll in a GED program. The mother appends a story of his receiving an award for outstanding work on his GED.

Redundancy is achieved not only through multiple tellings of the same story but also by its distribution among so many different tellers in different conversations to make different points. The structural possibilities of the kernel story allow different tellers and tellings to convey the same message in different ways, with different contextualizations and development. Shifting codes around the same message when it must be repeated contributes to a more wide-ranging redundancy. Furthermore, the task of telling is not limited to its protagonist—indeed he need not tell it himself—but is distributed as a responsibility throughout family. Support is displayed through the multiple tellers' attending to the tale and its significance to family more than by individual ownership of the story. The participation of the son-in-law, a relatively recent family member from the "other side," in a story about his wife's father also indicates how new members can broaden the range of redundancy.

A related form of redundancy functions to increase family participation in the tasks of storytelling, both narrating and listening. The courtship storytelling round described in the previous chapter, a group production distributed among four family women from two generations, illustrates this form of redundancy. The task of telling was first allocated to the protagonist, Nicole, with the presumption of her unshared experience and right to tell the story. Subsequently, the story is reworked by a generation of three sisters who claim access to ownership by filling in shared properties of the event. They participate through questions, clarifications, elaborations, and challenges to the story. This form of widening redundancy exemplifies the proposition "let us (all) tell your (singular) story" that Blum-Kulka (1997) identifies in Israeli families. From the perspective of task-ordering, the significance of the family's reworking of the story is not to retrieve additional basic information on details of the three-month hiatus, although that is one outcome, but rather to interpret the conjugal event from a family standpoint. The shift in task to interpreting content allowed the greater participation of the second generation in a third generation story. Individual telling rights and the self-accomplishment of the protagonist were not eliminated—Nicole does tell her story—however, interpretive procedures of the family standpoint are developed and highlighted by how the group participates (Langellier & Peterson, 1992). Forms of redundancy that increase involvement in family storytelling require frequent and face-to-face contact in order to assure familiarity with the story as well as participation in tellings. Such strategies may be less efficient as a tactic to increase redundancy—because each participant must become a family, not just an individual, narrator—but they may be more effective for the longer-term task of transmitting family culture.

A communication tactic that consolidates storytelling tasks in one person may achieve greater efficiency in the short run. That is, one person may tell all of the family's story, locating task-ordering in the hands of one or a few. Jewish American families in Blum-Kulka's (1997) study supported the rights of the individual teller who, in enacting the proposition "let *me* tell *our* story," performs a shared event as a monologue. In investing the power of narrative in one person, differences between personal and familial experience are elided or rendered ambiguous. This transmission tactic could be embodied by a traditional patriarch, such as the father who tells the family story through his public service, or by a traditional matriarch, such as Pauline, who locates family in the motherline. Less directly, family narrative may reveal icons who anchor family definition, for example, the *pépère* whose conviviality compelled family parties, or the matriarchal *mémère* whose demise left the family without a center around which to revolve. Alternatively, the biographical fusion of Louis and Bernice (described earlier in this chapter) may consolidate narrative in a generational dyad. The possibility for idiosyncratic rather than widely distributed commitment to family memory is captured by Alain (in Chapter 2) when he observes that "some are interested, some not." In this situation, a family must find somebody to pass on its culture and someone to listen. However, McFeat's (1974) findings on experimental small group cultures suggests that monads and dyads are at greatest risk for loss and distortion of information over time. Designating a "keeper of family stories" achieves efficiency but may imperil continuity if tasks of telling are not experienced by others. The death of a family storyteller can create a crisis if that role is not assumed by another family member nor distributed among members.

It is important to distinguish loss of information from loss of a task. As Stone (1988) puts it, "attention to the stories' actual truth is never the family's most compelling consideration. Encouraging belief is. The family's survival depends upon the shared sensibility of its members" (p. 7). The transmission of a shared sensibility to family culture is facilitated if tasks of retrieving, interpreting, and innovating information are invested in roles more than in individuals and, furthermore, if roles are fluid and mobile within and between generations. Allocating the tasks of transmission exclusively to elders or to women carries risks in an environment characterized by rapid change. The fusion of story and telling modes between couples may serve long-term transmission better than a rigid sexual division of labor. The tactical adaptations of co-narrating by the father-son and mother-daughter pairs (described above) accomplished, in different ways, the strategic tasks of transmission. Although the allocation of conversational and family culture maintenance to women has proven survival value, the fluidity and mobility by which men may also assume these tasks widens the range of redundancy and possibilities for cultural transmission, particularly as gender roles and family forms continue to change.

Finally, the tasks of interpreting and innovating information are critical to cultural survival and depend upon the narrative participation of younger generations who bring new information and difference into a family system. A diverse family system has more resources and adapts more readily to environmental changes. Information in families flows upward through generations as well as downward from elders. We conclude our discussion of transmission with an example of how one family responds to changes, internal and external, through generations. Our discussion here can only be suggestive because our research strategy was not longitudinal. This example reveals the task-ordering of two generations of the same family, observed first in a session with a mother, father, and daughter; and then a week later in a second session with the daughter. From the perspective of generations, there is a unique asymmetry between parents and children, who differ by bodily location, which can be viewed from parents' or children's standpoint. In distinction from biographical fusion between parents, illustrated by Louis and Bernice, parent-child reciprocity is a process of "biographical fission" in which "two actors who originally possessed a nearly identical biographical standpoint and relevance system gradually construct divergent standpoints" (McLain & Weigert, 1979, p. 177). Children bring difference into a family simply by growing up.

Aimee, now in her twenties, is the tenth of eleven children, and the only one of the children to go to college. She is now working toward a master's degree in French. In the session among mother (M), father (F), Aimee (D), and Kristin (K), Aimee has been discussing how her upbringing on the farm differed from other children in the area who were "mill kids." For several years she and her siblings worked in the family egg business, "picking eggs" before and after school, in the barn that housed 30,000 chickens.

> D: I never told anybody I <u>picked eggs</u> that's for sure
>
> M: what was so wrong about that?
>
> D: <u>noth</u>ing . <u>now</u>
>   I tell everybody now
>   when you're <u>twelve</u> you don't tell anybody you pick eggs

A moment later the mother says:

> M: [to Kristin] our daughter there she would think how
>   everybody should have a job not to pick eggs or whatever
>   and I think she's just begun to <u>realize</u>— probably a few more years
>   that it's <u>true</u>:
>   [to all] <u>somebody's got to pick eggs</u>
>   <u>somebody</u>'s got to shovel manure
>   if you're in <u>college</u> you are not out shoveling <u>manure</u>
>   so those poor guys that are out doing it
>   hey that's a job <u>we</u> don't have to <u>do</u>

> *D:*   and there was never any questioning either
>   we just had to do it
>
> *K:*   right
>
> *D:*   I never remember thinking oh god I don't want to do this

This exchange, which begins in narrative and transmutes to discussion that involves interpreting content—the meaning of picking eggs—provides an opportunity to chart changes in reciprocity of perspectives between parent and child. The daughter Aimee's statement "I never told anybody about picking eggs that's for sure" is challenged by the mother: "what was so wrong about that?" Aimee's response deflects conflict but suggests they may disagree over their standpoints on such labor as picking eggs. When she was young, the child and parental perspectives were merged, and the daughter says she did not question their work, either to her parents or to herself. As the locus of primary socialization, family originates the fusion of parent-child perspectives. In school, other perspectives enter and a splitting emerges, based on Aimee's awareness and probably embarrassment of being different from other children who do not have to pick eggs every day. The narrative offers some insight into the working-class milieu of a rural area where other families are by no means wealthy, although a hierarchy of occupations exists. Most families work at the mill in town, not on the farm where children's labor was necessary to contribute to the family business. The mother introduces a third marker of divergence, when Aimee goes to college and thinks "everybody should have a job not to have to pick eggs or whatever," a direction the mother frames as flawed and temporary because "somebody" has to do this work while others are in college. According to the mother, her daughter's perspective will realign with her parents and away from a college "we" who "don't have to do" such work. The mother speaks for her daughter, addressing Kristin, proposing an alternative interpretive frame for picking eggs. The daughter foregoes comment on these interpretations. Her "we" of "we just had to do it" refers to her siblings, and perhaps her parents in the past.

Conflict emerges not over basic information but over interpreted content. The task of interpreting content can break down the hierarchy of generations, but here the task-ordering reinscribes generation when the mother prescribes a family standpoint for her daughter. However, this task allocation simultaneously imbues the older generation with a new perspective, gleaned from the college experience of the daughter. Interpreted and innovated information may be problematic in terms of family consensus; however, it is crucial to adapting to change through generations. The participation of children in family storytelling adds new information and diverse viewpoints to family culture. As we turn to the second session of storytelling from this family, a follow-up interview with the daughter one week later, our intent is not to establish the accuracy or legitimacy of one interpretation or another, the parental or child perspective, but to look at how the second generation both preserves family sensibilities and introduces new information conducive to family change.

Aimee concludes her interview with Kristin in a summary statement that "I came back to language but not to religion." In distinction from her siblings, Aimee asserts that "I will teach my kids French," even if not the same French as her parents', nor in the same way, because she recognizes the conscious and consistent effort it will require in an environment so altered from the one in which she and her parents learned the language. Aimee embodies a strategy in which the third generation ethnic offspring reclaims her or his heritage (Bona, 1999). Her narrative embeds this reclamation in a lengthy and ongoing process of conflicting perspectives that contribute simultaneously to a fission with her parents and a rapprochement with family culture. The French language her family spoke at home was silenced in school. Aimee stopped speaking it for six years, but when she entered college her French was affirmed by outside perspectives for the first time. She elected to journey to France and learned the "standard" dialect, which her parents do not speak and which marks their North American French as "substandard."[5] In the process of her education in college and in France, Aimee lost her own childhood dialect, which she is now working to relearn. Her narrative on French language is ordered around a triumphant story of bringing friends from Germany to the farm in Maine to visit her parents, where they all manage to communicate in French of different dialects. In contrast to reclaiming French, Aimee has rejected the religion of her parents and family. Again, she attributes these new perspectives to college, where she wrote her honor's thesis on literary works that influenced her change. She has shared her thesis with her parents and discussed her reasons for rejecting religion with them. She reflects on the session with her parents the week before, where generational conflict over religion was discussed, including her mother's comment that "the kids'll come back [to the Church]." Aimee interprets this statement as both a message to her and about them: "maybe they need to believe that someday I'll come back."

As fusion of perspectives within generations is neither complete nor desirable, neither is fission between generations. This example of storytelling by a younger generation can be read as evidence of successful transmission: Aimee has fully assumed the narrative tasks of retrieving, interpreting, and innovating content. Moreover, she is infusing family culture with information that flows upward to her parents, introducing new interpretations on religion and innovating language practices. Discussions of family cultural survival often privilege and praise the task of retrieval in the face of environmental change at the same time they downplay and distrust the innovations of youth. However, the tasks of interpreting and innovating information are as crucial to cultural survival as is remembering. Diverging perspectives that create family fission emerge in encounters with different others, whether difference is discovered via education, travel, media, new technologies, or interaction. The innovation of information is urgent and decisive as family environments for task-ordering change in a global and multicultural world. What children and new members bring to family is not simply problematic for fusion and consensus because it simultaneously creates alternative ways to accomplish the tasks of family storytelling and cultural survival.

"That's why I did my *Réveillon*: to keep the family as long as we can"

Task-ordering has to do with "the possibility of communication among members in which *some* remain predominantly senders while *others* remain predominantly receivers, and each has or will experience the other's role" (McFeat, 1974, p. 114). Family storytelling is not limited to specific speech events, but it is enhanced by opportunities for families to gather face-to-face. In this final section on task-ordering we consider how families establish and continue rituals for "the possibility of communication"—conversation and storytelling. Family rituals make explicit the embodied and material conditions for doing family and doing family storytelling. They afford the times and places for families to communicate and to perform themselves to themselves in family rituals. Such events supply and support the conditions for participants to experience each other's role, the conditions that make possible the telling and hearing of family stories. If family storytelling depends on settings for interaction, how do families maintain and innovate rituals in the changing conditions, internal and external, they face over time?

The labor of retrieving, innovating, and interpreting information tends to privilege aspects of telling that transmit content, those stories visible and audible to families. We have also described a more invisible labor in storytelling, which is not only listening. In conversation, it is the labor that weaves conversation together: the generation and maintenance of interaction. Within family, it is the labor that creates, connects, sustains, and repairs relationships among members. Between families, it is the invisible and creative labor that knits households together, maintaining family, community, and work ties: for example, family dinners, birthday parties, holiday activities, communal meals, and festivals. All of this labor organizes situations and occasions for family ritual and storytelling. The ordering of occasions for storytelling must focus not just on the rituals themselves but on their preparation, which may require hours or even months of labor. As we have seen above, families divide the labor of storytelling, like household tasks, by generation and gender. In this respect, family rituals, or what Pleck (2000) calls "domestic occasions," are simply part of women's everyday work of cooking and cleaning and creating the family's social life (p. 15). They cluster with other high-frequency and low-status tasks of housework and feeding the family (DeVault, 1991). Di Leonardo (1984) names this labor *kinwork*, and she argues that it is especially the responsibility of ethnic women, regardless of individual class membership, to bind cultural identity. Taken together, conversational work and kinwork support the expressive and social rituals that perform and celebrate the family: talking and storytelling, eating, getting together. These rituals order the everyday and special times of family. The visits, cards and letters, gifts, phone calls, and e-mails, the organization of holiday gatherings, services, foods, goods, and money exchanged in ordinary and crisis times for families and communities are organized and facilitated primarily by women.

In her historical analysis of family ritual, Pleck (2000) links the sentimental family ritual with the ideology of domesticity that arose in the nineteenth century to distinguish the separate spheres of public and private life and to define middle-class identity. In this belief system, the ideal family resided in a quasi-sacred space made into a home and presided over by a middle-class mother who symbolized tradition and cultural identity. Her "valuable but invisible work both reflected and contributed to the unequal relations between men and women" (p. 15). Rituals showcased gender ideals in performance displays of women as nurturant in their service to the family, and of men as ceremonial heads of family waited upon by women. At the center of the sentimental domestic occasion, women were less free than men to reject group identity (see also Boscia-Mulé, 1999). If the middle-class homes they made were to be distinct from the public sphere of labor, women could not be constructed as workers. In the ideology of domesticity, housework and kinwork were constructed as a labor of love, with the sentimental domestic occasion proof and performance of love's labor. In postsentimental culture since the 1970s, the sentimental family ritual has diminished and changed but not disappeared. That is, only some aspects of daily life and special occasion are selected for tradition (McKay, 1994), and these selections often involve ethnic working-class women's work (Narayan, 1997). Pleck traces the rise, decline, and remaking of the sentimental occasion within the multiple forces that are simultaneously braking and accelerating changes in gender roles, precipitating and erasing ethnic identity, and resisting and incorporating consumer and popular culture.

One marker of postsentimental family ritual is the performance of ethnic identity and difference. After immigration to the United States, the transmission of cultural heritage, language, and religion was often delegated to women and located in the home. The home may be a refuge from the forces of assimilation, with family rituals that promote authentic and homey food and interaction. Pleck (2000, pp. 5–6) distinguishes an ethnic discourse on the decline of the family that differs from the mainstream lament on the loss of the family meal. The lack of a fixed time when the family eats and converses together is usually blamed on working mothers, supplemented by divorce, a decline in religious practices, the overly scheduled lives of children, a culture which is individualistic and narcissistic, and the ubiquitous television. By contrast to targeting the forces of consumer and popular culture, an ethnic discourse focuses on a decline in the sense of community, mourning a deterioration in family solidarity and kinship. In traditional Franco-American culture, specific rituals connect extended families and communities in daily, weekly, and special occasions. After-supper tea every day with *Mémère*, Saturday-night family gatherings, Sunday-after-Mass dinner at the grandparents' house, the weekly sewing circles, card games with family and friends, neighborhood parties, parish suppers, and community *soirées*—all were narrated by families in our corpus. Franco-Americans celebrate religious holidays. One narrator recalled Mardi Gras as a "big thing" in his town, observed somewhat like Halloween, with children going from house to house for candy. The tradition of *Réveillon* featured a party after the midnight Mass of the holy days of Christmas and New Year's. Parties were held in homes and featured ethnic and family foods, especially *tourtière*, or meat pie in southern Maine, and chicken stew in northern Maine. At the intersection of French ethnic and Roman Catholic religious identity, *Réveillon* is a unique source of holiday tradition for Franco-Americans.

Family members retrieved information about rituals as an exercise in nostalgia and loss, their recall often marked by sadness. One declared that "that's why I did my *Réveillon:* to keep the family as long as we can." Later she lamented that "we are down to nothing, and I find that so difficult." One *mémère* wept over the demise of dinners she regularly prepared for the extended family, times when everyone was together and "everybody was always happy." The senior generation retrieved information that the middle generation remembered as children and that the younger had not known. For example, while the elders recalled music and dancing in community halls and homes, and playing cards with friends and family, the middle generation remembered sleeping on porches and on beds piled with coats, or staying upstairs or in bedrooms while adults had their fun. A family home with two parlors was emptied for dancing, the room bordered with shoes and the long driveway lined with cars parked out to the road. One interviewee named these parties "big family fun," from accordion music to "fist fights in the yard." Another described making the rounds to family and neighbors, the men having a drink at each place. One family hosted *Réveillons* with up to seventy people and offering an array of foods—from *tourtière* to vegetable soup, potato salad, and shrimp fried rice—which she prepared weeks and even months in advance, a routine which her daughter says "she [mother] had down to a science."

Family markers such as weddings and funerals were homogenized in the 1950s (Pleck, 2000) as the result of intermarriage and the decline of the funeral as the grandest family event. A few older participants recalled wakes in the living room and the abundance of food provided by family and neighbors. One *mémère* talks about how church women labored to prepare food for weddings, a community event that exceeded family. Funerals were not narrated, although deaths divide family history into before-and-afters: *Réveillons* ceased after *Pépère* died; holiday gatherings at the grandparents moved to the next generation after *Mémère* died. These narratives equate a death in the family with the passing of a tradition. Franco-American families did not narrate family vacations to distant "America" sites. Instead they went to a nearby lake, a camp in the Maine woods, or to visit other family. Birthdays were not large events, perhaps because recent postsentimental celebrations focus on peer-culture and consumer services that supplant rather than reinforce ethnic culture (Pleck, 2000).

Retrieving information is an occasion for nostalgia that divides tasks by generation; and greater participation by younger generations in storytelling may have yielded more views of postsentimental ritual in Franco-American families. When participants interpreted information about domestic occasions of celebration, their meanings for family rituals were offered by multiple generations. Elders who witnessed a decline in sentimental and ethnic rituals in their lifetime articulate a felt absence. They point to a loss of opportunities and pleasures that family celebrations may afford: neighborhood and community parties where couples met and eventually married; a place where cousins got to know each other; the "big fun" of their gatherings across households. Their meanings intimated material constraints: families who could not afford to go out, eat out, go on costly vacations made their own fun—dancing, singing, playing cards, and socializing within the relations of kin and community. These interpreted meanings remind us that the goods and services of consumer culture, while available widely, are not equally accessible to all. Moreover, the Roman Catholic faith of the North American French embraces an antimaterialist strain at odds with consumer culture. Kin and communal gatherings afforded an opportunity to express the loving bonds of family and a sense of belonging through presence and participation.

Some participants, however, articulate the excesses of sentimentalism and the uncomfortable bindings of family obligation. They talk about families having to bundle up children and take them out of their own homes to grandparents, close or farther away, for Christmas. Another couple resented assumptions that their home was a hotel for extended family, providing room and board. A younger member talks about the sense of obligation to attend family gatherings that was "understood differently" within her generation and not enacted in the same way by all. A mother describes the pressure, emotional and financial, of selecting and shopping for the ever-expanding gift-giving at Christmas. Another bakes approximately twenty *tourtières* for Christmas, beginning months ahead. A daughter recalls that each year her mother stayed up all night preparing for Christmas day. Family rituals may generate more stress than they relieve, create as much conflict as they reduce, and kindle as many bad feelings as good (Pleck, 2000, p. 19). Other critiques of the idealized family and ideal family ritual include those mounted by feminists who decry the unequal burden of labor on women to create the perfect family and perfect ritual in the patriarchal family, by lesbian and gay theorists and activists who reveal the painful exclusions or closeting of homosexuality in the "straight" family, and race and ethnic critiques that resist the homogenized family and hegemonic culture.

Like mainstream families, Franco-American families in our corpus regret that gatherings of the extended family are confined mostly to weddings and funerals. However, rituals in which to enact and observe storytelling have diminished but not disappeared. When Franco-American families turn to the task of innovating information, they both revive and remake rituals. Some carry on ethnic family traditions, modified by contemporary circumstances. One father-son pair has shifted family holidays from the home to a ski chalet in winter, whereas another family organized a four-generation golf tournament in the summer. These modifications reflect their social mobility and middle-class status as well as the postsentimental move of family celebrations to activities of consumer culture. Those parents whose children have moved away, altering the pattern of frequent visits, keep in touch by phone or letter. Every Monday one mother writes her children living far from home. Others adapt holiday rituals that formerly revolved around the grandparents' home. Instead of holidays at the grandparents', they gather at the home of the biggest family so the children do not have to go out, or grandparents travel to see their children and grandchildren. Families eat out at a restaurant rather than preparing meals at home. One elderly couple whose family is small and scattered "came up with zero" plans and stayed home for the holidays. Although holidays are still defined as an occasion for extended family, more families are gathering as nuclear units or in specific sibling alignments: for example, "I see my closest sister regularly" but the rest of the family and the "whole family" more rarely.

These shifts suggest how French ethnic family rituals converge with mainstream patterns. However, some ethnic practices are retained and modified. For example, after Sunday Mass, a younger daughter picks up her mother and brings her to the oldest daughter's house for the afternoon, during which time other family members drop by as they can. One family organizes intergenerational card games, children playing with their aunts and uncles. Another family, whose members have moved away or passed away, has revived *Réveillons* to focus on the daughter's ties. The daughter has recently moved back to the family home, and the parties, prepared by her mother and her, span family, neighbors, and friends. Still other families are inaugurating new traditions in an effort to maintain opportunities for storytelling and family rituals. One example is a girl-cousin weekend organized periodically. Another is a family reunion every five years, or a special summer reunion for a grandparent's birthday. At the latter, the grandmother and two grandchildren created a game of family trivia in which two teams had to discover favorite foods, middle names, and other facts about the great-grandparents. One reunion, planned by family men, was an ambitious affair spanning a weekend and including a slide show, games, talent show, and Mass, as well as food and socializing. Around this special event, the planners developed an electronic archive of family photographs as well as a genealogy. Another father has taken his children on a "pilgrimage" to the Franco-American homeplace of his parents in Berlin, New Hampshire, and to French Canada and France, sites which he visits when he can. Another family is producing a video, a mechanism for cousins who no longer know they are related, to get acquainted. A few families were involved in Internet research on genealogy; however, no families in our corpus had webpages or weblogs, although that is becoming a more common practice (as we discuss in Chapter 5). Neither did any routinely communicate with each other through electronic mail, although individual family members use it for other purposes. Other families, of course, might differ in their uses of alternative and new technologies of transmission and storage of family stories.

Task-ordering that supports occasions for family storytelling continues to rely heavily on ethnic women's unpaid labor in the home, although the postsentimental shift to third-party services outside the home as well as greater participation by family men can lighten that burden. Some participants attributed changes in rituals to changing roles of women in family and society, citing women's entry into the workforce. Considering the powerful conservative discourse that blames feminism for the "decline" in the family, and that "kids today," enmeshed in consumer and popular culture, were not spared criticism, the relative lack of talk focused on women's work is interesting. Perhaps Franco-American women manage the "double shift" of work and homemaking. An alternative explanation might be that mothers are not criticized in Franco-American families. Regis Langelier (1996) explains the family's "tremendous need to protect the mother from any negative comments by other family members" as an instance of family homeostasis. Uma Narayan (1997) distinguishes feminist daughters' strategies for telling their mothers' stories inside the family—a personal project—from the political project of feminist analysis. We can also recall how a father's story about increasing his education (the GED story) was a family kernel, developed by multiple participants in diverse settings, but that the mother's story of continuing her education beyond his was told only once, by her, with women as audience. These juxtaposed stories show how family storytelling displays normative gender roles in the father's story and eschews the transgressive display in the mother's story. Finally, we note that women often continue to do the demanding and invisible labor to facilitate family storytelling willingly, choosing to take on the extra work of preparing family rituals. This labor offers an opportunity to perform their worth as homemaker and mother, validated and valued as the center of family culture. Task-ordering regulates a tension between access to and manipulation of information to control family activities. Doing the required and extra work can bring satisfaction, even power, for women's efforts.

The Politics of "Good Tellings" as a Strategy of Family Culture Survival

Families perform themselves with special urgency as they span generations and enter a new century of transformations, internal and external. As a small group ecology situated in a complex and changing environment, a family processes information as one form of cultural work. As families tell and listen to stories, they order the inflow, outflow, and distribution of information around the definitions of tasks. From the communication perspective of task-ordering, family is a site of struggle over how this cultural work gets done and who does it. Telling family stories is a strategy of cultural survival that requires participation for its success. "Good tellings" result in the accomplishment of the tasks of storytelling, but they simultaneously rely upon and reveal a politics of storytelling rights and responsibilities at work in the family.

The tasks of ordering basic, interpreted, and innovated information in families define generations. In one idealized variation, the senior generation (grandparents) retrieves basic information of family history and memory which the middle generation (parents) transmits and interprets to the younger generation (children). Younger generations innovate information that responds to changing environments, directing the flow of information upward as well as downward through family. This three-generational structure identified by McFeat (1974) and illustrated by some Franco-American families appears particularly suited to the organization of the nuclear family because it requires only intermittent contact with grandparents. Other families in our corpus maintained greater contact, however, some sharing the same household. And, we would expect to find alternative task structures for other forms of family. The three-generational structure of complementary relations also shifts when tasks of interpreting and innovating dominate interaction and as more symmetrical relations between generations emerge. In times of stress and rapid change, the grandparents' roles as legitimators of culture may wane as parents struggle to respond to environmental pressures. Our research corpus revealed fewer instances of young children narrating than did other studies (e.g., Blum-Kulka, 1997). Families we studied devised various ways to work together and apart on the tasks of transmitting content, forming subunits and alliances between spouses, cross-generational pairs, and family sides. For example, our corpus revealed how subunits work together in varieties of co-narration such as family fusion and fission, parallel labor, and motherlines. Different allocation of storytelling tasks differentiates families from one another.

Because generations are precisely relative, that is relational to each other, tasks of retrieving, interpreting, and innovating content may be collapsed between two generations or, as in the case of the interview between a family member and researcher, within one generation. However, if only information retrieval is accomplished, a pattern of task allocation and telling that privileges the storytelling rights of the senior generation, the family may not survive environmental demands of interpretation and change. Cultural memory is not adapted to new needs, and the family performs itself to itself, closing the boundary to the environment, other small group cultures, and new inflow of information. Conversely, a family which engages only in innovating information in response to environmental demands, privileging the rights of the youngest generations to narrate, will cease to have a culture to transmit to succeeding generations because memory work remains undone. The border to the environment is so open that generations of transmission are no longer created, and all information must be innovated or taken from sources outside the family. Within these politics of telling, the middle generation faces the greatest responsibilities for allocating and implementing the multiple tasks of telling that support transmission and the survival of small group culture, remembering the past and anticipating the future of the family.

A second strategy of cultural survival is the allocation of storytelling tasks by gender. The sexual division of labor in the family is elaborated, and extended by women's labor to make storytelling possible. Examining the labor of family women in the corpus revealed two tasks of storytelling in addition to the work of retrieving, interpreting, and innovating information—conversational work and kinwork. Conversational work facilitates storytelling itself through interactional tactics, while kinwork orders events and prepares occasions for storytelling through the organization of family gatherings, such as meals, visits, and holidays. This additional narrative labor is made weightier when ethnic women bear responsibility for transmitting cultural identity through homemaking as a haven and source of tradition. Class constraints may add another layer of stress; ethnic working-class women have limited access to consumer goods and services with which to provide celebrations of family. The special and often invisible labor of women to support conversation and kin is valuable, positioning women at the center of family, pragmatically and symbolically, and it serves cultural survival. In Aimee's family story about having to pick eggs as a child, her mother offers language descriptive of the layers of women's narrative labor: "somebody's got to pick eggs / somebody's got to shovel manure / if you're in college you are not shoveling manure / so those poor guys that are out doing it / hey that's a job we don't have to do." Picking eggs and shoveling manure serve as metaphor for family women's conversational work and kinwork that support storytelling and family culture survival. Like Aimee's mother, we wish to highlight the gendered politics by which family women assume a disproportionate burden for family storytelling.

Ordering tasks by generation and gender routinizes them and maintains the family over time. But the importance of generation and gender does not originate in the identity characteristics of age, authority, or sex. In communication terms, transmission requires only that some family members are principally tellers while others are principally listeners, and that each experiences the other's role. Thus, loss of information about family history or loss of an individual family member is less consequential than loss of a storytelling task. Stated in the positive, transmission is better served when tasks are invested in roles that are fluid among individuals and mobile between generations. Strategies that increase redundancy in messages (stories) and tactics that augment participation (telling and listening) of family members promote the flexibility and diversity that can adapt to internal and external changes for a family. Our analysis identifies two narrative possibilities that widen the range of redundancy and increase participation in family storytelling: the kernel story and collaborative telling.

The kernel story is communally owned, repeated, and widely known in the family. It is illustrated by the GED story told by different participants in different conversations to make different points. The structure of a kernel story is not found in the story itself but in the story's relation to family context, on which it depends for development. A kernel story is part of the conversation in which it occurs, and the conversation is part of the story. In the context of spiralling from story to conversation to story to conversation, different family participants make connections by substituting aspects of their experience for aspects of the story. The kernel story thus becomes a family story, communally shared, and it functions to promote group solidarity. A family may use a kernel story to retrieve sedimented meanings of the normative family and their own family history; alternatively, they may transgress and rework these meanings to innovate content to meet new environmental challenges. The kernel story forms a family culture and confirms its accepted values, and it transforms family culture by incorporating new values.

Collaborative tellings are illustrated by ways families work together in couples, pairs, sides, and lines. One example is the courtship story, a group production within two generations of family women, which exemplified the proposition "let us (all) tell your (singular) story" previously identified by Blum-Kulka (1997). Collaboration emphasizes group performance rather than individual participation. Participants employ a variety of strategies to support the work of storytelling. Increased participation has the potential to either solidify or to challenge group culture. Because they structure more symmetrical relations among generations, the tasks of interpreting and innovating information are more problematic for consensus than is retrieving basic information. We note some sources of tension and disagreement in tellings, but our corpus displayed more intrafamilial support than contestation. Although this may be a function of performance for an outside listener, McFeat (1974) notes that task-ordering requires consent and consensus in ways that content-ordering does not. Family members may disagree on content, for example, the details of a story, without disturbing small group culture. Collaboration suggests shared responsibility for speaking and listening rather than an assertion of individual rights. Ways of working together to accomplish the tasks of story-telling result in a process of collaborative canonization that contributes to family hegemony (Georgakapoulou, 1997) and fusion of family perspectives.

Taken together, kernel stories embody the major narratives of a family, and collaborative strategies show the kind of work required for their performance. These exemplars increase group participation in storytelling and enhance the generality, timing, sedimentation, and generic adaptions of stories by families we describe in the previous chapter. Elsewhere (Langellier & Peterson, 1992) we argue that the kernel story and collaborative tellings constitute a model of women (not women's) storytelling, carefully delineating that the use of this model is strategic rather than inherent or incidental, arising out of specific circumstances, constraints, and resources for storytelling. The differential use of strategies within particular speech contexts assumes the rationality of discourse as its explanation, rather than sex (biological differences) or gender (social power). Similarly, families' use of kernel stories and collaborative tellings responds to a realistic assessment of transmission possibilities: if care is not taken by participants to discover, share, and connect stories with each other and with themselves, they—stories and families—will cease to exist. The allocation of tasks by generation and by gender, wherein the middle generation and women assume greater responsibilities, are one but not the only way to do family. Task-ordering that disciplines by gender, particularly as it is over-determined by the sexual division of labor in the family, makes it difficult to challenge and change. However, to the extent that the tasks of storytelling are not inherent in age, sex, familial authority, or social power, they can potentially be undertaken by interested participants of either sex or any generation. Our corpus provided examples of men's interaction and kinwork as performance possibilities for family narrative.

Task-ordering generates internal rules for "good tellings" that promote cultural survival. We have adapted McFeat's informal ground rules for task-ordering to suggest how families foster transmission of small group culture (McFeat, 1974, pp. 155–56). We intend this summary list to be suggestive rather than normative:

1. Basic information about family history is not open to everyone. Retrieving basic information about family history tends to stabilize small group culture.

2. Family storytellers/narrators of any generation are valued over listeners by virtue of their control over basic information.

3. The senior generation (grandparents) are special people.

4. Interpreted and innovated information is open to any family member. Arguing over interpretations and innovations tends to minimize generational status differences.

5. Younger generations and new family members bring new information and introduce different perspectives into the family. New information tends to promote adaptation to changing environments.

6. Family members, sometimes as couples, cross-generational pairs, sides, and lines, develop a variety of ways to co-narrate and listen to stories. Task-ordering in the hands of one or a few tends to gain efficiency but risks distortion and loss of information.

7. Someone, usually but not necessarily a woman, assumes responsibility for fostering conversation and interaction among family members.

8. Family members, usually but not necessarily women, create and prepare occasions for family gatherings. Such occasions may be traditional, adapted, or innovated.

9. Family stories that are significant are coded in multiple settings by multiple family members.

10. Code-switching (different languages, different versions, different tactics, different media) around the same family stories promotes transmission.

11. If a family story is complex or transgressive, or family culture otherwise not easily transmittable, it may be simplified, muted, transmitted only under certain circumstances, or lost.

Families perform themselves in the shifting relations of communication among tellers, listeners, narrators, and characters. In ordering content they develop their stories to tell. In ordering tasks, they process this content in ongoing performances. Task-ordering as performance, a making and doing of family, adapts to different kinds of environments and different kinds of technologies of storytelling. The allocation of the work of storytelling and the definition of those tasks form different small group cultures. In the conversations and rituals of family, group identities are formed, solidified, and transformed. In the next chapter we examine family storytelling as group-ordering that responds to questions about who we are, especially questions about ethnic identity.

CHAPTER 4

Performing Families

Ordering Group and Personal Identities

On a daily basis, families "get a life" by producing and consuming narratives about themselves. Put another way, a person gets a family (life) by daily performances of telling and listening to its stories. Sidonie Smith and Julia Watson (1996) elaborate that "*this telling and consuming of autobiographical stories, this announcing, performing, composing of identity becomes a defining condition of postmodernity in America*" (p. 7; italics in original). In this chapter we examine family storytelling for its capacity to order group and personal identities: how American families get a life and how a person gets a family life through performing narrative. This final chapter in our discussion on family storytelling extends the meaning of getting a life to embrace "getting it," that is, understanding some consequences of cultural identity performance in the historical situation of postmodernity.[1]

According to Gillis (1996), the contemporary family is asked to create its own myths, rituals, and images, engaging with special urgency in a postmodern culture of performative display. In conversation, rituals, and storytelling, families perform themselves to themselves and to others. In these performances, families proclaim self-definitions of worth and vitality (Myerhoff, 1992). As Stone (1988) announces, "[family] stories last not because they're entertaining, though they may be; they last because in ways large and small they matter" (p. 5). To ask Butler's question, what matters for families and what families matter? What identities are at stake in the performing of their stories? For several centuries autobiographical storytelling has played a significant role in the making, unmaking, and remaking of "American" identity, and it continues to be a "palpable means through which Americans know themselves to be American and not-American in all those complexities and contradictions of that identity" (Smith & Watson, 1996, p. 6). How does family storytelling define "American" identity in postmodernity? How do groups of families negotiate their complex positioning within cultural uniquenesses and assimilation in multicultural America?

Storytelling participates in family as institution and as agency. As an institutional practice, performing family stories is part of a frame-up which takes up, circulates, and renews models of acceptable identity in society according to local norms: good mothers and fathers, good children, good families. This mapping may involve idealizations as the *family lived by* is mapped onto the *family lived with* (Gillis, 1996). The ordering of content (Chapter 2) can be stated in terms of what can be spoken and what stories or parts cannot be spoken, what narrative forms can be circulated and what stories cannot be readily understood or easily credited. Task-ordering (Chapter 3) can be stated in terms of who speaks and who listens, how alignments are solicited and acted out, and who is responsible for the work of storytelling. Families order and frame information selectively in terms of institutional needs and routines, for example, the particular generational and gender responsibilities for work, including creation of occasions for family storytelling. Simultaneously, performing family stories engages a possibility for agency to build personal and communal identities that resist major narratives of family. Resistance may take forms of struggle, refusal, repudiation, or contestation. Everyday occasions for family storytelling are multiple and dispersed; their situations vary by historical moment, place, participants, and purposes of narrating. Situated and embodied in performance, family storytellers may reframe meanings, redistribute tasks, and remake identities, both personal and communal.

The very idea of identity is imbricated in the conception of narrative performance (Bochner, 1994; Brockmeier & Carbaugh, 2001; Mishler, 1999); indeed, narrative is a privileged site of identity performance. Understood as performance, identity is not the act of a fixed, unified, or final essence that serves as the origin or accomplishment of family experience. Rather, in performing narrative, families struggle over personal and family identities that are always destabilized and deferred. Family is an ongoing formation rather than a natural, pregiven phenomenon. This non-essentialized conception of identity aligns post-structuralism with multiculturalism to decenter, destabilize, and multiply family identities and to resist recreating master narratives of the family. What we commonly call "the family" is not a single, naturally occurring biological phenomenon but variations in small group cultures produced in embodied, situated, and material performances such as family storytelling. Family storytelling is a multileveled strategic discourse carried out in diverse situations by multiple participants who order personal and group identities as family.

We emphasize once more that in our performance approach, family is both the medium and outcome of performing narrative. By medium, we mean the specific group and institutional arrangements in space which provide the environment for the storage, retrieval, and transmission of messages over time.

A family is an embodied communication medium that ensures the production and reproduction of stories and sensibilities through content-ordering and task-ordering. Content-ordering generates family stories whose situated tellings are allocated according to material relations of generation and gender. Task-ordering makes possible a third level of semiotic analysis; for what is constituted in performing family narrative is neither simply content nor only labor. This residue or excess may be thought of as identity. "The group is seen to 'explain itself to itself,' thus providing contexts that are intensely local. Outcomes tend to be group-specific" (McFeat, 1974, p. 61). The outcomes of performing narrative are local models of family identity: "who we are, where we came from, and where we are going." In narrative terms, family storytelling discursively produces and reproduces local notions of "goodness," that is, good stories, good tellings, and good families.

Let us briefly revisit Nicole's courtship story for an illustration of how a local model of identity is produced in family storytelling. When her mother and two aunts (three sisters) called for Nicole to tell the story of how she got together with her husband, she responded with the romance story we analyze in Chapter 2. As the sisters reworked this story, they ordered content that filled in the narrative gap of the three-month hiatus when Nicole's boyfriend "dumped" her. This content contributed the emotional meanings of her misery and the tender sensibilities of their emotional work and support during this "awful" time. As task-ordering (analyzed in Chapter 3), the narrative performance first allocated telling rights to the protagonist Nicole but then redistributed the telling among the three sisters in a collaborative performance that reframed the conjugal courtship into a family standpoint, transforming Nicole's "I" to the family women's "we." This "we" bears the marks of this particular family's dynamics, locale, and material constraints. The outcome, a local model of the family lived with, might be described as an intergenerational, working-class, woman-centered family identity that simultaneously embraces and subverts romantic ideals of love and marriage. The storytelling maintains a tension between Nicole's personal narrative of the romance plot that led to her marriage and the view of marriage as family business.

As a small group culture retrieves, interprets, and innovates information, it differentiates an internal boundary and a group identity. Group-ordering depends upon the maintenance of a boundary, but how this boundary is maintained is key for understanding local models of small group culture. McFeat (1974) argues against the notion that group identity is maintained by separating groups and segregating traits of groups such that they are most ideal and typical when they are isolated from others. Boundaries are maintained not through avoidance but through interaction between individuals and the group, and between groups. This interaction was illustrated in the collaborative production of Nicole's courtship story with extended family. As McFeat elaborates, groups "appear to require regulatory mechanisms which accommodate sets of contrary facts: what brings uniqueness and adaptation is opposed to that which brings disturbing features from the outside that will not go away" (p. 167). In performing family, group-ordering regulates tensions between individual interests and group interests, and among different family groups' interests. Differentiating boundaries among family groups constructs ethnic identities, such as Franco-American families.

Family stories embody individual, group, and ethnic tensions, and family storytelling is one site for the performative struggle over identities that matter. Our analysis of group-ordering in Franco-American family storytelling first describes how persons "get a family" and the regulation of individual and group relations in terms of family hegemony and intrafamilial contestation, including discussion of individualism and idealization as forces in performing family. Then we turn to group-ordering that differentiates boundaries around nuclear, extended, communal, and network relations to form families, including "getting an ethnic family." We conclude with a discussion of the politics of performing family in postmodernity that engages issues of white ethnicity, assimilation, and racism.

Getting a Family: Person-Group Relations

Phenomenologically speaking, the family is "an irreducible reality that is constituted by a plurality of actors and is, as it were, an added quality to the presence of an individual actor when he or she is acting *qua* member of the family" (McLain & Weigert, 1979, p. 172). The family is experienced as extending beyond the physical limits of the body, part of a we-relationship different from other social institutions. This we-relationship is embodied in the intimacy, immediacy, and intensity of family time and family space that structure a reciprocity of perspectives. The "I" of the person emerges from a familial "we." This "I" is a specifically "enfamilied self," a central source of identity performance bestowed and symbolized by personal and family names (p. 173) and narrated in family stories. The unique lived experience of family provides the enfamilied person with a biography that derives larger meanings from its location in the process of ordering activities in daily life (task-ordering) and the events of family history (content-ordering).

Naming Stories and Family Identities:
"Germaine and Patooooou"

In terms of group-ordering, names reveal the tensions of personal and group relations in family and of family in the social world. Names are bestowed in the family and validated in interaction with others. Family names establish temporality in genealogical lines, predominantly those of patrimony in the

United States. In Chapter 2 we discussed the way genealogy anchors patri-archy and the "purity" of, usually, white Anglo-Saxon identity. Four families in our corpus had done or were doing genealogies that trace their heritage to French Canada and sometimes to France. Personal names were also passed down from previous generations in a few families; for example, Bernadette was named after a deceased aunt. Nicknames sometimes mark families and children as French, for example, Blanc (white), Émile-a-Siméon (Simon's son), and Memorie (a variation on Emily). In a comical story, one participant per-forms the booming soprano voice of a mother calling her children—"Ger-maine and Patooooooou"—heard all the way across the river and to the town on the other side. Patou is an affectionate French American nickname that se-cures both a personal and ethnic group identity. Nicknames, especially for young people, may also be bestowed by those outside the family, a source of identity formation that flows inward and upward in family.

At the same time, names may reveal family tensions with the social world, its discursive and material constraints. One family session indexed all the family nicknames on the paternal side, including "Nigger" for the darkest one in the family. Perhaps like Bérubé, the daughter was aware that "the casual use of the word 'nigger' marked our family as low class, ignorant, and preju-diced" (1997, p. 51). In any case, she immediately followed this statement with the story of an athletic event at a nearby military base where this racial-ized naming was uncomfortably challenged by the presence of African Amer-icans. Interaction at the boundaries of family with outside groups complicated the nicknaming within the family and differentiated alignments of those fam-ily members who felt "they didn't mean anything by it" and those concerned with racism and the racialized context of American identities.

As an ethnic group, Franco-Americans had themselves been racialized and discriminated against, subjected to epithets such as Frenchy, Frog, and Ca-nuck. Linguistic, religious, and class conflict subjected Franco-Americans to two hundred years of discrimination, oppression, and poverty.[2] Ethnic fric-tions and class conflict pitted French workers against other immigrants in the white ethnic hierarchy of New England.[3] A language law in Maine, instituted in 1920 and repealed in 1976, suppressed French. Public schoolteachers ad-monished French children to "speak white," a racist form of ethnic shaming that drew on the promise of white privilege because of their European ances-try. Franco-American history attests to "race" as a malleable concept, a "float-ing signifier" that calls upon mutable historical and cultural discourse for its claims (Hall, 1992; Gilroy, 2000). "Whiteness" is a variable achievement in contested interactions with other groups (e.g., Ignatiev, 1995; Brodkin, 1998).

In the face of linguistic hostility, religious persecution, employment dis-crimination, and ethnic and racialized slurs, many French changed their fam-ily names to more English-sounding and English-spelling forms. One source on French Island history lists 152 Anglicized French names (*Nos Histoires de l'Ile*, 1999, p. 131–132). Some were Anglicized by translation (e.g., Leveque to Bishop, Deschene to Oaks), some by more English sounds and spellings (e.g., Ouellette to Willett, Labbé to Libby), and others more arbitrarily (e.g., Vachon to Cowan). Gerald, for example, narrates how his grandfather changed his French name to an English one in an effort to enhance his job opportunities. Like the patriarchal practice of women taking their husband's name, Anglicized family names obscure ethnic difference and intergroup conflict. Simultaneously, they make it more difficult to find and form ethnic group identities. Name changes are an example of environmental pressures and adaptions that destabilized Franco-American identity in terms of cultural history and family genealogy. Names—family, personal, and nicknames—both reflect and reveal identity issues internal to family, between individuals and the group, and between groups. Names inscribe family history, personalize the identity of individuals, and interact with groups and forces outside family boundaries, but they are not simply family matters. They interact across borders of identity with pressures and repercussions in a social world of discursive and material constraints.

The following story combines personal and family names with tensions between the enfamilied self, family group, and cultural identity. Introduced as the "birthday cake story," it is told by Lena, a mother in her sixties. Lena introduces the story by providing the family name of her French Canadian grandmother whose one-hundredth birthday the extended family is celebrating. She details the rollicking trip ("it was funny, a riot" and "I told you it was wild") on a school bus with forty-five family members driving thirteen hours north of Montreal for the big party. Lena's daughter listens with Kristin.

> *Lena:* at the party they had this hu:ge cake
> oh I'll tell you it was at least this big [gestures with arms]
>   if not bigger
> and it was uh bei::ge frosting
>   and all the writing was done . brown dark brown
> so in the middle there was my grandmother's name
>   which was Appaulienne
>   which is a derivation that I've got
>
> *Kristin:* okay
>
> *Lena:* she was Appaulienne
> so they had her name
> and then they had all of her children
>   there was eleven or twelve of them
> then they had all the grandchildren
> that went— she had 87 of them
>
> *Kristin:* oh my gosh

> *Lena:*   [quickly] so they're all written in brown except mine
> [slowly] mine is written red white and blue
> *Kristin:*   ooh
> *Lena:*   the only one born in the United States
> *Kristin:*   ooh
> *Lena:*   wasn't that dramatic
> that was <u>dramatic</u> for me

By the story's end the emotion has changed from one of gaiety about the trip and party to something more somber. What was dramatic for Lena was not the celebratory moment of unveiling the one-hundredth birthday cake, but the identities marked in the frosting and her difference from all the others. Comments later in the session connect the birthday cake story to other family themes. The *Réveillons* of family in the United States have stopped, extended family has moved back to Canada, and Lena is an only child with a husband whose only brother died in 1949: "we're basically alone, which is one thing I've always despised. I wanted a big family." She loved Canada and all the cousins there, and "When I went to Canada I never wanted to come home." She tells how she dreamed of going to Canada to be a schoolteacher and had a job offer when she was younger. "Oh, I was tempted," she says, "if it hadn't been for my mother . . . I should have been a Canadian girl." She continues that "I was one of those that listened to my family. They said no is no. It was not maybe." The story is told with resignation but also regret and some bitterness. Her storytelling weaves a retrospective with a hypothetical event, a prospective narrative that never takes place. Group-ordering in this family story mediates the tensions between personal desire and responsibility to family, and it appears to resolve these tensions by subordinating individual to family interests.

Notably, Lena is telling these stories to her daughter as well as to Kristin. The message to her daughter appears to be multiple and mixed. As a character in the story, the mother performs a daughter who is obedient and "good" in accordance with the parental authority characteristic of French American families (French, 1981). Yet her performance as narrator does not mask the cost of her dutifulness; it expresses what Dorothy Allison calls women's "loss of their own hopes, their own futures" (1994, p. 33). The telling secures a group identity for the family, but the attempt does not escape the ambiguities inherent in the boundary drawn. Performing family enacts U.S.-Canada border crossings, but the boundary differentiates the family as contradictorily nuclear and extended. The family bounded by nuclear relations has identified itself as an American family but according to the mores of parental authority in French families. The presence of the boundary reflects and perpetuates the ambivalence of Franco-American identity with ties to French Canada as well as notions of the "good" daughter. It also reveals generational conflict embedded in specific ethnic rules for legitimate ways to "leave" family—in this instance, a turning point not taken by Lena.

"Everything we wanted, everything we thought": *The Familial "We" and Group Identities*

Group-ordering may create local models that idealize or totalize the "we" of family. The we-relationship in which family interests prevail may be performed through daily life and in storytelling. Fifteen minutes into a session with a mother, father, daughter Aimee, and Kristin, the mother charges, "you haven't asked me how they [the children] behaved at the table," so Kristin quickly submits and dutifully delivers the question. "Good!" the mother answers in one word, and she then describes how their eleven children came promptly to dinner when she called and how they sat in birth order on long benches. She served each one, and there was "no fighting about who, where, and what" and "no fooling around." She states that she gave attention to the children as a group rather than individually. Each child had daily chores, including a routine of seven girls drying dishes which the eighth one washed. Aimee explained that one dried plates, one forks, and so on, and she confirmed that she enjoyed the order and stability of parental authority. In their joint storytelling, Aimee and her mother perform roles of "good" daughter and "good" mother. Kristin, although a family outsider, likewise enacted the "good" daughter within the family script and mother's directives (as discussed by Langellier & Hall, 1989).

However, this "we" of family was not easily translated to parties outside its boundaries whose ideology is based on individualism. Aimee and her mother narrate a story of failing to convince financial aid officers to increase Aimee's aid package after she is accepted to a prestigious private college in Maine. Aimee believes that the officials were unable to understand that her parents could not provide her with money that they did not give equally to their other children. The storytelling is emotionally charged, with the mother describing how she "cried and cried" on the trip home; both mother and daughter are tearful as they co-narrate the heart of the story. The story concludes with the information that instead of the expensive private school, Aimee attended the more affordable state university campus nearest home. In sets of matching evaluations that provide a resolution to the narrative, Aimee and her mother recoup the painful experience as more than a concession. The mother quotes statistics on the local university's high rating in liberal arts education, and Aimee finds the first teacher who affirms her North American French language and bilingual family background, and who encourages her first studies in France. The outcome of interaction with outside others—specifically, conflict over higher education—secures both group and personal identities.

Group-ordering may create local models where personal identity embodies family definition in a totalizing process which casts the specific values and practices of one member onto the whole group. Novelist Claire Messud (1999) writes that, "Without my father, the very notion of a family seemed a poor chimera, and all our history like so many arbitrary stories" (p. 328). One family member, by dint of character or fate, may define a family's identity. For example, the story of the father who had a life-threatening injury at age twenty (introduced in Chapter 2) braids the entire family narrative, weaving markers of family history into his personal story of perseverance and faith. Their courtship is linked to the night before the accident and embedded in the long convalescence in Providence, Rhode Island, where his wife-to-be sent cards and visited him. The birth of their four children is couched in a joking comment about his not taking so many pain pills so as to prevent their conception. Family livelihood is narrated in terms of the father's ability to do construction work, and when he could no longer withstand its physical demands, he prays in desperation for a job that he can do. A blueprint for an invention comes to him in a dream, and the income helps support them to retirement. The family story hinges not just on the father's strength and perseverance but on his faith, which thematically linked the telling of the accident story and the invention story: "the priest saved my leg," and the invention comes from God in a dream. The father takes the primary narrative role, but his story is supported, co-narrated, and elaborated throughout by his wife and daughter. The father's injury orders the family history; and his personal identity, reinforced by his religious belief, anchors the family definition.

Fathers may be family heroes, but mothers may be saints, an idealizing narrative strategy promoted in Yvonne's poignant story of her mother's death. In this story, without the mother the very notion of family is a "poor chimera" and their stories without order or force. A tribute by the daughter Yvonne, the story is simultaneously a testimony of her love and the legacy she inherits. The storytelling describes the ravages of her mother's cancer and the prognosis of her death by July. But the mother outlives the medical prediction. In a segment of reported speech, Yvonne quotes the doctors: "Is she holding off for a date or something?" to which Yvonne supplies the fiftieth wedding anniversary date in October. Yvonne also offers the indirect speech of others: "Others will say she [her mother] is a saint." The day of her mother's death—one day before the anniversary—is narrated in symbolic and spiritual tropes. On that early October morning, Yvonne and her husband step into the dawn to see what she identifies as two rainbows with handles touching, and what she interprets as a sign that "Mama's in heaven." Later in the session, Yvonne tells about the hospice training she and one of her sisters underwent. On separate teams in a training session, the sisters drew the same family picture: a grouchy father, two grouchy brothers, a mother with a halo and apron, and three sisters laughing. In her sister's drawing, Yvonne is distinguished by her eyeglasses, but she also sports a halo like their mother. Although her words stop short of saying her mother is a saint—others do that—her narrative performance bespeaks that idealized identity in its group-ordering of personal and family identities.

Family heroes and saints enjoy high tellability. Narrating the remarkable lives and deaths of extraordinary individuals orders family identity through ideal actors and totalizing actions. Recitations of their stories fill in identity and firm up the family boundary. One person's life simultaneously substitutes for the whole family's and obscures the whole. These narrative tactics fix characters and create family as a reification that stands over and against actual family members and families, those lived with. It is not just that real persons do not live up to the idealizations or are marginalized by totalizations, but that a model can become so hegemonic that it commands belief in a myth of unchanging continuity with the past and contributes to the ongoing construction of identity. Idealizing and totalizing strategies pick out certain characters and events over others in a process of cultural selection (Narayan, 1997; McKay, 1994). This cultural selectivity contributes both to myths and to stereotypes, for families and for ethnic groups. The story of Yvonne's "good" mother, for example, incarnates the icon of the mythic mother mooring the family. The "good" father story embodies the enduring faith in Roman Catholicism integrating Franco-American identity with religion.

"Mom, I don't believe in that": Intrafamilial Contestation and Personal Identities

Cultural selectivity of icons and images highlights the power of narrative as a cultural strategy to create an idealized whole of the family "we." Performing narratives of "good" family members and families not only wards off criticism and change, but it also conceals the negative pole of family and ethnicity. From a transnational feminist perspective, Narayan (1997) argues that intragroup contestation reveals cultural differences within groups that critique ethnic identities and traditions. In parallel fashion, family storytelling exposes intrafamilial contestation as well as family hegemony. For example, the we-relationship of Aimee's family cozily lined up on benches for dinner was not without conflict. In a separate interview Aimee discloses that although the girls got to the table first, the boys got the best food.[4] In another interview, a feminist daughter challenged her mother's favoritism to her sons, a charge the mother forcefully denied. The moment was tense and quickly passed, the conflict patched over with humor. But these examples suggest how feminist daughters may contest sexism in family culture: "Just as daughters seldom recount their mother's stories in the same terms as their mothers tell them, feminist daughters often have accounts of their mother-cultures that differ in significant ways from the culture's own dominant accounts of itself"

(Narayan, 1997, p. 9). Narayan distinguishes the morally delicate project of a daughter telling the intertwined story of her mother from the political project of retelling the mother-culture in feminist terms. Family experience is differentiated in terms of gender and generation, as we argued about task-ordering in Chapter 3. Disturbances from the outside that will not go away include the forces of feminisms and tensions introduced into family through youth culture.

Sons also participate in intrafamilial contestation that challenges the family "we." Alain, for example, tells a story of his rejection of a distinctive family role. It concerns the tradition of bloodstopping, a healing practice among the French that developed in the northern woods when accidents occurred and no medical help was available. The ability to heal depended upon the belief of both the bloodstopper and the victim. Alain's father was a bloodstopper, well-known and sought out within the ethnic community, and Alain is the son designated to succeed his father in the next generation. However, Alain states:

> I never <u>believed</u> in it
> and it's supposed to be passed on to me from my <u>father</u>
> my mother used to say I used to have wicked toothaches
>   she'd say well ask your <u>father</u>
>   he'd get rid of them
> I'd say Mom I don't <u>believe</u> in that
>   I'm a young man now
>   I don't <u>believe</u> in that
> so ah it never was passed on to me

Despite this disclaimer in which he declines the passing of his father's mantle, Alain offers a gripping story in which his father saves a man's life after a shooting accident. The historical moment may contribute to Alain's skepticism: bloodstopping animates the lore of older people and earlier times. Still, he continues to embrace the place of its roots, living on French Island where his father was born.

Alain narrates a turning point in his biographies away from his father, but he still obtains a personal identity within family definitions. His story opens up options, but does not undermine group identity. Personal differences become a greater concern in performing family because only certain kinds of biographical differences can be legitimated within the family world. The enfamilied self may legitimately "leave" family, for example, by getting married, going into the military, entering religious life, going away to college, or taking a distant job. However, any of these leavings might be contested.[5] On one level such leavings are symbolic, but as border crossings out of family, they are a site of narrative struggle and anxiety. Marriage, perhaps the most legitimated way to exit family, aligns a family member with a new family (the in-laws) and itself inaugurates a new family. Aimee says that "it's very hard to leave home," and in her family, she claims that marriage is the only acceptable way to leave the family. Families also may have proximity rules for how close to home children ought to stay, rules that may be constrained by gender (Stone, 1988). As important from family interests may be how a symbolic leaving is carried out. In a cursory narration, one mother told that her only son, while overseas in the military, married a woman the family had never met. The wedding in Wales not only violated the mother's expressed wishes, but it also excluded the family not only as participants but also as narrators—there is little story to tell. Another husband and wife suggest tensions around a son whose wife cares for her own mother, leaving little time or energy for visits to them. Young, single daughters and granddaughters who "live away" in other states raise a mix of concern and pride. Their future, in terms of family identity, is not yet known, their identities engaged, at least for the time being, with individual pursuits.

Divorce is a familiar way to leave a family. Legally accessible in the United States for generations, it is a commonplace in family histories. The Franco-American family's devotion to Catholicism held divorce in check in the first half of the twentieth century, but these families now divorce at the same rate as the national average. Divorce presents a narrative challenge in performing family because it disrupts narrative teleology, which is both retrospective and prospective. Retrospectively, a narrative ends before "till death do us part" and ruptures the myth of continuity. Prospectively, planning for the future, especially if there are children, is interrupted or dispersed across households. We noted in Chapter 2 that in family storytelling divorce stories lack the ready-made template such as that found in courtship stories. Although mentioned with some frequency or given in response to a question, they were not developed into family stories by participants for Kristin. They complicate the family "we" and expose tensions between individual and group interests and between personal and group identities. They accentuate the shifting, multiple, and ambiguous boundaries of family identity. At a family dinner, for example, a twelve-year-old grandchild was asked by her *mémère*, "what do you eat at home?" The granddaughter first distinguished between the before and after of her parents' divorce, and then what she eats at home with her mother and stepfather, and then with her father and stepmother.

To take another example from our corpus, an "illegitimate child" disturbs the boundary of family, even though it is not unusual in the social order. The youngest son of one family was unmarried with a child. The mother seemed to feel that this situation required an explanation to Kristin, which she supplied, conserving her son and bringing a grandson into the family narrative realm. But this boundary-setting raises a further question about who else is in family. Is the mother of the child? She is not in family pictures displayed in the house, which include the son and grandson. Both the retrospective and prospective teleology of family storytelling is complicated. This example clarifies, again, that no family is natural, and that all families are constructed in and through inclusions and exclusions that draw, undraw, and redraw boundaries of identity. Family is a set of discursive practices, storytelling one among them, as well as interpersonal relations.

New family members "enter" a family in ways other than by birth and through marriage. Adoption may be a muted or even proscribed story, or it may be highly tellable, with multiple versions for the child as listener, for family, or other adoptive parents. Some parents, particularly in transracial adoptions where their children visually differ from them, resent being called out by others, called upon to narrate personal and group identities. Under conditions where telling a family story is compelled, resistance resides in not telling. Sandra Patton (1996) explores narrative challenges of transracial adoptees: "In a society that defines 'real' families through biological ties, those of us with origin narratives beginning in a public agency rather than a human body cannot help but struggle with questions of who we 'really' are, who we might have been, and how our identities have been constructed" (p. 274). She calls for a genealogy of identity that goes beyond the family tree to the discursive orders of race and class, to forces outside and inside families that construct identity.

Group-ordering of family identities regulates individual and group interests. The we-relationship of family differs from other social institutions in terms of how the intimacy, immediacy, and intensity of lived time and lived space inform identity. In the process of group-ordering, families are partisans of the "we," the good-of-the-many which subordinates individual to family interests. As Stone (1988) elaborates,

> the fact is that the family, any family, has a major stake in perpetuating itself, and in order to do so it must unrelentingly push the institutions that preserve it—the institution of marriage especially, but also the institution of heterosexual romantic love which, if all goes the way family would have it go, culminates in marriage, children, and enhanced family stability. (p. 50)

The narrative logic from heterosexual romance to marriage to children not only stabilizes the family but also normalizes and naturalizes sexuality. Judith Roof (1996) calls this storytelling a "heteronarrative" of production and reproduction. Family storytelling ties sexuality into the service of family, restricting it to non-incestuous heterosexuality. The heteronarrative distinguishes "healthy" from "perverted" sexuality, and it constructs "gay" and "family" as mutually exclusive terms. "Thus, while healthy heterosexuality produces the proper reproductive narrative—like producing like and increasing (similar to well-invested capital)—perversions produce the wrong story: decrease, degenerescence, death" (p. 35). Roof also explores possibilities for counternarratives of sexual identity. Weston (1991) examines the "families we choose" constructed by lesbians and gay men to redefine family in more diverse and inclusive terms that reduce the opposition of "gay" and "family." Ruthann Robson (1994) argues, however, that the liberal redefinition of family, such as Weston advocates, may be less liberating than it promises if class relations are not considered. Liberal definitions of family rely upon functions as the formal relations of either spouse-spouse or parent-child, functions that "emphasize the economic, which is perhaps not surprising given our capitalist culture" (p. 988). She challenges that adopting the terms of a privileged category, such as "family," amounts to arguing for inclusion without sufficiently critiquing the privilege and category itself. From this perspective, arguments for inclusion may depoliticize, privatize, and domesticate counternarratives of family identities.

"I" and "We": Individualism and Performing Family

Group-ordering in family storytelling differentiates an internal boundary and a group identity. Local models of small group culture accommodate sets of contradictory facts and forces into group identities. In this schema, family storytelling regulates what brings uniqueness and adaptation of internal relations as opposed to what brings disturbing features from the outside that will not go away. Our discussion has emphasized the construction of the family identity as a small group cultural "we" in family stories, even as that group identity is complicated by intrafamilial contestation. We now extend the discussion by considering two additional issues in the politics of performing family: individualism as a force in family cultural formation, and the language of turning points in the narrative production of personal and group identity.

The sentimental family of the nineteenth century constructed home as a refuge from the individualism of industrializing forces. Individualism has a long history which is not new to families nor limited to the United States. Nonetheless, capitalist culture of the second half of the twentieth century intensified individualism to locate it not just outside of but also inside the postmodern (Bellah et al., 1985) and postsentimental family (Pleck, 2000). If what distinguishes the conditions of postmodernity in the last third of the twentieth century is how people get a life through telling their stories, these lives are imagined as possessions of individuals, and in turn, individual lives are seen as "representative" of a group (Smith & Watson, 1996). With regard to families, we have called this individualism a form of overpersonalization that allows praise and blame, celebration and criticism, to fall on individual family members or an individual family rather than on the discourses of power structuring family (Langellier & Peterson, 1993, 1995; Robson, 1994). Di Leonardo (1998) argues that the very notion of the unencumbered self is an American myth, an invented tradition of individualizing social orders (pp. 80–81).

We intervene in assumptions of individualism by taking the family group as the unit of analysis. The "I" of the enfamilied self emerges from the "we" of family culture; the enfamilied self is an encumbered self. Family story-telling reveals conflicts and contradictions in the formation of personal and group identities. The ordering of family identity occurs in interactions with others along group boundaries. To take an example from the formation of personal identity, consider that the courtship narrative is privileged in family storytelling, whereas the divorce story is muted. However, what love, marriage, and divorce share is a modern and postmodern grounding in the myth of individualism by which one enters or exits a family. That is, both romance and divorce invest in an ideology that views marriage as personal choice and fulfillment rather than an economic arrangement, alignment between families, or other social organization.

Conversely, the individual family member may be collapsed into the we-relationship of family. To take an example from group identities, individualism here draws an internal boundary around the nuclear family isolated from its environment. The story of the one-hundredth birthday party first creates family as an expansive, extended identity that crosses the U.S.-Canada border, and then the storytelling contracts that boundary to the proximity rules of the nuclear family. Indeed, the "American" family is identified as the nuclear family by this narrative logic. The adaptation of sewing sandwiches from the women's sewing circles on French Island to the daddy sandwiches of Alain's nuclear family shows a similar boundary shift that reflects changes in the amount of interaction among families (Chapter 2). The push to individualist discourse inside as well as outside families is powerful, and it denies the relational, interactional, encumbered self and family. Family storytelling narrates the ambivalences of identity formation, the tensions between family hegemony and intrafamilial contestation. It reveals rather than resolves struggles over personal and family interests.

Turning points narrated in family stories also engage the struggle between personal and group interests. The retrospective teleology of storytelling in which families look back produces turning points that construct identity. Making personal biographies and family histories is a production of visibility: special moments in individual and family life that stand out as turning points in identity formation (Sandell, 1999). Such moments function not just retrospectively but also prospectively, involving expectations, plans, and dreams for the future. In family storytelling, family members learn the special moments to record and anticipate. Family turning points such as courtships, births, and infant tales are generic and overdetermined. Their high visibility legitimates family interests of survival and reproduction, and their tellability fits in with retrospective-prospective trajectories of a family future. In these ways turning points help to seamlessly reproduce family ideology and hegemony.

The visibility of turning points depends upon the invisibility of other moments that make them possible. We discussed in Chapter 3 how the special occasions of family celebration depend on the invisible social relations and labor of family women. Moments that are not "special" to family interests—for example, infertility or the choice to be childless, children born to unmarried family members, remaining single, or homosexuality—are muted and marginalized in performing narrative. Simultaneously, however, family storytelling may give access to the veiled and muffled material circumstances and conditions that stand behind special moments. It may narrate habitual characters, actions, and the dailiness of family: for example, stories of the children's behavior at the table, preparing food, and nicknaming. These invisible moments have low tellability across family boundaries but may enjoy performance status within family.

Turning points within family culture may reveal differences among family members and family groups in the gaps and seams of group-ordering. Stories about rejecting a family tradition, changing a family name, or going to college when it is not part of family history suggest that family is a site of contestation and change. More explicitly, family hegemony may be contested by family members who challenge sexism or heterosexism, racism or classism as negative dimensions of family culture. Turning points highlight how intentional acts individualize a family member's life or a family life. In doing so, they point out the obvious: the subjectivity of family storytelling, which emanates from embodied and situated narrators. The family is not an undifferentiated whole, nor are families undifferentiated from each other. What might not be so obvious are the discursive forces that reify family, such as idealizations, genre, and the hegemony of heterosexism, sexism, racism, and classism. Family storytelling plays the tensions between individual and group interests, plies the edges of background and foreground, and obfuscates or emphasizes the ambivalences of boundary-setting in interactions with others. Turning points may either shore up or splinter the tradition of individualism.

"Well, we're all French, although . . .": Small Group Identities

As families perform themselves, they imagine and reproduce a group identity. No intrinsic criteria define an ethnic group. Identity construction is a reciprocal process of communication that sets boundaries and distinguishes "us" and "them" (Nakayama & Martin, 1999). A specific identity has meaning only in relation to other identities. According to Arjun Appadurai (1996), the performance of cultural identity is based less upon shared claims of blood, land, or language than on the work of imagination in a modern, global context. The nature of continuity of ethnic groups depends on the maintenance of a boundary through interaction rather than its avoidance. Constructed on the boundaries of group membership, ethnicity is malleable, historically contingent, shifting, and dispersed.

Family stories embody the built-in ambivalence of boundaries between "us" and "them." The assertion by one participant that "well, we're all French" is promptly unraveled by "although our children don't speak it." By this example we do not mean that speaking the French language is an essential criterion of ethnicity (people of many ethnicities speak French) but rather something more like: Franco-Americans are neither all like each other nor different from all other groups. No single criterion or combination of criteria—language (French), religion (Roman Catholicism), gender (male), age (elderly), or class (working)—defines what it means to be a Franco-American family. "Rather, 'Franco-American' names a terrain of contested affinities and commitments which shape participation of members within the social group and in contrast to other social groups" (Peterson, 1994, p. 65), participation which is localized and historicized. "We're all French, although" contains the structural ambiguity of the "all." Nor are we *all*, that is, entirely and purely, French. The history of French intermarriage with Native Americans is well documented, for example. If ethnic identity is a question of maintaining a boundary through interaction, who is in the circle of "we Franco-Americans" is not answerable outside specific situations and material conditions—nor outside family narrative.

In asking how families order identity in storytelling, we challenge assumptions about the "white ethnic community" (di Leonardo, 1998). The white ethnic community customarily assumes inner-city neighborhoods that are homogenous, self-reproducing, and long-term. The Franco-American manifestation is the Little Canada, *le Petit Canada*. But these neighborhoods were also ethnically heterogeneous, shifting between urban and rural settings, with families moving frequently to find or follow waged work (Louder & Waddell, 1993). Franco-Americans collected in some communities but also scattered throughout the Northeast and across the United States. Bérubé (1997) connects-the-dots of the "tortured geography" of Franco-American migration: Woonsocket, Rhode Island; Lewiston, Maine; Lafayette, Louisiana; Lowell, Massachusetts; Frenchtown, Montana; Cohoes, New York; Hollywood, Florida; Kankakee, Illinois; Ste. Genevieve, Missouri; and so on.

If never the discrete phenomenon assumed by "white ethnic community," Franco-Americans still established boundaries in interaction with other groups. Michael, who earlier in a storytelling session had described himself as "McDonaldized," questions if there is sufficient identity among Franco-Americans to build on for the next generation. His wife, Monica, responds:

> I guess I think that <u>all</u> of the stories
> that we talk about kind of fit in
>   that like

being Franco-American was . that was . that was
   even though that word "Acadian" was not in any vocabulary
   being Franco-American <u>was</u>
   it was just
   that's just who we were

In the sections that follow, we look at how family storytelling produces local models of group identities of "just who we were" in interaction over boundaries. Families differentiate boundaries around small groups, communities, and networks.

"We were just a French little community, our family itself"

The Gagnon family lives on a farm on a hill overlooking a pond in rural Maine. The parents married in the early 1960s; after a brief time living in town, they moved to a dilapidated, "almost decapitated" farmhouse that they gradually rebuilt and remodeled to house their eleven children. The father began working in the paper mill and then for a small company, but he wanted to be self-employed. On the farm he worked as a milkman, built an egg business, and started his own tire business. Self-employment kept both the father and mother at home, working and raising their large family. As the children grew up, they helped with the family businesses until the three sons took them over and built homes on the family property. The parents are now retired with several grandchildren. In the past they hosted extended family meals, reciprocated among households; and every Saturday night they went to *Pépère's* home to visit. This tradition stopped after he died in the mid-1980s. The parents have traveled little and say they do not enjoy it. Their children and grandchildren come to the farm to see them for visits, meals, and holidays.

Gagnon family stories differentiate the boundary of family group around their nuclear but very large family. In a session among mother, father, daughter Aimee, and Kristin, the mother states that the children were not allowed to sleep over at other's houses, whether family or friends.[6] She follows this family rule with a hypothetical story she told the children: "If a fire starts in that house, who are they going to save first? It's not going to be you." Aimee says they were permitted one friend a year to sleep over, but the experience rarely lived up to expectations, and her interest in doing it flagged. She played primarily with her brothers and sisters, nestled in the middle of the youngest group of three girls who shared a bedroom and bed. She states that with her big family she "had little need for friends." Home was a haven from school, "magical and safe," eagerly anticipated at the end of each day. She also recalls the school lunches, theirs homemade while other kids' were store-bought and packaged: "When you're a kid you don't want homemade. You want the Oreo cookies." Because they were considered poor, the family received bags of clothes, which the children then used for play clothes. The mother adds, "I cannot give clothes to a poor person to make him poorer"—they have to be decent. As bell hooks (2000) elaborates, "the poor are not fooled when the privileged offer cast offs and worn-out hand-me-downs as a gesture of 'generosity' while buying only the new and best for themselves" (p. 47).

Aimee summarizes, "we were the only ones still speaking French" through the 1970s, 1980s, and 1990s, and it was hard to adjust back to English after school vacations in French at home. Some of the Gagnon family dynamics seem to be based upon avoidance of interaction with others to keep outside disturbances at bay. The parents supported their children in school, but there was a sense that they distrusted education, particularly beyond high school. For some families, the language of school conflicts with the ethnic- and class-marked language learned at home, "a language that spoke through and held a deep mistrust of educated talk that doesn't come through when times get tough" (Bérubé, 1997, p. 58) and "where being smart meant being able to use your head and your hands to turn into projects that could feed, clothe, and house your family" (Doucet, 1999, p. 205).

Interaction over group boundaries crystallized in a cluster of family stories around dating, marriage, and divorce. The mother states, "it's harder to leave a large family," and *Pépère* [her father] hated to see us get married" because he loved them so much. In a second interview with Aimee, she states that marrying was the only legitimate way to leave family, although it was hard to leave in any way because of what was not talked about. Stories of dating and marriage were told by mother, father, and daughter, and they were dispersed across the two-hour session rather than in one round or series. The three share a laugh over the memory the mother narrates about a boyfriend watching TV when she called them for dinner. When he did not come immediately, she pulled the plug: "it was dinner or else." Later, in a more serious tone, she tells how the family ritual of saying the rosary in French after the evening meal stopped when Protestant girlfriends started to come over for suppers. The father mentions a spouse in the extended family who is French but "doesn't speak a word of French," a comment paired with the mother's story of another in-law who came from Canada speaking French but "got laughed at and will only speak English now."

At other points, Aimee offers two stories that are more overtly evaluated in terms of family boundaries. Aimee and her mother have been discussing the silent understandings that governed their family. Then Aimee says:

> I was telling Mom just the other day
> we have a brother who's getting divorced
> and the more I think about it the more it looks like
>   we were just a French little community

    our family itself . eleven people plus parents
and <u>one</u> person came in
    English . Protestant on top of that (laughs)
    and <u>she took over</u>
it was very much just like a silent <u>war</u>
we just [sound effect like a fading whistle]
everything <u>we</u> wanted everything <u>we</u> thought
    just kind got <u>bowled over </u>by one English-speaking Protestant
that was it . that was all we needed
    one person
and it's funny how it's destroyed the language
    nobody speaks French anymore amongst us
    once the older ones started getting married
because nobody else— before the English Protestant came
    nobody else really <u>questioned</u> that we spoke French
    nobody else made fun of it
    or tried to change us
    but this one

In a second interview, Aimee talks to Kristin about a cousin who tried to teach his wife French and, for her effort, she was "kind of made fun of." Aimee provides the explicit evaluation from a family standpoint that "outsiders should stay outsiders." The two stories contradict each other, the one criticizing the "take over" by an English-speaking spouse and the other mocking an in-law's attempt to learn French. In family systems terms, these paradoxical injunctions set up a double bind for new family members. They establish a boundary protecting French as the home language that differentiates "real" family as insiders, and they appear to discourage intermarriage. The ambivalence of the boundary is resolvable if family members marry French and Catholic. The mother says that in her generation, there was no "mixed marriages," to which the father appends, "you just didn't bring anyone home who wasn't French and Catholic." The mother adds that their Protestant neighbors could not go out with Catholic girls. Later, the father asks rhetorically but with vestiges of pain: "how do you think we felt when our oldest daughter didn't want to have a Mass [for her wedding]?" In the later interview with Aimee, she says that her father predicted this marriage would not last. It did not. The daughter divorced and is now married again with children.

This narrative motif about entering the family differentiates a boundary and founds family identity. The parents play out interaction with other groups not so much directly as through their children and grandchildren. The ambivalence built in to performing the Gagnon family moves around an inside-outside binary that creates an "us" and a "them." The "we" depends on inside knowledge, discussed in Chapter 2 as action- and performance-based rather than centered on talk. Tensions between groups constitute family identity regulating uniqueness, that is, "We were the only ones still speaking French," and adaptation, as when Aimee charges, "why are the French always the ones to adapt?" The disturbing forces from the outside that will not go away are, especially, the English language and other religions, but also the different perspectives that interactions, education, and travel open up.

This local model of performing family focuses on group-ordering to maintain its cultural identity, especially the preservation of French language use against enormous odds. Family attention to staying together and staying apart from outside disturbances focuses on the needs of the internal system. Group-ordering creates shared sensibilities among its members and orders tasks among them. The family is stabilized by the technology of speaking French and by the sexual division of labor, especially the mother's work in the home and in storytelling. The father's self-employment at the homestead also centered efforts internally, making a very modest but self-sustaining living. The internal focus on group-ordering creates difficulties in task-ordering relations with the environment, however, as outside forces press to change the family identity. Here Aimee's positioning is key; that is, she occupies a position both inside and outside, straddling and crossing family boundaries through advanced education, travel, and talk. As we developed in Chapter 3, she strategically positions herself both to protect family and to promote change.

"I am an Americanized family"

The first words spoken in an interview with Robert were "I am an Americanized family." The ambivalence built into this family narrative strains between the individual "I" and the "we" of family as Robert struggles over temporal horizons between the "then" of childhood and the "now" of adulthood. The biographical focus of Robert differs from the spatial tensions that order the inside-outside binary of the Gagnon family, discussed above. Robert contrasts his childhood in a small Franco-American town with his current life as an educator and father of two children. He describes his childhood as "very intense" in a "completely French" family and community. Robert continued his grade school education in the French language in a bilingual seminary run by a French Canadian order. "I was very Franco-American, very Catholic." His father was a woodsman who hunted, fished, practiced divining, and knew how to find spruce gum. Robert reasons that "I am not my father's son," although he states that his brother is. He refers here to the outdoor sensibilities his brother shares with his father, whereas Robert prefers gourmet cooking, travel, and an intellectual life. Robert is the only one in his family to graduate from college. Following the warmth and security of his ethnic childhood, his journey through higher education submitted him to negative valuations of being Franco-American when both his English (because of his French schooling) and French (because it is North American) were initially judged to be deficient. He persisted and earned a doctorate in French.

Robert's storytelling marks a boundary between the "then" of his Franco-American past and when his mother died, what he specifies as "the difference between living Franco-American and the intellectualized experience of being Franco-American." He presently teaches French language and Canadian studies, although his children do not speak French. He does not escape the tensions of the biographical boundaries of identity. He describes, for example, the "pilgrimage" to his hometown on which he takes his daughter and son. Although they have no family in French Canada nor in France, he has also taken his children there. His family practices Roman Catholicism, he states, as a way of maintaining ties to French Maine and to his heritage, although he distinguished his belief from that of his family's past: "it's not my mother's religion." He explains this difference with a story of how he confronted an antiabortion protester in front of a church. Robert's comment suggests that the Church is not a simple equation of religion with tradition and tradition with culture. Religion is a cluster of beliefs and practices, historically constituted, crossed by change, and internally contested (Narayan, 1997).

Franco-American cooking, both in a more daily sense and for special family celebrations at Christmas, expresses Robert's family identity. He makes *ployes* (Acadian buckwheat pancakes), *pâte chinois*, which he translates as shepherd's pie—"that's automatic"—and *tourtière* (meat pie) for the *Réveillon* he celebrates at home. Robert says:

> that's one thing I <u>do</u> do
>> one thing we <u>talk</u> about
>> and my kids <u>ask</u> for
> <u>Christmas</u> isn't <u>Christmas</u> without my <u>meat pies</u>

Cretons (pork crackling made into spreads), however, are "too charged with cholesterol": "to see you make *cretons* would make any nutritionist pass out and not revive for at least five hours." Robert has adapted these traditional ethnic foods to contemporary health standards.

Robert appears to be "Americanized" in the way of many ethnic families, a narrative moving from French origins to American ends. But Pleck (2000) challenges the conventional interpretation of immigrant history that each group arrived with a distinctive set of traditions, clung to them as they adapted to the new environment, and then abandoned their heritage and adopted mainstream cultural rituals as they moved into the middle class. She argues that it is wrong-headed to locate changes in ethnic celebrations as unidirectional assimilation because "everything is changing: the group's ritual, its sense of self-definition, its interaction with others, and the relationship of ritual to the group" (p. 13). In terms of family storytelling, both group-ordering of internal relations to form family identity and task-ordering around family relations to the environment are transforming.[7]

Robert's "Americanized family" focuses on the external needs of task-ordering and adapts to all these environmental forces with cultural uniqueness. Of the three things that most identify Franco-American culture—language, religion, and food—"people lose contact with them in that order" (Marion, in Kenney, 1999). Despite the pushes and pulls of environment, Robert's family storytelling creates a group identity that retains ethnic flavors. His family has adapted but not abandoned the French language, Catholic religion, and ethnic foods. The responses to external needs increase their interactions with other groups via education, travel, moves, and occupation. The French-Americanized family is not defined by language or any other single feature or combination of features but rather by the self-regulation of adaptations in specific locations and times while sustaining cultural uniqueness.

Because all families must order content for cultural survival, local models of group identity may center on either group-ordering or task-ordering. The Gagnon family emphasizes group-ordering to bind the family as insiders, creating tensions in the external demands of task-ordering. By contrast, Robert's family focuses on task-ordering that adapts to external forces but creates concerns about an "Americanized" group identity. These two group identities are similar, though, in that differentiation of an internal boundary surrounds the nuclear family with only limited inclusion of extended family and community relations. Robert's family identity allows more permeable boundaries with other groups through interactions in work, educational settings, and travel. Material conditions also contribute to differences in group identities. Whereas the Gagnons may be described as working class, Robert has undergone a migration to middle class. The internal task-ordering of the Gagnon family places the burden of family labor, celebration, and storytelling on the mother (that is, family women), reflecting an asymmetrical sexual division of labor in family and ethnic rituals. Robert's family appears to have incorporated some changes of feminism: a mother working outside the home and a father participating in childcare, cooking, and labor for holiday celebrations.

"What stories about being Franco-American would we pass on?"

Michael and Monica are a married couple with three young children living in the country in central Maine. Their house is a few miles from a small city and two hours from the mill town where they were raised, met, and married, and where their parents and surviving grandmother still live. Michael and Monica are college graduates. Monica continues educational development as she home schools their two older children. Michael has a doctorate and studied at

Oxford and in France. Kristin was invited to a four-generational family meal in the summer, occasioned by Monica's father's retirement.

Evolution in small group identity is reflected through storytelling from each generation. *Mémère* (Monica's mother's mother) was often sad as she narrated aspects of her past in English that is increasingly difficult for her to speak as she ages. Her family of French Canadian immigrants endured economic stresses and hardships. Early in life, her father suffered a work injury in which he lost two fingers, and "there was no worker's compensation in those days." Later on, her only son died at age twenty-five after a short illness, and then her husband died shortly after. Her daughter recalls a time her father was working two jobs while her mother worked another. *Mémère* herself lived for a time in Connecticut, where they moved for her husband to work for a large company that employed many Franco-Americans. In this more heterogenous urban setting, her lack of fluent English was very trying, and she was fearful of living for the first time in the same tenements with African Americans. Despite its economic hardships, she yearns for the family life before her husband's death, when their home was a gathering place and "everybody was happy." She now lives alone, and health problems prevent her from walking, getting out, and going to Mass. At one point in the session she weeps. In these awkward and emotional moments, the family engages in interpersonal management that diverts conversation to "safer" topics. As Bruner (1990, p. 126) describes in his session with a family, the researcher—Kristin—also "behaved family," drawn into established techniques for countering centrifugal pulls and conflicts.

Monica's father worked for years in the mill until losing his job in yet another economic decline. Searching for a new job was difficult and degrading, especially because he lacked a high school education. Now retired, the father speaks colorfully and performs stories with animation and dialogue. He loves talking politics and has clear views and perceptions of other families like his own. Michael says that when he wants to know how the vote will go on a local or state issue, he talks to his father-in-law. Monica's mother went to nursing school after their two daughters were in high school and has worked outside the home since. The parents are an example of the "invisible Americans" in the working classes of the last two decades of the twentieth century, what Lillian Rubin (1994) calls families on the faultline of increasing vulnerability to fates beyond their control.

The dinner talk is an intergenerational performance of identity. The meal consists of lobster salad (flight interruptions after the terrorist attacks of September 11, 2001, created a lobster glut that drove prices the lowest in years), garden vegetables, and side dishes. For a time the talk revolves around family foods. In one interaction, Monica asks her *mémère* how she made *herbes salées* (salted herbs). Monica's mother assists *Mémère*'s English, and her father inserts stories of eating mashed potatoes seasoned with *herbes salées* for the first time at *Mémère's* house. Kristin asks if lobster is a family food. "No, it's too expensive," Monica's father responds. He then tells stories of driving to the coast in summers to buy large, cheap lobsters directly from fishers which they carried home in coolers and ate at long tables in the garage, using hammers, pliers, and screwdrivers to crack hard shells and extricate the meat. Monica recalls her surprise the first time she saw people eat lobster inside the house. Dessert is a homemade cake with three-color frosting prepared by the children in celebration of the father's recent retirement. The cake is served to the chorus of "I am my own boss now" led by Monica and the three children. The children are thrilled about the frosting, and the seven-year-old granddaughter tells why: "Mom, you're letting us have <u>food coloring</u>!" This funny moment displays values of simplicity, frugality, and homemade celebration. The extended family celebration performs small group identity through its rituals, narrative, and conversation.

We save our discussion of the parent's generation for the next section in order to focus here on Monica and Michael's generation and to suggest some ambivalences in their family cultural work. The boundary that differentiates family identity includes extended family, but like the Gagnons and Robert's family, Michael and Monica do not live in the Franco-American community of their childhood. In an earlier session, Michael has asked Kristin, "what stories about being Franco-American would we want to pass on?" Their ambivalence about what to pass on suggests a view of ethnic culture that is not purely conservative and celebratory. Michael and Monica do not nostalgically fetishize all aspects of ethnic family culture. For example, they are unwilling to pass on excesses of parental authority, the cycle of punishments that Monica labels "abuse" in her father's childhood and family culture. They are critical of the sexism that limits family women's independence, their educational goals and career options. Against the ethnic norms that keep family secrets or bring family problems to the clergy, they support Monica's mother's decision to go into counseling for reasons not disclosed in the sessions.

Michael and Monica also struggle over class relations in their family identity and Franco-American history. When Michael acknowledges family stories of poverty among Franco-Americans, he asks, "do we want to pass on being poor?" Yet class migration has costs as well as benefits (hooks, 2000). Stories telling what happens in moving to a higher class expose unresolved conflicts over what is lost as well as gained. Bérubé (1997) narrates "the anguish of leaving a home you can't return to, while not belonging where you've ended up" (p. 45). Furthermore, he argues that "the class hardship narrative only reinforces class hierarchies in the telling. Even as it makes visible and validates the lives of working-class people, and evokes sympathy from middle-class listeners, it reduces us to either victims or heroes. Our lives become satisfying dramas of suffering that end in inspiring victory or poignant tragedy" (p. 63). The built-in ambivalences of class escape narratives may be painful and confounding. Among the costs may be shame associated with the route taken to escape, for example, the intellectual work that differentiates one from family of origin; anxiety about passing on, or passing as, what one is not; or worry that the escape serves the interests of middle-class benefactors but does nothing to improve working people's lives (Bérubé, 1997; Ryan & Sackrey, 1984; Thompson & Tyagi, 1996).

Interestingly, Michael and Monica's ambivalence does not revolve around the traditional Franco-American trilogy of French language, faith, and food. In a context much changed from that of their parents' lives, they teach their children some French, belong to a Catholic Church, and continue some ethnic food traditions. Monica especially embraces the way she was raised, calling it a "wonderful childhood." Michael contrasts his Oxford education with the immersion in the daily life of raising children "where your sense of your own identity comes through." In fact, Michael and Monica perhaps reserve their greatest concern for consumer, popular, and youth culture. Presently, they do not own a television, and they are home schooling their children. These tactics for group-ordering buffer them from outside disturbances and reorder tasks of entertainment and education within the family. But whatever the third generation passes on, the internal boundary that differentiates Michael and Monica's family identity, like that of the Gagnons and of Robert, is made more difficult in the absence of the ethnic community their parents more fully experienced.

"Well, we're all French, although . . .": Communal Identities

We now take up Monica's parents and the mill town of their home to begin our examination of family identities that extend to community. Lewiston was one of several New England towns that first attracted Franco-American immigrants to the industrializing Northeast. Located in southern Maine on the Androscoggin River, Lewiston built six textile mills between 1819 and 1869. French Canadians brought the first ethnic diversity to Lewiston, part of the one-hundred-year migration from Quebec to the United States, from 1830 to 1930. The exodus of one million French peaked in the 1880s, responding to hardships of economic depressions, indebtedness, and a lack of arable land, and to recruitment for cheap manual labor for the textile industry, paper mills, machine shops, and shoe factories. By 1900 French workers in the cotton industry surpassed all other ethnic groups in number and percentage (Roby, 1996a). By 1910 they formed the majority population in Lewiston. In the 1960s the average family in Lewiston was fourth or fifth generation with a residency of seventy years, and 20% had been in the United States over one hundred years. James Hill Parker (1993) suggests that in 1970 it was entirely probable that Lewiston had the highest proportion of Franco-Americans of any sizable U.S. city (p. 3). Lewiston still claims a Franco-American majority in population, the people whose pulse Monica's father embodies.

The cultural stability of Franco-Americans is a rare achievement among U.S. white ethnic groups. When French Canadians migrated south, they followed extended family and organized, to some extent, into neighborhoods and ethnic communities. Parish churches and bilingual parochial schools anchored the *Petits Canadas*, together with French-language newspapers, ethnic organizations, social clubs, hospitals, and orphanages. Reproducing rural villages in urban settings created structural bases that resisted assimilation. Proximity to French Canada also advanced and sustained ethnic identity as families crossed and recrossed national borders. Although these rural villages displayed a diverse class structure in the late nineteenth and early twentieth centuries, by the 1940s Franco-American communities were largely working class. Sacks (1993) argues that Euro-ethnic working-class communities reject the public-private dichotomy of bourgeois culture for the binary logic of "our world" and "theirs." "Our Franco-American world" joined family and community, work and politics, into a single sphere. Moreover, "our world" is primarily maintained by the kinwork of ethnic family women who provide the invisible labor to maintain family, community, and work ties, for example, through birthday parties, holiday rituals, communal meals, and festivals (di Leonardo, 1984).

"Being Franco-American, that was everything"

One thing that distinguishes Monica and Michael from their parents is that the latter still reside in an ethnic community in Lewiston.[8] Monica states that "My family has no idea how to even <u>talk</u> to someone about being Franco-American because it's just life . . . ingrained in everything we do but not that would make us special." Monica's parents narrate activities that enmesh families in the daily business of living. We have described one of their intergenerational family meals above. In other stories, the father depicts a friendly barter system of labor for vegetables that he engages in with a local truck farmer. When the family was young, the parents played cards on Saturday nights with family and friends while kids played together because, the mother explains, they could not afford to go out. Dances, such as the Fireman's Ball, were described as special annual occasions to see friends. The father tells stories around learning to dance and dancing partners; the mother tells about getting baby-sitters for these eagerly anticipated events. Their talk is animated and spirited, conveying the emotional significance of those social events with their mixture of French and English languages.

Monica's family did not emphasize the *Réveillon* as an ethnic ritual for family and friends. However, for the Lewiston family of Lena, another interviewee, *Réveillons* held center place; after their decline, she says, "I find it so difficult." *Réveillons* meshed sociality, music, and food across households to mark the religious holidays of Christmas and New Year's, although for Lena's family they signified the more general notion of house parties, what some other families call *soirées*. Ethnic holidays coinciding or falling near to the four dominant U.S. holidays of Christmas, New Year's, Easter, and the Fourth of July are more likely to survive migration (Pleck, 2000). Legislation in Illinois, for example, forbade the celebration of Bastille Day (July 14) and required Franco-Americans to observe only the Fourth of July. Lewiston is also the location of one of three Franco-American annual festivals in Maine, a celebration both Monica's and Lena's families anticipate and attend.[9]

Religious institutions, especially if they combine ethnicity with religion, are important in preserving group identities, as the role of the Catholic Church in current Hispanic and Mexican cultures testifies. The French expressed the relation of native tongue and religion by "*qui perd la langue perd la foi*" (who loses their language loses their faith).[10] On both sides of the U.S.-Canadian border established in 1842, a valiant effort to maintain and promote French ethnic culture was called *la survivance*. *La survivance* focused on the trinity of French language, Catholic faith, and large families to offset the sea of Anglos surrounding the French. *La survivance* in French Canada hitchhiked on migration to the United States and took the form of the French Cultural Movement, led by the Church and emphasizing religiosity, hard work, and Puritan values. One of its techniques was to establish ethnically based, or "national" parishes, coordinated with bilingual schools (Quintal, 1996).[11]

The first complete Franco-American parochial school in Maine was founded in Lewiston in 1878 by the Grey Nuns: *Paroisse Sainte-Pierre et Saint-Paul.* It was the third school in New England, which numbered over 200 national parishes. Lewiston has four Franco-American churches, three of which still held services in French in 1964. By 1972, all four parishes were bilingual. Parker (1993) writes, "it appears that the existence of French Masses may represent the one remaining vestige of French culture in an otherwise assimilated community" (p. 43). Michael and Monica were married at St. Peter and St. Paul's with their large extended families in attendance. Lena worked for twelve years administrating the church and school of the *Paroisse Saint-Croix* (Holy Cross Parish). She and her husband attend the Saturday night French Mass, which Lena calls one of the last in Maine to celebrate the liturgy in French. The sermon is in English. Their daughter usually attends the Sunday morning Mass in English, reading the epistles. Many Franco-American families collapse French and Catholic when talking about heritage because the two are so intertwined as to be inseparable. Families may nurture religious vocations, especially to send a boy to study for the priesthood, as in Robert's biography, but also a girl to the convent, as in Pauline's family. For other families, the Church is less marked ethnically; Roman Catholicism is the family religion but it is not specifically French. One couple, for example, found the local church, Franco-American in its origins, to be unfriendly; they now attend a parish with no French background in a larger, more ethnically mixed community. But not all those who identify as Franco-American secure that identification to religion. Aimee, in an excerpt discussed in Chapter 3, has turned away from the Catholic Church.

Religious institutions can help preserve group identities by extending the boundary of family to community relations. Communities with Franco-American parishes were also bolstered by other institutional bases. Lewiston was home to a French-language newspaper founded in 1880, *Le Messager*, and to French-language movie houses, theatre troupes, and a francophone radio station. In his study of the declining use of the French language in Lewiston, Parker (1993) argues that Lewiston was a central and vital locus of the French Cultural Movement, as evidenced by the church and school leadership, by 14,000 members in twenty-eight French-language organizations, and by political organizing that elected French mayors from 1932 to 1970. Lena recalled the festivity of the annual snowshoe parades that brought French Canadians to Lewiston. Monica's father embodies the pulse of Franco-American politics in Lewiston, which his son-in-law Michael monitors. All of these ethnic infrastructures declined by the 1950s, *Le Messager* surviving until 1968.[12]

Against the backdrop of 400 years of cultural survival and stability, Parker (1993) argues that the decline in the use of the French language in Lewiston in the 1960s was so dramatic as to be called a cataclysmic cultural change. He argues that the gradual, generational model of ethnic group breakdown cannot explain the case of Lewiston French. In the first place, French persisted well beyond the three-generation model of decline. In the second place, change was multigenerational rather than a provenance of the younger generation. He argues that Franco-Americans in Lewiston changed as a group, and by extension as whole families, in the 1960s from a bilingual population with a preponderance of French to a preponderance of English. Third, he explains the cataclysmic shift by the French Cultural Movement's concentration on an "ideal" model, promoted by the French elite and Catholic Church, that privileged Yankee and Puritan values over the "real" model of French and humanistic values. The "ideal" culture was born of their long-suffering history in Canada and emphasized religion, hard work, stoicism, and the other world. The "real" Franco-American culture, however, is performed in the routines, rituals, and relationships of the *Petits Canadas:* talking and laughing and gesturing, singing and dancing and card-playing, eating and drinking. Significantly, these "real" values emerge in the expressive, daily lives of family and their storytelling, and they do not limit ethnic identity to language. It is also notable that the argument of cataclysmic change focused on public sites for speaking French, specifically the Lewiston business district. Our data on family talk and storytelling challenge earlier conclusions about the totality and timing of cataclysmic change.

The cultural divide suggested by the difference between "ideal" and "real" Franco-American culture is echoed in a class divide over the terms of *la survivance* that culminated in a 1960s revolt against "the incantational, outmoded, and sometimes contemptuous speech of certain elders" advocating a renaissance of Franco-Americanism (Roby, 1996b, p. 624). These new voices argued that the exodus of a million French Canadians and their integration into American society had been seen only from the perspective of the cultural elite. In response to the view of ordinary, working-class people as victims of outside forces, they outlined a renaissance led by the young and the ordinary in all their variations: those who do or do not speak French, those who practice or do not practice Catholicism, those who do or do not support feminism, and those who are or are not heterosexual. These voices suggest that white ethic community must not be romanticized in ways that mask class inequities, gendered asymmetries, and the heterosexual privileging of "ideal" Franco-American culture.

This alternative vision positions Franco-Americans as active contributors to American history as well as links to the francophone world of North America. As in the case of Aimee within the family boundary, and Michael and Monica from Lewiston but no longer living there, every generation straddles "our" world and "theirs," with ties to both and inescapable conflicts. Class conflict within Franco-American culture suggests the intracommunal contestation that challenges ethnic hegemony, just as struggles around gender and sexuality within family do. These struggles are not simply generational because they are situated in larger social forces. The built-in ambivalences of the boundary between "our Franco-American world" and "their world" must consider multiple and shifting constraints on group identity.

When narrative emerges from a material, situated, and embodied space, family identity is inseparable from place. In this instance, the "we" is not only a family name but also a place shared with other families. A cultural boundary sometimes corresponds with a physical boundary to differentiate group identity. The topography of a river, one surrounding French Island in the Penobscot River and the other marking the border between the United States and Canada along New Brunswick, produce two additional variations of communal family identity.

"The relatives never liked it when my parents moved off the island": Staying and Leaving

People living on the the forty-seven acres of French Island "could <u>walk</u> to all the relatives" and did not need cars to visit each other. French Island was first settled in the 1830s and then further developed in the 1880s by French Canadians, part of the exodus that resulted in seven million French descendants in the Northeast alone. French Canadians first sought work in the estimated 200 sawmills dotting the five miles between Milford and Bangor, then the woolen mills, and later the shoe industry. According to Eugenie Nadeau Wollstadt, a local historian of *Nos Histoires de l'Ile:*

> I was on the fringes of the last generation to glimpse the full French Island phe-
> nomenon. A time when there was still no more pleasurable a way to spend Sun-
> day afternoon than in a rocking chair on *mémère* and *pépère*'s front porch. A time
> when we still crossed the ice in winter. A time when entire summers were spent
> at the river's edge. A time when any brief adventures away from the Island were
> usually to our Catholic church or school, mere extensions of our community. All
> that was ever needed or wanted was found there, on this tiny island mass in the
> Penobscot River called French Island, home. (*Nos Histoires,* 1999, p. 6)

Nos Histoires de l'Ile tells a collective story from its last keepers, a generation of elders dying out. The incantation of a "a time when . . ." marks moments that no longer exist. Many French-speaking residents of the last half
century have left the Island during war, for college, or to work. Houses have
been torn down or sold to landlords renting to college students. Even the river
has changed: it no longer freezes and is not safe for swimming, after the dams
and pollution of the paper mills. The river defined the community and shaped
the identity of this tiny land mass. It was playground to the children, power
for the lumber and paper industries, and transportation for all. People crossed
the ice in winter and rowed punts in summer. The bridge to Old Town both
extends the French community to the St. Joseph parish and parochial school
on the other side of the river and to the dominant English culture of other
white ethnics.

Counting for approximately 20% of Old Town's population, French Island
began a church and school in 1852. The Island was heavily but not wholly
French, and the Island School was public and English-speaking. Unless the
French children got one of the French-speaking nuns, they suffered punishments and insults for their language. Many of the families on the Island were
related and inter-related. Yvonne recalls that the Island was like a big family
where "everybody knew everybody." Extended families and boarders lived in
multistory houses with gardens plotted wherever space was available. Gerald
and Alain recall that when they were children, the buildings were so close
they could jump from roof to roof. In multigenerational homes, such as that
described by daughters Jeanne, Susan, and Annette and their mother, some
children shared bedrooms and used the living room for sleeping when *Pépère*
came to stay. Despite the density, the daughters report that they loved living
with *Pépère.* Their mother, however, hints more than once at the difficulty of
living in her father-in-law's house with him after his wife died. She is now in
"that big house, all alone." French people frequently took in boarders, both for

the money and because as a group they took care of their own. The teacher boarding with one couple stayed thirty-seven years, and the mother narrates that the occasional times spent alone with her daughter or her son were precious. Yvonne states that she was never alone and never felt crowded.

The stories from French Island create a place of intimacy, conviviality, music, and people walking, talking, and stopping by to visit: the "real" culture proposed by Parker (1993). Children swam, fished, skated, and pulled logs from the river, the length of the island and the river their playground so long as they stayed within range of their mothers' calls. Children were watched by grandparents, extended family, neighbors, and anyone who saw them. Recall Yvonne's story (analyzed in Chapter 2) of the phone call from a neighbor reporting to her mother about her children smoking cigarettes. Youngest children began school at Island School, but as soon as they were old enough, in the company of older siblings and guided by crossing guards, they walked to the other side of the river, back home for lunch, back to school, and then home again. Across the river, the town of Bradley, from which Mrs. Lillie Bouchard rowed or crossed the ice for the sewing circle nights, had no parochial school and was dominated by a paper mill. Pauline describes how the mill schedule punctuated the day, even though her father was not a mill worker, as children and adults headed home for lunches, called "dinners" by participants, and then suppers, when the mill whistles blew.

Gerald and Alain recall that across the bridge the children were sometimes called French Island bums in a chant invented by Old Town children. The Island had a working-class history and a reputation for being rough and tough. Some narrators told stories of hearing domestic disputes from the streets, of bootlegging, of Friday night boxing matches. French Island was right next to Indian Island, home of the Penobscot Nation. Alain says that as a child he and some other French children "chummed" with Native Americans, but social proscriptions muted both interactions and stories.

Yvonne says that "the relatives never liked it when my parents moved off the island because not many people had cars back then . . . and they couldn't see us as much." French Island is ordered by the close proximity of its residents. The binary logic of its narratives revolved around staying on or leaving the Island, sometimes moving just to Old Town where family visits continue, and sometimes "away" for good. The narrative of ethnic community suggested: you stay on the island; if you leave, it's where you come from and where you visit, but you rarely move back. A strong sense of family ties and community identity was retained, even when families crossed the river to live in Old Town. The French of Old Town maintain a low profile in public, locating French identity on the Island, in their church, and in homes. By the 1930s and 1940s, children spoke English even if their parents did not. A strong sense of family culture extending to community and place endures, but it is difficult now to find places where French is spoken in public settings or in homes. The family narratives of French Island are nostalgic tales set before change and loss. They center on group-ordering and remembering a family identity based in community and a place set off by the river. The boundary of small group identity differentiating French Island as a family-community separate from the mainland parallels the French-speaking Gagnons as a family separate from the mainstream.

"A lot of people come back": *Crossings and Backtracking*

In 1842 the boundary between the United States and Canada was established, dividing the St. John Valley between two national identities. At the very northern tip of Maine, the St. John Valley is home to 20,000 Franco-Americans descended from two French groups, Acadians and Québécois, who settled in the 1870s. Acadians, deported and scattered during the brutal Great Disruption, came back to Nova Scotia, settled temporarily in New Brunswick, and then permanently along the St. John River. There they were joined by Québécois from the St. Lawrence River valley. These Franco-Americans made their livelihood in the woods and on the potato farms of the valley. Driving through the St. John Valley today, one still sees the French Canadian system of long-lot farms, fields laid out in long rows perpendicular to the river to allow each family a small access to its resources.

The Valley, as it is called throughout Maine, includes the forests, potato fields, and lakes. The St. John River is an arbitrary border between bilingual Franco-Americans and the bilingual province of New Brunswick with its 250,000 French speakers. More a contact zone than a barrier, its bridges are crossed by hundreds of Americans and Canadians each day. Observing in the early 1990s, Doty (1991, p. 34) writes that "almost everyone in today's flourishing St. John Valley speaks or understands French," and "in speaking with one another people often move from English to French in mid-sentence." Its distance from the larger population areas of southern Maine, its proximity to Canada, its mythic beauty as Acadia, and its bilingual history combine to make the Valley a unique site of struggle over Franco-American identity.

The St. John River sculpts the memory and stories of a father as he tells a story about fishing with his brothers as a young child. The orientation of the story hints at the poverty of the family of twelve children in which not all the children have shoes. When his father returns with his earnings from the winter lumbering in the woods, his mother says, "Buy those kids some boots," which he does. When the boys go fishing, "we didn't want to dirty our new boots," so they carry them. The narrating father supplies a French word for the steel tub they put the fish in, and, to keep them clean, their new boots. He describes a way of fishing using baskets and potato peels, an illegal technique. Thus, it is one brother's task to watch for the game warden. "Someone's coming!" the brother suddenly calls. In their panic and haste, the boys throw the tub—and their precious boots—into the river and run. The father concludes that they searched for but never found their boots, nor did they get new ones, and "My god, did we cry." In his family of twelve children, six were Canadians and six were Americans, testimony to the crossings over the river's national boundaries.

Like New Brunswick that it borders, the Valley is bilingual and has been for generations within its families, towns, and farms. For example, Bernard's great-grandfather was French-speaking, as was his son Joseph, but most of Joseph's sons, including Bernard's father, could speak English, too. Bernard's mother was English but she spoke French. Bernard's generation was brought up speaking French, but they learned English, too. His first two children spoke French in the home, and the younger two understood French but spoke the English they heard in the neighborhood among peers. Bernard's son says, "I never spoke French until after I got out of college and I got into business." Doing business in the Valley often requires the French language.

Lois gives further insight into bilingual culture and communal identity with a pair of stories she tells about her two sons when they were very young. Lois's birth family spoke French at home, but both her parents also talked English, and she and her siblings were bilingual at young ages. Her husband tragically died when their sons were two and five years old. The first story is about the younger son, Mark. After the husband's death, an English-speaking brother-in-law "took Mark under his wing," and English became his first language. Subsequently, his mother sent him to the "Protestant" (public) school, from which he came home one day to say, "Mom, they call me *tête-pioche.*" Literally, this translates as "hoe-head," an old expression to designate a French person who does not speak French. He now speaks French as an adult in his job as a local police officer.

The second story is about Paul, the older son. By contrast to Mark, "Paul is French," Lois states, having learned French at home even though he "chummed" with English-speaking children. One of these children came to visit him at his *mémère's*, with whom he stayed during the day while Lois was teaching school. Lois describes Paul as "old beyond his years" because he lost his father at such a young age. He was concerned that having company would bother his *mémère,* and he was afraid she would be upset by their speaking English in her home. So he instructed his friend, "You stay where you stay, and I stay where I stay." Paul's social aptitude aside, people in the Valley do not stay put in one language or the other, nor on one side or the other of the St. John River. Like the Franco-Americans of the 1930s, bilingualism persists in Franco-American families in the Valley.

Parallel with the movement across the river, these stories suggest a movement between languages. Like Old Town and mill towns, the French language is learned at home; but a difference in the Valley is its public necessity, opportunity, and endorsement in workplaces. Professionals and business people invest in bilingualism to meet the needs of their community and those coming to trade or visit from French Canada. By comparison to Franco-Americans who are often invisible in their hometowns, the French in the Valley have high profiles as community members and movers. Recall the father-son pair's narration on family contributions to the local hospital, golf course, ski area, and insurance business from Chapter 3. Franco-Americans in the St. John Valley have claimed and achieved a large role in building and maintaining the Valley and its towns, and they take public pride in their accomplishments. Theirs is a public and present-tense definition of communal family identity.

The Valley still enjoys some institutional support of ethnicity, although like Lewiston and French Island, this, too, is under transformation. Of the Roman Catholic churches that center the towns, more are closing and priests are in short supply. Parochial schools have also been closed due to population decline and economic constraints. Still, the Valley boasts a bilingual education program in the public schools that has won state and national awards. Interested people may join *Le Club Français*, which meets monthly in one of the towns on the river and conducts its meetings in French.

The boundary of family encircles a community outside the home to produce a local model of group identity in the Valley. Of Dorene's three sons, two have stayed in the Valley and one lives in another part of Maine. The oldest she calls a "St. John Valley boy" who left home to work but returned at the first opportunity and has now taken over his father's business. Her second son works in the same business in a nearby town. The mother herself moved to the Valley from a Franco-American mill town in southern Maine to marry her husband from another Valley town. Coming to the Valley she now calls home, she says she never felt like an outsider because she knew both French and English.

As more than one participant voiced, people, especially young people seeking work, leave the St. John Valley, "but a lot of people come back." "Coming back" may refer to the Valley, religion, or language. Like French Island, the communal identity of the Valley embraces a sense of place even as that place is changed by outside forces. Participants not now living in northern Maine return to it. One couple keeps their local home for the winters, spending summers downstate near one of their daughters. Another couple reverses the movement, from downstate in winters to summers in the Valley. A third couple, now elderly and with health problems, has relocated in central Maine to be closer to medical facilities and their son's family, but the husband goes back to the Valley as frequently as he can with the express purpose of speaking French with friends. He has not found acquaintances nor a French community where they presently reside.

As discussed above, leaving a family or communal identity may entail a class migration. Some families in our sample from the St. John Valley do not narrate parties like those of the Lewiston families, nor the neighborhood fun of French Island residents, but instead family outings to golf, ski, and play bridge, activities characteristic of the middle class and not marked as ethnic. The St. John Valley, perhaps because of its geographical boundaries, displays the diverse class structure characteristic of earlier *Petits Canadas*. In the Valley, working-class Franco-Americans may be cleaning the homes of other more prosperous Franco-American families. To the extent that the Valley achieves a communal ethnic identity, it centers on the task-ordering of economic relations, particularly the bilingual business and professional community, that supports that group identity.

Family Network Identities

The variations in communal identities we have described are not ideal types but local models that emerge within particular relations of group-ordering families in specific locations and times. The models that differentiate their boundaries around the nuclear and extended family, those of the Gagnons, Robert, and Michael and Monica, struggle to create and maintain cultural identity. The models of Lewiston, French Island, and the St. John Valley lend modest support to the persistence of ethnic community and place, but they too are fragmented, contingent, and fragile. Our discussion of group-ordering and family identity unavoidably presents evidence of the decline of Franco-American identity. Still, we close with intimations of evolution. McFeat (1974) argues that small groups may join other small groups to maintain their cultural integrity; that is, families may contact and keep in touch with other families. If a group-based division of task-ordering evolves among families, the possibility of networks arises, such as the economic, recreational, and cultural links in the local model of the St. John Valley. The most familiar form of such networks is the family reunion that gathers extended family for celebration. Communal identities, however, create additional alternatives. At the Acadian Festival held each year in Madawaska, for example, one Acadian family is selected for a reunion that attracts hundreds of family members from across North America. In 1994, New Brunswick sponsored an enormous reunion of all Acadian families from all over the world. *Les Retrouvailles* was their first-ever reunion as an Acadian people after the devastating forced exile of the Great Disruption of 1755–1763. The two-week reunion included conferences, seminars, and a women's summit at the University of Moncton, a series of cultural events, and scores of Acadian family reunions. The Le Blanc reunion, for example, gathered five or six thousand descendants, and the entire occasion more than a quarter million Acadians. In this instance, a network of small group cultures formulated something akin to an assembly of family groups.

Electronic networking offers another alternative for small group evolution. According to McFeat (1974), "group-ordering inflow has to find media conducive to model construction" (p. 169). Although our research technique focused on face-to-face interactions, we were made aware that some families participate in "virtual communities" on the Internet, which support and extend small group identities. As one example, the Franco-American Women's Institute (FAWI), established in 1997, negotiates an ethnic identity within a feminist vision to become visible after generations of being unseen and to become vocal after generations of being unheard. Their website describes FAWI as the "first and only Institute of its kind to exist that is solely dedicated to the promotion, advocacy, research, and archiving of Franco-American women." FAWI adopts the language of family in its mission statement: "a NET designed to capture, catch, and free the diversity of expression of the women, their *mamans* and *maman's mamans*. Daughters, too. Because daughters are the best insurance for the future." The Institute emphasizes diversity and inclusiveness in terms of race/ethnicity (e.g., Québécois, Acadian, Métis, and Mixed Blood) and lifestyle (e.g., community women, academic women, women of faith, women of skepticism, women of the seam, women of sensuality, women who farm). The website includes an e-zine, numerous links to related sites, and English/French language options. Its mission is to archive heritage and to move into the next millennium as "an alive, present, and accounted for cultural group of women." This strategic adaption to changing social and technological conditions creates a virtual community of "kin."

Group-Ordering, Ethnic Identity, and the Politics of "Good Families"

The postmodern injunction to "get a life" is carried out as families tell their stories. In performing narrative, families are the communicative medium of storytelling—families tell stories; and families are the outcome of that ordering of information—storytelling forms families. Family is not a biological phenomenon guaranteed by nature but an ongoing performance and cultural formation. As a material expression, family storytelling is a performative struggle over personal, small group, communal, and network identities. In performing narrative, families become visible and audible both to themselves and to others. Group-ordering in family storytelling differentiates a boundary and an identity. Performing family produces local models which manage person-group and group-group tensions as complex positionings between family members, among families, and among groups of families. Our examination of group-ordering in Franco-American family storytelling suggests three conclusions.

First, boundaries between family and environment and among groups of families are differentially drawn, based upon embodied interactions in specific historical, social, and material locations. We describe two structural variations of group-ordering in our corpus: ones that differentiate family boundaries in terms of nuclear or extended families, and others that draw upon communities and networks for definition. Group identities centered upon nuclear and extended families include local variations based upon narrative ambivalences such as inside-and-outside and then-and-now positionings. Group identities centered upon communal variations of "our world" versus "their world" negotiate ambivalences around the passing on of traditions in family time and around leavings, crossings, and coming back to family space. Emerging network identities explore the North American French diaspora and virtual communities of new technologies. Family storytelling regulates diverse individual and group tensions to create a cultural "world of our own making," both for individual families and ethnic family groups.

The analysis of group-ordering in Franco-Americans storytelling illustrates Gillis's (1996) argument about the performance of identity by families in contemporary U.S. culture. More specifically, it articulates the role and significance of family storytelling in creating small group culture. Performing family storytelling embodies tensions between idealizations of *the family we live by*, which stabilize identities around myths of motherhood, fatherhood, and other cultural stereotypes, and the lived reality of group-ordering narratives which emerge in particular social situations and historical circumstances. Intrafamilial differences contest family hegemony and idealizations. The invented tradition of individualism is drawn upon not only to distinguish among family members but also to differentiate the contemporary nuclear family from the extended family of the migration period and earlier generations. But the myth of individualism is also challenged by the enfamilied self and in articulations of communal and network identities. Performing family storytelling offers a more complex story than the "American" family as an isolated nuclear unit. As Gillis suggests, each family makes its own world, but the boundaries of that world—who is in the family circle of "we"—are variable, permeable, and shifting within and between groups.

Second, local models of family identity always rely on task definition. Reliance on task-definition focuses on the needs of the external system, the group-environment relations which require adaptation to relatively unyielding conditions for cultural survival. These demands exert forces on family identity to adapt and change. From variations that focus on nuclear and extended family, Robert tells stories about how his family has become "Americanized" as task-orderings originally maintained by community are now assumed by the nuclear family. From communal variations, the family stories of Lewiston narrate a community changed by social, economic, and cultural forces. In both situations, families resisted the demand that they give up their ethnic differences. When surrounding conditions and circumstances support ethnic identity, as in the case of St. John Valley families where bilingualism continues to meet community and economic needs, ethnic identity is more easily maintained. Local models of family identity may also resist the external demands of group-environment relations. These local models prioritize internal relations and define identity in terms of staying together and staying the same. From nuclear and extended family identities, the Gagnons narrate the maintenance of French language in an isolated farm setting. From communal identities, French Island families invest in remembering their unique culture. Group-ordering, whether focused on external demands or internal relations, secures family identity at the same time it denies or deflects differences among family members and among groups of families.

Third, performing narrative is an evolving expression of family culture rather than a set of artifacts (McKay, 1994). The view of family story as cultural artifact suggests that group identity is fixed, static, and conservative, and it assumes that change is loss, distortion, or corruption. In this view, family storytelling can only serve a conservative function, restoring a past when families were more ethnically pure, sex roles more traditionally defined, and sexuality more firmly controlled. Interactions across boundaries in the group-ordering of identities, however, struggle with "outside disturbances that won't go away," such as popular and consumer culture, changing economic conditions, and race relations and feminisms. Emergent family culture resists purely biological and developmental explanations captured by terms such as "generation gap" or by essentialized and dehistoricized notions of white ethnic community. Family identity evolves in storytelling that contests the binary opposition of Franco-American with non-Franco-American (assimilated, intellectualized, McDonaldized). The evolving expression of performing family is not simply a story of silence, loss, and nostalgia but a complex narrative of adaptation to conflicting demands. Like the family storytelling of Robert, Aimee, and Michael and Monica, it engages change and differences coded in positive terms.

With McFeat (1974) and Foucault (1980) we have called these variations in family identities *local models* in order to resist the totalizing and purifying moves of either overpersonalization or overgeneralization. We have addressed overpersonalization, which severs the family from its social, economic, and historical circumstances, in terms of the invented tradition of individualism and the French family context in North America, the Northeast, and Maine. Family identity is never "just personal," nor even "just family" because it emerges in interactions with difference rather than in isolation. For example, family names are innovated and interpreted outside family, idealizations of individuals and families draw on canonical sources, communities are heterogenous and mobile. Nor can a family identity simply be taken as an ethnic group culture. Such overgeneralization, which makes a family-sized story into a group-sized story, obscures the variations in ethnic experiences inflected by gender, race, class, region, religion, and sexual orientation. We conclude our discussion by addressing issues in overgeneralizing ethnic identity. In performing family storytelling, what kind of "American" family do we get? What kind of "American" family are Franco-Americans?

By all accounts, the Franco-American family story is a muted voice in the making, remaking, and unmaking of American identity.[13] Some explanations hold Franco-Americans responsible for silencing themselves, emphasizing an internal cohesion which created ethnic enclaves and home cultures of "our world" where Franco-Americans resisted assimilation by hiding out (e.g., Langelier, 1996), maintaining a quiet presence (e.g., Hendrickson, 1980), or keeping on the move (e.g., Louder & Waddell, 1993). These accounts create heroes who preserve culture (Langellier, 2002) or blame the victims for losing their language, religion, or culture. Responsibility for cultural survival is variously lodged in *la survivance* of French Canada, in the French Cultural Movement of the U.S. elite, or in traditional ethnic women. Other accounts argue that Franco-American identity was silenced by others, pointing to external hostilities to French language use, anti-Catholic sentiments, class conflict over employment, and attacks on their "whiteness." These explanations shift blame to others, creating Franco-Americans as unmeltable ethnic heroes or vanquished victims of assimilation. Whether Franco-American identity is self-silencing or silenced by others, such accounts tend to slight mundane cultural practices, such as family storytelling.

The Franco-American silence may seem surprising, particularly by contrast with French Quebec, a site of vigorous and ongoing political struggle over North American identity. Quebec defines identity in opposition to British Canada, especially through the French language, drawing upon the rhizomatic relations of *la Francophonie.* In the francophone framework, Franco-Americans are twice immigrants, first from France to Canada, and second, from Canada to the United States. Franco-American identity in the Northeast emerged in opposition to Anglo-American, often specifically Yankee identities, but also in differentiation from other white ethnic immigrant groups, especially the Irish. Attention shifts from language and texts to performance and evolving family cultures, and analytically from *la Francophonie* as the basis for Canadian identity to white ethnicity in a U.S. context. Narratives of Franco-American families express the ambivalences of ties to French Canadian heritage and an American culture in its own right. As white ethnics they articulate the ambiguities of being simultaneously invisible and unmeltable. White ethnicity in the United States offers an alternative framework for interpreting Franco-American family identities. Family storytelling functions as a strategic performance of white ethnic identity that struggles against invisibility and assimilation. We discuss this strategic performance in terms of three explanations for white ethnicity: that it no longer exists, that it is symbolic and optional, and that it is discursive and material.

Franco-American family storytelling resists the erasures enacted by the white, Protestant, middle-class narrative reflected in Gillis's (1996) analysis of the American family. The Franco-American *family we live with* is inflected by boundary work and border conflicts that constrain race and ethnicity, region, religion, language, class, gender, and sexual orientation. Likewise, Stone's conclusions on ethnicity and migration expunge white ethnicity from family stories: "As for a correlation between the kinds of stories I heard and the home region or ethnicity of the teller: neither was as telling a factor as a family's tenure and status in this country" (p. 11). Her corpus tells the Assimilated Family Story and the pursuit, though not always successful, of the American Dream. Ethnicity is constructed as little more than family lore meaningful to past and elder generations. The Assimilated Family Story is the "old" ethnic narrative that asserts the acculturation of white European immigrants to which Franco-American family storytelling gives the lie. The politics of in/visibility narrate the achievement of assimilation and the ongoing silencing of ethnic difference. Franco-Americans, however, are not a new immigrant group, having resided in North America for 400 years and in the United States for 150, and entering over northeast borders in intermittent and unstable migrations with border crossings continuing to this day. Franco-Americans defy the straight-line theory of assimilation, the three-generational hypothesis of language loss, and cataclysmic cultural decline in the 1960s.

A second explanation of white ethnicity proposes that it has not disappeared but is only symbolic. In the context of the ethnic revival of the 1970s, Mary C. Waters (1990) studies white, middle-class, suburban Roman Catholic ethnics, especially Italians, Poles, and Irish. Notably, the book-length study mentions French ethnics just three times, none substantively. The new ethnicity is a symbolic identification with ancestry, invoked at the will of the individual and enacted situationally, often in leisure-time activities. For example, one participates in the St. Patrick's Day parade or a family celebrates a holiday with ethnic foods and rituals. Waters concludes that such ethnicity is an *option* exercised voluntarily for its pleasures. Invoked at the will of the individual or individual family, symbolic ethnicity is not something that influences one's life unless she or he wants it to. It carries no social costs and constrains no individual choices. It offers a sense of community, of connection through shared history, and some elements of a common culture.

The ethnic option fulfills the particularly American quest for community and for individuality. However, the study of Franco-American family storytelling renders the ethnic option problematic for a number of reasons. Its conceptualization of ethnicity as individualistic, voluntaristic, and without material constraints and consequences is not supported by Franco-American history and family storytelling. This new Ethnic Family Story (Rubin, 1994, p. 192)—"we came, we suffered, we conquered"—obscures differences among white ethnics, for example, the historical and contemporary class constraints on Franco-American families as well as the inflections of geographical region and rural experiences. Both the Assimilated Family Story of the "old" immigrants and the new Ethnic Family Story narrate the triumph of getting an American family and the American Dream of social mobility and invisibility.

Lillian Rubin also describes a symbolic ethnicity, but her study of race, ethnicity, and working-class families tells a more materialist story of the American family. In the social, political, and economic changes defining and re-defining family at the end of the twentieth century, she heard this story re-peatedly from her interviewees: "Each small climb was followed by a fall, each glimmer of hope replaced by despair. As the economic vise tightened, despair turned to anger" (pp. 240–241). For such "families on the faultline," the Amer-ican Dream—"if you work hard and play by the rules, you'll get a piece of the pie and surpass the generation before you"—has slipped away. For working-class families, being white does not assure dominance in a multiracial society organized around class privilege. The new immigration story of the White Eth-nic Family, "we came, we suffered, and we conquered," may be told without a single reference to race, and as Rubin notes, "it just happens that they're all white" (p. 192). Here white ethnicity describes a strategic response in a par-ticular historical and social circumstance, including "identity politics" and the competition for scarce resources within the economic shifts of the last thirty years as well as the historical changes brought about by the civil rights movement and immigration laws since 1965. Because the working class forms the largest, albeit invisible, group of families in the United States, working-class identity could unite families across races and ethnicities. Instead, Rubin argues that class resentment is mobilized as race anger directed at blacks and other minorities. At the same time that racial dissent has increased, white ethnicity has arisen.

According to Rubin, "Until new immigration shifted the complexion of the land so perceptibly, whites didn't think of themselves as white in the same way that the Chinese know they're Chinese and African Americans know they're black" (p. 182). Franco-American family storytelling accesses class and poverty quite directly but narrates race less directly. The historical emer-gence of Franco-American identity in opposition to Anglo-American language and culture (e.g., English, Yankee, Irish) deflects a discussion of race but does not escape racism. It has not yet come to terms with white skin privilege, and as bell hooks (2000) asserts, northern working-class people tend not to be sen-sitive to skin color privilege. A consideration of race also brings into focus both parallels and disjunctions of Franco-American migrations to the north-east with the southwest borderlands of Hispanic and Latina/o peoples. Paral-lels include the borderland migrations organized around extended family and continued border crossings. The issues of language (French and Spanish) and religion (Roman Catholicism) also suggest parallels. But skin color distin-guishes these ethnic groups and brings the relations of race and ethnicity to the forefront.

Issues of race and class in the construction of white ethnic identity can be situated within the "new ethnicities" described by Stuart Hall (1992). "New ethnicities" emerge in a second moment of black identity formation in Brit-ain. In the first moment blacks moved out of silence and invisibility as Other to the white British to become subjects rather than objects of representation practices. The second moment shifts from the struggles of representation to the politics of representation itself. The politics of representation are based on a sense of representation that is not simply mimetic. In Hall's words, "events, relations, structures, do have conditions of existence and real effects, outside the sphere of the discursive; but that only within the discursive, and subject to its specific conditions, limits, and modalities, do they have or can they be constructed within meaning" (p. 253). In this view ethnicity cannot be only symbolic because it has real effects. Representations of ethnicity in family storytelling have a formative, not merely an expressive, place in the constitution of social and political life. Performing family storytelling is an embodied, situated, and material practice with political consequences.

In fact, the "new ethnicities" of Britain overlap with the "ethnic revival" in the United States. Di Leonardo (1998) describes the discursive conditions most strongly when she identifies the moment in which white ethnicity articulated the "just right" family of multicultural America. For a decade of the 1970s ethnic traditions were refreshed in a U.S. "white ethnic revival," creating opportunity for families and communities to use celebrations as a special time to assert waning identities. The encumbered selves of ethnic families, particularly through the kinwork of women, created a sort of do-it-yourself domestic antimodernism, warm and homemade. According to di Leonardo, for a brief time on the heels of the civil rights movement and black power, the white ethnic family appropriated the just-right Baby Bear's chair between the "too cold" WASP family (modern, bloodless, bland, and unencumbered) and the "too hot" black family (primitive, wild, spicy, and overencumbered). In this formulation, white ethnic community emerged in opposition to and mimicry of civil rights and black power movements in the urban north as the "poor urban black" became the figure with which the "just right" of white ethnic community contrasted. White ethnic families were constructed as bearers of "good culture"—good families, mothers, fathers, and children—and long-lost "family values" in contrast to the "bad culture" of new immigrants, of gays, of feminists. She argues that the multicultural invitation to "honor our grandparents" and "our rich, rich culture" is a romantic celebration in the morality play of "American" identity that ignores the politics and material differences of history and political economy.

Di Leonardo's argument articulates a historical moment of unifying white ethnicity in the U.S. context. But the second moment of the "new ethnicities" invites a more differentiated and complicated narrative of Franco-Americans' relations to the past. On the one hand, the white ethnic family described by di Leonardo suggests more the "ideal" Franco-American culture than the lived realities of group-ordering in the storytelling of Franco-American *families we live with.* On the other hand, Franco-American identity emerged in opposition to Anglo-American identity, in Canada and the United States. Put another way, Franco-Americans are struggling over both what it means to be "American" and what it means to be "French," including contestations over language, religion, gender, and sexuality. Pleck's (2000) study of family celebration is also instructive. The rituals of the sentimental family based in domestic culture were invented between 1820 and 1890 among the white Protestant middle class, and Pleck argues that there was no comparable time for U.S. ethnic cultures, especially those inflected by Catholicism and working-class relations, such as Franco-Americans. French migration from Canada, for example, reached its height only at the end of this period and continued until 1930, when laws and economic forces closed migration. Both Quebec *survivance* and the French Cultural Movement in the United States long preceded the 1970s white ethnic revival.

We are not proposing that Franco-American family storytelling does not participate in old and new racisms—it does—but we encourage the problematizing of ethnicity *inside* group-ordering as well as in relation to racial groupings. In family storytelling Franco-Americans articulate multiple identities in their own terms, ethnic identities that are historically constructed and internally diverse. Telling Franco-American family stories invokes the positionings of language, region, and religion in the construction of ethnic identity. Analysis of such narratives of American identity are not just a "technology of the sacred" which makes visible and valuable yet another "rich, rich culture" for multicultural America (di Leonardo, 1998). Rather, attention to the performance of Franco-American family storytelling gives access to the complex politics of white ethnic narratives. Diversity among Franco-Americans and their differences from other U.S. white ethnic groups displaces the universal "white European American," whether assimilated or symbolic. Franco-American family storytelling complicates the narrative of "American" identity and reminds us that all persons speak from a historical and cultural family without being contained by it. In relation to Quebec identity movements, Franco-American identity decouples ethnicity from nationalism; in relation to U.S. identity movements, it decouples ethnicity from race. Diversity among white American ethnics and inside the notion of Franco-American family identity calls us to think more fully about the relations between racism and ethnicity and between antiracism and multiculturalism.

Finally, we argue that questions about the performance of family storytelling, for example, the loss of "family values," the costs of assimilation, multiculturalism and racism, resistance to hegemonic forms, and so on, are best answered within a multileveled and strategic model, such as the one developed in these three chapters that form Part II. Announcements on the decline of family and optional ethnicity are premature as people continue to get a family through daily practices of storytelling. The focus on identity and group-ordering can only be understood as particular tactics within the work of storytelling and task-ordering. Forms of task-ordering operate within the larger strategic context of content-ordering. Doing family constitutes a strategy for ordering cultural content and meanings in narrative. Within this strategic context, storytelling tasks are distributed among diverse participants in dispersed circumstances in order to perform narrative. The ordering of tasks, in turn, contextualizes the ordering of personal and family identities as tactics by which small groups articulate who they are to themselves and for themselves, for the diverse communities in which they live, and for society and future generations.

Part III

Storytelling Practices: Three Case Studies

We now turn to consider three case studies of performing narrative: storytelling in a weblog, breast cancer storytelling in a conversational interview, and a staged performance of storytelling. We take up these three cases after the extended analysis of family storytelling in order to disrupt analytic traditions that would explain communication as the action of individuals or as the result of self-expression. Family storytelling, taken as a research model, has the advantage of emphasizing the strategic distribution of knowledge and power in performing narrative. In the previous three chapters, we analyzed family storytelling as a communication practice, that is, as the multileveled ordering of strategies and tactics by which small group cultures produce and reproduce themselves as family in changing material conditions across generations. In the phenomenological tradition, we "bracketed" both the individual and the family in order to interrogate the operation of communication practices that define person and lived-world in doing family storytelling. For this reason, we clustered empirical accounts of family storytelling according to their lived-meaning or *theme*—that is, how they function relationally and contextually as communication practices—rather than use them to analyze the story of an individual or an individual family.

In the following case studies, we shift directions to move from a thematic analysis to one that *problematizes* performing narrative in particular cases. Foucault (2001) describes this form of analysis as an attempt "to analyze the way institutions, practices, habits, and behavior become a problem for people who behave in specific sorts of ways, who have certain types of habits, who engage in certain kinds of practices, and who put to work specific kinds of institutions" (p. 74). By making performing narrative problematic, analysis serves the goal of critique in the sense of offering an interpretive explication of a troubling situation rather than a calculus of celebration and suspicion. In these three case studies, we examine the way storytelling, "an unproblematic field of experience, or a set of practices, which were accepted without question, which were familiar and 'silent,' out of discussion, becomes a problem, raises discussion and debate, incites new reactions, and induces a crisis in the previously silent behavior, habits, practices, and institution" (p. 74).

The three cases we wish to "trouble" and problematize concern instances of storytelling that suggest boundary conditions for performing narrative. The case of storytelling in a weblog challenges the assumption of oral performance and presence that privileges "live" or face-to-face interaction as a necessary condition of performing narrative. In particular, we explore how storytelling in an age of digital reproduction constrains the bodily reflexivity by which webloggers participate in performing narrative. The case of storytelling about breast cancer challenges the assumption of coherence and expectations for recognizable beginnings, middles, and ends in performing narrative. This case troubles the therapeutic function of modernist illness and recovery narratives which positions narrators and audiences as survivors. The final case study, on a staged performance of autobiographical storytelling by a gay man, challenges the assumption of representational conventions that privilege normative visibility as a necessary condition for developing narrative identity and agency.

The following three case studies are organized to reflect the theoretical argument set out in the first chapter; that is, each case study explores how performing narrative is embodied, situated and material, discursive, and open to legitimation and critique. Furthermore, the progression of case studies parallels the structure of the strategic model we used to develop our discussion of family storytelling. While all aspects of the model are included in each case, we emphasize content-ordering in the critique of weblogs, especially issues of genre, generalizability, and timing; task-ordering in the critique of breast cancer storytelling, especially issues of decision-making and who gets to act and decide "what happens"; and group-ordering in the critique of staged performance, especially the representation and articulation of sexual identity and agency.

CHAPTER 5

Storytelling in a Weblog

Performing Narrative in a Digital Age

In his essay on the figure of the storyteller, first published in 1936, Benjamin (1969) argues that the storyteller in her or his "living immediacy" is no longer a present force but an increasingly remote and distant one. Benjamin attributes this change to the growing isolation of storyteller and audience from each other and to the devaluing of experience. If Benjamin was concerned about the isolation of storyteller and audience during the first part of the twentieth century when the explosive growth of technology transformed "a generation that had gone to school on a horse-drawn streetcar" (p. 84), then it seems reasonable to expect that he would express even greater concern at the beginning of the twenty-first century about the isolation of a generation that now can go to school on the Internet. If he was concerned by the diminution of experience and the "fragile human body" that occurred with the rise of mechanical warfare in World War I, then it also seems reasonable to expect that Benjamin would worry about computerized warfare in the twenty-first century as well as the uploading and downloading of virtual reality on the Internet that has come to replace the art of storytelling in which "experience [. . .] goes from mouth to mouth" (p. 84).

By resituating the traditional figure of the storyteller in the context of the contemporary fascination with the Internet, we extend Benjamin's analysis of changes in communication relations that accompany changes in technology. At the same time, however, we would like to hold in suspension two common tendencies in how we approach understanding historical changes in material conditions between the early twentieth and early twenty-first centuries; we would avoid technological determinism as well as nostalgia for an imaginary past that romanticizes oral culture. We suspend these tendencies, in part, by balancing the cautionary pessimism of Benjamin's essay "The Storyteller" with the cultural optimism of his essay "The Work of Art in the

Age of Mechanical Reproduction." In the latter essay, Benjamin suggests that changes in technology—the development of mechanical reproduction, in this case—detaches culture from the domain of tradition and thereby changes the mode by which we participate in its production. Rather than the cultural loss described in "The Storyteller," Benjamin suggests that changes in technology open up opportunities for cultural experience outside of either the traditional realm of high culture or the newer realm of commercially produced mass culture. Storytelling on the Internet provides a ready exemplar to question the changing relations of culture and technology as well as the tendency to privilege oral culture and "orality" in the analysis of storytelling.

One example of storytelling on the Internet can be seen in the explosive growth of the Internet-based online journal or diary. One of the authors of this book, Eric, first came across online journals while doing research on personal web pages and electronic self-publishing in 1998. The web page he stumbled upon was a dated entry in which the writer described a visit to the beach over the last weekend with friends and the changing nature of their relationships. Clearly, this site was more closely related to a personal diary or journal than it was to a personal home page. Nor was this website an isolated case, for a quick look at the listing of "friends" on the web page revealed links to a number of similar journals.

Diane Patterson (2000) writes that there were very few journals online when she began hers, *nobody-knows-anything.com*, in June 1996. Simon Firth (1998), in an essay posted on *Salon*, credits Carolyn Burke with the first online journal in January 1995.[1] By 2000, Blogger.com reported over 150,000 registered users of its web tools after a year in operation. Blogger.com is only one of several Internet sites for those interested in writing or reading journals and diaries; other such sites include Diarist.net, Diaryland.com, LiveJournal.com, and Pitas.com. Another type of site attempts to categorize or list the growing number of journals. At the close of 2002, for example, the list of "recently changed weblogs" on Dave Winer's weblogs.com (http://www.weblogs.com) may reach to over 1,200 entries on any given day; *Eatonweb Portal* (http://www.portal.eatonweb.com) provides a registry of over 8,000 journals that can be sorted alphabetically or by topic, language, or country.

While this amorphous group of Internet diaries, journals, home pages, and websites has no agreed-upon label, we will use one term that is commonly employed by practitioners (although not without controversy) and that is broad enough to suggest the variety of forms that it attempts to describe: *weblog*. An invented, portmanteau-style label, weblog has the advantage of suggesting the two forms that tend to predominate under its heading. Weblog suggests both a "log of web activity" that serves as a filter or portal to other websites, and a journal or "log published on the web." The use of the term "log," or "blog," recalls related computer terms such as server log and logfiles. Some weblog authors, or bloggers, argue against the inclusion of either filter-

or journal-style versions in their definition of weblogs. Rebecca Blood (2000) attributes the combination of both filter- and journal-style versions in a more inclusive definition of weblog to Brigitte Eaton's practice of accepting any site with dated entries in the *Eatonweb Portal* list of weblogs. Blood concludes that since this "was the most complete listing of weblogs available, Brig's inclusive definition prevailed."

The emphasis on dated entries is shared by both filter- and journal-style weblogs, although in the latter case the weblog is oriented less around links with commentary and more around recording the reflections, thoughts, and observations of the writer. These journal-style weblogs resemble their print and handwritten cousins with the important distinction that nearly all weblogs maintain a reverse chronology (the most recently posted goes on top) in their entries rather than the progressive chronology typical of print or handwritten journals and diaries. The mix of observation and reflection in storytelling is illustrated by the first part of an entry taken from *clinkclank*, the journal we will use to illustrate our analysis in this chapter.[2] The entry is entitled "trapped by technology."

> This morning the garage door opener jammed, and we couldn't manually open it. It was a moment of absurdity, being trapped inside the garage. J. muttered something about this thing needing rebooting, and I couldn't help but think of that Far Side cartoon with the phone ringing and the cows: "And here we sit, without opposable thumbs."
>
> However, there was a sticker on the wall with a phone number and instructions to call if the garage door was stuck—a sort of Wonderland touch, at this point. J. called them and they told him how to jostle the emergency thingie to un-stick it, which worked. Only now do I realize that the garage door people had assumed (correctly, of course) that we were calling on a cell phone and thus were able to follow their directions on the spot. (4/20/2001; http://clinckclank.net/clonk/000020.html)

In this entry, *clinkclank* epitomizes the tension that Benjamin finds in the explosive growth of technology. Here one form of technology, the garage door opener, increases the potential for isolation (literally) while another form, the cell phone, works to decrease that isolation.

Blood (2000) attributes the rapid growth in journal-style weblogs in 1999 to the arrival of free web-tool packages and software, such as those provided by Greymatter, MoveableType, Pitas, and Blogger, which greatly simplified the process of composing and publishing weblogs. Widely available web tools, templates, and automated update services make it possible for anyone with computer access and rudimentary skills to publish a weblog. Pitas.com asks on its signup page if "you're sick of editing html pages all the time and then ftping them to your site? Well you're in luck! Pitas.com is now offering free and easy to update pages with an easy-to-use web interface." Blogger.com, which describes itself as "push-button publishing for the people," announces on its home page that "Blogger offers you instant communication power by letting you post your thoughts to the web whenever the urge strikes." Writers use such services to create online identities and journals with titles such as *gee-off, blogstalker, undo, pixgrrl, myuki, funkytrash,* and *mangledoll.*

Weblogs chronicle daily events, interactions with friends and romantic partners, drinking adventures, bad haircuts, favorite foods and recipes, rants about current events and music, impromptu movie and book reviews, and all the details, trivial and otherwise, of daily life. As *jish.nu* writes, "part of the reason [to keep a weblog] is to share my writing with my readers, but another reason is for historical or documentation purposes. I like to keep track of interesting sites I find, events in my life, and how I felt at a particular moment in time" (http://www.jish.nu/about). Amidst the lists, fragmentary details, and ephemera of daily life are stories—sometimes implicit and sometimes explicit, as when *clinkclank* titles the following entry "stories from l.a."

> I'd forgotten about this one.
>
> We are sitting on the patio of a Japanese-California fusion restaurant. All very L.A. down to the brushed-aluminum and tiki-style outdoor lamps. At the table next to us sits a man and woman, fifties or so, clad in brightly casual clothing, and talking too loudly and too near to allow us our own conversation. The man is planning a trip to Bali, which he pronounces Baahhh-lee.
>
> "You should go sometime, you'd love Baahlee. Tell you what, I'll bring you something. I'll bring you . . . some art."
>
> "I really need some furniture—you could bring me a piece of furniture! Furniture from Baaahlee!"
>
> "No, no. They make really nice art, they do. You know, like ob-jeckts deh-art. I'll bring you some, an ob-jeckt—"
>
> "You know Sally?—She went to Baahlee, and got all this furniture, for her whole apartment it was only $1500. And it was just wonderful, it was just like Pottery Barn. This heavy table, and chairs, and it's all just beautiful, just like Pottery Barn!"
>
> I turn to J., and say (to paraphrase Kyle Baker [embedded link to http://www.kylebaker.com/www/book/wihs.htm]), "These people are in hell, and they don't even know it." (5/29/2001, http://www.clinkclank.net/clonk/000143.html)

We know this weblog entry is an example of storytelling because the writer announces it as one instance of a larger group of stories ("stories from l.a. I'd forgotten about this one"). Furthermore, the entry exhibits those characteristics that narrative researchers use to identify the recapitulation of past experience as constituting a personal narrative event. That is, there is a verbal sequence of clauses that contain the structural elements of a "fully formed narrative" (Labov & Waletzky, 1967), as we identify in the analysis of Pauline's "family classic" about her mother sliding under the car (Chapter 2). The story has an abstract (this is an L.A. story), orientation (who is involved, where the action takes place), complicating action (first this happens, then this happens), evaluation ("All very L.A.," "these people are in hell"), and resolution ("I turn to J., and say"). It contains many of the same theatrical devices and poetic features (e.g., the shift from past tense to narrative present, dialogue, suggestion of expressive phonology and intonation) that render the text self-focusing, increase reader involvement, and display the writer's competence.

But does posting stories on a weblog constitute what Benjamin would recognize as storytelling in its "living immediacy?" Do weblogs come from and return to "living speech?" Or, as we would pose the question, how do weblogs perform narrative? Let us begin by looking at the systems of relations among storytellers and audiences in weblogs—in short, at how storytelling in weblogs is embodied.

Into the Abyss of the Inanimate:
The Cyber Storyteller

Benjamin distinguishes storytelling from other forms of narrative by insisting that it constitutes a particular kind of communication relationship between audience and storyteller, not merely the dissemination of information or the recapitulation of past experience. The storyteller, as we discussed earlier, "takes" from experience in order to "make" experience for an audience. By contrast, Benjamin argues, "the novelist has isolated himself" or herself (p. 87). Again, when discussing storytelling from the perspective of the audience, Benjamin states that a woman or "man listening to a story is in the company of the storyteller; even a [woman or] man reading one shares in this companionship. The reader of the novel, however, is isolated, more so than any other reader" (p. 100). Benjamin uses the isolation of the storyteller from the audience to distinguish storytelling from other forms of narrative. As the last quotation makes clear, however, he does not base his description of storytelling on a distinction between speaking and writing, between hearing and reading, because it is possible for a person to read a storyteller. Instead, Benjamin emphasizes the shared companionship of audience and storyteller: the audience is "in the company" of the storyteller.

What does it mean to be "in the company" of the storyteller, and does reading a weblog put us in the company of a storyteller? An excerpt from the weblog *clinkclank* illustrates this question. In an entry entitled "half a conversation," *clinkclank* records:

> Michael writes me to say "When I read a blog I feel sort of like I'm corresponding with someone, except that I'm not obligated to hold up my end of the conversation." This makes me laugh, because I have a long history of shy friends who would confide that they really appreciated the fact that they could spend time with me and only talk if they wanted to, instead of that awkward silence-dashing need. (5/3/2001, http://www.clinkclank.net/clonk/000187.html)

This extract from *clinkclank* suggests that weblogs resemble but are not the same as correspondence and conversations. Reading a weblog is "sort of like" corresponding with someone, "sort of like" a conversation. The changing relation between storyteller and audience in weblogs reflects what Benjamin would call a "new kind of perception." He attempts to unravel these changing relations in his essay on "The Work of Art in the Age of Mechanical Reproduction," in which he contrasts the relationship of audience and performer in theater with the relationship of audience and performer in film. The audience in theater is in the company of the performer, just as it is in storytelling. This joint companionship makes it possible for the performer to adjust to the audience and for the audience to adjust to that adjustment within the duration of the performance. In film, by contrast, the performer cannot adjust to the responses of the audience within the duration of the film—a "feeling of strangeness [. . .] overcomes the actor before the camera" (p. 230) Benjamin writes—because the audience is "beyond the reach" of the performer. The performer in film can adjust her or his performance in future films, but this adjustment takes place after or between entire performances.

The distinction here is between adaptive action that occurs within a single performance (where theater is the exemplar) and adaptive action that occurs upon a class of performances (where film is the exemplar)—what Gregory Bateson (1979) identifies as the difference between feedback and calibration. The performer in theater makes continuous changes in her or his performance based on the *feedback* of the audience, while the performer in film must wait until after the film is completed to *calibrate* changes in her or his future performances. While both feedback and calibration are adaptive actions of audience and performer, one is only "sort of like" the other.

What makes it difficult to untangle the ways that feedback and calibration are "sort of like" each other is that they are not in a simple relation of opposition that Benjamin's comparison initially suggests. Bateson reminds us that feedback and calibration overlap and spiral as well as alternate. For example, a performance in theater—Benjamin's exemplar for feedback—is based upon numerous rehearsals in which the performer repeats and revises a series of actions in order to *calibrate* her or his character as a whole for performance. Rehearsal is an occasion for training or disciplining the body so that it can productively respond to *feedback* in performance. In a similar way, performance in film—Benjamin's exemplar for calibration—is based upon recording several "takes" of the same scene and then selecting from among them. However, within each "take" the performer responds to *feedback* from the director, other performers, as well as staff and crew in what constitutes a kind of "model" audience and upon which the performer builds a particular *calibration*. In this case, each separate scene is an opportunity for the bodily responsiveness of the performer to be "taken" by the discipline of the camera and later editing. As Benjamin reminds us, "The audience's identification with the actor is really an identification with the camera. Consequently the audience takes the position of the camera; its approach is that of testing" (pp. 228–229), or what Bateson calls calibration. In this way, we see that the audience of film *calibrates* its response to a film through *feedback* in talking with friends and reading critics both before and after watching a particular film performance. Feedback and calibration alternate and overlap.

Rather than the mutual communication and reflection that engage audiences and performers in theater, weblogs approximate—they are "sort of like" —the adaptive action of continuous feedback. Weblogs approximate the adaptive action of feedback by reducing the size of the class of performances in which calibration takes place to smaller units: for example, through the posting of brief log entries, updates, and responses rather than the longer essays or novels invoked by Benjamin's contrast of novelist-audience relations. Weblogs are more like writing and reading correspondence than they are like writing and reading a novel or newspaper. Weblogs approximate the adaptive action of feedback by reducing the interval or delay between calibrations: for example, through daily postings and through the more rapid exchanges made possible by e-mail notes or Internet chats. Weblogs are more like engaging in conversation than they are like watching or "talking back" to a film. In phenomenological terms, communication in weblogs is better described as interactive than as intersubjective.

We use the terms *interactive* and *intersubjective* in order to avoid reducing the differences between theater and film, or between storytelling in conversation and storytelling in weblogs, to an opposition between unmediated and mediated communication or between reality and virtual reality. This easy and commonplace opposition is troubling for at least two reasons. First, it ignores how person-to-person relations are always already mediated by discourse (as we discuss in the chapters on family storytelling). Second, it obscures how person-to-person relations are always already imbued with the imaginary and virtual (an extended discussion of this point can be found in Morse, 1998). We do not leave one world of interpersonal interaction, for example, in order to enter another world of cyberspace to read a weblog. Our interpersonal world is already saturated with the virtual and imaginary in our pre-reflective relations with others.

At the same time, however, we want to avoid collapsing the differences between interactivity and intersubjectivity to the point that they are indistinguishable. To say that our only access to weblogs is through bodily participation is not the same as saying that there is no difference between person-to-person and person-to-technology relations. An example of a stance that collapses this difference in relations can be seen in the comment by one of Sherry Turkle's (1997) interviewees for her book *Life on the Screen,* who says that "RL [real life] is just one more window" (p. 13). With the metaphor of a window, the interviewee collapses the social and material context in which he lives to one of several possible "worlds" he can choose; he takes experience, as Turkle puts it, at (inter)face value.

Turkle sees the struggle to understand the relations of people and things marked out in how we conceptualize the computer as tool, as mirror, and as a "looking glass" or gateway. In this analytic move, Turkle recalls Benjamin's description of the "feeling of strangeness" that overcomes the performer before the camera. This "feeling of strangeness" is not unique to film, Benjamin points out; it is basically the estrangement that a person feels "before one's own image in the mirror. But now the reflected image has become separable, transportable" (pp. 230–231). In order to understand our bodily participation in weblogs, therefore, we must examine and clarify the labor of vision by which we participate in images.

For a description of vision and our relation to mirror images, we turn to an extended quotation from Merleau-Ponty's (1964a) essay on "Eye and Mind":

> The mirror image anticipates, within things, the labor of vision. Like all other technical objects, such as signs and tools, the mirror arises upon the open circuit [that goes] from seeing body to visible body. Every technique is a "technique of the body." A technique outlines and amplifies the metaphysical structure of our flesh. The mirror appears because I am seeing-visible [voyant-visible], because there is a reflexivity of the sensible; the mirror translates and reproduces that reflexivity. My outside completes itself in and through the sensible. (p. 168)

When "bloggers" sit down or stand in front of computer screens in order to read or write weblogs, they do not leave their bodies behind. Despite the rhetorical flourishes in which enthusiasts and detractors alike talk about disembodied communication and virtual selves, weblogs arise on the open circuit that goes from seeing body to visible body. Commonplace statements of being "sucked into the computer," "lost to the world," and "transported into cyberspace" may come close to describing how the bodily focus of attention shifts in using a computer (and we will argue later that these rough approximations are inadequate at that as well), but they fail miserably as descriptions of the bodily participation in the labor of weblogging. A person can read or write a weblog only to the extent that she or he is bodily capable of doing so. That is, reading and writing weblogs requires bodily discipline (the ability to orient, reach for, and grasp or accomplish a task) and a disciplined body (a body trained to read and write, to manipulate a keyboard, to use computers and access the Internet).

Weblogs appear because of bodily participation in them, "because I am seeing-visible." The question is not one of disembodiment, but of how reading or writing a weblog "translates and reproduces" the reflexivity of the sensible. What, in other words, is *clinkclank* getting at by saying that a weblog is "sort of like" a conversation? In the following passage, Merleau-Ponty continues his description of how the mirror translates and reproduces the reflexivity of the sensible:

> The mirror's ghost lies outside my body, and by the same token my own body's "invisibility" can invest the other bodies I see. Hence my body can assume segments derived from the body of another, just as my substance passes into them;

man is mirror for man. The mirror itself is the instrument of a universal magic that changes things into a spectacle, spectacles into things, myself into another, and another into myself. (p. 168)

A weblog, just like the mirror image, is an "outside" that the body takes up and invests through the labor of vision. The mirror image and the weblog are not puzzles to be thought about or completed in reflection, but openings in the body's reflexivity that are lived through. The invisibility of this bodily participation—of vision in act—is what makes it possible for weblogs to appear. Weblogs are a spectacle, both a sight and a site; that is, weblogs are the instrument of a universal magic that changes "writing" into a "reading" and "reading" into a "writing."

In a similar way, the body's invisibility is evident in the reflexivity of speaking and listening that *clinkclank* describes when she comments that her shy friends "confide that they really appreciated the fact that they could spend time with me and only talk if they wanted to." In the "realm of living speech," as Benjamin calls it, the reflexivity of speaking and listening is not fixed in a particular pattern of exchanges; it is possible for the conversational task-ordering of taking turns to be set aside while one person does most of the talking. Both *clinkclank* and her shy friends are comfortable in their ongoing relationship—they maintain their bodily capability of both speaking and listening—even while one person temporarily foregoes the obligation of reciprocal exchange to "hold up my end of the conversation." Clearly, weblogs also forgo the obligation of reciprocal exchange, an exchange that approximates the continuous feedback immanent in conversation. However, both conversation and weblogs are "techniques of the body" that outline and amplify bodily reflexivity. In a weblog, the body's contact with an image "on the screen" is not virtual but lived through. What is immanent in this lived experience and cannot be guaranteed is the "shared companionship" of the audience and storyteller.

A weblogger may desire that her or his use of computer technology remain transparent and "unmediated" in the experience of reading or writing a weblog. But desire operates here to incorporate technology and not vice versa: that is, while technology extends the body's capability to participate in storytelling, it does not make the body into an extension of the computer. As Merleau-Ponty summarizes, "Our organs are no longer instruments; on the contrary, our instruments are detachable organs" (p. 178). It is the lived-body, the conscious experience of communication, that provides the basis for its technological extension in reading weblogs. However tempting it is to mistake the invisibility of bodily reflexivity for the transparency of our reversible relations with technology, we must take care not to confuse the lived-body with the body-object, our "detachable organs" with "instruments." Vivian Sobchack (1995) warns against this temptation to confuse flesh and hardware, consciousness and computation, in the technologically enhanced body. She argues that "the increasing transparency of one's lived-flesh enabled by new technologies as well as the ubiquitous visibility of new technologies leads to euphoria and a sense of the limitless extension of being beyond its materiality and mortality. This, however, is 'false' consciousness—for it has 'lost touch' with the very material and mortal body that grounds its imagination and imagery" (p. 211).

The question that Benjamin poses about what it means to be in the company of the storyteller results in a deliberate ambiguity when we consider weblogs. To the question "does reading a weblog put us in the company of the storyteller?" we must answer *both* yes *and* no. Based on the analysis of the body's labor of vision in reading a weblog, we would respond that, *yes*, the "living immediacy" of the storyteller is immanent in weblogs as it is in conversational storytelling. Storytelling, whether in weblogs or in conversation, arises on "the open circuit" of bodily reflexivity. In reading a weblog, the body assumes segments—traces of verbal material—derived from the body of the storyteller in writing. At the same time, and because the body's reflexivity comprehends both possibilities, we do not confuse storytelling in weblogs with storytelling in conversations. The analysis of storyteller-audience relations and adaptation through feedback and calibration would lead us to respond that, *no*, the reader of weblogs is not in the company of the storyteller as she or he is in conversation. While weblogs may approximate, they do not replace the adaptive action of continuous feedback. But neither does physical presence alone put us in the company of the storyteller—for the tired audience member slumped over and sleeping in the last row of a large auditorium can hardly be said to be engaged in that adaptive action either.

Weblogs extend the body's capability for storytelling. Thus, weblogs function as storytelling to the extent that they emphasize rather than mask or disavow our participation. Weblogs function as "cyber storytelling" because they extend the body's reflexivity, not because they absorb the body or transport it to another world. The audience of the weblog is not "beyond the reach" of the storyteller, as Benjamin would put it, because the audience "grasps" the weblog through the labor of vision. Neither the person before a mirror nor the person before a weblog can reach out and touch the image; however, the body takes up both images in the "action at a distance" that is vision. Thus it is the materiality and mortality of the lived-body that grounds our potential to "join the company of the storyteller" in weblogs.

Storytelling in the Context of Digital Reproduction

Weblogs extend the bodily capability to participate in storytelling. The social and material context for bodily participation, however, is not uniform and homogeneous. As Benjamin points out, there is a difference in the situation of the person who feels estranged before the image in the mirror and the person who feels estranged before the image in film. In the latter situation—brought about by what Benjamin calls the age of mechanical reproduction—the "image has become separable, transportable" (p. 231). Mechanical reproduction makes possible a greater separability and transportability of images and of cultural texts in general. Before the age of the printing press and photography, such cultural texts were reproducible through the work of copyists and forgers. The author of a handwritten journal or diary constructs an original that is open to reproduction in limited ways; the journal can be hidden, circulated among friends, talked about with others, copied by hand. In an age of mechanical reproduction, the reproducibility of the journal changes; the journal can be put into print and published in books, newspapers, or magazines, it can be typed rather than handwritten, it can be photocopied and distributed by mail, broadcast on television, or read aloud over radio.

The historical development of mechanical reproduction thus alters the relations of cultural objects to their context. Techniques of mechanical reproduction make it possible to detach cultural texts from the domain of tradition where the authenticity of a work was guaranteed by its unique existence. Mechanical reproduction increases the availability of copies and increases access to cultural objects by bringing them out of the cathedral, studio, or auditorium and into daily life and domestic space. A journal, for example, is not limited to the few persons who can read the original. It can be published or broadcast and read or listened to by a large public. Readers no longer need access to an original to discuss its meanings and significance. As Mark Poster (2001) summarizes, "handwriting introduces one relation of the writer and reader to the text; typewriting and print, different ones" (p. 80). The plurality of copies in the age of mechanical reproduction, in other words, recontextualizes how writers and readers of journals relate to them. Reproducibility becomes an intrinsic rather than incidental part of journals. As Benjamin states, "the work of art reproduced becomes the work of art designed for reproduction" (p. 224). The public that reads a published journal recognizes that it was written by an absent author, and authors in an age of mechanical reproduction produce journals with the understanding that they may or will be reproduced and read by a public, by absent readers.

In an age of mechanical reproduction, the separability and transportability of images and texts are part of their taken-for-grantedness, part of their social and material context. In her discussion of "why web journals suck," Patterson (2000) begins with the premise that journal authors "put them on the Web for an audience." However intimate their contents may be, the claim that they are "private and not for readers is disingenuous at best." *Gingerbug* reflects a similar sentiment in the weblog *Interview* (http://www.interview.diaryland.com) that she created to make it possible for diarists to "have their say" rather than rely on rankings provided by the weblog and journal service providers. In her response to the question of why keep a journal online, *Gingerbug* writes: "Like most on-line diarists though, one of my main reasons for all the public writing is, of course a degree of morbid fascination with the workings of one's own mind—and the faint hope of being noticed in some sense. By someone at least. Otherwise the therapeutic written form of introspection might as well happen in one of those dusty old notebooks" (http://www.interview.diaryland.com/gingerbug.html).

Weblogs make public what is usually thought of as personal. In reflecting upon the first web pages published in the mid-1990s, *clinkclank* writes that "there was this rush in self-publishing; suddenly, we were all struck by the excitement of sharing our *selves* with the world [. . .] nothing was too trivial for the personal homepage: pet pictures, lengthy bios, favorite recipes, and lists, lists, lists" (5/2/2001, http://www.clinkclank.net/clonk/000188.html, emphasis in original). After a few years, and with the introduction of templates and automated update services, the excitement of reading these pages faded, and she read only a few sites that belonged to friends. Then, she writes,

> Skip ahead to the present, when I've slowly added more blogs to my daily reading. I was initially put off by those always-linked blogs: lemonyellow? sippey? There must be a reason why people point to these as exemplar blogs, but they make me sad, with their sparse and impersonal feel—like they are being updated out of duty, not desire. But the number of blog-voices are growing, and I'm seeing the earnestness, the questioning and quirkiness, the concern and humor once more. [. . .] So I've been reading more blogs. (5/2/2001, http://www.clinkclank.net/clonk/000188.html)

The weblogs that regain *clinkclank*'s attention are not the "sparse and impersonal" ones, but ones that are "earnest" and "quirky"—in short, weblogs that are written by someone in their particularity, not just anyone.

Thus, even though weblogs are published to a public, they are differentiated from what Paddy Scannell (1996) calls the "for-anyone structures of publicly available anonymous (mass produced) usable things" (p. 174). Scannell uses this distinction between a text written for-someone and a text written for-anyone to characterize how radio and television programs have an embedded orientation or directionality. Such programs address their audiences as particular someones and not as a group or public. In a public event, such as a political speech or a theatrical performance, there is a one-to-many structure to communication in which the audience is addressed as a collective. By contrast, Scannell argues, broadcasts address the audience in a one-to-one fashion; an audience member is not addressed as part of the many, a collective, nor as an eavesdropper on someone else's conversation. Broadcast programs, he concludes, have a "for-anyone-as-someone structure" (p. 13); that is, they combine the for-anyone structure of public communication with the for-someone structure of interpersonal communication.

Weblogs share the for-anyone-as-someone structure with broadcast programs and other forms of mechanical reproduction. We would make explicit the complementary relationship of production and consumption implied by Scannell's formulation. That is, the directionality of journals contextualizes their writing as well as their reading. Journals are written with what we would call the as-someone-for-anyone structure—just as they are read as having such directionality. An author makes public or publishes (as-someone-for-anyone) a journal which an individual reader can find in print or on the Internet and read (for-anyone-as-someone). The for-anyone-as-someone structure of weblogs is evident in *clinkclank*'s entry entitled "not a stalker, just a dolphin":

> When I was in college (cue joints popping and gray hairs emerging), there weren't that many women with personal websites. Add to that the fact that my name appeared near the top of any alphabetical lists, and you get an epoch where most of the people you meet grin knowingly and say *Ahhh, I know you.* I had to fight the urge to do exactly that to *Jish* [embedded link to http://www.jish.nu] today at lunch. (1/9/2002, http://www.clinkclank.net/clonk/000044. html)

What *clinkclank* describes here is the inappropriate application of a model of interpersonal communication to relations that emerge in weblogs. That is, *clinkclank*'s readers—and *clinkclank* herself—may confuse familiarity with a writer's work (a pubic *you*) for the familiarity of an interpersonal relationship (a personal *you*); they may confuse the as-someone-for-someone structure of conversation with the for-anyone-as-someone structure of weblogs. But *clinkclank* resists confusing her affective involvement in reading the "separable and transportable" weblog, *jish*, with the person, Jish, she talks with at lunch. She does not "stalk" Jish by assuming a personal relationship where there is "only" the trace or appearance of one in her web surfing (playing in the surf, as a dolphin would).

At the same time, however, we must not confuse the for-anyone-as-someone structure of weblogs with a "many-to-many" model of communication as Poster (2001, p. 16) does in attempting to distinguish between the constitution of text-audience relations on the Internet and in broadcasting and print. The "many" of the weblog audience are not the collective group found at a public event but dispersed and isolated readers, as are broadcast and print audiences. The "many" of weblog authors are not a collective but dispersed and isolated individuals, as are authors of print and broadcast journals. Two distinctions that Poster develops, however, are helpful for understanding the difference between reproduction on the Internet and reproduction in broadcasting and print. First, weblogs are digital reproductions; second, weblogs do not require the extensive material conditions for production and distribution that print and broadcast do.

For Benjamin, mechanical reproduction differs from manual reproduction in its process. Benjamin gives the example of the photograph that reproduces a painting in a different way than a forged painting reproduces a painting. In mechanical reproduction, there is a difference in the "medium" or the "capacity to do physical work" (Wilden, 1987a, p. 72) between the original and the copy

that does not exist in manual reproduction—even if the organization of information or "message" remains roughly the same in both cases. For example, to
photocopy or mechanically duplicate someone's journal requires a different
kind of work than it does to "forge" a journal by sitting down at the same type-
writer and typing the same words on the same kind of paper. A weblog, constructed by manipulating a computer keyboard, further modifies the kind of
work it takes to reproduce a journal. Because a weblog does not, by definition,
exist as a "log" until it is posted to the "web," the distinction between original and copy is further reduced if not eliminated. The "original" weblog of the
author is accessed in the same way as the "copy" of the reader—both versions
are reproductions in that the author and reader gain access to the same source
(i.e., the server where the weblog is stored) and download the weblog by entering the same computer commands (i.e., entering the address for or clicking
on a particular website). In some senses, digital reproduction would appear to
be closer to forgery and manual reproduction than it is to mechanical reproduction in that weblogs are *replications* in the semiotic sense (Eco, 1976); that
is, copies are made in the same material continuum (the same physical work)
as the original.

It is important to emphasize that this distinction in forms of reproduction
concerns types of *coding* and not other communication elements or functions. Poster (2001) would generalize from a difference in coding to a difference
between speech and language and on to "authors analogue and digital." But
both speech and writing are linguistic messages and, as such, are digital representations used to refer to the surrounding context. As Poster says, "the
word *tree* does not look like a tree" (p. 81)—to which we would add, nor does
the spoken word *tree* sound like a tree. The difference here is not between
speech and writing because both employ analog and digital coding. Wilden
(1987a) clearly states this point: "analog and digital coding are found in all
communication systems. [. . .] The two forms of coding do not oppose or contradict one another ('either/or') but complement each other ('both-and')"
(p. 225). Both speech and writing rely on analog coding of sensing-sensible participants. As Poster notes, "spoken words rely on the ear [and voice] for copy-
ing and reproduction; writing depends rather upon the eye [and hand]" of *embodied participants* (p. 80; our additions and emphasis). The construction of
"digital authors" and readers does not occur, as Poster suggests, "entirely on
the screen, determined entirely by words entered on the keyboard" (p. 75) but
in the context of work by a disciplined body—a body whose varied capabilities include playing with language and moving among speaking, reading, writing by hand, and composing at the keyboard.

Poster's distinction between the work of digital reproduction and that of
manual or mechanical reproduction is helpful, however, when considering
how digital coding facilitates reproduction and distribution of cultural texts
such as weblogs. The second distinction that Poster develops concerns the

contrast between the historical and material conditions of print and broadcasting and those for Internet use. The development of print and the multiple copies of mechanical reproduction ruptured the institutional relations in which writing was produced and distributed; mechanical reproduction moved cultural texts from the realm of craft to that of industry, from the hand work of copyists to the standardization and part-interchangeability of the printing press, from distribution within social elites to mass marketing. As Poster comments, "a printing industry, a market for books, an educational system all developed around the page" (p. 93) and mechanical reproduction. While the so-called "fourth estate" made possible by the printing press may have challenged the traditional elites of the first three estates (nobility, clergy, and middle class), the requirements of capital—especially access to systems of production and distribution—limited the "democratizing potential" of mechanical reproduction. Freedom of the press, the common saying goes, only exists if you happen to own one. In a similar fashion, broadcasting functions as a capital intensive industry: nearly anyone can make a film, video, or recording, but without access to production and distribution systems, these efforts remain amateur (i.e., of limited production values) and marginal (i.e., of limited distribution) cultural texts.

Poster argues that digital reproduction on the Internet accomplishes for production and distribution what mechanical reproduction accomplished for the availability and consumption of cultural texts—decentralization. He writes: "the Net is highly decentralized: for a small fee and subject to no regulatory body, anyone using the proper protocols and having a telephone line can connect to it. This decentralization enables anyone connected to have a position of enunciation, sometimes to the chagrin of existing authorities" (p. 45). Other scholars, such as Robert McChesney (2000), take a more cautious position:

> We should be careful not to extrapolate from the experience of activists what the Internet experience will look like for the bulk of the population. [. . .] in the big scheme of things, having the ability to launch a website at nominal expense is only slightly more compelling than saying we have no grounds of concern about monopoly newspapers because anyone can write up a newsletter and wave it in their front window or hand it out for their neighbors. (p. 15)

Weblogs, with their emphasis on the particular and the personal, provide a good example of what Internet experience might look like for "the bulk of the population." Despite McChesney's suggestion otherwise, weblogs benefit from the "distributed network" structure whereby "routers allow data to flow to its destination by any route that is available to it" (Poster, 2001, p. 46), especially in comparison with the centralized distribution networks (of telephone, cable, television, radio, and so on) which regulate what can be broadcast or published in print.[3]

While monopoly and corporate concerns might be working to take advantage of the Internet—and this is especially evident in the creation of macro-portals that compete or attempt to replace the micro-portal function of filter-style weblogs—webloggers are not excluded from the beginning because they lack the "start up" and capital necessary to gain access to the limited and highly controlled broadcast spectrum and to print distribution networks. Monopoly publishers and broadcasters may control all the available "shelf space" in the marketplace of ideas under mechanical reproduction, but digital reproduction opens up that market by expanding both the shelf space (through the rapid growth of websites) and the range of ideas that can be placed there.

In an entry entitled "when corporate blogs attack," *clinkclank* speculates on the difficulty corporations face in appropriating weblogs for commercial interests:

> OK, so we were talking on this mailing list about the seeming inevitability of corporations faking weblogs to hawk their products. And I said, I don't know, but somehow that doesn't strike me as very exciting reading . . .
>
>> I woke up this morning with the worst breath ever. Thank God for Crest, I muttered to myself as I staggered into the bathroom. I brushed my teeth vigorously, then stepped into the shower.
>>
>> Damn! I was out of Pantene, which meant my hair wasn't going to have that healthy, lustrous sheen this morning. At least I could be Sure about my deodorant.
>>
>> Stepping out of the bathroom, I almost tripped over my cat, Proctor. "Fine, fine, I'll get you your Iams", I said. I was pretty hungry myself, now, so I opened the refrigerator. "Eh . . . there's milk, beer, purple stuff . . . yes, there's Sunny D!" I chugged half the carton and pumped my fist in the air. I grabbed a can of Pringles off the counter and shoved it into my bag, ready for the day.
>
> All right, corporate America, here I come. Now to sit back and watch those checks flow in . . .
> (11/13/2001, http://www.clinkclank.net/clonk/000101.html)

This entry by *clinkclank* suggests that the content of weblogs, and not just their production and distribution, make them resistant to corporate interests and commercialization. Of course, there are other ways to appropriate weblogs and other exploitative functions that weblogs may serve. Before we consider these possibilities, however, let us turn to weblogs as cultural texts and explore how they order discourse.

A Performance of One Sort or Another: Ordering Discourse in Weblogs

Weblogs extend the body's capability for storytelling in a context of digital reproduction. How, then, does this particular social and material context order discourse in weblogs? For Benjamin, the changing relations between story-

teller and audience in the age of mechanical reproduction results in an emphasis on information rather than the "living speech" of storytelling. Cultural
texts such as newspapers, Benjamin argues, do not practice storytelling; they
disseminate information. Information is "shot through with explanation"
which "lays claim to prompt verifiability" by appearing to be "understandable
in itself" (p. 89). Whereas events in storytelling may be related with the greatest accuracy, as Benjamin states, "the psychological connection of the events
is not forced upon the reader. It is left up to him [or her] to interpret the way
he [or she] understands them, and thus the narrative achieves an amplitude
that information lacks" (p. 89).

Newspapers and broadcasting work to appear "understandable in themselves" because they cannot count on the participation of audiences. The development of the for-anyone-as-someone structure, Scannell (1996) points out,
provides one way for authors to address this problem of a voluntary audience
not amenable to direct coercion. Existing forms of public communication,
such as a speech or lecture or sermon, are inappropriate when the audience
can put down the newspaper or switch off the radio or television. Instead,
Scannell argues, the texts of print and broadcasting adopt "a more informal
discursive style as markers of a general sociable intent" (p. 24) in which the
"appropriate expressive idiom" is the one in which the audience reads, hears,
or views the text. In brief, these texts emphasize an informal or conversational
sociability—what Poster (2001) calls an "economy of sharing" on the Internet
(p. 58)—because that is the context in which audiences encounter them.

At the same time that the texts of print and broadcasting adopt this conversational idiom, they obscure the fact that authors and audiences do not
have the same "discursive rights" as do conversational participants. As we discussed earlier, audiences cannot take speaking turns as they might in a conversation. However, as Scannell remarks, these texts do not conceal or hide
the fact that this conversational idiom is a performance; indeed, they emphasize and highlight their performative nature. We are reminded constantly, and
in a multitude of ways, that a television drama is not real life, a newspaper report is not the event it describes, and listening to a "live" interview on radio
is not living it. Broadcast texts, in short, perform a conversational idiom; they
are not themselves conversations. In this way, the very limitation of a voluntary audience not amenable to direct coercion is used to guarantee the "truth"
of its status—it is only a program, you can always turn it off. But conversational participants, even though they enjoy reciprocal speaking turns, do not
have the same "discursive rights" as broadcast and print audiences. Conversational participants cannot "turn off" or "put away" their conversation the
way they could a program or newspaper; conversational participants must engage in some form of leave-taking behavior in order to disengage. In other
words, what broadcast and print texts conceal is not their own performative
nature but the performative nature of the conversational idiom itself. As Scannell (1996) concludes: "what radio and television do—in a very pervasive way

—is to render transparent that social life [. . .] is a performance of one sort or another" (p. 57).

Broadcasting, conversation, and weblogs are all performances "of one sort or another." Their differences are not to be found in an exclusion of the performative from conversation, nor in the opposition of performance and daily life, but in the types of performative conventions they employ and emphasize. In tracing out the implications of electronic reproduction, Scannell (1996; also Frith, 1996) describes how the development of the microphone transformed the performative conventions found in pre-electronic amplification sites such as theatres and auditoriums:

> Techniques of mass-performance had to be developed in order to project to large audiences over large orchestras in large auditoriums. All these were instantly reversed by the microphone: instead of loudness, softness; instead of singing to many, singing to one; instead of the impersonal, the personal; instead of the extraordinary, ordinary voices. Thus, public performative values were displaced by private performative values that privileged the particular and the personal. (p. 69)

Weblogs emphasize similar performative values of the particular and the personal. They are not the diaries of the "best and brightest" found in libraries and taught in schools, nor the journals of the "rich and famous" found in bookstores and made into films; nor are they written in the "informational" style of news reports, the "studied eloquence" of public speeches and sermons, or the "commercialized" style of advertising (as the previous excerpt from *clinkclank* illustrates); nor are they read in a group of people or a public gathering. Weblogs are written by ordinary people, not extraordinary ones; in a personal voice or register of discourse, not a public one; to be read by one person at a time, not many people all at once.

As a discourse event, weblogs work to distinguish their performative values from those of related cultural forms—what Foucault calls the formation of external rules or systems of exclusion by which we distinguish performances of "one sort" from performances of "another sort." Let us examine another story from *clinkclank*, "stating the obvious," to illustrate the operation of these external rules in weblog storytelling. This story is seventeenth in a series of twenty-six entries posted on the days following the author's birthday. *Clinkclank* introduces the series in this way: "I just celebrated my birthday yesterday, and so in celebration I bring you 26 entries (gradually) devoted to navelgazing narcissism. Let the fun begin!" (1/22/2002, http://www.clinkclank.net/clonk/000036.html). This form of birthday self-celebration recalls family storytelling events where a gathering of kin occasions stories about one or more of its members. A birthday in contemporary U.S. cultures focuses on celebrating the individual, typically with gifts and food (especially the birthday cake) for the person being celebrated (Pleck, 2000). As is characteristic of such events, *clinkclank* writes stories of childhood exploits, relations with family members, school tales, adolescent crushes, college adventures, and work-related experiences. "Stating the obvious" is one such story in this weblog celebration:

> It was winter break of my senior year in college, and I was hanging out with my best friend from high school. We'd headed in separate directions for college, and both of us had been relieved to discover that Out There, in the world, there are places much larger and more imaginative than Riverside, CA.
>
> Let's walk around the school, he suggested, and we did. It was twilight, and this was before high schools everywhere put their campuses under lockdown. We strolled right through the student parking lot and walked around.
>
> At night the campus looked so small and empty. Or maybe it was just the realization that while once this had been so much of our universe—where we'd dreaded and complained and mocked others before they could get to us—now it was utterly insignificant.
>
> *You didn't offer to take me to my senior prom,* I said accusingly. Not that it mattered anymore, but I had been annoyed by the omission then.
>
> *I didn't realize I should,* he said, *I'm sorry.* And then he took a deep breath, and I knew what he was going to say, because it was something that I'd figured out years before.
>
> *Cindy, I'm gay.* he said. All in a rush, white frozen breath pluming out over him. Anxious to see what I was going to say. This is where I was supposed to say something worthy of a made-for-TV movie.
>
> I spoke. *Well, DUH,* I said.
>
> This was obviously not what he was expecting, and he stood there—and I continued, *I KNOW. I went to college too, y'know.* And then we started laughing, and I gave him the requisite hug, and everything continued along as it had been. (2/8/2002, http://www.clinkclank.net/clonk/000084.html, emphasis in original)

What initially distinguishes the weblog version of this birthday celebration from the everyday version, as cued by *clinkclank*'s comment about "navel-gazing narcissism," is that the celebrated is also the celebrant. *Clinkclank* takes on the storytelling tasks typically performed by other family members or friends at a birthday celebration. The readers of the weblog can "attend" the celebration, but they do not do the work of remembering and telling stories during the event. *Clinkclank* writes about herself to herself for potential others to read—she performs as narrator, character, and audience—in telling "26 short stories about cindy."

Not only does this weblog celebration differ in its spatial distribution of storytelling tasks but also in how these tasks are distributed through time. Stories are posted irregularly: one story might be posted on one day, followed by two or three stories the next, followed by a gap of two or three days before another story appears. "Stating the obvious" is posted more than two weeks after the birthday itself. Readers, checking the website on an occasional basis, may read a group of stories posted over several days at one sitting. This irregular, intermittent, and dispersed order distinguishes the weblog celebration from an event in someone's home as well as from print or broadcast forms of birthday celebrations. Weblog participants, if they read the weblog contemporaneously, cannot read all the stories in one setting, nor can they skip ahead to read the last ones as they might with a print collection—even assuming the existence of such a print collection focusing on an "ordinary" person. Nor does this weblog celebration follow the format of a predictable schedule that one finds in broadcast celebrations, such as the radio broadcast of one symphony or major work each day until a composer's birthday.

The work to distinguish the performative values in weblogs from related cultural forms also can be seen within the discourse. "Stating the obvious" falls in the genre of personal experience stories, but *clinkclank* uses her response to her friend's coming out in order to distinguish her story from those found in other cultural forms. Rather than "something worthy of a made-for-TV movie," she responds with *"Well, DUH."* This contrast between the unsaid possibility of "something worthy of a made-for-TV movie" and her spoken colloquialism functions in three important ways. First, it establishes the sincerity of her response to her best friend within the structure of the narrative. *"Well, DUH"* is not polished or elegant language; it suggests an unrehearsed and unplanned—hence, genuine—reaction. Her next comment clarifies that what she "figured out years before" takes place after their interaction in high school: *"I went to college too, y'know."* This comment maintains the non-literary form of the slang "duh" and forestalls the potential protestation that her friend might make ("if you knew, then why didn't you say something?"). The performative values for the aesthetics of speech at this point are taken from the realm of conversation rather than that of broadcasting and made-for-TV movies. Thus, the blatant disregard for the quality of her language guarantees the sincerity of *clinkclank*'s unguarded and open response. Something more aesthetically pleasing, polished and clever, would be seen as studied or composed and thus false and insincere.

Of course, her response *is* composed; that is, it takes place within a narrative that *clinkclank* has written; it is—in the broadest sense of the word—a fiction, a making she performs. The second function served by this contrast with made-for-TV movies concerns the sincerity of the storyteller herself in relation to the form of her storytelling. Indeed, the evaluative remark that "This is where I was supposed to say something worthy of a made-for-TV movie" is made within the narrative event but not in the narrated event of the twilight conversation between friends. So why this remark at this point in the discourse? In part, because the form of the story evokes the form of made-for-TV movies: it concerns a socially relevant topic (gay sexuality) posed as a relational issue between individuals, it focuses on the topic from a mainstream (heterosexual) perspective, and it emphasizes interaction and emotion (expressing feelings) rather than action in developing the conflict and resolving the drama. Furthermore, the narrative employs visual elements that suggest the made-for-TV form: the move from a wide-angle description of the campus to a close-up on facial reactions, the compression and expansion of time (their walk around the school takes less narrative time than their dialogue), the alternating cuts between speakers, and the attention to minor but revealing visual details ("white frozen breath pluming out over him"). The story *clinkclank* tells is significant both because she has selected it as "an experience" to include in the twenty-six entries celebrating her birthday and because of the care she takes to tell the story. If the unstudied and impulsive *"Well, DUH"* works to guarantee the sincerity of "Cindy" as a character in the story, then the care taken to develop a dramatic narrative or "good telling" works to guarantee the sincerity of *clinkclank* as a narrator. "Cindy" says what she means (that is, without thinking about it), while the narrator means what she says (that is, upon careful reflection).

The combination of these two functions is productively paradoxical, what we elsewhere (Peterson & Langellier, 1982) have called a creative double bind: only by being insincere in making up a "good telling" can a sincere or "good story" be told. At the same time, a good or "tellable" story is one that is about *an* experience—something out of the ordinary—in which the sincerity of the storyteller is established through the ordinariness of the telling rather than the extraordinary events of the story. The productive aspect of this paradoxical combination is illustrated within the discourse by the self-knowing and mocking humor of the narrative voice (and the combined use of present and past tense) in "This is where I was supposed to say something worthy of a made-for-TV movie" and by the laughter of the characters as a resolution within the story.

The third function served by the contrast between this story and other cultural forms builds upon the creative ambiguity put into play by the tension between the sincerity of the character and that of the narrative voice. *"Well, DUH"* surprises the reader of the weblog as well as the best friend within the story. *"Well, DUH"* may be another way to say "that's obvious," but it is hardly the obvious response a weblog reader might anticipate even given the title of the entry, "stating the obvious." The narrative carefully builds to the point of self-disclosure—*"Cindy, I'm gay"*—that ordinarily would be the dramatic climax or turning point in a coming out story. However, the narrative defers this climax until Cindy's response; indeed, this story is not about coming out but about Cindy's experience of her friend's self-disclosure—as is evident in her recognition of reciprocity, "the requisite hug," demanded by the situation. Why and for whom does one state the obvious or that which usually "goes without saying?" Certainly, the positive affirmation of gay sexuality cannot be taken for granted and is not obvious at the time in which the story is set, in the latter half of the 1990s, whether between friends or in society at large. While Cindy's knowledge and acceptance of her friend's sexuality may be "obvious" to her, it is not so obvious for her friend ("This was obviously not what he was expecting") nor is it for the reader.

The reader is guided, or misguided, textually by the reference to the senior prom ("*You didn't offer to take me to my senior prom*") and contextually by the heterosexual normativity of society toward either a romantic or an uncertain interpretation of the relationship between Cindy and her best friend. At the same time, the reader is warned to expect something unusual textually by the narrative asides (both "I knew what he was going to say" and "I was supposed to say something worthy of a made-for-TV movie") and contextually by the familiarity of the dramatic structure employed in the narrative. The reader is set up to be surprised by the disclosure and Cindy's response at the same time that she or he is forewarned to expect something unexpected. Thus, the creative ambiguity put into play by the tension between the sincerity of the character (Cindy) and the narrator (*clinkclank*) solicits the reader's engagement and participation; "stating the obvious" invites a dual identification of surprise and knowingness within the context of an ongoing relationship between storyteller and audience. The closing line, "and everything continued along as it had been," captures this interlaced ambiguity: Cindy's relationship with her friend remains unchanged (the story reveals a "good" or moral character), the narrator's relation to the telling is consistent with narrative conventions (her telling is "good" or aesthetically pleasing), and storytelling is a way to continue in relationship with an audience (storytelling is "good" socially or, as *clinkclank* says in the introduction to the series of birthday stories, "fun").

The participation of the audience in storytelling cannot be guaranteed. However, storytelling does not elicit the participation of audiences through claims to the "prompt verifiability" of information, as Benjamin finds in newspapers. Rather, storytelling invites participation by "leaving it up to" the reader to interpret the way she or he understands the events. Readers of "stating the obvious" have no way to verify if the events happened as *clinkclank* describes them, no way to confirm what was said on that twilight walk around the high school, no way to substantiate that the events ever took place at all. The "amplitude" that storytelling achieves, as Benjamin puts it, relies on audience engagement that is "contextually marked, collaboratively mediated, provisional" (Smith & Watson, 1996, p. 9). Certainly readers can construct less charitable readings of "stating the obvious" that would refuse to join in the laughter of the "we" that concludes the story. These readings might note how the "anxiety" around gay sexuality is located in her friend's concern about disclosure and not in herself, how Cindy's undesirability as a prom date is explained by her friend's sexuality and not anything in her character, or how the conclusion of "everything continued along as it had been" negates the lived reality of coming out. Or a reader may find these less charitable observations a reason to believe in the sincerity of *clinkclank* and to dismiss the possibility that the story is fabricated or that Cindy's response is contrived, implausible, or self-serving.

We mention these possible readings to emphasize the variability of audience engagement in storytelling, not to claim privileged access to interpretation and understanding. We do not *see* what is *really* going on by engaging in interpretation and criticism. As Merleau-Ponty (1964b) reminds us, seeing without participating transforms others into visible things and teaches us "only our bias of looking without understanding" (p. 312). The person "who sees believes himself to be invisible: for him his acts remain in the flattering entourage of his intentions, and he deprives others of this alibi, reducing them to a few words, a few gestures" (p. 311). In order to participate in storytelling, we cannot be that unacquainted spectator whose acts of understanding remain in the flattering entourage of our intentions while depriving *clinkclank* of this alibi and reducing her to the few words of her story. Our participation in storytelling, much as what is obvious in "stating the obvious," is contextually marked, collaboratively mediated, and provisional.

Consuming Digital Lives

The provisional and collaboratively mediated quality of discourse in weblogs, and Internet-based interaction in general, has occasioned much discussion about the "truth" or "authenticity" of that discourse. The possibilities for deception, impersonation, gender swapping, and virtual cross-dressing on the Internet has been seen as cause for both celebration and castigation. In his discussion of home pages on the Internet, Steven Rubio (1996) considers the possibility that the author of a particular home page is a fabrication. He decides that "it doesn't matter whether Walter [the author] is being truthful on his home page. Or rather, it matters, but only in relation to the judgment we make regarding the aesthetic value of his home page." Rubio argues that readers are interested in the style of the home page rather than the reality of the author, what he calls the "representation of his life rather than his actual life." Identity becomes, as Rubio describes it, "a text available for criticism," a reduction of the interpersonal, social, and moral realms to the aesthetic.

Yet, as our previous analysis suggests, storytelling in weblogs relies on social and moral assessments as well as aesthetic ones. Furthermore, the possibility for authorial deception and impersonation is not limited to weblogs or to the Internet. Certainly there is a tradition of such happenings in literature, as exemplified by the unreliable narrator and by authors writing under pseudonyms; it is also found in daily life, as exemplified by instances of cross-dressing and passing (Butler, 1990a, 1990b, and 1993; Garber, 1992). Foucault (1976) reminds us that this ambiguous interplay of secrecy and disclosure occurs "even in true discourse, even in the order of published discourse, free from all ritual" (p. 226). What weblogs share with daily life is a disposition to trust in appearances, all the while remembering that "appearances can be deceiving." Scannell (1996) describes this disposition toward trust in storytelling: "In ordinary circumstances we are inclined to take at face value the truth claims of storytellers unless or until we begin to have good grounds for suspicion" (p. 105).[4]

Let us consider an example of the operation of this disposition to trust and the development of suspicion in a pair of entries from *clinkclank* entitled "craig's lust" (a word play on a listserve name, "Craig's List") and "passive aggressive monsters" posted the following day.

> I subscribe to Craig's List for a number of reasons, but the absolute number-one reason is that you occasionally get posts like this:
>
>> subject: Jim Watts who lives in the Richmond, click here
>> Dear Jimmy,
>> Instead of sulking over your old girlfriend, dating girls who just don't like you, and complaining to ALL your friends why don't you go after the girl who IS interested in you???? She does exist and you know who she is . . . . . just think about it for a minute. . . .
>>   Besides, most of the girls think you have a small penis.
>> —a friend who is tired of listening
>
> I live in the Richmond, so now if I ever encounter anyone named Jim there I will have to wonder if this is him. (4/25/2001, http://www.clinkclank.net/clonk/000193.html)

The initial post strikes *clinkclank* as interesting and perhaps funny, in part because she and the subject of the post both live in the Richmond district of San Francisco. Her response is not "is this true?" but what she would think if she encountered someone named Jim. As Scannell would say, *clinkclank* takes the post at face value. The post triggers the "ambiguous interplay of secrecy and disclosure" that Foucault describes insofar as it suggests the possibility of meeting someone named Jim about whom she may or may not know something that he would not expect her to know.

The subsequent posts by this "friend" on Craig's List, however, lead *clinkclank* to recontextualize her initial response in a follow-up entry titled "passive aggressive monsters":

> The poster of yesterday's message has been repeating it today, variations on a theme, which makes it a lot less interesting. Said person also made a point of claiming to be a guy, which pretty much proves to me that it's a bitter, bitter ex-girlfriend. I don't know, this was funny, but in the same sort of way as that psycho ex-girlfriend website—you hope that it's parody so that you can laugh at it, but also cringe thinking that it might not be. I am, however, also tempted to post to Craig's List saying "I slept with Jim Watts and he has a big penis". You know, as some sort of karmic rebalancing. (4/26/2001, http://www.clinkclank.net/clonk/000192.html)

The unexpected repetition and "variations on a theme" create grounds for sus-picion; the "friend" is now seen as unbalanced and bitter, someone who is "obsessed." Because "said person also made a point of claiming to be a guy," *clinkclank* reinterprets the gender and renames this "friend" an ex-girlfriend. The ambivalence of her response—she both laughs and cringes—along with her feeling of responsibility to "re-balance" yesterday's message suggest that the weblog is not merely the representation of a life and "a text available for criticism." Rather, *clinkclank* is also engaged in making social assessments as to how interesting or repugnant the entry is and moral assessments as to its genuineness. The combination of these varied assessments are used to legiti-mate or "re-balance" *clinkclank*'s responsibility for repeating what she now sees as potentially unfounded gossip. In this sense, she performs in her second weblog entry the re-balancing that she is only tempted to perform for Craig's List: that is, the second entry works to repair the damage created by the first.

In working to remedy her initial "bias of looking without understanding," *clinkclank* reflects on her responses and her responsibilities. Her effort is less a question of calculating how much she can believe or trust what she reads—a kind of physics question on the inertia of trust and suspicion—than it is an attempt to clarify her participation in a shared communication context. That is, she works to locate these acts in the "entourage of their intentions," their lived context, rather than assume the context as given or "understandable in itself." By making explicit this question of "in whose interest" a weblog op-erates, we underscore our concern for the strategic function of performing nar-rative and the distribution of power in communication relationships.

Contrary to critics such as Rubio (1996), some writers trumpet the poten-tial of weblogs to benefit groups and communities whose interests are mar-ginalized in society, whose lives are ignored or distorted by mass media, and whose members are isolated from each other. In describing the appeal of Inter-net journals for women, Laurel Sutton (1999) writes: "Women who have been permitted only to write for themselves can now compose their public history, filled not with historical events or momentous deeds but the detail of every-day life" (p. 175). Similarly, Tim Archer (2002) argues that weblogs are "espe-cially relevant for gays and lesbians" because "with the number of queer blog-gers on the 'net, the reality of our existence is available to anyone online. Not everyone may want to read about these lives, but the stories we tell are avail-able in abundance." Jon Katz (2000) writes that geeks "don't suffer alone any-more. They tell their stories to one another almost continuously" (p. 142). The Internet provides "a medium in which they can express, instantaneously and eloquently, the reality of their lives, both to one another and to the rest of the world" (p. 152). For marginalized groups, weblogs are seen as a way to docu-ment and make sense of their lives, a way to overcome social isolation and alienation, and a way to resist mainstream cultural forms and practices.

But this potential for resistant social and cultural action is not a common emphasis for weblog service providers. For example, Pitas.com conceptualizes the interest in weblogs as an opportunity to avoid the work of production for the "fun" of self-expression:

> you can update from any web browser, without fussing around with uploading, editing pages, and all that time-wasting junk. You can customize it to look however you want, or to use one of the templates we've made already, and you can give your friends access to it so you can all have a page you all contribute to [. . .]. What fun! Don't you like fun? Of course you do. (http://www.pitas.com/)

Another site, Diarist.net, takes this reduction of self-expression to fun further when it defines expression in online journals as self-exploitation. As the subtitle to the Diarist.net guide to setting up an online journal suggests: "you too can be an online exhibitionist." This orientation is made more explicit in the description of "Clix," the Diarist.net daily list of most active online journals. "*Clix* is for those of us willing to embrace our inner *hit slut*, our subconscious *page pimp*" (http://www.diarist.net/clix/about.shtml; emphasis in original). Both of these sites make a weblog "understandable in itself," as Benjamin would say, by reducing the possibilities for expression to "having fun" and "exhibitionism."

The potential for self-exploitation in weblogs has also attracted the attention of mainstream journalists. A feature in the *Washington Post* (Cha, 2001) poses the issue in terms of a moral panic: "Teens Tell Secrets, Get Gifts, Attract Nuts, Scare Mom." Rather than investigate how weblogs maintain existing relations among teenage friends or how geographically dispersed teens can create community around marginalized identities, the *Washington Post* article focuses on weblogs as relations of exchange. The feature quotes one teen, Nay (short for Renee), on the social relations engendered by weblogs: "I've met a lot of cool people. They give me advice and I give them advice. We're all strangers, but in a way we're all friends, too" (Cha, 2001). The *Washington Post* underscores the exchange-based nature of the audience relationship by emphasizing the practice of readers sending gifts to weblog authors. In addition to advice, teen weblog writers such as Nay receive e-mail responses, "lewd come-ons," and gifts of CDs and cordless phones. Nay writes: "It's really weird to get all this stuff. Sometimes I wonder what people want in return [. . .] I'm not like 'Buy me this!' like some of the other girls. I'm not holding this over anybody's head. But I guess I don't try to stop it either, because it's kind of fun" (Cha, 2001). The ambiguous interplay of secrecy and disclosure in weblogs is nicely captured in the way Nay qualifies her statements: "it's *kind of* fun" and the audience are "all strangers, but *in a way* we're all friends, too" (emphasis added). Weblogs, in the terms of our earlier discussion, are "sort of like" corresponding with strangers who are, "in a way," friends.

The qualifications that Nay employs in her description mask her bodily participation in weblogs—she seemingly does not do anything; the advice just happens to show up on her computer monitor, gifts just happen to show up in the mail. The difficulty in untangling the political function of the ambiguous interplay of secrecy and disclosure is that, to borrow a phrase from Merleau-Ponty (1964b), "there is a trick with mirrors here between what is written and what is lived" (p. 310). Posing the problem in terms of exchange, and as a moral panic over naive girls accepting gifts from older men, as the *Washington Post* does, distracts us from understanding this "trick with mirrors" by which weblogs function. We are not arguing that there is no value to concerns raised over teen weblogs and interaction with "friendly strangers" (e.g., readers who make sexual propositions to teen writers) and "strange friends" (e.g., readers who use weblogs to libel teen classmates); however, framing the discussion in these terms obscures rather than interrogates the political function of weblogs. The challenge here is to not let the technological reproduction of storytelling in weblogs shift our attention from conscious experience to the consumption of experience.

The reduction of storytelling to an exchange of self-revelation for attention and gifts from "an audience of total strangers" would appear to confirm Rubio's suspicion of weblogs and Internet-based communication as a reduction of the social realm to the aesthetic. Critics such as Rubio do not indulge in sensationalism or moral panic but question the kind of community and social relations that weblogs facilitate. In this case, the possibilities for cultural self-expression are seen as masking and obscuring social relations rather than re-structuring them: the homeless are forgotten in our fascination with home pages, as Rubio says. In the epilogue to his essay on mechanical reproduction, Benjamin warns about just this consequence in the rise of fascism. Benjamin argues that fascism seeks to maintain social control by organizing the prole-tarian masses around the chance to express themselves rather than the right to change property relations. As Benjamin states, "Fascism seeks to give them an expression while preserving property. The logical result of Fascism is the introduction of aesthetics into political life" (p. 241). From this perspective, weblogs are seen as a reduction of the complexities of communication rela-tions to an aesthetics of self-expression.

The problem with this reduction of storytelling to an aesthetics of self-ex-pression is that it tends to position webloggers as cultural dupes who have been led to exploit themselves for fun and profit before others do it for them. While storytelling in weblogs entails relations of exchange—indeed, that is much the point of our earlier discussion on calibration and feedback—we want to avoid collapsing social relations among weblog authors and audiences in producing and consuming weblogs to the single moment of exchange. Story-telling in weblogs, as we have developed it, is a bodily practice of discourse in a particular social and material context. The relations of weblog authors and audiences in storytelling are not pre-given, fixed, or stable but open to chang-ing as well as reproducing those relations which they perform. In this instance, the example of marginalized groups is instructive. As Archer (2002) points out, "there are some who are uncomfortable with the exhibitionism they detect in weblogs. [. . .] However, coming across sites [by gays and lesbians] does make me believe that by having a forum and an audience for their concerns, queer youth will have an easier time coming out than we had even ten years ago." Performing narrative in weblogs may work to undermine and expose existing social relations and conditions, thereby making it possible for marginalized groups to change them.

At the same time, however, the strategic function of performing narrative requires that we not romanticize these possibilities for change and resistance. The fact that performing narrative in weblogs is provisional and collaboratively mediated does not guarantee change or restructuring of social and political relations. In fact, as John Clarke (1991) cautions in his critique of consumption, the image of cultural creativity by a freely choosing consumer—such as the "freedom" of self-expression in weblogs—is precisely the view of capitalism that capitalism would most like to promulgate. In other words, how can there be problems in existing social relations if everyone has the same opportunities for self-expression? Of course, phrasing the question in this manner obscures both the structural inequities of current social and political arrangements as well as the move by which it makes these structural inequities a matter of individual responsibility. "In short," as Zygmunt Bauman (2001) summarizes, "individuals are doomed to seek 'biographical solution of systemic contradictions'" (p. 23) as one way to create the meaningful continuity that society can no longer provide.

Weblogs offer marginalized groups one possibility to intervene in existing social and political relations by changing the ordering of cultural content (making the reality of their lives visible and public) and the ordering of tasks (shifting the production and consumption of weblogs so they are by, about, and for a marginalized group). Thus, weblogs offer a possibility but not a certainty for strategic intervention in mainstream cultural forms and conventions that go beyond the minor tactics of self-expression, the "biographical solution" that Bauman describes. While we would argue that the mutual fit between consumer culture and the "biographical solution" offered by weblogs is not as perfect as Bauman describes it, weblogs—like other forms of cultural innovation—can be appropriated, coopted, and normalized by the consumer culture within which they operate. Stephen Duncombe (1999) describes the cautionary example of *U Don't Stop*, a zine which combines basketball, politics, and hip hop but is produced by two members of an advertising firm and copyrighted by Nike. The zine illustrates the commercial appropriation of the "anti-commercial" ethos of zines; it employs the countercultural elements typical of zines, including a "hand scrawled introductory rant" and "crossed off words kept in the text" (p. 33), but in this case they work to reinscribe rather than resist commodity consumption.

The development of weblogs, as we have argued in this chapter, is a cultural innovation that refigures storytelling in an age of digital reproduction. Although weblogs incorporate the possibility of self-exploitation in recapitulating past events, in expressing feelings, in exchanging information, they are not limited to these possibilities. The storyteller-as-consumer in a digital age reconfigures but does not replace other social relations and identities. The weblog is, in an expression we take from Clarke (1991), "a highly contradictory ensemble of diverse cultural elements." For example, despite *clinkclank's* skepticism that weblogs could be coopted by commercial interests (as evidenced in the entry "when corporate blogs attack"), she performs an explicit form of self-commercialization on her web page. In earlier versions of the weblog, a sidebar contained a link, under the ironic title of "buy my love," to an Amazon.com wish list of books. Here weblog readers could, much the way the *Washington Post* fears, realize their storytelling relationship in a commodity form—they could "express themselves" and their appreciation for *clinkclank* by purchasing a book for her. In the revised version of the weblog posted after June 2, 2002, this link is removed. However, a new link— "Conquer the Kitchen"—connects readers to a page that describes the personalized "hands-on learn how to cook in your own home" lessons offered by the author. Another link, "Cooking and Eating," takes the reader to the author's site of a subscription newsletter of essays, articles, and cooking tips that specialize in Asian, Mexican, and Indian cuisine.

Clinkclank's consumer identity accompanies and resituates other cultural identities—it does not replace them. For example, below the sidebar that contains "buy my love" is another one entitled "daily hits" with names and links to nearly a dozen other weblogs that *clinkclank* reports reading on a regular basis. In this instance, these loosely interrelated weblogs resemble more the "fellowship of discourse" that Foucault describes than they do a community, a term perhaps too readily applied to any group of discourse participants.[5] Not only her affiliations but also the stories she tells reveal this struggle over group-ordering in weblogs: *clinkclank* tells stories about her Mexican American ancestry and her blue-collar family; stories that position her in relation to family, friends, and co-workers; stories that chronicle her diverse interests in reading books, playing soccer, learning Mandarin, and cooking food; stories that work through her domestic life with a romantic partner and her professional life as a computer interface/interaction designer. The variety and volatility of these interests do not displace the material and historical conditions in which weblogs are produced and consumed. Rather, what weblogs "express" is the struggle over identities—interpersonal, social, moral, aesthetic—in uncertain and unstable conditions by making that struggle concrete and accessible.

As storyteller, the weblogger does not consume a life in performing narrative. The storyteller, as Benjamin writes, does not "swallow up the material" of a human life "as the fire devours logs in the fireplace" (p. 100). The relationship of the storyteller to the material of human life is productive. That is, as Benjamin concludes, the very task of the storyteller is "to fashion the raw material of experience, [her or] his own and that of others, in a solid, useful, and unique way" (p. 108) for oneself and for others. We join in the company of the storyteller in reading and writing weblogs to the extent that we participate in this struggle to make lived experience solid, useful, and unique.

CHAPTER 6

Breast Cancer Storytelling

The Limits of Narrative Closure in Survivor Discourse

Cultural history authorizes narrative practices. Before the latter half of the twentieth century, illness narratives, or pathographies, as they have been called in their written form, were rare.[1] As part of life, illness in itself did not warrant narrative performance; stories of disease were interruptions in life narratives or enveloped within other narrative frames. After 1950, and in ensemble with several other kinds of survivor stories, the illness narrative emerged, proliferated, and evolved to a genre of storytelling, of which breast cancer storytelling may be considered a subgenre. In this cultural shift, the speaking subject is interesting—that is, the subject matters—because she or he is ill. Anne Hunsaker Hawkins (1993) organizes pathographies in three groups: testimonial narratives of the 1960s and 1970s that bear witness to the experience of illness, complement medical accounts, and offer advice and a model for readers; angry pathographies of the 1970s that expose and denounce the medical system and technology as dehumanizing, sometimes brutal, and indifferent to the emotional and psychological needs of the individual; and alternative pathographies of the 1980s that supplement biomedical models with healing and holistic therapies plumbing inner resources of the psyche and spirit in a mythos of healthy-mindedness. Susanna Egan (1999) calls the genres of terminal illness after World War II the rediscovery of death as a significant point of departure for life writing and storytelling. Indeed, Benjamin (1969) asserts that the storyteller borrows his or her authority from death: "Death is the sanction of everything that the storyteller can tell" (p. 94).

The term *illness narrative* differentiates disease as a diagnostic entity encoded by medical discourse, from illness as lived experience perceived and responded to by a sick person in a social and cultural network of relationships

(Kleinman, 1988). Disease converts a person to a patient, the body to an assembly of fixable or replaceable parts, and the personal narrative to a medical report or clinical history. Illness is a call for stories; the body needs a voice, which disease takes away (Frank, 1995, 2002). The storyteller narrates a story *of* the body *through* the body, reclaiming the capacity to tell, and to hold onto, her or his own story against the medical chart as the legitimate story of illness. When disease disrupts the orderliness of life, interrupts its continuity, and endangers its coherence, the storyteller faces the task of suturing body and spirit. The narrator's task is not only to describe the biographical disruption of disease but also to order, interpret, and create meanings that can bind body and meanings together again. In short, illness narratives are part of the process and performance of healing (Mattingly & Garro, 2000), a kind of secular healing ritual in a society of survivors (Couser, 1997). Performing narrative provides therapy for both narrator and audiences (Park-Fuller, 2000).

The illness narrative is a modern adventure story constructed around recovery and healing. Survival stories recount disasters of the body and the battle to stay alive physically at the same time they combat the disembodiment of medical practices and the stigma of cultural discourses first described by Susan Sontag (1978) in *Illness as Metaphor*. Hawkins (1993) argues that narratives of illness are "all variations on a long-standing heroic paradigm of the struggle of brave individuals confronting what appear to be insurmountable forces" (p. 2). For storytellers, the narrative is an opportunity to exert agency and empowerment in a disruptive and dehumanizing experience; for audiences the illness narrative negotiates the anxieties of their temporary able-bodiness and the specter of death. In whole or part, illness stories are retrospective narratives, written or told from a relatively secure vantage point of recovery or remission, where threat of recurrence is closed off, even if contingently and incompletely.

Breast cancer storytelling is sufficiently common and widely circulated to compose a subgenre of illness narrative. Not only can breast cancer alter the course of a woman's life narrative, but it also engages gendered and sexual meanings of breasts (Langellier & Sullivan, 1998). Because breasts are the most visible and tangible signifier of womanliness in Western culture, breast cancer is assumed to produce special problems over and above those experienced by other cancer patients, problems specifically associated with feminine identity, body image, and sexuality. So large has the discourse of breast cancer grown that, as Barbara Ehrenreich (2001) writes, "Today [. . .] it's the biggest disease on the cultural map, bigger than AIDS, cystic fibrosis, or spinal injury, bigger even than those more prolific killers of women—heart disease, lung cancer, and stroke" (p. 45). Breast cancer storytelling is conscripted in the struggles over the bodies of women, extending identity politics to illness in battles between good medicine/science and bad disease.

Breast cancer storytelling is, by definition, narrated by survivors who lived to tell the tale: "Although some of these women suffered recurrences, and some have died of their cancer, their narratives tend to end with recovery of some tentative assurance of health and vitality" (Couser, 1997, p. 39). G. Thomas Couser argues that the self-reconstruction of the breast cancer narrative follows the comic plot of a happy ending. Resolution through healing, if not cure, constructs the narrator as better off not just physically but also in moral dimensions of achieving normalcy (Mattingly & Garro, 2000, p. 29). The commanding investment in recovery funds the drive for narrative closure. The comic closure of a resolution serves multiple and compelling interests. The narrator secures both an emotional and narrative denouement, others with cancer feel the comfort of hope, and additional listeners or readers ward off the fear of disease and death. Thus, breast cancer storytelling functions therapeutically for all participants.

When diagnosed with breast cancer, Ehrenreich (2001) recognizes that she battles not just the disease but also breast cancer culture itself and the narrative constraints of breast cancer storytelling.[2] Among websites, newsletters, support groups, national organizations, and races for the cure that make up breast cancer culture, she identifies the "heavy traffic" and force of personal narrative. These personal narratives are testimonials to survivorship. "The effect of this relentless brightsiding is to transform breast cancer into a rite of passage—not an injustice or tragedy to rail against, but a normal marker in the lifestyle, like menopause or graying hair" (p. 49). Passing through the requisite ordeals of diagnosis and treatment, the initiate emerges from this liminal state to the new and higher status of survivor. The experience is not only over but constructed as a blessing in disguise, a test of one's makeup and a creative transformation—a makeover—to enhanced character. The chance to find oneself or a better self casts breast cancer storytelling as a progress narrative of self-realization and self-actualization. In her harshest criticism, Ehrenreich writes that contemporary breast cancer culture participates in "normalizing cancer, prettying it up, even presenting it, perversely, as a positive and enviable experience" (p. 53). Breast cancer storytelling celebrates survivorhood, mutes mortality, and underplays causes of the disease in general and environmental factors in particular.

Ehrenreich's critique works both within and against the generic constraints of breast cancer storytelling and its therapeutic functions. Her essay unearths the underlying anxiety of breast cancer storytelling to expose the falsity of comic closure: that breast cancer may recur, that it is a systemic rather than a localized disease, that there is no definitive cure, and that its causes remain unaddressed. Her concern is with those who do not survive and the narrative constraints of the illness narrative. In this chapter, through a case study using the critical-interpretive framework we develop in this book, we explore the concern that the language of survival and closure is the only language available for breast cancer storytelling. We first discuss embodiment as the ground for narrative and experiential possibilities about breast cancer. Second, we explore material and situational constraints that lead to only some of these possibilities being realized in performing narrative. Then we analyze discursive regularities that inform the breast cancer plot and the only partially successful effort to tell a counternarrative.

The storytelling we analyze in this chapter is drawn from a larger corpus of breast cancer narratives based upon interviews conducted with women with breast cancer.[3] The interviewee, Jane, is Eric's cousin. We selected her interview for analysis because it both illustrates and challenges the master narrative of breast cancer; and because Jane did not survive. As researchers at this writing, we know what she did not but what she feared at the telling: how her story ends. This knowledge must affect our hearing and analysis because we can no longer read her story simply as closure, as therapy, as self-actualization —as a survivor.[4]

"Well, I don't know where my beginning really is": Breast Cancer and Embodiment

At the time of the interview, Jane, an educator with dual citizenship (U.S. and Canadian), was fifty-four years old and six months past her diagnosis with Grade Three breast cancer.[5] During those six months, Jane underwent a quadrantectomy, a mastectomy, chemotherapy, and, just three weeks before the interview with Kristin, a second, elective, mastectomy. Despite these definite and decisive medical markers, she begins her narrative by questioning its beginnings: "well, I . . . I think I'll start at my beginning, which is, well, I don't know where my beginning really is, now that I look back on it." "*My* beginning" signals the hallmark of illness narrative: the experiencing patient's voice and point of view. Elliot Mishler (1984) terms this the "voice of the life-world" in distinction from the "voice of medicine." The voice of the life-world restores the person to the medical project and situates the psychological, social, and cultural experience of illness within the narrator's life and the meanings of that life. "My beginning" is ambiguous, enigmatic, and contested as Jane assesses her risk factors: searching her family background for cancer, recalling her first personal encounters with breast cancer in friends from Edmonton and Halifax, and examining the personal history of her breasts, including cysts that put her on a course of annual mammograms twelve years earlier, and participation in a five-year national breast cancer study.

Our analytic beginning is with embodiment and the social relations in which the body is both part and participant. The lived body sees and is seen, feels and is touched, is sensible to itself and accessible to others. This bodily capability grounds the experience and narrating of breast cancer. Breast cancer storytelling is a site of embodied memory and knowledge. Breast cancer increases awareness of physicality and feelings of mortality, heightening sensibilities to the body. To take one example from the interview, Jane details the ordeal of chemotherapy in sensate smells of cooking, smoke, soaps, and perfumes that nauseated her, and the tastes of juices that burned her throat and water that tasted "minerally." Flat ginger ale, the only drink she can tolerate, leads to yeast infections: "I mean it's just never-ending. You get one thing and then another." The present tense "get" suggests that the bodily sensations linger long after their effects have faded. Going into the soap aisle of a grocery store still nauseates her. She incorporates her friend Gillian, a breast cancer survivor, as a voice of counsel and support in her story: "Gillian had said to me, 'now on the first day of chemo, when you eat lunch, eat something you don't care if you ever eat again, because you may never want it again, see.'" These bodily memories of the trauma of chemotherapy are not only vividly, intensely recalled but also triggered by somatic association with particular tastes, smells, sounds, or places when nausea can return. "Like the scars that become the permanent reminders of the tissues below the skin, these bodily memories mediate against a complete forgetting" (Stacey, 1997, p. 100). In performing narrative the past may be either remembered or experienced (Young, 2000).

The medical report offers an external perspective of disease and disavows a particular authorship, or any authorship at all. By contrast, the illness narrative embodies a specifically located "I." This "I" participates in a system of relations among storyteller, narrator, character, and audience. Narrator and characters perceive their experiences in the narrated event (the "told"), and storyteller and audience express their experience in the narrative event (the "telling"). Breast cancer storytelling typically adopts a perspective internal to the realm of events, with the embodied "I" at the center. The internal perspective of this "I" is associated with subjectivity, emotional engagement, and the authoritative but restricted knowledge of experience. Jane presents her story as evidence of human agency and mastery of her body within the medical context of her illness. Subjected to breast cancer and submitted to its painful treatments, she narrates her illness as a series of decisions she herself makes, in consultation with health professionals, her mentor Gillian, a small circle of close friends, and a wider network of acquaintances. After the discovery of a suspicious lump that requires biopsy, she debates between her general practitioner and a breast cancer specialist for care, finally choosing the specialist: "I'll go with the worst case scenario just in case it turns out that way [cancer], which I was right." The "I'll go" phrase first positions her as narrator and major character in the narrated events; she then shifts to storyteller in the phrase "which I was right" in the narrative event with the interviewer/audience, Kristin. The "which I was right" is a retrospective insight after the narrated event and also incorporates herself as audience. Her next decision, between a quadrantectomy and a mastectomy, similarly shifts among embodied relations of perception and expression. Jane chooses a quadrantectomy, which her surgeon states is as effective as a mastectomy 95% of the time, except in cases of a very aggressive cancer. "Well, I [narrator] was in the 5% so . . . that didn't work out too well [for the storyteller]." She undergoes a mastectomy three weeks later.

The opportunity to negotiate treatments indicates current doctor-patient relations that allow collaboration, an outcome of the women's health movement of the 1960s and 1970s. Doctor-patient collaboration also reflects the state of knowledge about cancer (there is no definitive cure) and its treatments (no one treatment has proven efficacy over other choices). Jane's storytelling suggests how she embraces decision-making with the understanding that she may choose wrong: "I got into the 5% of the other one. Who knows what'll happen?" Collaboration brings both empowerment and anxiety, depending upon the outcome: satisfaction or disappointment. Jane's storytelling highlights interviews with professionals and talk with friends as she deliberates alternatives and negotiates her options. Whatever her decisions, however, they are couched within the unchosen context of having breast cancer and that she will undergo a range of treatments. Ehrenreich (2001) charges that "the career of the breast-cancer patient has been pretty well mapped out in advance for me: You may get to negotiate the choice between lumpectomy and mastectomy, but lumpectomy is commonly followed by weeks of radiation, and in either case, if lymph nodes turn out, upon dissection, to be invaded—or 'involved,' as it's less threateningly put—you're doomed to chemotherapy, meaning baldness, nausea, mouth sores, immunosuppression, and possible anemia" (p. 44).[6] Collaboration with doctors is, in other words, more one-sided than mutual in its contents.

Jane, however, features a series of non-medical decisions in her narrative performance: whether to attend support groups (no), to participate in the Reach to Recovery program (no), and to get a prosthesis (no). Decision making about the body in illness increases the vulnerability and drama of breast cancer storytelling; it invites audience empathy. When describing how she begins to lose her hair after three weeks of chemotherapy, Jane launches the most highly dramatized, expressive, and humorous storytelling in the interview. Gesturing to her head, her volume and intensity increase as she asserts, "I'm gonna control my hair first, if it's gonna start to go. I'm gonna shave it because I do it to me, and I'm the one who decides whether this is coming off, you see." The first segment of the story of going "wigging" with her two friends starts with trying on turbans and ends in all three "dying laughing" at how bad Jane looks. She then obtains a wig but says:

> *Jane:*　I've never worn it once
>
> *Kristin:*　I was gonna ask that
>
> *Jane:*　ne:ver wore the wig once 'cause I never liked it
> 　　　　It was hot
> 　　　　I mean with hot flashes

> All you'd need to do would be
> > to put your wig o:n [voice up on wig; Kristin laughs]
> > and you'd just want to di::e
> So . I: never ever used the wig
> I have have a baseball cap

The lines about the hot flashes refer to severe menopausal symptoms Jane has suffered for three years, a narrative line we take up below. Jane performs these lines, an imagined event for her narrator-as-character, with vocal animation and humor.

Jane's story continues with her trip to a hairdresser after her hair begins to come out, performing dialogue as a character internal to the narrated event: "when I need to get it cut, will you cut it off?" she asks the hairdresser. He takes Jane to a storeroom without a mirror and away from other clients' view of her. He cuts her hair very short, but he will not comply with her request that "I want this Yul-ed," that is, to be shaved like Yul Brynner. Three weeks later, she goes to a different hairdresser, who likewise resists shaving her head but does finally cut all her hair off using an electric clipper. This time Jane does not have the option of a separate room, and "the people in there were watching," she narrates. She concludes the story in the position of storyteller, with an external evaluation for Kristin and the absent audience: "I didn't like it [being bald]. You know you get used to it, looking at yourself bald. But it wouldn't be a choice of mine if I, if I didn't have to do it, let me tell you."

Even though the story heightens the agency of the narrator-character, and its telling is enhanced with gestures and vocal animation, sprinkled with humor and punctuated by shared laughter, a current of anxiety flows beneath and around it. Young (2000) writes that "fear is experienced as an intense alertness at the rim of my auditory, visual, and tactile field" (p. 81). The embodied narrator in breast cancer fears for her somatic self and feels her mortality. Jane had a mammogram and manual exam six months earlier, "and they find nothing. And how does it [lump] get to be an inch in six months?" The lump was "a bit huge . . . and so I was very concerned about that. I thought, this thing's gotta be growing fast." When chemotherapy is prescribed because recurrence with the multifocal involvement of her cancer typically happens within a year, Jane says:

> they don't know if it [chemotherapy] will do any good at all
> the only thing they'll know is if it doesn't work
> > and then you—
> it comes back
> and then they [doctors] explained it would come back
> > and then the major organs
> > and there would be no cure
> and you know after that they just try to control it

Jane takes a breath after this line, and then she describes the cancer clinic for chemotherapy as "not interested in anything but treating you, in treating the cancer and there was no psychological element in the place." Again, Gillian appears as a character in the story: "The thing Gillian told me was 'get a therapist!'" Jane begins in indirect discourse ("the thing Gillian told me was") as an external narrator but midway she shifts to Gillian's reported speech and to the internal character whom Gillian addresses. Entering into the narrated event bodily and combining their two voices gives the moment emotional emphasis, and Jane presents this as her wisest decision. In another passage she explains that her friends are there for advice, support, and help but she does not burden them with demands for therapy: "I don't want them to have to be my psychiatrist." She suggests that it is the psychiatrist with whom she discusses her emotions, attitudes, and especially her fears about dying.

Jane underwent a mastectomy in light of the multifocal and aggressive form of cancer. The second mastectomy, however, was elective, and, as she clearly states, not preventative—"I knew it wasn't gonna spread to that breast, so that wasn't it." We discuss the narration of the second mastectomy in terms of embodied knowledge and knowledge production: the lived body's simultaneous participation in reflective and pre-reflective experience. As a story *of* the body, Jane shares her body in illness with friends, with the researchers, with those who read this chapter. As storytelling *through* the body, she shows, that is, makes visible, her body in illness. The lengthy segment on the second mastectomy takes a further step into showing the body and is keyed and propelled by Jane's statement "so, of course, I'm large-breasted." She situates the second mastectomy within the physical and psychological "down time" of chemotherapy, and her speech here is accented but pitched low and cadenced quite slowly:

> I mean I couldn't do anything anyway
> and then I was <u>think</u>ing al<u>ready</u>
>   of having the <u>left</u> breast taken off
> because . the <u>weight</u> of that thing
>   <u>pull</u>ing on <u>this</u> side was <u>hurt</u>ing [gestures to each side as she speaks]
> I mean it was was like this the <u>right</u> side never healed
>   I mean I <u>knew</u> that it was
>   it was . the <u>nerve</u> endings take really a long time to regenerate
>   and that you know it's ah like you've
>   see? [Jane holds her shirt out to show Kristin]
>   any material on it
>   would hurt and irritate it
> and um . so::
> I more and more I thought ah
> [softly] I'm gonna get you know the second mastectomy

Jane makes her body visible in the narrative event of telling with the interviewer. She reiterates that it was the "unbalanced, the hurting part of it," and "then I started to get the aches in my shoulder." When she asks her surgeon about a second mastectomy, the surgeon requests that Jane delay her final decision until her chemotherapy is finished, "even though I wasn't going to change my mind." Jane narrates the second mastectomy in the narrative context of large breasts, lack of balance, pulling, pain, and aches. She presents a narrator-storyteller who is deliberative but decisive.

Kristin asks Jane if she considered other alternatives, such as a prosthesis, reconstruction, or a breast reduction. "I did, I did," she responds and narrates each option in turn, calling on bodily knowledge and relational comparisons. Her sister had undergone reconstruction and "I listened to that story . . . and all the hell she's been through with that stuff. And I thought, there's no way [spoken forcefully]. No, I never ever considered it [reconstruction]." She has, however, considered breast reduction. She discards this option for two reasons: first, a two-year wait for such "cosmetic" surgery, and "I thought, two years, I mean I might be—you're telling me I might be dead in two years . . . why would I wait two years?" Second, she recounts the story of a cousin who underwent a similar surgical procedure (a "tummy tuck"), which she describes as a far more painful procedure with a longer recovery than a mastectomy, and "for what?" she asks. Then she continues,

> Jane: and the other thing
> I mean I have to admit in my life
> because I— I mean I'm very active
>   and I was always doing things outside
>   and playing sports and having
> and running, you know
>
> Kristin: right
>
> Jane: and carrying this weight
> there were times I'd think
> [her voice rises in pitch] I'm gonna have these things
> you know . taken off

Here the weight of her breasts is associated not only with pulling, pain, and aching after the mastectomy but also with obstructing Jane's routine physical activities. Before narrating the second mastectomy, she has described her return, less than three weeks after surgery, to playing golf, riding a bike, and throwing and batting a baseball. Breast cancer delayed her travel sabbatical and activities of hiking, biking, and snorkeling. In her spare time, she does house projects for family and friends, such as painting and minor repairs. Jane assesses what her breasts allow her to do, more easily or less easily, rather than how they look to others. In doing so, she intervenes in the objectified view of breasts as the measure of femininity in Western culture in the evaluating gaze. She also indirectly challenges the view that women's breasts are for the other—husband, lover, baby—rather than for self (Young, 1990). She considers that her large, heavy breasts that inhibit an active life could have been "taken off" before breast cancer "except":

> except that they were—
> [said low, confidentially] my nipples worked really well you see
>   that was what I liked [chuckling]
>   and I thought no:: that was a big problem [Kristin laughs with Jane]
> And I used to think the worst thing
>   if I'm gonna get <u>punished</u> for something
>   I'm gonna get <u>breast</u> cancer
>   and have to <u>lose</u> these things right
>   because they really sexually work
>   [makes squealing sound] <u>EEEEOOW</u> [Kristin laughs with her through next line]
>   you know I can almost get an orgasm from <u>nipples</u> you see
> and some women have nipples that don't do anything

Jane's narration now shifts from breast as object of gaze to breast as touched and touching, and from feeling the weight and pull of breasts negatively to positive sensations of pleasure. Iris Marion Young (1990) writes that "for many women breasts are a multiple and fluid zone of deep pleasure quite independent of intercourse, though sometimes not independent of orgasm" (p. 194). As an active and independent zone of sensitivity and eroticism, the sensual breast opens up possibilities of women-centered meanings in patriarchal culture, of a woman's breasts as her own. However, what intervened for Jane was menopause, after which her nipples did "<u>nothing</u>. It [erotic sensation] went from a <u>plus</u> ten on a scale down to <u>one</u>, so luckily this [cancer] happened <u>after</u> menopause." She elaborates that "Because I had <u>passed</u>, and I knew I wasn't going to get it <u>ba:ck</u>, it was harder dealing with <u>that</u>, knowing that . . . It made me <u>mad</u> at the time, you see. So, um, I had already dealt with that before this [cancer] happened." Had cancer come in her forties, she reasons, it would have been a greater loss, but now, after menopause, "I have no regrets."

After the second mastectomy, the constant reminder of pain on the right side is gone. "I'd rather have a matched pair," she says. If she got a prosthesis, she could now get an "A" bra cup size, and an A "sounds good" after "a life of Ds and double Ds." About the option of a prosthesis, she says:

> the other thing was to get a prosthesis you see
>   to match this left breast would have been
>   [pitch rises] it would have had to weigh five pounds
> now how would—
> and I put that that um temporary prosthesis I got from the Cancer Society
>   put this in the bra right

> well you <u>walk</u>
> in <u>two</u> seconds this is down here
> and this one's up here
> it's over there

Although objectified as things, breasts are not stable objects. The prosthesis and breast move. As Iris Young (1990) notes, breasts radically change their shape with body position and movements; standing up, lying down, bending over produce very different contours. "Many women's breasts are much more like a fluid than a solid; in movement, they sway, jiggle, bounce, ripple even when the movement is small" (p. 185).

The fluid being of breasts is situated in her body history when Jane explains that "I think part of it, you know, living with large breasts all your life, people don't understand what you're carrying around." She talks about the difficulty of running, premenstrual pain before menopause, and her fear, that, like her mother, her breasts would get even larger after menopause. The interviewer asks if she has had to adjust to looking different:

> Kristin: what about— do you think about ah how you look?
>
> Jane: me?
>
> Kristin: did you have to adjust to how you feel you look and others look at you or not?
>
> Jane: well what I notice first is that I have a stomach [Kristin laughs; Jane joins in]
> I could never see my stomach . no

Jane's response precipitates a laugh from Kristin because it is amusing and unexpected. Rather than seeing from the glance or gaze of the other, Jane speaks from the modality of the body of self as self observed (van Manen, 1998). She is looking at her stomach, and with her shirtfront raised, the breast area and mastectomy scars are visible. She points out to Kristin the scars from the quadrantectomy, the first mastectomy, and the second, which are not yet matched up but "I think in the end they may be," she says. The scar "looks pretty good now," she muses, which Kristin confirms.

Jane concludes the narrative of her second mastectomy, speaking again in the modality of the self observing her own body by looking in the mirror. Her speech is fragmented and unfinished but thoughtful:

> Jane: so when I look in the mirror
> you know I I look different
>   but it doesn't
>   I don't have a
>   it doesn't really right now
>   I mean I haven't had the
> that's not my problem
> I'm I figure that's the least of it you know
>
> Kristin: mhmm

> *Jane:*   so it's a
>   in a way
>   in a way it's kinda nice they're gone you know
>   with all the things I like to do
>   as long as I can keep doing the things I like to do
>   which I hope I can
>   and uh I don't have regrets that way . no
>   I might have but I don't think I will
> *Kristin:* mhmm
> *Jane:*   but it's like you say I think it's because of the
>   you know the history

In the first set of lines, Jane seems to be talking to herself, looking at herself, living her feelings pre-reflectively. The address appears to shift more to Kristin with the line "that's not my problem." The disfluencies in Jane's speech suggest that even if how she looks is "the least of it," she has yet to comprehend and incorporate all the changes cancer has wrought as she continues to live and tell her story. But she situates the comparison of past and future within her body history, a history of large breasts, painful premenstrual syndrome, the loss of erotic sensation in her nipples after menopause, and then the breast cancer through which she loses one breast. The second mastectomy responds to her body history prior to breast cancer, to the exigency of becoming one-breasted, and to a future—whatever time she has left—of "doing the things I like to do."

Like their breasts, women's body histories are fluid and changing, and it may be possible for Jane to form a new and positive body identity (Langellier, 2001). Jane's embodied storytelling reflects a desire to regain control of her body and to reclaim her life narrative, a desire always deferred and unfulfilled. "Well, I don't know where my beginning really is, now that I think back on it" captures the teleology of breast cancer storytelling and the mutable and transmutable possibilities for its beginnings and ends. The lived body is the locus of possibilities for memory and anxiety, knowledge and emotion. The embodied storyteller remembers, knows, feels, and acts in the "kingdom of the ill" (Sontag, 1978) and in the world.

"I knew for me it was big, since I was alone": Constraints on Breast Cancer Storytelling

The body of the breast cancer storyteller is a material body. Although embodiment makes possible a range of personal and interpersonal dimensions of illness, only some possibilities are realized in performing breast cancer narrative. The material body is constrained by cultural inscriptions, institutional practices, and situational relations that inform performance. Jane, like the large majority of those who write pathographies of breast cancer, is a literate, white, middle-class woman (Couser, 1997).[7] From the outset of her interview she calls attention to her privileged status: "I got really speedy treatment, and I'm sure that happens, I mean it's who you are. I know my position [an educator] and it comes into play here." In several variations she reiterates that medical treatment is a question of "who you are" and "who they know." Her general practitioner, for example, "was very well connected" and got her a timely appointment with a "booked up" psychiatrist. The psychiatrist, also an M.D., had very specific knowledge of cancer, its treatments, and their effects, which she brought to the therapy, a factor Jane constructs as an advantage over a psychologist or counselor. Jane sought out and selected female doctors whenever possible. As characterized above, she narrates her story as a series of decisions she makes, based upon networking and discussion with professionals and friends, to select healthcare providers as her needs unfold. She constructs a narrative of options, good care, and respect from medical professionals.

Jane also develops the critical importance of "knowing how to do it," by which she means being able to identify issues in breast cancer and to ask informed and strategic questions about treatments. What helped her in her crisis was "my friend Gillian who'd just been through it." Jane explains that, like herself, Gillian is "single" and "she has no family there [Halifax], so we were all the ones that were around." Following all the steps with Gillian, Jane knew what to expect and ask. Around Jane as the bodily center of the narrative, Gillian is the most individually developed character, spiraling through its plot. "Gillian and I will talk and say, 'what do you think?'" Gillian never told Jane what to do but helped her explore issues and options by willingly sharing her experiences and skillfully asking questions. The circle of friends who supported both Gillian and Jane also plays a critical role in the narrative. Friends visited Jane in the hospital and welcomed her home, accompanied her to appointments, and cooked, cleaned, and cared for her throughout chemotherapy. As Couser (1997) notes, supportive family and friends people pathographies, creating scenarios where no woman suffers in isolation. Jane encapsulates the unusual array of resources she enjoyed when she says, "I know for me it [the support from Gillian and other friends] was big . . . since I was alone."

Near the end of the narrative Jane asks, "now how many people have that?" —the exceptional support system of Gillian and friends—and she answers her own question: "most women don't." For example, Jane tells a story about a woman, also recovering from a mastectomy, with whom she shared a hospital room. Because she has friends ready with food and support, Jane can go home the day after her mastectomy, whereas the woman who shares her room and has been there for five days cannot. Jane describes her as a woman in her sixties from an "out-port town" who is waiting for a representative from the Cancer Society to visit:

> they [my friends] <u>always</u> came to visit you see
>   and <u>chat</u> and all the rest . so um
> and then this poor woman's sitting there with <u>no</u>body
>   I mean I didn't see a <u>per</u>son with her
>   And I thought <u>well</u> this is bad you know [takes a breath]
> so I'm dressing to go [home]
>   and <u>in</u> comes this lady from the Cancer Society
>   with a <u>fur:</u> coat on okay
> now in Halifax we have the
>   the <u>ritz</u>iest part of town of the city is called the South End
>   that's on the <u>end</u> where the peninsula
>   where the <u>water</u> and . alright?
> and <u>all:</u> I could think of that
> this is a do-gooding lady
>   meaning very well
> and here's this poor woman from a very small community
>   way: out in the middle of nowhere
>   and this fur coat's coming in
> and I thought oh my god
> if that had come at me you know I [laughingly]
> I wouldn't . that would be the end of me

Jane's story suggests several constraints—interpersonal, material, and in-stitutional—on this other woman's breast cancer experience. To the lack of interpersonal resources of supportive friends and family, Jane's storytelling constructs differences in material resources through the synecdochal "fur coat coming in" that contrasts the "poor woman" from a small and remote community with the ritzy, urban matron from the city. The storytelling further suggests a criticism of institutional practices of the Cancer Society that does not consider differences among women, such as social class. Jane distinguishes herself from the poor woman by virtue of the interpersonal and material resources that make the Cancer Society lady an option she can forego.

However, the national system of medical care in Canada does cover this woman's hospitalization and treatments, and it offers mental health benefits as well, should she request and qualify for them. Jane notes the ease, both emotional and practical, that her insurance provides. "All I had to do was to show my card, it takes two minutes" to get medical care. Moreover, she says "I have known none of the worries" about coverage nor the load of paperwork and bewildering forms that she has worked through for her mother's health in-surance. Because insurance offers mental health coverage, Jane suggests that Canadians do not face the stigma of mental illness that the U.S. medical and insurance systems engender. Nonetheless, she faces "a big problem" in that, given her kind of cancer, she could not now obtain health insurance in the United States for two years, nor afford it should a policy be available. "If I ever get to retirement . . . I had the option [with dual citizenship]" of returning to the United States, a choice she now comprehends, with great regret, is no longer possible.

The "if I ever get to retirement" intimates the timing of storytelling, a situational constraint that underwrites the entire narrative performance: "the fear of it coming back," as Jane states. At the telling, Jane did not know that she would die within eighteen months, exactly two years from her diagnosis. She narrates from the time and place of coming through surgeries and chemotherapy but without the relative stability of remission and infused with the foreboding of recurrence. Pathographies of breast cancer are usually written during the equilibrium five years after diagnosis, the medical signpost for "cure." That circumstance of timing, coupled with the privileged status of the narrators, their high-quality and respectful medical care, and the active support of family and friends, constructs breast cancer narratives as "best-case scenarios" (Couser, 1997, p. 38). The danger of the best-case scenario is not only that the breast cancer experience of a privileged group is universalized—African American women, for example, have a poorer survival rate than do white women, poor women receive lesser quality care and respect, some women are isolated and alone in their illness—but also that the situational conditions of narrative production are obscured. We conclude our discussion of constraints on performing breast cancer narrative by briefly considering the situation of the interview and Jane's address to other audiences.

The interview is an oral, face-to-face, collaborative form. Throughout the interview, Jane states a preference for talk over writing about breast cancer: "I'd rather talk about it." Although she keeps a notebook in which she records key symptoms and questions for doctors, she says, "I've never been a journal person, I've never been a diary person." She talks especially with friends, and perhaps the interview extends that circle, in Jane's preferred mode of communication, as an opportunity to share her experience and show her body in illness. As a collaboration, the interview is co-produced by Jane and Kristin. For example, in the stories about hair loss (discussed above), shared laughter increases as the narrator's adventures with turbans, wigs, and hairdressers unfold. Hair loss is not funny—indeed it is most often narrated as an assault and trauma—and Jane could have narrated these experiences very differently. But they emerge in this narrative performance as opportunities for humor within a tragic story. Moreover, they emphasize Jane's agency in the face of terminal illness as well as the buoyant support of friends. Jane's animated performance and Kristin's shared laughter encourage the inclusion and elaboration of these events. Other topics, more anxious for the interviewee and more uneasy for the interviewer, are quickly and slightly developed; for example, talk with the psychiatrist and "the fear of it coming back."

> *Kristin:* have you changed what you talk with her about as time has gone on?
> *Jane:* we:ll yeah
> now
> you me
> [quickly] cause I I mean to me— the the the serious matter is you know how do you
> you learn— I mean it's live— learning to live with it
> *Kristin:* mhmm
> *Jane:* [slowly, softly] the fear of it coming back
> *Kristin:* mhmm
> *Jane:* it's big
> *Kristin:* mhmm
> *Jane:* I haven't conquered that one yet
> *Kristin:* mhmm

The question asked by Kristin in the past tense is answered in present tense fragments, punctuated by pauses, unfinished because unknown or resisted or unspeakable. In the first lines, Kristin does not respond audibly. When she does, Jane names "it" as the fear of recurrence. The interaction shifts so that each of Jane's fragments is followed by Kristin's positive minimal response, a pattern which appears to facilitate the speaking although it remains fragmented and spare. We will return to this talk about fear of dying in our discussion of the ordering of discourse, below, but our concern here is to call attention to variations in co-production within the interview. Comparing the hair-loss segments with the fear-of-recurrence segments intimates a "let's go here" and "let's not go there" collaboration between the participants.

Breast cancer storytelling is as much about the power to be heard and listened to as it is to tell. To the extent that the interview is therapeutic for Jane, she responds to Kristin's questions at the same time she addresses the self-audience that is there and alive to hear (Frank, 1995). But Jane also speaks to other audiences, absent audiences beyond the interview situation, especially other women with or at risk for breast cancer (Minister, 1991; Frank, 2002). She narrates from a position of privilege: treatment options, interpersonal resources, and institutional support in the form of high-quality medical care and mental health care, empathy and respect from health professionals, and insurance coverage. Simultaneously, she calls attention to her privilege, marks its differences, and extends it to all women. She speaks for herself and her embodied particularities—"I knew for me"—but she also points to other women's stories—"other women don't"—for example, the woman who shared her hospital room. Her storytelling talks within and talks back to the medical institution and cancer culture, as we will develop further by turning from the capabilities of embodiment and constraints of performing to the breast cancer narrative itself.

"Call it what it is": Ordering Breast Cancer Discourse

In the culture of breast cancer, as Ehrenreich (2001) observes, "cheerfulness is more or less mandatory, dissent a kind of treason" (p. 50). Couser (1997) makes a similar observation with regard to breast cancer narratives. He writes that "the breast cancer narrative like that of autobiography generally is a comic one; it ends 'happily,' with some significant recovery; the narrators are healed if not cured. Without exception, then, the narrators are, or claim to be, better off at the end than at the beginning" (p. 39). Couser attributes the absence of unhappy and negative outcomes in breast cancer narratives to the simple fact that they are told overwhelmingly by women who have the physical resources and emotional well-being to narrate their experience and thus should not be considered "representative" of breast cancer experience. Women who do not survive breast cancer cannot narrate their experience. But the emphasis on the comic plot and cheerfulness, as we discussed earlier, is not only a consequence of who lives to tell the tale but also an expression of desire. As Couser notes, women are unlikely to invest in the efforts of narration when facing death: "few people want to read (and no one wants to write) an autopathography with a tragic plot" (pp. 39–40).

The emphasis on the comic plot and cheerfulness in breast cancer story-telling suggests the operation of discursive rules organized around a series of exclusions: the prohibition of talk about uncertainties and death, the division of discourse into what does and does not belong to breast cancer experience, and the oppositional construction of truth in breast cancer narratives. The prohibition of talk about uncertainties and death can be seen in the avoidance of the use of the "C-word," cancer, both in early stages of diagnosis and in general talk after diagnosis (Stacey, 1997). To some extent, the avoidance of the term may reflect the uncertainty of knowledge by medical personnel regarding the yet-to-be-analyzed lump. For example, in Jane's interaction with her doctor during the initial breast examination, she reports the doctor saying "I think there's something here." Jane picks up this term in the description of her own response: "and when I felt it, it was [pause] it was definitely something." After viewing the results of the mammogram, Jane reports the doctor's careful selection of language. "She wouldn't say what it was, but she just said that whatever it is, it has to come out." However, there is a difference in the meaning of uncertainty when it reflects the understandable reluctance of medical personnel to make a premature diagnosis and in the meaning of uncertainty when it reflects the lack of medical knowledge about cancer. For example, Jane states that "what I learn more and more in this is that they know very little about breast cancer if they don't get it when it's less than a centimeter and it's Grade One." Because the "something" in her breast is larger than a centimeter, multifocal, and Grade Three, her prognosis is unknown. As Jane states, "it's all guessing, they don't know."

While critical of medical discourse, Jane is more scathing in her critique of the enforced cheerfulness—what she calls "that friggin positive stuff"—enacted by acquaintances, colleagues, and a representative from the Cancer Society.

>   *Jane:*   I mean this <u>pos</u>itive thing
>   I think is the <u>wor:st</u> thing that you can say to somebody
>   cause here you <u>are</u>
>   got this <u>terrible</u> news
>   you might <u>die</u>
>   and . ah . nobody . I don't think
>   nobody knows what that means
>   and
>   *Kristin:*   mhmm
>   *Jane:*   I'm still trying to figure out what does it mean to be positive
>   and of course the psychiatrist always says
>   we're working on it
>   what does it mean to be positive
>   you see . um
>   it's like you're supposed to go around with a <u>smile</u> on your face and pretend
>   and I mean <u>forget that</u>
>   that's not how you <u>feel</u>
>   it's <u>awful</u>
>   so people that say that to you
>   I just want to punch them

For Jane the injunction to "be positive" is enacted in sympathy cards, motivational tapes, hospital visits, and telephone calls by well-meaning individuals across a range of interactions. As we discussed earlier, the "relentless brightsiding" of such comments works to normalize breast cancer and transform it, in Ehrenreich's terms, into a rite of passage rather than "an injustice or a tragedy to rail against" (p. 49). Enforced cheerfulness makes it possible to avoid talking about what it means that "you might die," as Jane voices it.

The exclusion of discourse about uncertainty and death informs what is seen as belonging to breast cancer experience. For example, in describing the interaction with her oncologist over his refusal to sign a long-term disability form, Jane describes the division and rejection of her lived experience. He insists that she can be back to work in three weeks even though, as Jane responds, "this is my third chemo and I can hardly walk to the bathroom and I'm supposed to be back working in three weeks?" She notes that the oncologist "never once asked me how I felt," "what it's been like at home," or "what kind of work I do." Nor do the innumerable forms she completes on diet and vomiting and "all the physical things" contain even "one psychological question." She remarks that the oncologist warned her by saying: "'I don't deal with whole persons' [. . .] and he certainly didn't." She situates his division of breast cancer discourse and the refusal to "deal with whole persons" as a defensive measure, a way to manage the reality that "so many of them die on them."

The efforts to avoid talking about death and to exclude consideration of death and dying from breast cancer discourse are repositioned as not true to experience. Jane opposes the false cheerfulness of greeting cards and people that say "be positive and pray hard and I know the Lord will be this" with her preference for the truth spoken by "the people that said 'this is shit,' you know, call it what it is." The injunction to "call it what it is" rather than to "be positive" is captured by the account Jane gives of her telephone interaction with "the cancer lady," a breast cancer survivor and representative of the Cancer Society who telephones after Jane begins chemotherapy. "This lady starts telling me" about how "I had cancer eighteen years ago and I'm doing so well and you've gotta be positive." Jane responds that it makes "you want to get your frying pan out and hit them over the head." At another point, she clarifies, "I mean, it's . it's a nice story but the . point is, I mean I know enough to know that every cancer's different." The relational truth that Jane recounts —that "every cancer's different" and that she might die—is excluded by the universalizing move of the comic plot; she does not find it an occasion for cheerfulness or to "be positive."

The "cancer lady" tells "a nice story" of breast cancer diagnosis, treatment, and recovery. This nice story, what Couser calls the breast cancer master plot, illustrates the internal distribution and ordering of discourse features. Couser (1997) writes that the following features of the master plot appear regularly in breast cancer narratives, typically distributed in the same order: "discovery by the author of a suspicious lump in her breast; diagnosis of cancer; the assessment of treatment options; some form of surgical treatment, lumpectomy or mastectomy; some form of adjuvant treatment—radiation, chemotherapy, hormone therapy, or a combination of these; recovery and resolution in the form of favorable reports and restoration of (relative) peace of mind" (p. 42). Couser describes other recurring features that supplement the master plot: discussion of decision-making on choices of reconstructive surgery and prosthesis, shopping for a wig or prosthesis, alternative or supplemental therapies, and fears about making wrong decisions.

The narrative that Jane constructs in her interview also incorporates the features of the master plot that Couser describes even while it varies from it. Jane reflects that her familiarity with breast cancer began two years earlier when her friend Gillian was diagnosed with breast cancer. In the absence of family, Jane and other friends as "the ones around her" became Gillian's support group. Jane's recollection of this time includes an explicit recognition of the regularity of narrative features and their distribution. As Jane states, "I was familiar with her story and had followed all the steps with her." Because of this experience with Gillian, she says, "I had a very good idea of what was gonna happen or what could happen and what were the big issues" in her own case. Not surprisingly, then, Jane utilizes the "steps" of this familiar narrative in recounting her own experience. We organize the following summary of Jane's narrative according to the steps of Couser's master plot.

1. *Discovery of a Suspicious Lump:* Jane describes "this thing," found during an annual examination with her doctor. She contextualizes the discovery by recounting the date of her last mammogram (six months earlier), her practice of regular self-examination and yearly mammograms, and discusses her family history and personal factors that put her at greater risk for breast cancer. She then returns to describing the scene with her doctor and how her doctor used her "connections" and "kept pushing it" to get her "speedy treatment" for the biopsy and lab work.

2. *Diagnosis of Cancer:* Jane then turns to the results of the core biopsy and names the "whatever it is" as a diagnosis of "definitely cancer," "infiltrating duct cancer."

3. *Assessment of Treatment Options:* Jane spends little time talking about the diagnosis and immediately turns to discuss her decision-making about treatment, including the choice of surgeon, problems scheduling operating room time, delaying her sabbatical travel plans, when to break the news to her family (before or after Christmas), and the choice of a quadrantectomy rather than a mastectomy.

4. *Surgical Treatment:* Jane describes her surgery in a highly condensed form: "I had the quadrantectomy done." The lab results after the surgery return her, in terms of the master plot, to the previous step of diagnosis (Step 2) because "I found out it was this Grade Three cancer, and multifocal." Again, she spends little time describing the mastectomy surgery: "then she [surgeon] did that." Following this brief comment, Jane returns to assess the treatment options (Step 3) regarding chemotherapy, the choice of oncologist, and her selection of a psychiatrist following Gillian's recommendation that she "get a therapist."

5. *Adjuvant Treatment:* Jane then describes scheduling chemotherapy and sessions with the psychiatrist. She interweaves descriptions of her loss of control during chemotherapy, "the chemo was the pits," with her sessions with the psychiatrist, who says, "you're in control and we're only gonna talk about what you want to talk about." In this segment of the interview, Jane also relates "this hormone story" (discussed in the following section of the chapter), as well as her shopping trip for wigs and hats and her experiences getting her

hair cut. The descriptions of humorous episodes, "wigging" and haircuts, are counterposed to descriptions of diet and dealing with the "rounds of chemo" and the accompanying debilitation, diarrhea, and vomiting.

6. *Recovery and Resolution:* The interaction with "the cancer lady" comes at this point in the interview. In addition, Jane considers the options of a prosthesis, breast reconstruction, and breast reduction. She relates her decision process for a second mastectomy (described in an earlier section), how she looks and feels after the second mastectomy, how other people respond to how she looks, her fear of recurrence ("I still have a fear of it coming back"), and her struggle "just trying to survive." She contrasts the care and support she receives from her circle of friends and the psychiatrist with the lack of care and support she finds with her oncologist and others who express a "be positive" attitude.

Familiarity with and recitation of "all the steps" of the master plot position Jane as a knowledgeable speaker. That is, the narrative repetition and sameness of the master plot work to establish Jane as a subject who knows what questions to ask and "what were the big issues." Performing the breast cancer master plot builds authority for Jane as a speaking subject by incorporating her reading and research on breast cancer, her knowledge of family history, her experience of Gillian's and of her sister's breast cancer cases, and her background in science education. The narrative repetition and sameness that position Jane as a knowledgeable speaker, however, simultaneously and paradoxically function to de-authorize her by reinforcing the medical plot. Jane summarizes this de-authorization when she cites her psychiatrist saying "everybody's controlling your life now; you have no say." Or as Jane asks:

> what can you say to the oncologist?
> no . don't use adriomyacin?
> I can't
> you gotta go with— some things you gotta go with

Jane locates her lack of a speaking position not as a failure of personal capability, captured in the fragmentary false start of "I can't," but in the generalized plural subject, the "you" of "some things you gotta go with," which speaks in the voice of medicine.

Not all interaction with medical personnel works to de-authorize Jane as a speaking subject. In addition to the interaction with her psychiatrist, Jane's discussion with her general practitioner on hormone therapy during menopause suggests collaboration, as is illustrated in the use of "we" in the following segment where she describes the dosage she took when "we started the hormone" therapy to treat her sleeplessness:

> so then we went up to the point 1.2
>   we <u>doubl</u>ed it you see

and um then that <u>stopped</u> it
    that stopped that
so the first time I got some <u>sleep</u> in eighteen months
    which was <u>really</u> quite nice

The shared speaking position suggested by this use of "we"—even though Jane is the only one taking the hormone therapy—stands in marked contrast to the description of her interaction with the oncologist who does not "deal with whole persons." Consider the use of "we" in the following description of going to the cancer clinic to meet with the oncologist:

simply go in and
    what kind . you know
    this is the <u>cancer</u>
    this is the <u>chemo</u>
    these are the <u>chemicals</u> we're gonna use
    this is how it's gonna <u>go</u>

The use of "we" in this excerpt refers not to any shared speaking position with Jane but to the authority of the medical establishment in treating the "cancer's person," as Jane puts it later in the interview. The cancer, chemo, and chemicals are ex-nominated; that is, they are not located in relation or reference to Jane. The process of chemotherapy replaces the lived-body as subject in this discussion.

The struggle to construct a speaking position in discourse also is evident in the way Jane performs the narrative of her breast cancer. In particular, this struggle can be seen in one of the few segments that is marked by numerous pauses and hesitancy in speaking. Earlier we discussed how the pauses and hesitancy in this segment illustrate the constraints of the interview situation and the relationship between Jane and Kristin. Now, we consider this interaction in terms of the narrator's relationship to the story she relates, that is, to her constitution as a speaking subject. In this segment, the first part of which was cited earlier, Jane is discussing her interaction with her psychiatrist when the talk turns to her present concerns:

   Jane: she's a good
           she's a good person to talk with
Kristin: have you changed what you talk with her about as time has gone on?
   Jane: we:ll yeah
           now
           you me
           [quickly] cause I I mean to me— the the the serious matter is you know how do you you learn— I mean it's live— learning to live with it
Kristin: mhmm

Jane: [slowly, softly] the fear of it coming back

Kristin: mhmm

Jane: it's big

Kristin: mhmm

Jane: I haven't conquered that one yet

Kristin: mhmm

Jane: but I . but I can <u>see</u> that
now that I'm <u>feeling</u> better physically
   I mean I'm a . much
   I'm much better able to cope with that?
   I mean I can . like I'm a
I can start to talk about it
where before I don't think I . I
I wasn't ready then

Kristin: mhmm

Jane: it was like it
all I was doing was day to day
she'd say now don't worry
you gotta
[louder, firmly] I have to learn to live with it now [clears throat]
   instead of the future
   I'm a very future person

The pauses and hesitancy perform the uncertainty that she narrates. They mark out the variable position of the speaking subject ("you me / cause I") and how discourse works to name what is yet unspoken. In this particular excerpt, we see Jane struggle to name what it is she is learning to "start talking about." She tentatively and indirectly names "the fear of it coming back" even though this phrase embeds another "it" within it. "It" can be understood as the cancer; however, the substitution of "cancer" in this sentence is still an indirect form of addressing the uncertainty Jane faces. Elsewhere in the interview Jane describes this uncertainty as the possibility "that you might die." In this segment, she works to make the distancing of a "you" statement into an "I" statement of personal responsibility. She rejects the false start of "you gotta" for the specific "I have to learn to live with it now." This excerpt also suggests her use of the breast cancer plot in the lines that suggest that "I'm feeling better physically." However, this description of her condition does not effect the comic closure that Couser describes as characteristic of such narratives. It is not just the fear of dying but its immediacy that she "has to learn to live with." Jane locates the possibility of closure in an uncertain future—an uncertainty she performs in formulating her condition as something that she is doing but has yet to accomplish.

"That's what I forgot":
Counterstories and Closure

Just as Jane reworks the comic closure characteristic of the master plot, she reworks the beginning as well. After talking through her loss of control during chemotherapy and her initial sessions with the psychiatrist, she notes that a typical question in those early times was "how are you feeling?" She situates the occurrence of this question by recalling that she was having hot flashes at the time, and this recollection triggers another one.

> *Jane:* cause I had trouble with the <u>hot flashes</u>
> cause I had to go <u>off</u> the hormones
> oooh that's what I forgot to do . to do
> put in this story
> was this hormone story
>
> *Kristin:* yes
>
> *Jane:* I never
> I . I avoided hormones because I was afraid of the breast cancer risk
> although they were saying
> > oh it's very little
> > and a::ll this
> > and no don't do that

The phrase "this <u>hormone</u> story" suggests both a revision to the opening of the interview where Jane is uncertain about where to locate "my beginning" as well as an alternative or counterstory to juxtapose to the story advanced by the breast cancer master plot. Similar to the discussion of her family history and other possible risk factors that Jane introduces after she describes the discovery of a suspicious lump, the introduction of the hormone story works to refashion the implied causality of the linear medical plot. Breast cancer is something to be discovered by an individual and her doctor; it "just happens" in the master plot. The focus on the individual in the master plot emphasizes genetic and lifestyle factors as possible causes for cancer and makes it difficult to speak about environmental factors.

Rather than a cancer story that begins with discovery of a lump, Jane suggests that her story should begin with the decision to undergo hormone therapy for menopause. She describes the severity of her symptoms—"I was having a hell of a menopause"—that lead her to schedule an appointment with her general practitioner (G.P.):

> I didn't sleep for
> I hadn't had sleep for eighteen months when I finally went
> > this again would have been about March '94
> I hadn't slept for at least eighteen months

> because I was awake every
> at least every hour with hot flashes all night long
> so I was getting sleep deprived

After trying several over-the-counter sleep aids, Jane repeats that she is "so desperate from lack of sleep" that she goes to talk with her G.P. about what to do. Her description of the G.P.'s response makes clear her reluctance to consider hormone therapy:

> *Jane:* she said we:ll
> you know I said my sister's got breast cancer so that puts me in a higher risk category see
> and she said ye:ah but that doesn't mean that you would get it you know
> and that was one of the times that I thought
>   you know this is
>   well it's interesting their <u>attitudes</u> of the connections between the hormones and
> and <u>she</u> had been <u>one</u> person
> um . we <u>talked</u> about it for <u>years</u>
> and . and she had been a . very much <u>against</u> it
> and then when the . when the evidence came out about the [takes breath]
>   um . you know— the heart disease and the <u>osteo</u> relationship with the hormones
> <u>she:</u> became— she <u>converted</u> over [takes breath]
> not that she she didn't <u>push</u> it on me or anything
>   but she said you know I <u>think</u> that
>   that there's a <u>lo:t</u> to this where before I would have said <u>no</u>
> but you mean given the risk after that
>   you know I . there's gonna be risks in anything you do
>   and I'm having a lot of trouble
> so I finally gave in and said okay I'm gonna try this thing
>   I'm so desperate to do
>   to get some sleep to try something to curb this
>   and I was
>   the psychological ups and downs
>   I mean it was like . God
>
> *Kristin:* mhmm
>
> *Jane:* it was very bad
> and it had been going on for three years at that point
> so um
> we started the hormone

As she does throughout the interview, Jane describes the interaction with her G.P. as one of shared decision-making. In this segment, she struggles to maintain that narrative positioning. She claims that her G.P. "didn't push" the hormone therapy, but then a few lines later Jane counters that assertion with "I finally gave in." While it is possible to understand her decision as a capitulation to the suggestions of the G.P., Jane immediately moves to clarify it as a response to the length and severity of menopause, to the lack of sleep and "the psychological ups and downs."

The narrative positioning in this segment, therefore, is less focused on the question of responsibility for making a tough decision to begin hormone therapy than it is about the possibility of a connection between the treatments and cancer.

> *Jane:* so that was in
>   that was in March '94
>   and then
>   so I always wondered if there was a connection between that and the tumor
>   now the tests came back
>   they do all these tests on this tumor
>   and it came back that it was not estrogen receptor sensitive
>   so but nobody has been able to say
>   or nobody will say categorically it didn't ha:ve anything to do
>   but of course in my mi:nd
>   I mean I can't
>   I . I . I . I
>   it may not have affected that tumor
>   but maybe the conditions around
>   or the environment somehow
>   cause I was on that higher dosage
>   and that was just the time
>   I mean within that six months this thing goes from— something that doesn't
>   and that when I had that last mammo mammogram in May they did a
>   they did a
>   you know they did a self-exam there as well
> *Kristin:* so you feel pretty satisfied it wasn't there
> *Jane:* [loudly] I really wonder
>   we:ll it certainly wasn't something that anybody picked up
> *Kristin:* mhmm
> *Jane:* so how did it get so big so fast?
>   and that's wh— that's when they were doubling the hormones

The specificity of knowledge regarding dates (March '94, May), hormone dose (1.2), diagnostic tests (estrogen receptor), and recall of dialogue all work to establish the certainty and importance of the hormone story. However, despite these certainties, Jane is unable to satisfy her suspicion of a connection between the hormone therapy and the growth of the tumor in her breast. Jane summarizes the uncertainty explicitly when she concludes, "so I don't know if there's a connection, that the why part you know [. . .]. I mean I'm sure I'll never know." Furthermore, she performs the uncertainty in the repetitions and false starts ("I . I . I . I") in her speech as she works to clarify the reasons for making such a connection.

In the hormone story, Jane works to understand the vexing issue of what caused her breast cancer, targeting pharmaceutical and environmental causes. She tries to locate her place in the story she tells and the life she lives, and to maintain her worth as a person able to act and make decisions even in uncertain conditions with inadequate and incomplete information. We interpret the inclusion of the hormone story, "what I almost forgot," as an effort to resituate both the disembodied story of medical discourse and the comic master plot of breast cancer narratives. The hormone story draws attention to the material conditions and cultural relations which shape the experience of living with breast cancer. As a counter to medical discourse, Jane reinscribes her body—her fears, her sleeplessness, her emotional oscillations—in the story she tells. This effort illustrates Smith and Watson's (2001) argument that autopathography is useful because it "critiques social constructions of the disabled body and incorporates a counternarrative of survival and empowerment that reclaims the individual's or a loved one's body from the social stigmatization and the impersonalization of medical discourse" (pp. 187–188).

By telling the hormone story, however, Jane attempts more than survival and empowerment. The hormone story also works to counter the closure of the comic plot of the survivor story by insisting upon an ambiguous narrative beginning and trajectory. Survivor stories are usually positioned as empowering in and of themselves; because they are told by survivors, they transgress dominant discourse (Alcoff & Gray, 1993). However, Ehrenriech (2001) counters that in the case of breast cancer, the dominant discourse infantilizes women with its emphasis on pink ribbons, stuffed teddy bears, and cosmetics: "America's breast-cancer cult can be judged as a mass delusion, celebrating survivorhood by downplaying mortality and promoting obedience to medical protocols known to have limited efficacy" (p. 52). From this perspective, survivor stories discipline the body and recuperate rather than transgress medical discourse and the comic master plot.

The tendency for dominant discourse to recuperate the transgressive potential of breast cancer storytelling is recognized by some narrative performers and theorists. For example, Linda Park-Fuller, author and performer of "A Clean Breast of It" (Park-Fuller, 1995), writes of her struggle to displace the victim/victor scenarios prevalent in popular culture. She struggles with the desire for narrative closure that would help her "put the disease-experience behind" and her misgivings about what that closure might mean if she should have a recurrence. In a similar way, Jackie Stacey (1997) wonders what is excluded by the kind of closure brought on by the "triumph-over-tragedy" genre—what Park-Fuller calls the victor scenario. Such stories "encourage us to believe that suffering makes us wiser and serve to heroise those who suffer most" (p. 15). In short, they function as a "fantasy of control" whereby story-tellers forestall death and contradict "the knowledge of one's own mortality" (p. 242). In her performance, Park-Fuller (2000) employs a Brechtian distanc-ing device of "a timer to sound every twelve minutes—signaling the symbolic frequency that people die from breast cancer in the U.S., and calling listener attention to the fact that some stories are absent while mine is told" (p. 33). This device helps to defer the move to closure in survivor storytelling and draws attention to the absences and ambiguities, the omissions and gaps, in personal testimony.

In Jane's storytelling, the inclusion of the hormone story displaces the con-ventional beginning of the dominant discourse. Instead of beginning with the disembodied discovery of a suspicious lump, Jane remembers her lived expe-rience of "a hell of a menopause" and the hormone therapy that may have af-fected "the conditions around / or the <u>environ</u>ment somehow." Instead of the enforced cheerfulness and "that friggin positive stuff," Jane attempts to "call it what it is" and to authorize herself as a speaking subject. Instead of the con-ventional comic closure of survival and the heroic scenario of victory over cancer, Jane voices "the fear of it coming back" and the uncertainty of "learn-ing to live with it." Throughout her storytelling, Jane works to counter the forms of closure that would impose a superficial order upon her account of breast cancer. She explicitly includes the pains and fears, the uncertainties and ambiguities, that both medical discourse and the "triumph-over-tragedy" sur-vivor story would mobilize but then put to rest.

We have described the ways in which Jane's storytelling works to counter or transgress medical discourse and the comic master plot. However, we are reluctant to label these fragmentary and dispersed efforts a "counterstory," as Hilde Lindemann Nelson (2001) defines it, because even when storytelling works to counter dominant discourses at the level of tactics, such efforts may not be effective strategically. Smith and Watson (1996) remark that this abil-ity of dominant discourses to recuperate transgressive efforts can be seen in self-help groups where "a person's efforts to make a gesture of tactical resist-ance to a stereotypic communal notion of the unspeakable can be co-opted and re-ordered into the community's normative patterns of speakability" (p. 16). Nelson recognizes the complexity of such narrative intervention when she insists that *both* dominant discourses—what she calls "master narra-tives"—*and* counterstories are inconsistent, tangled, organic ensembles rather than static, uniform, and singular narratives. Just as there is no "one-size-fits-all" master narrative, so, too, there is no corresponding all-encompassing counterstory to resist it (p. 169). Instead, let us conclude our analysis by spec-ifying the variable ways that Jane's storytelling operates according to the strategic hierarchy of content-, task-, and group-ordering in performing narra-tive.

First, at the strategic level of content-ordering, Jane's breast cancer story-telling works to contest what Nelson calls the "epistemic rigging" by which medical discourse and the comic master plot hide their coercive force. Nelson suggests that dominant discourses hide their coercive force through natural-izing, normalizing, and privatizing content. For example, Jane's hormone story counters the presumption that breast cancer is inevitable or natural for certain women with particular hereditary or lifestyle choices. If hormone replace-ment therapy can affect the growth of cancer or the environment within which cancer grows, then it is reasonable to look to other environmental fea-tures as causal factors. This form of critique is difficult to conduct—and it may be for this reason that Jane does not pursue it—because it easily can be-come a form of "blaming the victim," where Jane (or her general practitioner) are blamed for making a bad choice to go on the hormone replacement ther-apy. Jane's storytelling contests the normalizing of breast cancer storytelling in her rejection of the "nice story" of taking a positive attitude and recovery told by the "cancer lady." In emphasizing her friends and community support, she counters the privatizing of breast cancer whereby women are hidden away from sight (such as the scene with the hairdresser) and isolated in hospital rooms and treatment programs. Such storytelling contests existing discourse topics, narrative plots and positions, and cancer-as-warfare metaphors.

Second, when we turn to the level of task-ordering, it is important to em-phasize that the combinations of medical discourse and the comic master plot found generally in breast cancer storytelling cannot be described as some-thing imposed upon storytellers. For example, Jane's storytelling incorporates medical discourse as a tactical move to reclaim authority and what Linda Al-coff and Linda Gray (1993) describe as the "expert" position in discourse. Jane repudiates, when she can, efforts to silence her or to de-authorize her speech. She uses her familiarity with the comic master plot to restructure listener ex-pectations. As Nelson argues, efforts at this level "don't merely *reflect* a shift in understanding. They set out to *cause* a shift" (p. 156); that is, they attempt to change the ordering of tasks. In her storytelling, Jane shifts the sedimenta-tion of discourse tasks—who gets to speak, who is seen as authoritative, who gets to listen, and so on. Another example of this effort comes when Jane tells how she gave family members copies of Dr. Susan Love's book (2000) to read, thereby shifting and redistributing the educational labor of explanation. But such tactics are not always effective, nor are they easily applied in all situa-tions. As Jane discovers in her interaction with the oncologist, "some things you gotta go with."

Finally, at the level of group-ordering, Jane's storytelling works to refuse pre-given identities. She struggles to redefine the triumph-over-tragedy scenario that would position her as the comic hero. At the same time, however, she obviously does not want to fall back into the victim/victor duality, which would require that if she rejects the comic structure then she must assume the role of a tragic hero. She summarizes this alternative when she describes how her community of friends and colleagues were shocked to discover "you know, there's somebody else down the tubes." Jane, in much the way that Nelson suggests, sets out to repair the damage to her identity (p. 154) in the stories told by medical discourse and the comic master plot. But tactical changes in group-ordering may not effect change in either level of task- or content-ordering. No amount of narrative repair or storytelling will alter the uncertainty of living with breast cancer ("it's tough enough just trying to survive") and the uncertain trajectory that will eventually end in death ("you might die").

Jane answers the call of the ill body for a voice with a complex and contradictory narrative performance. She both constructs and deconstructs the normative breast cancer narrative as she simultaneously invests in and disavows medical discourse, and as she expands and delimits the comic closure of survivorship. Our examination of Jane's breast cancer storytelling recalls Foucault's argument that the relations of power are dispersed throughout the social field and can attach to strategies of resistance as well as to domination. There are no inherently liberatory or repressive narrative practices (Sawicki, 1991). In performing a breast cancer story, a woman can function as an agent of mundane resistance. But because of the multileveled relations of power, resistance cannot be guaranteed by any particular text, even when it opposes the normative story; by any particular telling, even when it contributes to healing; by any particular hearing, even when it achieves personal and cultural witness to a life or death. Even had Jane chosen silence as a form of resistance to breast cancer storytelling culture, that silence would resonate with ambiguities of embodiment and discourse.

CHAPTER 7

Performing Narrative on Stage

Identity and Agency in an
Autobiographical Performance

The possibility of performing narrative on stage brings us to the third and final case study. While it may appear counterintuitive to wait until the end of a book on *performing* narrative to discuss staged performances of storytelling, we have deferred discussion until this point for three related reasons. First, we deferred this discussion in order to emphasize that staged performances are one permutation of storytelling in daily life, along with storytelling in families, in conversations between friends, in weblogs, in therapeutic dialogues, and in the discourses of organizations and institutions. We want to avoid making performance on stage into a metaphor for performance in the rest of life and vice versa: not "all the world's a stage," nor is a stage all of the world. Second, we emphasize the continuities among the many permutations of performing narrative in order to challenge the discontinuity assumed by a modernist view of performance that separates "art" from "life," and the aesthetic realm from that of daily life. In performing narrative, participants draw upon and combine a variety of discursive resources and conventions in a particular social and material condition in order to, as Merleau-Ponty says, turn back on the world to signify it. Finally, we emphasize these combinatory possibilities in order to understand how they are productive for a lived-body engaged in storytelling. Performing narrative is both a *doing* and a *making*—both *praxis* and *poiesis* in the Greek tradition. Performing narrative is the communication practice of storytelling; performing narrative ranges across all our daily "doings," our ways of "making do," and the more public ceremonies in which we make a "to-do" of storytelling.

Performing narrative on stage draws from rich and varied traditions in the United States.[1] Even within the last century, these traditions include a wide range of performance events and practices: cultural or folk performances (such as those found at storytelling festivals, at folk art revivals, at county fairs, at civic centennial and bicentennial celebrations), performances in mass or popular entertainments (such as those found in vaudeville and variety shows, in travelogues and public lectures, in Chautauqua circuit programs, and in stand-up comedy), performances in religious ceremonies (such as the performance of stories from the Bible, storytelling within sermons, or reenactments found on holy days), performances in schools and educational institutions (such as poetry recitals, oration contests, performance of literature festivals), and, of course, performances in the world of high culture and theater (such as one-person shows, monologuists, traveling theater troupes, and performance art). During the 1960s and 1970s, at a time when performance art was emerging in unconventional spaces and storytelling was undergoing a folk revival, minority groups and activists were discovering the efficacy of performance as political action by "staging" protests and interventions to advocate for civil rights, to protest government action or inaction, and to gain visibility and educate the general public. By the end of the twentieth century, performance and politics intersected in efforts to redefine the public sphere and possibilities for social and cultural change (Kistenberg, 1995; Madison, 1998; Schlossman, 2002).

In this chapter, we focus on one example drawn from performance practices that emerged at the end of the twentieth century: queer solo or autobiographical performance. Commenting on the boom in queer solo performance at the end of the century, David Román suggests that autobiographical material is attractive to both performers and audiences because it reworks a model of identity politics that emerged from three decades of gay and lesbian liberation efforts (Hughes & Román, 1998). In particular, the performance of autobiography makes lesbian and gay identity visible in a society that ignores, marginalizes, and erases its existence. At the same time, the changing variety of autobiographical performances emphasizes the dynamic and historically contingent meanings for "lesbian," "gay," and "queer" life. Autobiographical performance, Román argues, "comes out of a sense of community and thus helps inform and shape our understanding of identity and community. Queer solo performers trouble the comfort of community even as they invest in it" (pp. 4–5). Thus queer solo performance makes the construction of identity and community in performing narrative thematic and problematic.

Embedded in Román's comment are two assertions that highlight the performative nature of identity: first, identity is not a substance or possession of an individual apart from any community or material context; identity "comes out of a sense of community." Second, identity is not an individual or communal attribute that is essential or ahistorical; identity changes in performances that "trouble" and help inform and shape it. As we discussed in Chapter 4, the performative sense of identity is based in what Hall (1992) describes as "a 'difference' that is positional, conditional, and conjunctural," not "a 'difference' which makes a radical and unbridgeable separation" (p. 257). In this chapter, we describe how a solo narrative performance by Craig Gingrich-Philbrook, "The First Time," engages these positional, conditional, and conjunctural differences in order to trouble our sense of identity and community and to intervene with an audience in a particular historical situation.[2]

This analysis of "The First Time" emerged from ongoing discussions between Eric and Gingrich-Philbrook, the author/performer, over the function of gesture, transcription practices, and conventions in personal narrative performance. We analyze "The First Time" in order to illustrate how performing narrative on stage uses the tensions and ambiguities of experience to critically participate in, to help inform and shape, the production and reproduction of identities. At the same time, we use this analysis to critically participate in, to help inform and shape, research on staged performances of narrative. This chapter, therefore, has a dual focus: the shaping dimensions of identity politics in a case of performing narrative on stage, and the shaping dimensions of the struggle for agency in performance and in research on such performances.

Our analysis proceeds in four stages. First, we describe "The First Time" by presenting a transcription that emphasizes the patterning or poetic structure of the performance. In the section that follows it, we reconsider the bodily experience of audience and the methodological move from the order of experience to the order of analysis. The ambiguity of conscious experience in performance and in reading a transcript makes storytelling possible—the "trope of repetition" (Atkinson & Silverman, 1997) that operates the first and every time in staged performances. This critical participation provides the basis for locating four themes about identity in the performance of "The First Time." The definition of these themes initiates the third stage of our analysis. We explore the reflexivity between conventional performance and performing conventions in order to unpack the production and reproduction of identities. Performing narrative engages, reiterates, and repeats conventions of stage performance as well as conventions of performing sexuality. In the final stage, we resituate our analysis of "The First Time" as part of the struggle for agency in research —a question of not only what constitutes a "good" story and "good" storytelling, but also what constitutes "good" research. Following Román's argument, our analysis troubles the comforts of research practices even as it invests in them. Now, let us turn to a transcription and description of "The First Time."

Craig Gingrich-Philbrook's "The First Time": Performance and Transcription

Craig Gingrich-Philbrook performed "The First Time" at the first Annual Performance Studies Benefit for the Southern Illinois Regional Effort for AIDS (SIREA) in July 1992. A brief performance of just over six minutes, "The First

Time" nonetheless illustrates the elements of narrative patterning and "stand-up theory" that Gingrich-Philbrook considers central to his work. In his introduction to the performance script for "Refreshment," a longer work performed for a later SIREA benefit, Gingrich-Philbrook (1997) comments on how he engages the critical responsibility of unpacking everyday experience in his performances. "I also find it useful to recall that autobiographical performers can speak for a particular confluence of shared events and can call the others assembled there to witness a pattern, see how one thing resembles another, or recognize how something previously taken for granted by the assembly is not what it seems" (p. 353). This approach employs performance as a form of "stand-up theory," that is, as a form of praxis or "a prolonged conversation helping us get clear on what happened and what we can do about it" (Zita, 1998, p. 188).

Gingrich-Philbrook uses performance to clarify "a particular confluence of shared events." He calls on the audience to participate in three tasks: to witness a *pattern*—a particular ordering, iteration, or citation in that confluence of shared events; to see how one thing *resembles* another—how this pattern is conventional in its reiteration and representation of events; and, finally, to *recognize* or rethink *the taken-for-granted* in order to discover how this "pattern of resemblances" in the shared events is not what it seems, that is, to interrogate the normativity of the conventions witnessed by the audience.

In a similar way, we use the following description, transcription, and analysis of "The First Time" not as a vehicle to "replay" a past event or "explain" the performance but as part of a "conversation helping us get clear on what happened and what we can do about it." Following Gingrich-Philbrook's suggestion, we call on readers to witness a pattern, see the conventions, and interrogate the normativity of this particular case of performing narrative on stage. The transcription follows the format suggested by Dell Hymes (1996) for patterning performance according to its "poetic structure" on the basis of repetitions, parallel topics and structures, and discourse functions (Peterson & Langellier, 1997). The transcript is patterned into *lines* (which begin at the left margin, numbered sequentially in the right-hand column; a bracket indicates a continued line) and *verses* (which may be composed of more than one line; linked or subsequent lines indicated by indentation), groups of verses that form *stanzas* (grouped according to internal repetition and common focus; indicated by spacing between stanzas and labeled in the right-hand column by an uppercase letter), groups of stanzas that form *scenes* (as suggested by repetition, parallel structure, and common discourse topic; indicated in the right-hand column by a lowercase roman numeral), and sets of scenes as *acts* (organized by discourse function and dramatic structure; indicated in the right-hand column by an uppercase roman numeral).

In "The First Time," Gingrich-Philbrook describes watching a televised public service announcement on HIV/AIDS prevention, his bodily response to it, and his attempt to make sense of that response. As we discuss in the analysis below, the confluence of shared events that he "stands up" and "unpacks" is the pattern of representation that takes heterosexual identities as normal and normative. At the same time, Gingrich-Philbrook uses the repetition of key elements in the performance—the multiple levels of "witnessing" in which the audience witnesses the performer witnessing the television commercial—to destabilize what Diamond (1992) calls the "mimetic pleasure of identification" (p. 390). That is, he uses the parallels between the event of watching a television commercial and the event of watching a performance to question the conventions of identification and representation that inform both of them. During the performance, Gingrich-Philbrook remains seated in an institutional-looking padded chair that is placed at a slight angle to the audience near center stage. He begins the performance with his left leg crossed over his right (left ankle on right knee), his hands resting on his legs, and elbows on the chair arms. The text of the performance is contained in Table 1 (pp. 224–226).

The First Time and Every Time

What is going on in this example of performing narrative on stage? In Chapter 1, we argue that if there is a beginning point to storytelling, then it is to be found in the bodily participation of audience. The mundane experience of audience, as we point out in the section on the embodied context of performing narrative, expresses an important ambiguity: to ask about bodily participation in performing narrative is to interrogate the conduct of an audience that includes actual, potential, and virtual audiences. The solo performance of autobiographical narrative, such as "The First Time," emphasizes the storyteller as audience to her or his experience; Gingrich-Philbrook "takes" from his experience and "makes" of it a "story" for an audience. At the same time, of course, there are other audiences participating in this example of performing narrative. There is an audience before whom Gingrich-Philbrook performs. This audience, sitting in a small performance studies theater in Carbondale, Illinois, in July 1992, can also "take" their experience of the performance and "make" of it a "story." Similarly, as researchers, we audience the performance. We "take" our experience of the performance and "make" of it a "story" for analysis and discussion.

   While there is some truth to this description of bodily participation, it is incomplete and misleading. What we have constructed by posing the problem of audience in this way is a linear progression of events. Let us make this chronology explicit. This limited description suggests that first one thing happens and then another and then another: first Gingrich-Philbrook audiences the commercial and breathes fire, then he makes his experience into a story that he rehearses, then he performs it for an audience, then researchers take

TABLE I   "The First Time" by Craig Gingrich-Philbrook

	Act	Scene	Stanza	Line
the first time that it happened I was watching television and this commercial came on	[frame]		(A)	
and in the commercial there was a row of women dressed in bright, red, blood, red velvet dresses that went from their throats down to their ankles	[I]	[i]	(B)	5
and then facing them was a row of men in tuxedos and then another row of women in their matching dresses and then a row of tuxedos and then a women in dresses row and then a row of tuxedos			(C)	10
and they were all dancing to this beautiful music they were waltzing			(D)	
and the whole thing was shot from above 　　　sort of off at an angle so they looked sort of like all of the Nazis moving in unison in 　　　　　　　　[those documentary films 　　　like The Triumph of the Will or those pictures of all of the mass marriages that the Reverend 　　　　　　　　[Sun Myung Moon had			(E) .	15
the women would turn in slow motion and the dresses would sort of fill and billow 　　　like the dresses that my sister liked when she was a kid they would just bloom 　　　all at the same time 　　　all in the same way		[ii]	(A)	20 25
and then the men next to them would sort of raise their arms 　　　to spin them 　　　all the same way "hi, I'm a man, I can spin a woman" over and over again			(B)	30
and then they started to change partners they would move in the opposite direction			(C)	
and then they would spin and bloom and then they would change partners and then they would spin and bloom			(reprise)	35
and I was trying to figure out what this could be a commercial for it didn't look like stain remover and I couldn't see any ice, so it wasn't the Ice Capades		[iii]	(A)	

TABLE I (Continued)

	Act	Scene	Stanza	Line
and then the announcer came on and said something like			(B)	
"a lot of people are changing partners now				40
and we need to be careful				
it's okay to change partners				
but you have to play by the rules"				
I never thought that I would go from thinking that something				
[was beautiful			(C)	
to being made so incredibly angry so quickly				45
it's true that men and women dancing together get AIDS				
it's true				
but I knew the organization that funded this commercial			(D)	
that probably got a lot of its money from gay men and				
[lesbians attending benefits				
would never make such a beautiful image of my people				50
they would never relate us—our promiscuity—				
to something so elegant as people changing partners in a waltz				
wearing beautiful expensive dresses				
shot in a artsy-fartsy-kind-of-camera-angle that must of cost a				
[lot of money				
no, not that any of that money would ever be spent making us look				
[beautiful and traditional				55
and then it started to happen	[II]	[i]	(A)	
in my feet				
they got really cold				
and my lower legs started to kind of cramp				
and the cramp moved up into my thighs and into my pelvis				60
and I had that sensation of imminence			(B)	
sort of like the onset of orgasm when one thinks				
maybe this isn't the best time for this				
maybe I can't live through this				
maybe I don't want this right now				65
but I can't stop it				
and then it shot up my spine		[ii]	(A)	
and I felt like I was having a stroke because my head was				
[drawn tightly to one side				
and my lower jaw drawn down				
and then it happened				70
the fire shot out of my mouth				
about a yard				
a big, red, blooming, column of fire				
and I could just sit there			(B)	
and I couldn't stop it				75
I knew I couldn't stop it				

(continued on next page)

TABLE I (Continued)

	Act	Scene	Stanza	Line
and I kept wondering what it was eating up		[iii]	(A)	
what it was burning				
something I might need later				
like my heart				80
but then, just like after a long car trip			(B)	
when you're emptying your bladder				
I sort of felt this sensation of diminishing				
and it stopped				
and whereas before there was a sound almost like			(reprise)	85
a hundred people shaking out sheets				
over and over again				
a big rumbling				
there was suddenly just silence				
and I could hear the birds outside				90
and I thought well that was rich	[III]	[i]	(A)	
I wonder if it's gonna happen again				
it wouldn't be very good if it happened in bed				
but it would be okay if I was shaking the hand of the President				
and I thought that maybe this was a hereditary thing			(B)	95
and that I should try to seek treatment for my outrage				
so I called up my mother				
and I said "Mom, listen, this is gonna sound kind of strange but			(C)	
has anyone in our family ever breathed fire?"				
She thought for a moment and then said				100
"well, no, honey				
no one's ever breathed fire				
but your Uncle Bobby used to shoot ice cubes out of his ass"				
and I said "no, no, Mom				
I'm not talking about that				105
everybody knew he was gonna do that				
he'd get this weird look on his face and disappear into				
[the kitchen"				
I'm talking about anger	[coda]			
I'm talking about a birthright				
I'm talking about something beautiful				110
something that has changed the way I will live what is				
[left of my life				

their experience of performance (based on repeated viewing of a videotape of the performance) and make it into a transcript, then readers of this chapter take this transcript in an effort to make sense of it, and so on. This description is incomplete because it collapses the ambiguity of the different ways the experience of performing narrative comes into consciousness. The "first time" of breathing fire, let us say, may give rise to another "first time" of performance, which in turn gives rise to the "first time" analysis. But we collapse the ambiguity of multiple first times when we take our consciousness of this recursive experience—even though they are different, they are all about the same thing—and straighten it out into a linear progression of "first one thing then another first." Furthermore, this description is misleading because it obscures the participation of the audience by taking the audience out of the situation, thereby making the experience neutral or objective where what happened is what "anyone" might experience. This description also is misleading because it takes one experience as universal for all forms of consciousness— that is, that "everyone" has the same experience. This description reduces consciousness of bodily experience by making it a possession of "anyone" and "everyone."

Our methodological digression emphasizes the importance of beginning with audience. As Lanigan (1994) states, "since the phenomenologist is looking at the *logic* inherent in the *phenomenon*, s/he uses a *method* that starts [in the order of experience] with her/himself as the (1) experiencer who (2) experiences the (3) event or thing experienced" (p. 112, emphasis in original). In this case, we begin with the order of experience, that is, with our experience as audience to a performance event as the basis for describing what happened in "The First Time." In order to analyze and describe this event of performing narrative on stage, we reverse this 1-2-3 logic and move from the event experienced (3) to how the experience was taken and not given (2) to us as audience (1). Methodologically, experience functions as a rule for making a judgment, not as a guarantee of objectivity or authenticity. The accuracy or value of experience is found in the reversible move from the order of experience to the order of analysis. This method, Lanigan argues, is the process by which we move from experience "to discover a particular phenomenon in consciousness [. . .] and then back as a judgment using the very discovered logic of the phenomenon in which the researcher's *consciousness* of the phenomenon" becomes the basis for understanding the experience (p. 112). To begin with audience, in the case of "The First Time," means beginning not with the event itself or the performance itself or the transcript itself but with a bodily memory of the event, with an experience of the performance, with a reading of the transcript and analysis. The movement from experience to consciousness and back—of participating in the performance, of reading the transcript and analysis—becomes the basis for the interpretation of "The First Time."

Our methodological digression also emphasizes that the ambiguity of conscious experience is not a problem to be resolved by collapsing experience into a linear progression of events (with a beginning, middle, and end), but constitutes a resource for understanding them. Merleau-Ponty (1964b) writes that "our present expressive operations, instead of driving the preceding ones away—simply succeeding and annulling them—salvage, preserve, and (insofar as they contain some truth) take them up again; and the same phenomenon is produced in respect to others' expressive operations, whether they be past or contemporary" (p. 95). In the recursive operations of performing narrative, a storyteller takes up her or his experience of events, salvaging, preserving, and working them over. Even when narratives of personal experience appear in supposedly spontaneous conversation, Atkinson and Silverman (1997) remark, they are "rehearsed and reproduced" in that they are "couched in an idiom that reflects prior narration" (p. 314). Storytelling cites and recites experience, performing narrative on stage iterates and reiterates that experience. Reading a transcript and analysis is not the end in a line of "first" experiences, but an occasion to take them up and experience the production of what is reproduced the first time and every time.

When we ask about what is going on in this example of performing narrative on stage, we have already taken up "The First Time" as another instance —and not the first—of storytelling, of performance. From the opening line, "the first time that it happened," we are engaged in shifting our embodied awareness to focus on an emerging performance and forming an horizon of silence and attention out of which Gingrich-Philbrook speaks. The "first time that it happened" also functions to orient the audience to a narrative, to focus on this particular telling of something that happened in the past. The opening line also functions within the narrative as the first part of the story, as the focal point or initial action upon which the story will build. This shifting focus, much like the operation of a gradual close-up in film, creates the illusion of one locus of action. But when one walks around a tree, the other side of the tree does not cease to exist just because it recedes in the field of vision; so too, these multiple and shifting foci do not disappear as the discourse moves along.

The simultaneity of these multiple and shifting foci is perhaps most evident in the final stanza (lines 108–111). The final stanza suggests the culmination of events within the story. In this case, the comment that begins with "I'm talking about anger" is a part of one character's dialogue, an extended answer to a previous comment made by another character, his mother. The final stanza also functions as a coda (following Labov & Waletsky, 1967) in that it serves as a perspective on what the narrator has been talking about in the entire performance and thus returns the narrative to the present act of narrating. Additionally, the stanza functions as an address to the audience. When Gingrich-Philbrook uncrosses his legs and leans forward to look directly at the audience to speak these last lines, he addresses the audience—whether for understanding, appreciation, action, or applause. To take the example of film once again, the final lines can be seen as reversing the close-up that began the performance: the shifting focus creates the illusion of one locus of action that gradually enlarges from the world of the story to the act of narrating and then to the performance situation.

Typically, the conclusion of a performance or of a personal narrative is seen as the denouement or resolution of the action, of "what finally happened." In this instance, however, the final verses raise more questions and appear to resolve very little: What happened? Did fire shoot out of his mouth? Did it happen more than once? Did it happen at all? What is the "something" he is talking about? Are the four things he talks about in the final stanza (anger, a birthright, something beautiful, something that has changed the way I will live what is left of my life) the same or different things? One way to answer these questions would be to interpret the final stanza as a weak story ending or a poor performance. However, given the careful narrative plotting and skillful handling of the performance, this interpretation is not very satisfying. Another possible interpretation, that the story is merely an anecdote, is rejected by Gingrich-Philbrook within the story when he refuses the potential resolution that his mother offers in her example of Uncle Bobby—breathing fire is not a humorous idiosyncracy or personal quirk. In order to "get clear on what happened," we take the final stanza not merely as a last segment in a series of events, but as crystalizing four key themes which compose a focusing system "out of which we are invited to build an overall interpretation of the narrative" (Gee, 1991, p. 33). Rather than recount the linear locus of action, let us explore how the focusing system operates throughout the performance.

The first theme, "I'm talking about anger," is foreshadowed in the comparison of the dancers to Nazis moving in unison and to mass marriages (lines 17–20) and stated directly in line 55 ("being made so incredibly angry"). In addition, anger is suggested by vocal intensity, intonation and rate of speech during the final two stanzas of Act I. The physical manifestation of that anger as breathing fire is detailed in Act II but, unlike the anger expressed in the previous two stanzas, the emotional tone of these lines suggests surprise or concern and perhaps fear. In Act III, anger surfaces again in the form of humor ("but it would be okay if I was shaking the hand of the President") and in the reference to "seeking treatment for my outrage." The theme of anger is initially posed as a response to the theme of "something beautiful" in lines 44–45 where the performer states "I never thought that I would go from thinking something was beautiful / to being made so incredibly angry so quickly." This verse functions as an emotional pivot for the performance, as is indicated both by the thematic opposition it expresses and by the three-second pause— the longest in the performance—that precedes it.

The theme of "something beautiful" is evoked by the descriptions of the dance in Act I as well as the explicit comments about "this beautiful music" (line 13), "something was beautiful" (line 44), "a beautiful image" (line 50), and "making us look beautiful" (line 55). The thematic opposition between beauty and anger is also suggested by a gestural inversion that links Act II as a reaction to Act I. In the first stanza of Act I, the performer marks his description of the dresses the women wear with an iconic gesture: he brings both hands to his throat and sweeps the left hand down to his ankle suggesting the shape of the dress. This movement employs a character-based perspective that locates the dress on the performer's body rather than in front of him in an imaginary space such as might be created by an observer or narrator. An inversion of this throat-to-ankle movement occurs in Act II when the performer points to the growing sensation of cold and cramping that moves up his body and results in fire shooting out of his mouth. In this act, the performer's hands sweep up his body toward his hips (lines 57–60), and then he rotates his head to the extreme right (lines 68–70). These two images also are linked in language through the use of the words *red* and *bloom*. The description of "bright, red, blood, red velvet dresses" initiates the first sweeping gesture (they "bloom" shortly thereafter in line 23). The second sweeping gesture culminates in the description of "a big, red, blooming column of fire" (line 73).

The bodily performance of this inversion suggests a type of regurgitation which purifies, a kind of abjection (Kristeva, 1982). That is, taking in or consuming the beauty of the commercial results in the production of anger which is expelled in the violence of breathing fire. Julia Kristeva describes the child's experience of gagging and nausea at being offered milk by parents:

> "I" want none of that element, sign of their desire; "I" do not want to listen, "I" do not assimilate it, "I" expel it. But since the food is not an "other" for "me," who am only in their desire, I expel myself, I spit myself out, I abject myself within the same motion through which "I" claim to establish myself. (p. 3)

The performer wants none of the commercial, the sign of social desire: his body expels it. Yet he questions the cost of that expulsion when he wonders "what it was eating up / what it was burning / something I might need later / like my heart" (lines 77–80). As Kristeva remarks, the subject experiences abjection when it "finds the impossible within; when it finds that the impossible constitutes its very *being*" (p. 5). The performer finds that he has "taken in" the impossible—the heterosexual promiscuity of the commercial—and that he has participated and taken pleasure in its construction. He *identifies* with the dancers and the dance, he *performs* them. In this way, the question of identification in abjection raises the third theme of "a birthright."

The theme of "a birthright" can be located in the concern that breathing fire "was a hereditary thing" (line 95) and is indirectly referenced through the comment about "my sister" (line 22) and the use of pronouns to distinguish "my people" (line 50), "us—our promiscuity" (line 51) and "making us look beautiful and traditional" (line 55). But it is the detailed focus on the performer's body (feet, legs, thighs, pelvis, spine, head, jaw, mouth, heart, bladder) and bodily processes (orgasm, urinating, cramping, hearing, watching) that grounds this theme. This focus on the body in speech has its parallel in the performer's deictic use of his body as a form of visual display in taking on a character perspective. In each of the three stanzas and reprise of Act I, Scene ii (lines 20–35), Gingrich-Philbrook shows the action of blooming and spinning by pointing to and locating them on his body. To suggest how the women's dresses billow or "bloom" when they turn, he extends his hands below his knees and then opens his arms outward as he raises them to about knee level (lines 21 and 23). To suggest how the men in the dance "spin" their partners (lines 26–29), he raises his right hand from just above his knee to the extreme upper right area out from the side of his head and then repeats the motion on each line.

In these "spin and bloom" moves of the dance, the performer takes on a character-based perspective that locates the action on his body rather than in an imaginary space in front of him as would be the case with an observer or narrator-based perspective. He embodies a woman wearing a dress and then he embodies a man spinning a woman. This embodied identification is the basis for the ironic comment of line 29: "hi, I'm a man, I can spin a woman." In this line the performer repeats the arm swing established in the previous lines (within the narrative) but shifts vocally to comment on the absurdity of this action as a basis for establishing sexual identity (the narrator's perspective on the story). The distance between identification and critical commentary results in shared humor (audience laughter) and increased identification between the performer and the audience.

The shared humor is extended shortly afterward in line 37 when, in trying to figure out the point of the commercial, Gingrich-Philbrook comments that "it didn't look like stain remover." The laughter occasioned by both this line and line 29 helps dispel any foreboding from the earlier references to Nazi marches and mass marriages. So when the commercial announcer speaks in the next stanza, the audience is in much the same situation that Gingrich-Philbrook describes as his initial experience. That is, the use of humor initially positions the commercial as "light entertainment" for the (mostly) unsuspecting audience. It thus replicates the narrative situation of watching the commercial by reinscribing it within the performance setting where the audience will be surprised by both the commercial and the performer's response to the commercial. The commercial makes explicit that one form of birthright is sexual identity and thereby suggests that the first line of the performance ("the first time it happened") be understood as a reference to the initiation of sexual activity (and echoed in line 62: "sort of like the onset of orgasm").

Of course, the more obvious meaning for the commercial is stated by the performer in line 46: "it's true that men and women dancing together get AIDS." This meaning locates the final focusing theme of the performance, "something that has changed the way I will live what is left of my life" (line 111). The commercial, then, falls in the category of public service announcements, although clearly the public it serves—suggested by the heterosexual pairing of dancers—is that of the straight community. The commercial is not unusual or atypical for the time period of the performance (1992) in which, after years of silence and inactivity, the U.S. government finally acknowledged HIV/AIDS as a significant health issue that required public intervention. Even then, however, the emphasis is on heterosexual interests and how HIV/AIDS affects sexual activity among heterosexuals. Despite the supposed inclusiveness of the pronoun, the authoritative "we" used by the commercial announcer in "we need to be careful" (line 41) excludes gay men and lesbians. The performer reacts to this and the prescriptive "you have to play by the rules" (line 43) by distinguishing himself ("my people" and "us"). Again, these lines serve multiple functions: they function within the story as part of the narrative, and they are a commentary on the narrative which functions to distinguish the sexual identity of the performer and challenge the supposed homogeneity of the public "we" used within the narrative of the commercial. At the same time, the use of "my people" also serves to separate the performer from the audience and to challenge the nature of their relationship—is the audience part of the homogeneous "we" used by the commercial announcer or part of the "my people" and "us" used by the narrator? It is this latter function that best illustrates the performative construction of identity in storytelling.

Moving in Unison: Conventional Performance, Performing Conventions

In the first act of the performance, Gingrich-Philbrook displays the sexual identity of the dancers. He *displays* them in the sense of metaphorically putting on their clothes, exhibiting their gestures, and speaking their language, in order to *play* out the conventionalism of normative heterosexuality, in the sense of criticizing or poking fun at those conventions. This play with display (a type of critical cross-dressing, so to speak) relies on the reflexivity of the body in performance to function at multiple levels. As Richard Bauman (1992) remarks, "the display mode of performance constitutes the performing self [. . .] as an object for itself as well as for others" (p. 48). David Halperin (1995) argues that one "discursive counterpractice" for disrupting heterosexist discourse is appropriation and theatricalization. In this case, the play of display makes the operation of normative heterosexuality into an "object" of performance available to both performer and audience for examination and criticism.

At the same time, however, Act II of the performance suggests that this appropriation and theatricalization, the play with display, is not without consequence. Portraying the heterosexual promiscuity metaphorically represented in the dance—even for critical purposes—leaves little space for "our promiscuity" (line 51) and no way to make "us look beautiful and traditional" (line 55). One possible response to the ubiquity of heterosexual promiscuity would be increased representations of gay and lesbian promiscuity. Rather than take up this possibility by presenting a competing narrative that might displace existing conventions of sexual identity, Act II turns instead to focus on the violence that existing conventions inscribe on the bodies of lesbians and gay men. While Act II documents and performs the effects of this violence, the fantastic form that this effect takes (breathing fire) has the function of refocusing attention on the act of representation itself—what Bauman (1992) calls the "formal reflexivity" of signification about signification. The performer's account of breathing fire raises questions about the nature of its representation, about its believability—what William Labov (1997) defines as the credibility of the narrative. Unlike the examples that Labov cites (jokes, tall tales, dreams), however, the experience of breathing fire is reported seriously. In fact, from the perspective of Labov's approach to narrative, the emphasis on bodily sensations and processes is a tactic for increasing the "objectivity" of the observations. The performer constructs the story of breathing fire as an internal sensation that becomes external; observations of sense experience in Act II replace observations of emotional reaction in the conclusion of Act I. By increasing the objectivity of how he narrates, the performer increases the credibility of his experience (see Labov, 1997, p. 412).

The juxtaposition of Act I and Act II brings out the parallels between the representation of the commercial and the representation of breathing fire. The audience can accept the performer's claim that "it's true that men and women dancing together get AIDS" (line 46) because it is located within the narrative construction of dancing as a metaphor for heterosexual promiscuity. The claim that the performer breathed fire is similarly true for the audience because it is located within the narrative construction that represents a past event. That is, Gingrich-Philbrook does not witness actual sexual activity when watching the television commercial, nor does the audience witness actual fire coming out of the performer's mouth during the performance. The parallels between these two acts of representation are further strengthened by the way the comment about the benefits that "funded this commercial" (line 48) implicates the SIREA benefit in which the performance takes place. The implied challenge of this juxtaposition is not to the truth status of the narrative reports but to the participation and identity of the audience and performer. In other words, is the audience attending Gingrich-Philbrook's benefit performance positioned in the same way as the gay men and lesbians whose attendance at benefits led to the creation of the commercial? Does the audi-

ence participate and identify with the performer in the same way that Gingrich-Philbrook participates and identifies with the commercial?

Act III addresses the tension created both by the representation of breathing fire and by the juxtaposition of the two forms of representation. The audience laughter at the end of each of the three verses that open Act III can be
understood as a response to this tension. In a similar way, the mother's response can be seen as an attempt to resolve the tension by reinterpreting the
fantastic (breathing fire) as the ridiculous (shooting ice cubes). The audience
again responds with laughter at the end of each of the three verses that form
the third stanza. The performer, however, refuses to collapse the narrative juxtaposition between Acts I and II into an opposition of beauty and anger,
heterosexuality and homosexuality, normal and abnormal. Rather than provide a clear "what happened next" in response to his mother's comment, the
performer maintains the ambiguity of multiple levels of representation and refuses to resolve them. The final four lines of Act III offer a parallel opportunity for the performer to conclude the performance the way that the announcer does in the commercial—to tell the audience what the performance
means and how they should respond. But to conclude the performance in such
fashion would be to adopt both the disciplinary conventions of heterosexuality and the very form of representation that is being criticized.

The coda leaves open the question of "what happened then" both within the
narrative and within the narrator's perspective on the narrative. It is in the relationship of performer and audience that the performance returns to "the
time of the telling." In a sense, the performer refuses the commercial's injunction to "play by the rules." The coda does not return to the bipolar definitions of heterosexual identity offered in the commercial as a model for all
sexual relations. Nor does the coda play by the representational rules that
would reduce the complexity and ambiguity of lived experience by opposing
one form of representation (of the commercial) with another, somehow more
authentic, form of representation (of anger or breathing fire). Instead, the ambiguity of the coda challenges audience members by denying them an explanation or "easy answer" and acts more like a nagging puzzle, a loose tooth to
worry at and fuss over.[3]

Benjamin argues that "half the art of storytelling is to keep a story free from
explanation as one reproduces it" (p. 89). The ambiguity of the performance
prevents the easy pleasure of identification either with the narrator of the
story or with the performer of "The First Time." If they identify with the narrator, then the audience risks being duped like the gay men and women attending benefits that funded the commercial. If they identify with the performer, then they risk being duped by or dismissing a fantastic event. Instead,
the coda offers an opportunity for the audience to reconsider their participation both in the cultural conventions of the commercial and in the representational relationships of performance, an opportunity to interrogate rather

than assimilate the identities produced in the context of their emotional response, their laughter, their applause.

"The First Time" illustrates how the bodily reflexivity of the performer can be used to "unpack" the reiteration and reproduction of the conventions of normative heterosexuality. What Gingrich-Philbrook learns from watching the television commercial is that his pre-reflective experience is no guarantee of value. His easy enjoyment of a television commercial teaches him to interrogate his experience of breathing fire. Otherwise, how is he to know the difference between the "good" experience of breathing fire from the "bad" experience of institutionalized heterosexism? Even more importantly, how is his breathing fire different from the homophobia that spews forth from the bigot who complains about "all that gay sexuality stuff being shoved down my throat"? How can he distinguish conventions that open up rather than close down possibilities for identity?

What the audience learns in performance, in turn, is the potential for the reiteration of representational conventions to reinscribe rather than disrupt the often imperialistic relations by which performers and audiences appropriate their own experience and the experiences of others in the act of identification. Gingrich-Philbrook does not perform his story only to move his audience to understand his outrage. If that were the case, then why would he include, at the end of the narrative in Act III, the deliberation about whether his experience of breathing fire is going to happen again? Rather, he works carefully to avoid the easy answers of either a "sublime" and justifiable outrage or a "ridiculous" and personal idiosyncracy. Gingrich-Philbrook prepares for, but cannot guarantee, audience response—he suggests and then refuses several possible explanations in order to maintain the ambiguity of lived experience. He takes on a more difficult task than talking about his experience; he interrogates his and the audience's participation in the heterosexualizing practices of representation and cultural reproduction. For the audience to participate in the autobiographical performance as Gingrich-Philbrook initially participates in the commercial is to continue rather than to question the conventions that constitute and normalize identity and difference.

In this performance, Gingrich-Philbrook engages Jill Dolan's (1993) challenge for theater to explore the "various identity configurations of production and reception" and "to teach spectators to be moved by difference, to encourage them to experience emotion not as acquiescent, but as passionate, and motivating toward social change" (p. 436). The performance provides the opportunity to explore the identity configurations in the performer's relation to experience and to the audience. Performing narrative on stage has the potential to teach about difference and motivate toward social change, but its lessons are not true or self-evident merely because they have been lived through together with performer and audience. Performance functions as a joint activity of bodies, a conventional performance that makes visible performing conventions, and not merely a means for transferring experience between performer and audience. Performance has the potential to open up possibilities for learning about difference and the operations of identity rather than didactically to prescribe or reinscribe particular identity configurations.

At the same time that we emphasize performing narrative as strategic, interested, and not neutral for performers and audiences—that is, the potential of performance to trouble as well as reinscribe conventions which reproduce existing power relations—we also emphasize it as strategic, interested, and not neutral for researchers and readers of research. Paul Atkinson and David Silverman (1997) find fault in this latter area occasioned by what they describe as the "Romantic impulse" in research on personal narrative. Atkinson and Silverman argue that even when researchers recognize that experience is always already narrated, "they can still contrive to represent narratives of personal experience as warranting more authentic data or insight than other forms of account and representation" (p. 316). In describing and analyzing autobiographical performance, such as we do in this chapter and this book, researchers risk romanticizing performance as more authentic or valuable because it is based on personal experience. This tendency to "romanticize the immediacy and presence of performance," as Pollock (1998b, p. 40) describes it, privileges performance by positioning it as innocent of the analysis and critique that researchers bring to it, as spontaneous and unadulterated by the theoretical and methodological interests that inform researchers and readers.

We would modify Atkinson and Silverman's argument. Although both the current version of romanticism and the earlier artistic movement that began in the late eighteenth century can be described as forms of antimodernism, the current or new romanticism is better described as a type of antimodernism posing as postmodernism. Where the old romanticism turned away from an increasingly urbanized and industrialized society toward an idealized nature, the new romanticism turns away from an increasingly fragmented and technologized subject toward a naturalized ideal of experience. In storytelling, the new romanticism is evident in the tendency to view experience as privileged content, as authentic "because-I-lived-it." Such ordering of content privileges subjects as heroes of their own discourse. As Joan Scott (1993) summarizes in her critique of how the evidence of experience is used in narratives of difference: "They take as self-evident the identities of those whose experience is being documented and thus naturalize their difference. They locate resistance outside its discursive construction and reify agency as an inherent attribute of individuals, thus decontextualizing it" (p. 399). In "The First Time," Gingrich-Philbrook uses the conventions employed in narratives of difference to question rather than to naturalize the identities they construct. By performing these conventions, he makes them discussable.

In staging narratives of difference before an audience, such as the encounter with heterosexism in "The First Time," it is difficult to avoid romanticizing experience and putting into play what Bérubé (1997) calls the rhetoric of hard-ship. Bérubé describes this rhetorical move as a storytelling strategy that tries to mitigate difference and oppression by appealing to the sympathy and under-standing of the audience, of those "more fortunate" than the speaker (p. 62). This move positions the narrator/performer as a victim/hero in a struggle against the impossible odds of oppression. In performance, this appeal to the audience is made explicit because the audience is a collective body engaged by the storyteller—construction of the narrator's identity in an experience of oppression is articulated with the construction of the performer's identity as a subject who now has control of (that is, can perform) that experience. This storytelling strategy constructs the audience as those who are able to share in the experience with the performer (responding with laughter, sorrow, anger, amusement, and so on) and who, by virtue of their shared action with the per-former, are able to distance themselves from the action of oppression and their participation in those social structures.

The new romanticism employs the task-ordering enacted by such strategic appeals to construct the audience as privileged witnesses, as ones with greater sympathy and understanding than those in the narrated experience (or the rest of an oppressive society), as ones who see what is really going on, as authen-tic "because-I-witness-the-person-who-performs-it." In this instance, it is the vision of the audience, to paraphrase Scott, that "becomes the bedrock of evi-dence on which explanation is built" (p. 399). Performance is naturalized in that the conventions by which experience is reproduced—the task-ordering of stage performance—are taken for granted. Performance and cultural repro-duction are seen as "unconstrained" and "honest" accounts of something that "really" happened to the person in front of the audience. In "The First Time," Gingrich-Philbrook resists this naturalization of experience by making ex-plicit the parallels between watching the commercial and watching his per-formance. He troubles the performance conventions that would naturalize the participation of audience and performer.

In research and analysis, the new romanticism naturalizes experience as an enduring and stable order, as authentic "because-I-recorded/transcribed/analyzed-it." The methods of research and analysis make experience visible for readers; they make experience "eminently reproducible," as Atkinson and Silverman (1997, p. 313) remark. The problem here is not the traditional con-cern over narrative authority in research (a question of content-ordering), nor is it the more contemporary concern over what Alcoff (1991–92) calls the problem of speaking for others (a question of task-ordering); rather, the prob-lem at this level is that the new romanticism takes the biographical conven-tions and cultural resources of the "interview society" as natural, given, and universal (a question of group-ordering). The background practices of talking about experience are reproduced and reinscribed in research and analysis. As Gingrich-Philbrook (2000b) comments, when as researchers and critics "we uncritically presume the possible commensurability of our account with the 'actual' context, we proceed unaware of our role as would-be omniscient narrators of cultural practices" (p. 378). The cultural conventions that make experience visible within society, the would-be omniscience under the new romanticism that Gingrich-Philbrook describes, are taken up by researchers when they uncritically transcribe and analyze the experience of performance. Just as a naturalized and conventional performance is no guarantee of the truth of the experience it performs, so too the commensurability efforts of researchers and critics cannot be guaranteed by adopting the habitual practices—however normative and naturalized—of the society in which the research takes place. Let us trouble the analysis of performing narrative on stage by examining the habitual practices by which research makes experience visible and discussable.

Breathing Fire: The Strategic Production of Identity

In performing narrative, a storyteller takes up her or his experience of events to salvage, preserve, and work over that experience. In the same way, when we analyze staged performances we take up these experiences, as Merleau-Ponty would say, rather than simply succeeding or annulling them. Analysis does not establish a replica of the performance event in an enduring and stable order, as the new romanticism would have it; rather, analysis provisionally and historically participates in performing narrative by taking up the experience of performance. "It is not individuals who have experience," Scott (1993) argues, "but subjects who are constituted through experience. Experience in this definition then becomes not the origin of our explanation, not the authoritative (because seen or felt) evidence that grounds what is known, but rather that which we seek to explain, that about which knowledge is produced" (p. 401). Performing narrative involves a struggle for agency rather than the expressive act of a pre-existing, autonomous, stable self that serves as the origin for or authority on experience. Researchers who study performance are not the omniscient source or origin of knowledge but participants in a struggle to articulate and situate storytelling within the material conditions of institutions and the forces of discourse that constitute subject positions and order context. Researchers constitute themselves as subjects in the inquiry into the experience of performing narrative.

Part of the struggle to articulate and situate the habitual practices of research on storytelling comes in the difficulty of disrupting the comforts of the familiar. How can we research performing narrative on stage while simultaneously calling into question the comforts of "the interview society," its resources and conventions? Darlene Hantzis (1998) suggests that "we begin by acknowledging the ease of muting critique in the telling of 'my' story and resist that ease even as it marks the story as unstable and open to interrogation" (p. 205). The ease of muting critique is not a concern limited to storytellers or audiences per se (as is suggested by the respective privileging of those positions adopted by the new romanticism) but shared by researchers in the conduct of inquiry. Even as researchers mobilize the background practices and analytic conventions of the interview society to establish "an interpretation," which—as one of many possible interpretations—is unstable and open to interrogation, they simultaneously utilize those same practices and conventions to support that interpretation and guard against "aberrant decodings" (Eco, 1990). What Hantzis challenges researchers to acknowledge are the practices and conventions, the comforts of research, that are mobilized in conducting "my" or "our" inquiry.

Those most at ease and comfortable in an interview society are those whose stories are already recognizable as stories that are good, satisfying, and pleasing and those whose agency as storytellers and audiences has already been established as meaningful and significant. Similarly, those researchers most at ease and comfortable in an interview society are those who study good stories by good storytellers and whose research practices perform, enact, and reiterate the conventions of "good research" in the historical circumstances in which they are situated. The extent to which any particular research project is comfortable and satisfying depends upon how it constitutes both itself and what good research is. For example, Mishler (1999) identifies the research expectation for coherent stories (with recognizable beginnings, middles, and ends) as a shaping feature of the sense-making that takes place in interview-based storytelling (p. 15). Research is performative, and as a performative, Butler (1993) reminds us, "*it draws on and covers over* the constitutive conventions by which it is mobilized" (p. 227, emphasis in original). Research is always already strategic in that it maintains and reinscribes the constitutive conventions it mobilizes.

In earlier chapters, we touched on the performative nature of research when we discussed how as researchers studying family storytelling we participate in performing family even as we question that participation. We cannot stand outside the family, or even a family, in order to study it. This "law of participation," as Lanigan (1992) describes it, is what makes research possible and what limits it. Our participation, while more or less evident in the conduct of inquiry, is nonetheless formative. For, as Merleau-Ponty (1964b) emphasizes, "it is in the actual practice of speaking that I learn to understand" (p. 97). This turn to explicate the performative nature of research is a methodological consequence of the process by which we understand performing narrative on stage as researchers. Let us emphasize, as we do in the beginning of this chapter, that the use of experience as a rule of judgment does not guarantee objectivity or authenticity. The effort to analyze performing narrative on stage, to move from the order of experience to the order of analysis, requires that we maintain the ambiguity of conscious experience. It is not an invitation for us as researchers to take center stage and become the focus of research as subjects. Such a move replicates but does not explicate the logic inherent in the phenomenon; it repeats but does not interrogate conscious experience. We are interested in explicating how the logic of performing narrative makes possible "good research" as well as "good stories" and "good storytelling."

In this chapter we have focused on how queer solo performance renders the construction of identity and community in performing narrative thematic and problematic. "The First Time" draws upon the ambiguities of conscious experience to intervene in a specific historical context—what Butler (1993) has described as "the killing inattention of public policy-makers on the issue of AIDS" (p. 233). In a similar way, this research project draws upon the conscious experience of performing narrative to intervene in a specific context—not an inattention to narrative by researchers but the very normativity and conventionality of narrative research itself. We take our cue here from Roof's (1996) critique of how narrative theory and research recuperates lesbian and gay sexualities within normative practices or what she calls the "heteronarrative." Roof argues that the turn to theatricalization and performativity may not disrupt normative practices because such a turn depends "upon another, more secure (if not unified) identity or ego elsewhere that perceives and critiques the fiction of unity in the first place" (p. 182). Research participates in this heteronarrative to the extent that it takes as its goal to make visible the "real story," the revelation of what "really happened," that reimposes the retrospective teleology of narrative resolution and closure.

In the performance of "The First Time," Gingrich-Philbrook disrupts the narrative frame that would exclude lesbian and gay identities in the first place; that is, he makes visible the oppressive experience of normative heterosexualities represented by the dance and narratively explained by the announcer of the commercial. Furthermore, he disrupts the effort to recuperate them as "alternative" identities within the same narrative structure; that is, he questions the conventions by which performance makes narrative visible. He resists the narrative possibility for performance to explain itself and the experience of breathing fire—a possibility he refuses by maintaining the ambiguous response of "what I'm talking about." It would be unfortunate, then, if research should move to accomplish the very narrative closure that the performance resists, if research should attempt to provide the explanation or answer that the performance refuses. Instead, as suggested by Román's description of queer autobiographical performance used to open this chapter, research should trouble the comfort of the research community even as it invests in it.

By way of conclusion, let us suggest two specific "comforts" of the research community that would benefit from the kind of troubling suggested by Roof's (1996) analysis: "1) a belief in the social and ideological efficacy of narrative as a transformative agency; and 2) faith in the social and ideological agency of identification" (p. 148). Researching narratives that go against or fall outside normative boundaries of what constitutes a "good story" or "good story-telling" is no guarantee of social and ideological agency. While locating previously excluded narratives may contribute to change, such research is open to recuperation as a minor tactic to the extent that the "new" narratives are simply reinserted as variations in group-ordering without altering the existing task-ordering of narrative research. The very visibility of such variations can be deployed to resist change in the task- or content-ordering of research: why is change needed if existing practices already make queer autobiographical performance visible? Our analysis and discussion of "The First Time" within various research communities is open to similar recuperation. The risk of providing a transcription and analysis is that such efforts reinscribe conventional research practices: collect and transcribe "new" or "unusual" narratives, analyze them, show how they transform existing social practices and theories of narrative. This form of reduction limits the transformational efficacy of narrative to tactical changes in group-ordering—whether that of the research community or of social and cultural communities—and leaves undisturbed the larger strategies that order research according to particular kinds of contents and tasks.

Furthermore, narrative research may reduce the processes of identification to the discovery of sameness rather than a "management of differences" (Roof, 1996, p. 160). The reduction of identification to a discovery of sameness comforts researchers by assuring their place and that of the "different" and "strange" within the research corpus. The danger here is for research to emphasize understanding in the very narrow sense of visibility, of showing what "others" are "really like" so that "we" will know "them"—what Ann duCille (1994) calls the "I once was blind but now I see" narrative. Roof argues that lesbian and gay experience is susceptible to such narrative assimilation because assimilation requires lesbian and gay invisibility as the retrospectively constructed initial condition out of which visibility will be discovered as the correct knowledge of narrative closure. As Scott (1993) concludes, "making visible the experience of a different group exposes the existence of repressive mechanisms, but not their inner workings or logics" (p. 401). Thus, identification may be organized around maintaining the repressive mechanisms that make difference visible rather than challenging the logic of visibility and its operation in performing narrative (Reinelt, 1994).

Let us emphasize that visibility is not unimportant but that it functions strategically. The social and ideological efficacy of narrative cannot be guaranteed by what story is told, how storytelling tasks are distributed, or by the identities it constitutes. In "The First Time," the focus on the "killing inattention" of public discourse on AIDS is used not for visibility (i.e., to replace the heterosexual dancers with lesbian and gay couples) but for critique. It is not enough just to perform the experience of breathing fire, to theatricalize political rage in Butler's terms (1993, p. 233), because the visibility of experience alone will not clarify how experience is produced or what breathing fire "was eating up." Nor is it enough just to identify with the experience in researching and analyzing it. Roof (1996) writes that "in concrete terms this means emphasizing, privileging, locating the repetitions that constitute the terminally unfinished presence of existence, putting repetition, alternation, and accrual in the place of progress and closure" (pp. 182–183).

We insist on maintaining the ambiguity, the differences and strangeness of "The First Time," of performing narrative on stage. This ambiguity makes it possible for us to trouble the comforts of research even as we engage in them. Research and analysis on performing narrative are participatory; that is, they are a way to continue performing narrative. Research and analysis do not finish or complete performing narrative. With Merleau-Ponty (1964b), we see the ambiguity of participation as a reason for optimism: "If no work is ever absolutely completed and done with, [. . .] [i]f creations are not a possession, it is not only that, like all things, they pass away; it is also that they have almost all of their life still before them" (p. 190). In performing narrative we discover the human capacity to continue storytelling.

Coda

With these words, soul, eye, and hand are brought into connection. In-
teracting with one another, they determine a practice.
—Walter Benjamin (1969, p. 108)

In the tradition of Labovian narrative analysis, the coda is an optional element of a fully formed narrative. Like its musical referent, it brings a story to a formal close, something akin to "That's it. We're finished," or as one of our colleagues describes it, "the end the end." The coda echoes and reverberates with the performance it brings to a close. Thus it encapsulates and reiterates the narrative even while moving on. "That's it" signals a return to the narrative present of our ongoing interaction. Along with Benjamin's angel of history, we keep an eye to the past while we back into the future. Storytelling is always on the move, using discourse in a particular situation to materialize the embodied efforts by which we legitimate and critique communication practices. Or to paraphrase Benjamin's more elegant conclusion contained in the epigraph above: with these words we bring into connection soul, eye, and hand, and determine a practice. Performing narrative is the communication practice of storytelling.

"We're finished" simultaneously announces the possibility of another story even as it draws performing narrative to a close; it opens the floor to others' stories, to conversation, and to critique. A coda then, analogous to the speech act of "here, I would like to recount a little story," performs the invitation to continue storytelling. A coda intervenes by performing narrative for "one more time," whether one more last time or one more first time. If the beginnings of storytelling are ambiguous, so, too, are its endings. We embrace this ambiguity in order to avoid collapsing our multilevel critique into oppositional criticism: no exclusionary choice between celebration and suspicion, no nostalgia for the storytelling of years gone by, no condemnation or moral panic. The ends of performance are not in any story's ending but in continuing storytelling as a communication practice. By approaching narrative as a communication practice, we emphasize our participation and variable engagement. Performing narrative is strategic: we could do it differently—after all, a coda is one more variation—and certainly we invite you to do so.

Storytelling gathers an audience—temporarily, situationally, and provisionally—around a narrative performance. A coda offers to release that gathering to the experiential moment of performing narrative in which we learn something about ourselves and the world.

Notes

Part I: A Communication Approach to Storytelling

1. Riessman (2002) argues that part of the struggle of "doing justice" in narrative research comes in the way researchers recognize and position themselves in their writing. She writes, "finding ways to include ourselves responsibly and skillfully, not confessionally, is difficult" (p. 209). In writing this book, we attempt to make our participation in performing narrative visible and discussable without naturalizing or conventionalizing our research practices. We discuss this problem in greater detail in Chapter 7.

2. The discussion of the performance-performativity relationship is multidisciplinary and recently collected under the rubric of performance studies. For discussions from communication scholars, see Conquergood (1991, 1998), Gingrich-Philbrook (1997, 1998, 2000a, 2000b), Langellier (1989, 1998, 1999, 2001), Madison (1993, 1998), Peterson (2000a, 2000b), Peterson and Langellier (1997), Pollock (1998a, 1999), and Strine (1998). From theatre scholars, see Carlson (1996), Case (1990), Case, Brett, and Foster (1995), Diamond (1996, 1997), Dolan (1993), Hughes and Román (1998), Parker and Sedgewick (1995), Phelan and Lane (1998), Reinelt and Roach (1992), Román (1998). For some discussions in folklore and narrative studies, see Bauman (1986, 1992), Bauman and Briggs (1990), Georgakopoulou (1997, 1998), Hymes (1996), Maclean (1988), Myerhoff (1992), Sawin (1992), and Wolfson (1978).

Chapter 1: Performing Narrative in Daily Life

1. Semiotics and phenomenology have a long tradition in both narrative studies and performance studies. An overview of these traditions is beyond the scope of this book. For a few examples in narrative studies, see Eco (1994), Frank (1995), Ricoeur (1980), and Young (1987, 2000). In performance studies, see Butler (1990b), Carlson (1990), Eco (1977), Helbo (1987), Phelan and Lane (1998), and States (1992).

2. We take "bodily conduct" in the phenomenological sense of a system of behavior—what Merleau-Ponty calls a "postural schema." The body is not an agglomeration

of sensations or a collection of behaviors, some of which we would allocate to "narrator" and others to "character." As Merleau-Ponty (1964a) insists, the body "is first and foremost a *system* whose different introceptive and extroceptive aspects express each other reciprocally, including even the roughest relations of surrounding space and its principal directions. The consciousness I have of my body is not the consciousness of an isolated mass, it is a *postural schema*. It is the perception of my body's position in relation to the vertical, the horizontal, and certain other axes of important coordination of its environment" (p. 117, emphasis in original). Radley (1995, 1997) underscores the importance of focusing on bodily conduct in narrative research in his discussion of the "elusory body."

3. For a critique of the representational view of narrative, see Brockmeier and Harré (2001); in performance studies, see Peterson (1983) and Diamond (1997). Performing narrative is not a matter of *representing* in the here and now something that happened then and there. As Merleau-Ponty (1964a) writes, "The picture and the actor's mimicry are not devices to be borrowed from the real world in order to signify prosaic things which are absent. For the imaginary is much nearer to, and much farther away from, the actual—nearer because it is in my body as a diagram of the life of the actual, with all its pulp and carnal obverse [*son envers charnel*] exposed to view for the first time. [. . .] And the imaginary is much farther away from the actual because the painting is an analogue or likeness only according to the body; because it does *not* present the *mind* with an occasion to rethink the constitutive relations of things; because, rather, it offers to our *sight* [*regard*], so it might join with them, the inward traces of vision, and because it offers to vision its inward tapestries, the imaginary texture of the real" (emphasis in original, pp. 164–165).

4. See Wilden (1987a, p. 175) and Foucault (1976) in *L'Ordre du Discours*.

5. As performing narrative is a strategic practice, so, too, is transcribing "what happened" in a performance, as the researchers "take" what they consider to be significant and meaningful and "make" it appear for study. The transcript does not contain or even represent the performance. As Merleau-Ponty (1964b) phrases it: "every attempt to close our hand on the thought which dwells in the spoken word leaving only a bit of verbal material in our fingers" (p. 89). We discuss the problem of transcription elsewhere (Peterson & Langellier, 1997). For other discussions and alternative models of performance transcription, see Fine (1984, 2003), Madison (1993), Mishler (1991), and Riessman (1993).

We transcribe the audiotapes to suggest the "bits of verbal material" taken in performing narrative. We hope both to retain the "feel" of telling and to promote readability. We preserve false starts, repetitions, and self-interruptions while segmenting the speech into lines that reflect the speakers' rhythms and meaning units. A period (.) indicates a pause within a meaning unit. We use indented lines to group phrases on a single topic that were spoken together. Underlined words indicate increased intensity; capitalized WORDS indicate greater volume. The use of one or more colons (:) indicates a sound elongation; a dash (—) at the end of a word indicates an abrupt cut-off of sound, often a self-interruption or shift in the direction of thought. Notes in brackets (e.g., [laughter]) provide clarification by describing vocal or gestural qualities, identifying speakers, and indicating inaudible speech or questionable transcription. We further describe performance features in the discussion and analysis of the narrative.

For the purposes of confidentiality, we use pseudonyms for the participants and for the people they name in their storytelling, or family roles (e.g., mother, father, granddaughter). We use *Kristin* to refer to the on-site author throughout our discussions in Chapters 1 through 4 and in Chapter 6. In all other instances, the terms *researchers* and *we* are used to refer to both authors.

6. Merleau-Ponty (1964b) writes: "For the speaking subject, to express is to become aware of; he does not express just for others, but also to know himself what he intends. Speech does not seek to embody a significative intention which is only *a certain gap* simply in order to recreate the same lack or privation in others, but also to know *what* there is a lack or privation of" (p. 90, emphasis in original).

7. For a discussion of capta and the research process, see Lanigan (1994).

Part II: Family Storytelling

1. For these reasons it is important to consider family storytelling in different contexts with different material and situational constraints, including interviews with family members (e.g., Stone, 1988; Weston, 1991; Hall & Langellier, 1988), family gatherings with a researcher present (e.g., Blum-Kulka, 1997), and family storytelling *in situ* (e.g., Ochs & Capps, 2001).

2. Franco-Americans claim a North American French identity that has persisted for 400 years in two countries, the United States and Canada. Descendants of the seventeenth-century settlers of the New World, they include Acadians deported between 1755–1763 (the Great Disruption) from Nova Scotia and New Brunswick, and Québécois farmers of whom one million streamed to the rapidly growing industries of the Northeast between 1865 and 1930. The first major non-English-speaking population in the Northeast, Franco-Americans accounted for one in five New Englanders by 1900, and they number seven million today, some still bilingual. Approximately one quarter to one third of Maine is of French heritage, making Franco-Americans the state's largest ethnic group. Historically, Franco-Americans in the Northeast are working class and Roman Catholic. For discussions of Franco-American history, family, and identity, see, for example, Bérubé (1997), Chodos and Hamovitch (1991), Doty (1995), Doucet (1999), French (1981), Langelier (1996), Langellier (2001), Langellier and Peterson (1999), Louder and Waddell (1993), Peterson (1994), Quintal (1996), Robbins (1997), and Wartik (1989).

Chapter 2: Ordering Content and Making Family Stories

1. Developed in 1967 by Labov and Waletsky, this heuristic model defined personal narrative on two levels of clause and overall structure. First, fixed referential clauses recapitulating in temporal order "what happened" correspond to narrative (i.e., the narrated event, the "told," the enhancement of experience), and free evaluative clauses answering to "so what's the point?" correspond roughly to the personal, the attitude of the narrator toward the incident, its significance (i.e., the narrative event, the

"telling," positioning and identity). Second, a fully developed narrative has six structural components: abstract ("what, in a nutshell, was this about?"), an orientation ("who, what, when, where?"), complicating action ("and then what happened?"), evaluation ("so what?" "so what's the point?"), resolution ("what finally happened?"), and coda, which puts off further questions about the narrative events and returns the verbal perspective to the present. For several discussions of the legacy of the Labovian model, see the special issue of the *Journal of Narrative and Life History* (Bamberg, 1997a).

2. For a recent rethinking of models of "women's narrative," see Sawin (1999).

3. Although our purpose here is to illustrate content-ordering in family storytelling rather than to analyze local norms of Franco-American families, we want to note that the persistence of French language use in the Northeast defies the three-generation hypothesis of language loss and the straight-line theory of irreversible ethnic decline and assimilation (Gordon, 1964). We return to issues of the situational and material constraints of language in the next two chapters.

4. After the session, however, his wife and daughter gave Kristin a "mother's book" to read. This book, filled out by hand in its entirety by the mother, is a version of the do-it-yourself autobiography genre, detailing the turning points in a mother's life from childhood onward.

5. Annette's lines can be read as a family injunction against divorce. See Bell (1988) for methods analyzing linked stories in a corpus.

Chapter 3: Family Storytelling

1. In a rapidly changing world, stories provided by grandparents as a class of legitimators may be considered increasingly irrelevant by parents and children (McLain & Weigert, 1979, pp. 182–183).

2. For a critique of popular and mass-marketed autobiographies, see Sandell (1999).

3. For analysis of the performativity of gender and language, see Bucholtz, Liang, and Sutton (1999) and Cameron (1998).

4. See Cameron's (1992) integrational approach to women and language for an explanation of gender performance similar to the one we argue for here.

5. For discussions of North American French, see Maury and Tessier (1991).

Chapter 4: Performing Families

1. By considering postmodernity as a historical situation, we reject the bifurcation of modernism and postmodernism, whether in terms of aesthetic or epistemological practices and effects. Postmodernism broadens rather than rejects modernism. Mumby (1997) argues that the continuum of modernism and postmodernism articulates "increasingly transgressive orientations toward the notions of 'representation' and 'correspondence' as critical attributes of knowledge" (p. 23). The historical situation of postmodernity allows for knowledge which is historicized, narratives that are localized, and identities that are situated within structures of culture and power. For dis-

cussions of postmodernism and communication studies, see Grossberg (1992), Mumby (1997), and Hegde (1998).

2. For example, an 1880 Massachusetts labor report characterized the French as "the Chinese of the East." Using French Canadians to argue against a ten-hour work day, the report concludes, "Now, it is not strange that so sordid and low a people should awaken corresponding feelings in the managers, and that these should feel that, the longer hours for such people, the better, and that to work them to the uttermost is about the only good use they can be put to" (Wright, 1881). An 1892 editorial in the *New York Times* on the French Canadians in New England ("The French Canadians") stated that "No other people, except the Indians, are so persistent in repeating themselves. Where they halt they stay, and where they stay they multiply and cover the earth" (p. 4). We thank our University of Maine colleagues Jacques Ferland, for the Massachusetts labor report reference, and Yvon Labbé, for the *New York Times* editorial.

3. One 1918–19 study ranked Franco-Americans lowest among white ethnic groups, far behind the first-ranked "native white Americans" but ahead of tenth-ranked "Negroes" (Doty, 1995). In the mid- and late 1880s and again in the 1920s, French Catholics and Jews were the targets of cross-burnings by the Ku Klux Klan. In Maine, a flourishing and active Klan, numbering 150,141 members in 1925, waged campaigns against the Catholic Church and foreign-language schools (Doty, 1995).

4. See DeVault (1991) for the gendered dynamics of family meals.

5. In our corpus, a mother's decision to go into counseling for undisclosed "recollections" was actively resisted by some family members. There is little research on family therapy and Franco-Americans. Langelier (1996) describes a history of self-help and reliance on kinship networks and priests among Franco-Americans. "Personal problems, especially family issues, are considered too intimate and private for a stranger (therapist). Thus they operate according to a familiar blue-collar ethnic: Work out the situation as best you can—then try to be tolerant" (p. 486).

6. hooks (2000) calls the parental authority blindly trusted by children in her working-class home a form of family fascism: "A crucial aspect of our family fascism was that we were not allowed much contact with other families. We were rarely allowed to go to someone else's house" (p. 29).

7. Roby (1996b) specifies some of the outside forces that pressed Franco-Americans to greater assimilation. The economic crash of 1929 heavily impacted the textile and shoe industries of New England that employed Franco-American workers, and it put an immediate end to migration from Quebec. Some families returned to Canada, but those who stayed favored a better integration into American society. "The family and bonds of solidarity were subjected to strong centrifugal forces" (pp. 616–617). World War II drew Franco-American men and women from their *Petits Canadas,* and many were no longer interested in returning. Those who were ridiculed for their imperfect English in military service wanted to protect their children from this pain. Families moved from ensuring their children be bilingual to fostering unilingual speakers of flawless English. World War II also swelled the patriotism of Franco-Americans and brought them closer to other Americans. The prosperity and rise of consumer culture after the war, together with the ubiquity of television and other media (newspapers, magazines, cinema, video, and radio) brought "American" behaviors into the

home, particularly to women and children. Finally, the *Petits Canadas* broke up, disassembling the institutional, social, and economic infrastructures, such as the parish church, parochial schools, French-language newspapers, mutual aid societies, ethnic businesses, and social clubs, that sustained ethnic communities. To these forces, Pleck (2000) adds gender and ethnic women's kinwork. "The process of adjusting to life in the United States usually involved accommodating to a different gender division of labor, with the responsibility for making or retaining ritual, preserving a foreign language or dialect, or transmitting a religious heritage given over to women" (p. 13).

8. Lewiston has a *Petit Canada*, but Franco-Americans are dispersed throughout the city of 36,000. Although known as a Franco-American city, it has been home to a variety of immigrants, most recently an infusion of Somalis fleeing civil war.

9. Lewiston's *Festival de Joie* emphasizes its Franco-American heritage but also celebrates multicultural diversity. Lewiston was the first town in Maine to host a Franco-American festival, beginning in 1975. The festival changed its location in 2001 to the Little Canada neighborhood of Lewiston. Some adults see the festival as a successor to the house parties of earlier times. The festival features family-oriented fun and entertainment.

10. After 1763, when the Treaty of Paris ceded all of Canada to the British after the French defeat on the Plains of Abraham and after the Acadians were deported in the Great Disruption, French officials fled Canada but 70,000 *habitants* remained. Connections between France and New France were cleaved, and immigration from France was closed off. In the absence of state representation, the French turned to the Church, which filled the vacuum of power.

11. The most militant advocates of the national parish asserted that the French language must occupy the central position in the parish and schools, and they were locked in struggle with the dominant Irish Catholic hierarchy. The program, however, was unsuccessful in resisting the incursion of English, particularly after Vatican II (1962–65). By the 1970s only 55 of 277 Franco-American parishes in New England could still be considered national parishes (Roby, 1996b).

12. The decline in the use of the French language was accelerated by economic forces that shifted occupations from the mills and factories, where speaking French was not a disadvantage, to service occupations that required English. Ethnic organizational deactivation, changes in ethnic voting patterns, the decline in parochial schools, and the increase in intermarriage are additional forces eroding French language and culture. Roby (1996b) attributes the break-up of the *Petits Canadas* to the shift from bilingualism to unilingual English; the decline of the national parish and the remaining parochial schools teaching less French, the prosperity that allowed people to move from ethnic enclaves, and the turn in economic infrastructure from downtowns and neighborhoods to the malls. About his native Lewiston, Ledoux (2000) writes, "the community I grew up in was the last generation of Franco-Americans to learn French before learning English, the last generation to live in family groupings where French was necessary and in which links to Quebec were active and regularly renewed" (p. 4).

13. This discussion of alternative explanations for Franco-American silence is indebted to our University of Maine colleague, Susan Pinette.

Part III: Storytelling Practices

Chapter 5: Storytelling in a Weblog

1. Barger (1999) claims to be the first to use the term *weblog* in the title of his filter-style web page, *Robot Wisdom Weblog*, in December 1997. But Barger and others point to precursors such as the first websites (at CERN and NCSA) that contained lists of and links to new sites as they came online. Another early weblog, Winer's *Scripting News*, grew out of his existing newsletter *DaveNet* (Barrett, 1999). These filter-style weblogs, also described as microportals or newspages, list the websites that the weblog author finds of interest—typically accompanied by pithy commentary—with the most recently added material placed at the top of the page. There are several competing histories on the development of Internet journals and weblogs. Compare, for example, Barrett (1999), Blood (2000), Patterson (2000), and Winer (2001).

2. We selected *clinkclank* to illustrate the argument in this chapter because it has been published for several years, it is regularly updated and appears likely to continue into the foreseeable future, and it is not password protected. Several sites initially monitored by Eric are no longer in existence or are now password protected. Although some webloggers do not identify themselves by name in their weblogs, Cindy Alvarez has a copyright notice on the *clinkclank* webpage as well as links to an online resume, cooking lesson service, and newsletter that she offers. These elements would suggest that public attention to her website would not be unwelcome. For consistency of reference, we use *clinkclank* in the text to refer to the writer of the weblog. In addition, excerpts from the weblog are referenced by the date they were originally posted and by their archive web address (http://www.clinkclank.net/clonk) as reflected by the restructured archive on June 2, 2002.

The weblog excerpts are reprinted as faithfully as possible and may include misspellings and grammatical errors present in the original. The only alteration we make is to indent new paragraphs when the change in formats makes the excerpt difficult to read.

3. We agree with Poster that weblogs benefit from what is now a mostly unregulated distributed network structure. However, we do not agree that nodes and switching centers are beyond control by corporate or state interests. Such an assumption, captured in the popular saying "information wants to be free," ascribes desire to information and participates in an "ideology of boundless communication" (Mattelart, 2001).

4. In addition, see Eco's comments (1994) on the reader's "trust" in the text and its importance in navigating a fictional world.

5. Contrast this claim to group identity with the situated social space shared by families in the particular Franco-American communities described in Chapter 4. The fellowship of discourse developed in weblogs—at best an aggregate of dispersed individuals—approximates but does not constitute "community." Evidence for the recognition of this distinction by webloggers can be seen in the recent development of meetings or "meets" with "face-to-face peer" interaction organized by location. For an example, see http://www.meetup.com.

Chapter 6: Breast Cancer Storytelling

1. See Frank (2002) for some notable examples of early illness narratives. Hawkins (1993) defines pathography as a "form of autobiography or biography that describes personal experiences of illnesses, treatments, and sometimes death" (p. 1). Couser (1997) uses the term *autopathography* to characterize first-person narratives of illness or disability that depathologize the writer's condition. Although autopathographies include medical conditions and treatments, their focus is on survival and reclaiming the body from social stigmatization and the impersonalization of medical discourse. See Smith and Watson (2001) for relations of autopathographies to other genres of life narrative. Social scientists of medicine and healing who study oral narratives tend to use the term *illness narrative*, the term we adopt here.

2. Ehrenreich (2001) incorporates critiques from feminist, socialist, and environmental perspectives that call attention to the causes, rather than cures, of cancer, carcinogens in particular.

3. Seventeen women, ages 32 to 64 years and diagnosed with breast cancer, participated in interviews conducted by Langellier and Sullivan (1998). Three women were interviewed a second time, after they underwent additional treatments. Four women had recurrences at the time of the interviews. Jane's interview with Kristin was conducted in July 1995. For more details, see Langellier and Sullivan.

4. See Couser (1997), especially pp. 54–76, for discussion of how knowledge of a breast cancer writer's death changes reading. Also see Egan (1999).

5. In the interview Jane refers to her cancer as "Grade Three," which we interpret as nuclear grade, a measure of how many cells are dividing and how actively. The most aggressive cancers tend to have many cells dividing at the same time because they are growing rapidly. Pathology reports usually grade on a scale of 1–3 or 1–4, with the higher number being the worst (Love, 2000, pp. 329–330). The extent of breast cancer is also reported in a staging system, from 1 to 4. Stage 3 is a large tumor with positive lymph nodes or a tumor with "grave signs." See Love (2000, pp. 336–346).

6. Ehrenreich (2001) continues, "These interventions do not constitute a 'cure' or anything close, which is why the death rates from breast cancer have changed very little since the 1930s, when mastectomy was the only treatment available. Chemotherapy, which became a routine part of breast-cancer treatment in the eighties, does not confer anywhere near as decisive an advantage as patients are often led to believe, especially postmenopausal women like myself—a two to three percentage point difference in ten-year survival rates, according to America's best known breast-cancer surgeon, Dr. Susan Love" (pp. 44–45). Jane is postmenopausal.

7. The notable exception is Audre Lorde in *The Cancer Journals* (1980) and *A Burst of Light* (1988).

Chapter 7: Performing Narrative on Stage

1. For overviews of this tradition, see Carlson (1996), Strine, Long, and HopKins (1990), and Gentile (1989).

2. Portions of this chapter appeared in Peterson (2000a and 2000b). We gratefully acknowledge Craig Gingrich-Philbrook for providing a videotape that made the initial

transcription and analysis of this performance possible. We have elected to emphasize a thematic description and analysis for the purposes of our discussion. Readers interested in additional information regarding the use of gesture (following McNeill, 1992) and its importance in transcribing this performance should consult Peterson (2000a).

3. Elliot Mishler (1999) observes that some stories resist attempts to make them "coherent" and gives the example of stories told by Holocaust survivors in Lawrence Langer's (1991) analysis (also see Harvey, Mishler, Koenen, & Harney, 2000).

References

Alcoff, L. (1991–92). The problem of speaking for others. *Cultural Critique, 20,* 5–32.

Alcoff, L., & Gray, L. (1993). Survivor discourse: Transgressive or recuperative? *Signs, 18,* 260–290.

Allison, D. (1994). *Skin: Talking about sex, class, and literature.* Ithaca, NY: Firebrand Books.

Anderson, B. (1991). *Imagined communities: Reflections on the origin and spread of nationalism.* London: Verso.

Appadurai, A. (1996). *Modernity at large.* Minneapolis: University of Minnesota Press.

April, S., Brouillette, P., Marion, P., & St. Onge, M. L. (1999). *French class: French Canadian-American writings on identity, culture, and place.* Lowell, MA: Loom Press.

Archer, T. (2001). Online article: Wag the blog. *Trade: Queer Things, 8* [Electronic version]. Retrieved February 14, 2002, from http://www.tradequeerthings.com/online.html.

Armstrong, N. (1994). Fatal abstraction: The death and sinister afterlife of the American family. In M. Ryan & A. Gordon (Eds.), *Body politics: Disease, desire, and the family* (pp. 18–31). Boulder, CO: Westview.

Atkinson, P., & Silverman, D. (1997). Kundera's *Immortality:* The interview society and the invention of the self. *Qualitative Inquiry, 3,* 304–325.

Baldwin, K. (1985). "Woof!" A word on women's roles in family storytelling. In R. A. Jordon and S. J. Kalčik (Eds.), *Women's folklore, women's culture* (pp. 149–162). Philadelphia: University of Pennsylvania Press.

Bamberg, M. (Ed.). (1997a). Oral versions of personal experience: Three decades of narrative analysis. *Journal of Narrative and Life History, 7,* 1–415.

Bamberg, M. (1997b). Positioning between structure and performance. *Journal of Narrative and Life History, 7,* 335–342.

Barger, J. (1999). Weblog resources FAQ. Retrieved February 14, 2002, from http://www.robotwisdom.com/weblogs.

Barrett, C. (1999). Anatomy of a weblog. Retrieved February 14, 2002, from http://www.camworld.com/journal/rants/99/01/26.html.

Bateson, G. (1979). *Mind and nature: A necessary unity*. New York: E. P. Dutton.

Bauman, R. (1986). *Story, performance, and event: Contextual studies of oral narratives*. Cambridge: Cambridge University Press.

Bauman, R. (1992). Performance. In R. Bauman (Ed.), *Folklore, cultural performances, and popular entertainments: A communications-centered handbook*. New York: Oxford University Press.

Bauman, R., & Briggs, C. L. (1990). Poetics and performance as critical perspectives on language and social life. *Annual Review of Anthropology, 19*, 59–88.

Bauman, Z. (2001). Consuming life. *Journal of Consumer Culture, 1*, 9–29.

Bell, S. (1988). Becoming a political woman: The reconstruction and interpretation of experience through stories. In A. D. Todd & S. Fisher (Eds.), *Gender and discourse: The power of talk* (pp. 97–124). Norwood, NJ: Ablex.

Bellah, R. N., Madsen, R., Sullivan, W. M., Swidler, A., & Tipton, S. M. (1985). *Habits of the heart: Individualism and commitment in American life*. New York: Harper and Row.

Benjamin, W. (1969). The storyteller [and] The work of art in the age of mechanical reproduction. In H. Arendt (Ed.), *Illuminations* (H. Zohn, Trans.) (pp. 83–109 and 217–251). New York: Schocken.

Bennett, G. (1986). Narrative as expository discourse. *Journal of American Folklore, 99*, 415–434.

Bérubé, A. (1997). Intellectual desire. In S. Raffo (Ed.), *Queerly classed* (pp. 43–66). Boston: South End.

Blood, R. (2000). Weblogs: A history and perspective. Retrieved on February 14, 2002, from http://www.rebeccablood.net/essays/weblog_history.html.

Blum-Kulka, S. (1997). *Dinner talk: Cultural patterns of sociability and socialization in family discourse*. Mahwah, NJ: Lawrence Erlbaum.

Bochner, A. (1994). Perspectives on inquiry II: Theories and stories. In M. L. Knapp & G. R. Miller (Eds.), *Handbook of interpersonal communication* (2nd ed., pp. 21–41). Thousand Oaks, CA: Sage.

Bona, M. J. (1999). *Claiming a tradition: Italian American women writers*. Carbondale: Southern Illinois University Press.

Boscia-Mulé, P. (1999). *Authentic ethnicities: The interaction of ideology, gender, power, and class in Italian-American experience*. Westport, CT: Greenwood.

Brandes, S. (1975). Family misfortune stories in American folklore. *Journal of the Folklore Institute, 12*, 5–17.

Briggs, C. L. (1993). "I'm not just talking to the victims of oppression tonight—I'm talking to everybody": Rhetorical authority and narrative authenticity in an African-American poetics of political engagement. *Journal of Narrative and Life History, 3*, 33–78.

Brodkin, K. (1998). *How the Jews became white folks and what that says about race in America*. New Brunswick, NJ: Rutgers University Press.

Brockmeier, J. (2001). From the end to the beginning: Retrospective teleology in autobiography. In J. Brockmeier & D. Carbaugh (Eds.), *Narrative and identity: Studies in autobiography, self and culture* (pp. 247–280). Philadelphia: John Benjamins.

Brockmeier, J., & Carbaugh, D. (2001). *Narrative and identity: Studies in autobiography, self and culture*. Philadelphia: John Benjamins.

Brockmeier, J., & Harré, R. (2001). Problems and promises of an alternative paradigm. In J. Brockmeier & D. Carbaugh (Eds.), *Narrative and identity: Studies in autobiography, self and culture* (pp. 39–58). Philadelphia: John Benjamins.

Bruner, J. (1990). *Acts of meaning.* Cambridge, MA: Harvard University.

Bruner, J., & Weisser, S. (1991). The invention of self: Autobiography and its forms. In D. R. Olson & N. Torrance (Eds.), *Literacy and orality* (pp. 129–148). Cambridge: Cambridge University Press.

Bucholtz, M., Liang, A. C., & Sutton, L. A. (Eds.). (1999). *Reinventing identities: The gendered self in discourse.* New York: Oxford University Press.

Butler, J. (1990a). *Gender trouble: Feminism and the subversion of identity.* New York: Routledge.

Butler, J. (1990b). Performative acts and gender constitution: An essay in phenomenology and feminist theory. In S. Case (Ed.), *Performing feminisms: Feminist critical theory and theatre* (pp. 270–282). Baltimore: Johns Hopkins University Press.

Butler, J. (1993). *Bodies that matter: On the discursive limits of "sex."* New York: Routledge.

Cameron, D. (1992). *Feminism and linguistic theory* (2nd ed.). New York: St. Martin's.

Cameron, D. (1998). Gender, language, and discourse: A review essay. *Signs, 23,* 945–973.

Carlson, M. (1990). *Theatre semiotics: Signs of life.* Bloomington: Indiana University Press.

Carlson, M. (1996). *Performance: A critical introduction.* New York: Routledge.

Case, S. (Ed.). (1990). *Performing feminisms: Feminist critical theory and theatre* (pp. 270–282). Baltimore: Johns Hopkins University Press.

Case, S., Brett, P., & Foster, S. L. (Eds.). (1995). *Cruising the performative: Interventions into the representation of ethnicity, nationality, and sexuality.* Bloomington: Indiana University Press.

Cha, A. E. (2001, September 2). Dear web diary, SO much to tell! Teens tell secrets, get gifts, attract nuts, scare mom. *The Washington Post,* p. A01.

Chodorow, N. (1978). *The reproduction of mothering: Psychoanalysis and the sociology of gender.* Berkeley: University of California Press.

Chodos, R., & Hamovitch, E. (1991). *Quebec and the American dream.* Toronto: Between the Lines.

Clarke, J. (1991). *New times and old enemies: Essays on cultural studies and America.* London: HarperCollins.

Collins, P. H. (1991). *Black feminist thought: Knowledge, consciousness and the politics of empowerment.* New York: Routledge.

Conquergood, D. (1991). Rethinking ethnography: Towards a critical cultural politics. *Communication Monographs, 58,* 179–194.

Conquergood, D. (1998). Beyond the text: Toward a performative cultural politics. In S. J. Dailey (Ed.), *The future of performance studies: Visions and revisions* (pp. 25–36). Annandale, VA: National Communication Association.

Cook-Gumperz, J. (1995). Reproducing the discourse of mothering: How gendered talk makes gendered lives. In K. Hall & H. Buchohltz (Eds.), *Gender articulated: Language and socially constructed self* (pp. 401–420). New York: Routledge.

Coontz, S. (1992). *The way we never were: American families and the nostalgia trap.* New York: Basic Books.

Coontz, S. (1997). *The way we really are: Coming to terms with America's changing families.* New York: Basic Books.

Couser, G. T. (1997). *Recovering bodies: Illness, disability, and life writing.* Madison: University of Wisconsin Press.

Crossley, N. (1996). Body-subject/body-power: Agency, inscription and control in Foucault and Merleau-Ponty. *Body & Society, 2*(2), 99–116.

Davis, F. (1979). *Yearning for yesterday: A sociology of nostalgia.* New York: Free Press.

DeVault, M. L. (1991). *Feeding the family: The social organization of caring as gendered work.* Chicago: University of Chicago Press.

Diamond, E. (1992). The violence of "we": Politicizing identification. In J. G. Reinett and J. R. Roach (Eds.), *Critical theory and performance* (pp. 390–398). Ann Arbor: University of Michigan Press.

Diamond, E. (1996). Introduction. In E. Diamond (Ed.), *Performance and cultural politics* (pp. 1–12). New York: Routledge.

Diamond, E. (1997). *Unmaking mimesis: Essays on feminism and theater.* New York: Routledge.

di Leonardo, M. (1984). *The varieties of ethnic experience: Kinship, class, and gender among California Italian Americans.* Ithaca, NY: Cornell University Press.

di Leonardo, M. (1998). *Exotics at home: Anthropologies, others, American modernity.* Chicago: University of Chicago Press.

Dills, V. L. (1998). Transferring and transforming cultural norms: A mother-daughter-son lifestory in process. *Narrative Inquiry, 8*, 213–222.

Dolan, J. (1993). Geographies of learning: Theatre studies, performance, and the "performative." *Theatre Journal, 45*, 417–441.

Doty, C. S. (1991). *Acadian hard times: The farm security administration in Maine's St. John Valley, 1940–1943.* Orono: University of Maine Press.

Doty, C. S. (1995). How many Frenchmen does it take to . . . ? *Thought & Action: The NEA Higher Education Journal, 11*(2), 85–104.

Doucet, C. (1999). *Notes from exile: On being Acadian.* Toronto: McClelland and Stewart.

duCille, A. (1994). The occult of true black womanhood: Critical demeanor and black feminist studies. *Signs, 19*, 591–629.

Dufresne, J. (1996). Telling stories in *mémère's* kitchen. In C. Quintal (Ed.), *Steeples and smokestacks: A collection of essays on the Franco-American experience in New England* (pp. 660–669). Worcester, MA: Editions de l'Institut Français.

Duncombe, S. (1999, December). DIY Nike style. *Z Magazine*, pp. 32–35.

Eco, U. (1976). *A theory of semiotics.* Bloomington: Indiana University Press.

Eco, U. (1977). Semiotics of theatrical performance. *The Drama Review, 73*, 107–117.

Eco, U. (1990). *The limits of interpretation.* Bloomington: Indiana University Press.

Eco, U. (1994). *Six walks in the fictional woods.* Cambridge, MA: Harvard University Press.

Edelman, H. (1999). *Mother of my mother: The intricate bond between generations.* New York: Delta.

Edelsky, C. (1981). Who's got the floor? *Language in Society, 10,* 383–421.

Egan, S. (1999). *Mirror talk: Genres of crisis in contemporary autobiography.* Chapel Hill: University of North Carolina Press.

Ehrenreich, B. (2001, November). Welcome to cancerland: A mammogram leads to a cult of pink kitsch. *Harper's Magazine,* pp. 43–53.

Ernaux, A. (1990). *A woman's story* (T. Leslie, Trans.). New York: Quartet Books.

Fine, E. C. (1984). *The folklore text: From performance to print.* Bloomington: Indiana University Press.

Fine, E. C. (2003). *Soulstepping: African-American step shows.* Urbana: University of Illinois Press.

Firth, S. (1998, July 3). Baring your soul to the web. *Salon.* Retrieved on February 14, 2002, from http://www.salon.com/21st/feature/1998/07/cov_03feature.html.

Fishman, P. (1983). Interaction: The work women do. In B. Thorne, C. Kramarae, & N. Henley (Eds.), *Language, gender, and society* (pp. 89–101). Rowley, MA: Newbury House.

Foucault, M. (1976). *The archaeology of knowledge and the discourse on language* (A. M. Sheridan Smith, Trans.). New York: Harper Colophon.

Foucault, M. (1980). *The history of sexuality, Volume I: An introduction* (R. Hurley, Trans.). New York: Vintage.

Foucault, M. (2001). *Fearless speech* (J. Pearson, Ed.). Los Angeles: Semiotexte.

Franco-American Women's Institute [FAWI]. Retrieved on July 12, 2002, from http://www.fawi.net.

Frank, A. W. (1995). *The wounded storyteller: Body, illness, and ethics.* Chicago: University of Chicago Press.

Frank, A. W. (2002). The extrospection of suffering: Strategies of first-person illness narratives. In W. Patterson (Ed.), *Strategic narrative: New perspectives on the power of personal and cultural stories* (pp.165–177). Lanham, MD: Lexington.

French, L. (1981). The French Canadian American family. In C. H. Mindel & R. W. Habenstein (Eds.), *Ethnic families in America: Patterns and variations* (2nd ed., pp. 326–349). New York: Elsevier.

The French Canadians in New England. (1892, June 6). *The New York Times,* p. 4.

Frith, S. (1996). *Performing rites: On the value of popular music.* Cambridge, MA: Harvard University Press.

Garber, M. (1992). *Vested interests: Cross-dressing and cultural anxiety.* New York: Routledge.

Gee, J. P. (1986). Units in the production of narrative discourse. *Discourse Processes, 9,* 391–422.

Gee, J. P. (1989). Two styles of narrative construction and their linguistic and educational implications. *Discourse Processes, 12,* 287–307.

Gee, J. P. (1991). A linguistic approach to narrative. *Journal of Narrative and Life History, 1,* 15–39.

Geissner, H. K. (1995). On responsibility. In J. Lehtonen (Ed.), *Critical perspectives on communication research and pedagogy* (pp. 17–29). St. Ingbert: Röhrig Universitätsverlag.

Gentile, J. S. (1989). *Cast of one: One-person shows from the Chautauqua platform to the Broadway stage.* Champaign: University of Illinois Press.

Georgakopoulou, A. (1997). *Narrative performances: A study of modern Greek storytelling.* Philadelphia: John Benjamins.

Georgakopoulou, A. (1998). Conversational stories as performances: The case of Greek. *Narrative Inquiry, 8,* 319–350.

Gillis, J. R. (1996). *A world of their own making: Myth, ritual, and the quest for family values.* New York: Basic Books.

Gilroy, P. (2000). *Against race: Imagining political culture beyond the color line.* Cambridge, MA: Harvard University Press.

Gingrich-Philbrook, C. (1997). Refreshment. *Text and Performance Quarterly, 17,* 352–360.

Gingrich-Philbrook, C. (1998). Autobiographical performance and carnivorous knowledge: Rae C. Wright's *Animal Instincts. Text and Performance Quarterly, 18,* 63–79.

Gingrich-Philbrook, C. (Ed.). (2000a). The personal and political in solo performance. *Text and Performance Quarterly, 20,* vii–114.

Gingrich-Philbrook, C. (2000b). Revenge of the dead subject: The contexts of Michael Bowman's *Killing Dillinger. Text and Performance Quarterly, 20,* 375–387.

Gordon, M. M. (1964). *Assimilation in American life.* New York: Oxford University Press.

Grossberg, L. (1992). *We gotta get out of this place: Popular conservatism and postmodern culture.* New York: Routledge.

Grossberg, L. (1993). Can cultural studies find true happiness in communication? *Journal of Communication, 43*(4), 89–97.

Hall, D. L., & Langellier, K. M. (1988). Storytelling strategies in mother-daughter communication. In A. Taylor & B. Bate (Eds.), *Women communicating* (pp. 107–126). New York: Ablex.

Hall, S. (1992). New ethnicities. In J. Donald & A. Rattansi (Eds.), *"Race," culture and difference* (pp. 252–259). London: Open University and Sage.

Halperin, D. M. (1995). *Saint Foucault: Towards a gay hagiography.* New York: Oxford University Press.

Hantzis, D. M. (1998). Reflections on "A Dialogue with Friends: 'Performing' the 'Other/Self' OJA 1995." In S. J. Dailey (Ed.), *The future of performance studies: Visions and revisions* (pp. 203–206). Annandale, VA: National Communication Association.

Hartmann, H. I. (1981). The family as the locus of gender, class and political struggle. *Signs, 6,* 366–394.

Harvey, M. R., Mishler, E. G., Koenen, K., & Harney, P. A. (2000). In the aftermath of sexual abuse: Making and remaking meaning in narratives of trauma and recovery. *Narrative Inquiry, 10,* 291–311.

Hawkins, S. H. (1993). *Reconstructing illness: Studies in pathography.* West Lafayette, IN: Purdue University Press.

Heath, S. B. (1983). *Ways with words: Language, life and work in communities and classroom.* Cambridge: Cambridge University Press.

Hegde, R. S. (1998). A view from elsewhere: Locating difference and the politics of representation from a transnational feminist perspective. *Communication Theory, 8,* 271–297.

Helbo, A. (1987). *Theory of performing arts.* Philadelphia: John Benjamins.

Hendrickson, D. (1980). *Quiet presence.* Portland, ME: G. Gannett.

Henley, N. M., & Kramarae, C. (1991). Gender, power, and miscommunication. In N. Coupland, H. Giles, & J. M. Wiemann (Eds.), *"Miscommunication" and problematic talk* (pp. 18–43). Newbury Park, CA: Sage.

Hochschild, A. (1989). *The second shift: Working parents and the revolution at home.* New York: Viking.

hooks, b. (2000). *Where we stand: Class matters.* New York: Routledge.

Hughes, H., & Román, D. (Eds.). (1998). *O solo homo: The new queer performance.* New York: Grove.

Hymes, D. (1996). *Ethnography, linguistics, narrative inequality: Toward an understanding of voice.* London: Taylor and Francis.

Ignatiev, N. (1995). *How the Irish became white.* New York: Routledge.

Johnstone, B. (1990). *Stories, community, place: Narratives from middle America.* Bloomington: Indiana University Press.

Kalčik, S. (1975). ". . . like Ann's gynecologist or the time I was almost raped": Personal narratives in a women's rap group. In C. R. Farrer (Ed.), *Women and folklore* (pp. 3–11). Austin: University of Texas Press.

Katz, J. (2000). *Geeks: How two lost boys rode the Internet out of Idaho.* New York: Broadway Books.

Kenney, M. (1999, October 21). *Ils se souviennent:* The quiet presence of New England's Franco-Americans. *The Boston Globe,* p. D01.

Kleinman, A. (1988). *The illness narratives: Suffering, healing and the human condition.* New York: Basic.

Kistenberg, C. J. (1995). *AIDS, social change, and theater: Performance as protest.* New York: Garland.

Kramarae, C., & Jenkins, M. M. (1987). Women take back the talk. In J. Penfield (Ed.), *Women and language in transition* (pp. 137–156). Albany: State University of New York Press.

Kristeva, J. (1982). *Powers of horror: An essay on abjection* (L. S. Roudiez, Trans.). New York: Columbia University Press.

Labov, W. (1997). Some further steps in narrative analysis. *Journal of Narrative and Life History, 7,* 395–415.

Labov, W., & Waletzky, J. (1967). Narrative analysis: Oral versions of personal experience. In J. Helm (Ed.), *Essays on the verbal and visual arts* (pp. 12–44). Seattle: University of Washington Press.

Langelier, R. (1996). French Canadian families. In M. McGoldrick, J. Giordano, & J. K. Pearce (Eds.), *Ethnicity and family therapy* (pp. 477–495). New York: Guilford.

Langellier, K. M. (1989). Personal narratives: Perspectives on theory and research. *Text and Performance Quarterly, 9,* 243–276.

Langellier, K. M. (1998). Voiceless bodies, bodiless voices: The future of personal narrative performance. In S. Dailey (Ed.), *The future of performance studies: Visions and revisions* (pp. 207–213). Annandale, VA: National Communication Association.

Langellier, K. M. (1999). Personal narrative, performance, performativity: Two or three things I know for sure. *Text and Performance Quarterly, 19,* 125–144.

Langellier, K. M. (2001). "You're marked": Breast cancer, tattoo, and the narrative performance of identity. In J. Brockmeier & D. Carbaugh (Eds.), *Narrative and identity: Studies in autobiography, self and culture* (pp. 145–184). Philadelphia: John Benjamins.

Langellier, K. M. (2002). "Performing family stories, forming cultural identity: Franco-American *mémère* stories. *Communication Studies, 53,* 56–73.

Langellier, K. M., & Hall, D. L. (1989). Interviewing women: A phenomenological approach to feminist communication research. In K. Carter & C. Spitzack (Eds.), *Doing research on women's communication: Perspectives on theory and method* (pp. 193–220). New York: Ablex.

Langellier, K. M., & Peterson, E. E. (1992). Spinstorying: An analysis of women storytelling. In E. C. Fine & J. H. Speer (Eds.), *Performance, culture, and identity* (pp. 157–180). Westport, CT: Praeger.

Langellier, K. M., & Peterson, E. E. (1993). Family storytelling as a strategy of social control. In D. Mumby (Ed.), *Narrative and social control* (pp. 49–76). Newbury Park, CA: Sage.

Langellier, K. M., & Peterson, E. E. (1995). A critical pedagogy of family storytelling. In J. Lehtonen (Ed.), *Critical perspectives on communication and pedagogy* (pp. 71–82). St. Ingbert: Röhrig Universitätsverlag.

Langellier, K. M., & Peterson, E. E. (1999). Voicing identity: The case of Franco-American women in Maine. In E. Slembek (Ed.), *The voice of the voiceless* (pp. 135–145). St. Ingbert: Röhrig Universitätsverlag.

Langellier, K. M., & Sullivan, C. F. (1998). Breast talk in cancer narratives. *Qualitative Health Research, 8,* 76–94.

Langer, L. L. (1991). *Holocaust testimonies: The ruins of memory.* New Haven, CT: Yale University Press.

Lanigan, R. L. (1988). *Phenomenology of communication: Merleau-Ponty's thematics in communicology and semiology.* Pittsburgh, PA: Duquesne University Press.

Lanigan, R. L. (1992). *The human science of communicology: A phenomenology of discourse in Foucault and Merleau-Ponty.* Pittsburgh, PA: Duquesne University Press.

Lanigan, R. L. (1994). Capta versus data: Method and evidence in communicology. *Human Studies, 17,* 109–130.

Lanigan, R. L. (2000). The self in semiotic phenomenology: Consciousness as the conjunction of perception and expression in the science of communicology. *American Journal of Semiotics, 15 and 16,* 91–111.

Lanza, C. D. (1994). "Always on the brink of disappearing": Women, ethnicity, class, and autobiography. *Frontiers, 15*(2), 51–68.

Ledoux, D. (2000). *La survivance*: Giving voice to Franco-American experience. *Portland: Maine's City Magazine.* [Electronic version]. Retrieved on July 18, 2002, from http://www.maine.rr.com/Around_Town/portlandmonthly/default5.asp.

Linde, C. (1997). Narrative: Experience, memory, folklore. *Journal of Narrative and Life History, 7,* 281–289.

Lorde, A. (1980). *The cancer journals.* San Francisco: Aunt Lute.

Lorde, A. (1988). *A burst of light: Essays.* Ithaca, NY: Firebrand Books.

Louder, D. R., & Waddell, E. (1993). *French America: Mobility, identity, and minority experience across the continent* (F. Philip, Trans.). Baton Rouge: Louisiana State University Press.

Love, S., with Lindsey, K. (2000). *Dr. Susan Love's breast book,* 3rd ed. Reading, MA: Addison-Wesley.

Maclean, M. (1988). *Narrative as performance: The Baudelairean experiment*. New York: Routledge.

Madison, D. S. (1993). "That was my occupation": Oral narrative, performance, and black feminist thought. *Text and Performance Quarterly, 13*, 213–232.

Madison, D. S. (1998). Performance, personal narratives, and the politics of possibility. In S. Dailey (Ed.), *The future of performance studies: Visions and revisions* (pp. 276–286). Annandale, VA: National Communication Association.

Maltz, D., and Borker, R. A. (1982). A cultural approach to male/female miscommunication. In J. J. Gumperz (Ed.), *Language and social identity: Studies in international sociolinguistics* (pp. 196–216). Cambridge: Cambridge University Press.

Mandelbaum, J. (1987). Couples sharing stories. *Communication Quarterly, 35*, 144–170.

Mattelart, A. (2000). *Networking the world, 1794–2000*. (L. Carey-Libbrecht & J. A. Cohen, Trans.) Minneapolis: University of Minnesota Press.

Mattingly, C., and Garro, L.C. (Eds.) (2000). *Narrative and the cultural construction of illness and healing*. Berkeley: University of California Press.

Maury, N., & Tessier, J. (1991). *À l'écoute des francophones d'Amérique: Exploitation de documents sonores*. Montréal: Centre éducatif et culturel.

McChesney, R. (2000, April). The Titantic sails on: Why the Internet won't sink the media giants. *Extra! The magazine of FAIR, 13*(2), 10–15.

McFeat, T. (1974). *Small group cultures*. New York: Pergamon.

McKay, I. (1994). *The quest of the folk: Antimodernism and cultural selection in twentieth-century Nova Scotia*. Montreal: McGill–Queen's University Press.

McKenzie, J. (1998). Genre trouble: (The) Butler did it. In P. Phelan and J. Lane (Eds.), *The ends of performance* (pp. 217–235). New York: New York University Press.

McLain, R., & Weigert, A. (1979). Toward a phenomenological sociology of family: A programmatic essay. In W. R. Burr, R. Hill, F. I. Nye, & I. L. Reiss (Eds.), *Contemporary theories about the family* (pp. 160–205). New York: Free Press.

McNeill, D. (1992). *Hand and mind: What gestures reveal about thought*. Chicago: University of Chicago Press.

Messud, C. (1999). *The last life*. New York: Harcourt Brace.

Merleau-Ponty, M. (1964a). *The primacy of perception* (J. Edie, Ed.). Evanston, IL: Northwestern University Press.

Merleau-Ponty, M. (1964b). *Signs* (R. C. McLeary, Trans.). Evanston, IL: Northwestern University Press.

Minister, K. (1991). A feminist frame for the oral history interview. In S. B. Gluck & D. Patai (Eds.), *Women's words: The feminist practice of oral history* (pp. 27–41). New York: Routledge.

Mishler, E. G. (1984). *The discourse of medicine: Dialectics of medical interviews*. Norwood, NJ: Ablex.

Mishler, E. G. (1991). Representing discourse: The rhetoric of transcription. *Journal of Narrative and Life History, 1*, 255–280.

Mishler, E. G. (1999). *Storylines: Craftartists' narratives of identity*. Cambridge, MA: Harvard University Press.

Modleski, T. (1982). *Loving with a vengeance: Mass-produced fantasies for women*. New York: Methuen.

Morse, M. (1998). *Virtualities: Television, media art, and cyberculture.* Bloomington: Indiana University Press.

Mumby, D. K. (Ed.). (1993). *Narrative and social control: Critical perspectives.* Newbury Park, CA: Sage.

Mumby, D. K. (1997). Modernism, postmodernism, and communication studies: A rereading of an ongoing debate. *Communication Theory, 7,* 1–28.

Myerhoff, B. (1992). *Remembered lives: The work of ritual, storytelling, and growing older.* Ann Arbor: University of Michigan Press.

Nakayama, T. K., & Martin, J. N. (Eds.). (1999). *Whiteness: The social communication of identity.* Thousand Oaks, CA: Sage.

Narayan, U. (1997). *Dislocating cultures: Identities, traditions, and third world feminism.* New York: Routledge.

Nelson, H. L. (Ed.). (1997). *Feminism and families.* New York: Routledge.

Nelson, H. L. (2001). *Damaged identities: Narrative repair.* Ithaca, NY: Cornell University Press.

Ng, F. M. (1994). *Bone.* New York: HarperPerennial.

Nos Histoires de l'Ile Group. (1999). *Nos Histoires de l'Ile: History and memories of French Island, Old Town, Maine.* (Available from H. Lacadie, 131 Bosworth Street, Old Town, ME 04468 or from http://www.old-town.org/nos/home.html.)

Ochs, E. (1997). Narrative. In T. A. van Dijk (Ed.), *Discourse as structure and process* (pp. 185–207). Thousand Oaks, CA: Sage.

Ochs, E., & Capps, L. (2001). *Living narrative: Creating lives in everyday storytelling.* Cambridge, MA: Harvard University Press.

O'Connell, S. P. (2001). *Outspeak: Narrating identities that matter.* New York: State University of New York Press.

Park-Fuller, L. (1995). Narration and narratization of a cancer story. *Text and Performance Quarterly, 15,* 60–67.

Park-Fuller, L. (2000). Performing absence: The staged personal narrative as testimony. *Text and Performance Quarterly, 20,* 20–42.

Parker, J. H. (1993). *Ethnic identity: The case of the French Americans.* Washington, DC: University Press of America.

Parker, A., & Sedgewick, E. S. (Eds.). (1995). *Performativity and performance.* New York: Routledge.

Patterson, D. (2000). Why web journals suck. Retrieved February 14, 2002, from http://www.nobody-knows-anything.com/websuck.html.

Patterson, W. (Ed.). (2002). *Strategic narrative: New perspectives on the power of personal and cultural stories.* Lanham, MD: Lexington Books.

Patton, S. (1996). Race/identity/culture/kin: Constructions of African American identity in transracial adoption. In S. Smith & J. Watson (Eds.), *Getting a life: Everyday uses of autobiography* (pp. 271–296). Minneapolis: University of Minnesota Press.

Peterson, E. E. (1983). Representation and the limits of interpretation. *Literature in Performance, 3,* 22–26.

Peterson, E. E. (1987). The stories of pregnancy: On interpretation of small group cultures. *Communication Quarterly, 35,* 39–47.

Peterson, E. E. (1994). Diversity and Franco-American identity. *Maine Historical Society Quarterly, 34,* 58–67.

Peterson, E. E. (2000a). Narrative identity in a solo performance: Craig Gingrich-Philbrook's "The First Time." *Narrative Inquiry, 10,* 229–251.

Peterson, E. E. (2000b). One more first time: A response to Katz and Shotter. *Narrative Inquiry, 10,* 475–481.

Peterson, E. E., & Langellier, K. M. (1982). Creative double bind in oral interpretation. *Western Journal of Speech Communication, 46,* 242–253.

Peterson, E. E., & Langellier, K. M. (1997). The politics of personal narrative methodology. *Text and Performance Quarterly, 17,* 135–152.

Phelan, P., & Lane, J. (Eds.) (1998). *The ends of performance.* New York: New York University Press.

Pleck, E. H. (2000). *Celebrating the family: Ethnicity, consumer culture, and family rituals.* Cambridge, MA: Harvard University Press.

Plummer, K. (1995). *Telling sexual stories: Power, change and social worlds.* New York: Routledge.

Pollock, D. (Ed.). (1998a). *Exceptional spaces: Essays in performance and history.* Chapel Hill: University of North Carolina Press.

Pollock, D. (1998b). A response to Dwight Conquergood's essay "Beyond the text: Toward a performative cultural politics." In S. J. Dailey (Ed.), *The future of performance studies: Visions and revisions* (pp. 37–46). Annandale, VA: National Communication Association.

Pollock, D. (1999). *Telling bodies, performing birth: Everyday narratives of childbirth.* New York: Columbia University Press.

Poster, M. (1978). *Critical theory of the family.* New York: Seabury.

Poster, M. (2001). *What's the matter with the Internet?* Minneapolis: University of Minnesota Press.

Quintal, C. (Ed.). (1996). *Steeples and smokestacks: A collection of essays on the Franco-American experience in New England.* Worcester, MA: Editions de l'Institut Français.

Radley, A. (1995). The elusory body and social constructionist theory. *Body & Society, 1*(2), 3–23.

Radley, A. (1997). The triumph of narrative? A reply to Arthur Frank. *Body & Society, 3*(3), 93–101.

Radway, J. (1984). *Reading the romance: Women, patriarchy, and popular literature.* Chapel Hill: University of North Carolina Press.

Reinelt, J. (1994). Staging the invisible: The crisis of visibility in theatrical representation. *Text and Performance Quarterly, 14,* 97–107.

Reinelt, J. G., & Roach, J. R. (Eds.). (1992). *Critical theory and performance.* Ann Arbor: University of Michigan Press.

Ricoeur, P. (1980). Narrative time. *Critical Inquiry, 7,* 169–190.

Riessman, C. K. (1990). *Divorce talk: Women and men make sense of personal relationships.* New Brunswick, NJ: Rutgers University Press.

Riessman, C. K. (1993). *Narrative analysis.* Newbury Park, CA: Sage.

Riessman, C. K. (2002). Doing justice: Positioning the interpreter in narrative work. In W. Patterson (Ed.), *Strategic narrative: New perspectives on the power of personal and cultural stories* (pp. 193–214). Lanham, MD: Lexington Books.

Robbins, R. C. (1997). *Wednesday's child.* Brunswick: Maine Writers and Publishers Alliance.

Robson, R. (1994). Resisting the family: Repositioning lesbians in legal theory. *Signs, 19*, 975–996.

Roby, Y. (1996a). A portrait of the female Franco-American worker (1865–1930). In C. Quintal (Ed.), *Steeples and smokestacks: A collection of essays on the Franco-American experience in New England* (pp. 544–563). Worcester, MA: Editions de l'Institut Français.

Roby, Y. (1996b). From Franco-Americans to Americans of French-Canadian origin or Franco-Americanism, past and present. In C. Quintal (Ed.), *Steeples and smokestacks: A collection of essays on the Franco-American experience in New England* (pp. 609–625). Worcester, MA: Editions de l'Institut Français.

Román, D. (1998). *Acts of intervention: Performance, gay culture, and AIDS*. Bloomington: Indiana University Press.

Roof, J. (1996). *Come as you are: Sexuality and narrative*. New York: Columbia University Press.

Rosenblatt, P. C. (1994). *Metaphors of family systems theory: Toward new constructions*. New York: Guilford.

Rubin, L. (1994). *Families on the faultline: America's working class speaks about the family, the economy, race, and ethnicity*. New York: HarperCollins.

Rubio, S. (1996, February). Home page. *Bad Subjects: Political Education for Everyday Life, 24*. Retrieved February 14, 2002, from http://www.eserver.org/bs/24/rubio.html.

Ryan, J., & Sackrey, C. (1984). *Strangers in paradise: Academics from the working class*. Boston: South End.

Sacks, K. B. (1993). Euro-ethnic working class women's community culture. *Frontiers, 14*(1), 1–23.

Sandell, J. (1999). Making histories. *Bad Subjects: Political Education for Everyday Life, 45*. Retrieved July 12, 2002, from http://eserver.org/bs/45/sandell.html.

Sarris, G. (1990). Storytelling in the classroom: Crossing the vexed chasms. *College English, 52*, 169–185.

Sawicki, J. (1991). *Disciplining Foucault: Feminism, power, and the body*. New York: Routledge.

Sawin, P. E. (1992). "Right here is a good Christian lady": Reported speech in personal narratives. *Text and Performance Quarterly, 12*, 193–211.

Sawin, P. E. (1999). Gender, context, and the narrative construction of identity: Rethinking models of "women's narrative." In M. Bucholtz, A. C. Liang, & L. A. Sutton (Eds.), *Reinventing identities: The gendered self in discourse* (pp. 241–258). New York: Oxford University Press.

Scannell, P. (1996). *Radio, television and modern life: A phenomenological approach*. Oxford: Blackwell.

Schely-Newman, E. (1999). Mothers know best: Constructing meaning in a narrative event. *Quarterly Journal of Speech, 85*, 285–302.

Schlossman, D. A. (2002). *Actors and activists: Politics, performance, and exchange among social worlds*. New York: Routledge.

Scollon, R., & Scollon, S. B. K. (1981). *Narrative, literacy, and face in interethnic communication*. Norwood, NJ: Ablex.

Scott, J. W. (1993). The evidence of experience. In H. Abelove, M. A. Barale, & D. M. Halperin (Eds.), *The lesbian and gay studies reader* (pp. 397–415). New York: Routledge.

Silberstein, S. (1988). Ideology as process: Gender ideology in courtship narratives. In A. D. Todd & S. Fisher (Eds.), *Gender and discourse: The power of talk* (pp. 125–149). Norwood, NJ: Ablex.

Smith, S., & Watson, J. (Eds.). (1996). *Getting a life: Everyday uses of autobiography.* Minneapolis: University of Minnesota Press.

Smith, S., & Watson, J. (2001). *Reading autobiography: A guide for interpreting life narratives.* Minneapolis: University of Minnesota Press.

Sobchack, V. (1995). Beating the meat/surviving the text, or how to get out of this century alive. *Body & Society, 1,* 205–214.

Sontag, S. (1978). *Illness as metaphor.* New York: Farrar, Straus and Giroux.

Spender, D. (1980). *Man made language.* London: Routledge.

Stacey, J[udith]. (1990). *Brave new families: Stories of domestic upheaval in late twentieth century America.* New York: Basic.

Stacey, J[ackie]. (1997). *Teratologies: A cultural study of cancer.* New York: Routledge.

States, B. (1992). The phenomenological attitude. In J. G. Reinelt & J. R. Roach (Eds.), *Critical theory and performance* (pp. 369–379). Ann Arbor: University of Michigan Press.

Stone, E. (1988). *Black sheep and kissing cousins: How our family stories shape us.* New York: Times Books.

Strine, M. S. (1998). Articulating performance/performativity: Disciplinary tasks and the contingencies of practice. In J. S. Trent (Ed.), *Communication: Views from the helm for the 21st century* (pp. 312–317). Boston: Allyn and Bacon.

Strine, M. S., Long, B. W., & HopKins, M. F. (1990). Research in interpretation and performance studies. In G. Phillips & J. Wood (Eds.), *Speech communication: Essays to commemorate the seventy-fifth anniversary of the Speech Communication Association* (pp. 181–204). Carbondale: Southern Illinois University Press.

Sutton, L. A. (1999). All media are created equal: Do-it-yourself identity in alternative publishing. In M. Bucholtz, A. C. Liang, & L. A. Sutton (Eds.), *Reinventing identities: The gendered self in discourse* (pp. 163–180). New York: Oxford University Press.

Tafoya, T. (1989, August). Coyote's eyes: Native cognition styles. *Journal of American Indian Education* (Special Issue), 29–42. [Reprinted from (1982) 21(2), 21–33.]

Tannen, D. (1984). *Conversational style: Analyzing talk among friends.* Norwood, NJ: Ablex.

Tannen, D. (1990). *You just don't understand: Women and men in conversation.* New York: William Morrow.

Taylor, K. (1993). The storytelling wake: Performance in the absence of established ritual. *Southern Folklore, 50,* 99–111.

Thym-Hochrein, N. (1981). "Peter left because": A comparative study of oral family histories. *ARV: Scandinavian Journal, 37,* 61–68.

Thorne, B., & Yalom, M. (1981). *Rethinking the family: Some feminist questions.* New York: Longman.

Thompson, B., & Tyagi, S. (Eds.). (1996). *Names we call home: Autobiography on racial identity.* New York: Routledge.

Turkle, S. (1997). *Life on the screen: Identity in the age of the Internet.* New York: Touchstone/Simon and Schuster.

van Manen, M. (1998). Modalities of body experience in illness and health. *Qualitative Health Research, 8,* 7–24.

Wartik, N. (1989). *The French Canadians*. New York: Chelsea House.

Waters, M. C. (1990). *Ethnic options: Choosing identities in America*. Berkeley: University of California.

Watson, J. (1996). Ordering the family: Genealogy as autobiographical pedigree. In S. Smith & J. Watson (Eds.), *Getting a life: Everyday uses of autobiography* (pp. 297–323). Minneapolis: University of Minnesota Press.

West, C., & Zimmerman, D. H. (1983). Small insults: A study of interruptions in cross-sex conversations between unacquainted persons. In B. Thorne, C. Kramarae, & N. Henley (Eds.), *Language, gender, and society* (pp.102–117). Rowley, MA: Newbury House.

Weston, K. (1991). *Families we choose: Lesbians, gays, kinship*. New York: Columbia University Press.

Wilden, A. (1987a). *The rules are no game: The strategy of communication*. New York: Routledge.

Wilden, A. (1987b). *Man and woman, war and peace: The strategist's companion*. New York: Routledge.

Winer, D. (2001). The history of weblogs. Retrieved February 14, 2002, from http://newhome.weblogs.com/historyOfWeblogs.

Wolfson, N. (1978). A feature of the performed narrative: The conversational historical present. *Language in Society, 7*, 215–237.

Woodward, K. (1999). Inventing generational models: Psychoanalysis, feminism, literature. In K. Woodward (Ed.), *Figuring age: Women, bodies, generations* (pp. 149–168). Bloomington: Indiana University Press.

Wright, C. D. (1881). *Uniform hours of labor: Twelfth annual report of the Massachusetts Bureau of Statistics and Labor*. Boston: Bureau of Statistics and Labor, State of Massachusetts.

Yocum, M. R. (1985). Woman to woman: Fieldwork and the private sphere. In R. A. Jordan & S. J. Kalčik (Eds.), *Women's folklore, women's culture* (pp. 54–64). Philadelphia: University of Pennsylvania Press.

Young, I. M. (1990). *Throwing like a girl and other essays in feminist philosophy and social theory*. Bloomington: University of Indiana Press.

Young, K. (1985). The notion of context. *Western Folklore, 44*, 115–122.

Young, K. (1987). *Taleworlds and storyrealms: The phenomenology of narrative*. Dordrecht, Holland: Martinus Nijhoff.

Young, K. (2000). Gestures and the phenomenology of emotion in narrative. *Semiotica, 131*, 79–112.

Zipes, J. (1997). *Happily ever after: Fairy tales, children, and the culture industry*. New York: Routledge.

Zita, J. N. (1998). *Body talk: Philosophical reflections on sex and gender*. New York: Columbia University Press.

Index